Lonely 🌐 planet

WHERE
TO GO
WHEN
with **Kids**

The Ultimate Month-by-Month Family Trip-Planner

Contents

April

68-87

Palau, Micronesia
Japan
Dordogne, France
Grand Riviere, Trinidad & Tobago
Central Otago, New Zealand/Aotearoa
Seville, Spain
Mexico City, Mexico
Massachusetts, USA
Beijing, China
Phillip Island, Australia
Thailand
Whistler, Canada
Arizona, USA
Cairo, Egypt
Tromsø, Norway
Seoul, South Korea
London, England
Athens, Greece
Duin- en Bollenstreek, Netherlands
Ionian Coast, Sicily
Puerto Rico, USA
Hill Country, Sri Lanka
Jordan
Algarve, Portugal
Giant's Causeway, Northern Ireland

May

88-107

New York City, USA
Darjeeling, India
Icefields Parkway, Canada
London, England
Oslo, Norway
West Cork, Ireland
Sahara Desert, Morocco
Loire Valley, France
Tree Hotel, Sweden
Okinawa, Japan
Santorini, Greece
Barefoot Island, Fiji
Altiplano de Granada, Spain
Montréal, Canada
South Wales Valleys
Maui Mermaid School, Hawai'i
East Coast, Sri Lanka
Venice, Italy
Watercress Line, England
Shark Bay, Australia
Paris, France
Orlando, USA
Damaraland, Namibia
Legoland Billund, Denmark
Mt Vesuvius, Pompeii &
Herculaneum, Italy

June

108-127

Dolomites, Italy
Mass MoCA, USA
Grindelwald, Switzerland
Rila Mountains, Bulgaria
Kuala Lumpur, Malaysia
Knepp, England
Interrailing, Europe
Snowdon & the North, Wales
Stockholm Archipelago, Sweden
Florence, Italy
Aitutaki, Cook Islands
Hiddensee, Germany
Okavango Delta, Botswana
De Kusttram, Belgium
Lake Tekapo, New Zealand/Aotearoa
Queensland, Australia
Angkor Wat, Cambodia
Detroit, USA
Alentejo, Portugal
East Tyrol, Austria
Parc Astérix, France
Kluane National Park, Canada
Golden Circle, Iceland
Great Smoky Mountains, USA
Eastern Hokkaidō, Japan

Contents

July

August

September

4

October

188-209

South Coast, Cyprus
Nara, Japan
San Francisco, USA
London, England
Parque Nacional Los Glaciares, Argentina
Fuji-Hakone-Izu National Park, Japan
Southern Sardinia, Italy
Kathmandu Valley, Nepal
Western Crete, Greece
Lake District, England
Paro Valley, Bhutan
Exmoor, England
Nova Scotia, Canada
Corfu, Greece
Split & the Cetina River, Croatia
Transylvania, Romania
Boyne Valley, Ireland
Oʻahu, Hawaiʻi
Sicily, Italy
Turquoise Coast, Türkiye
East Coast, Australia
Cuzco & the Sacred Valley, Peru
ʻUpolu, Samoa
Caribbean Coast, Costa Rica
New England, USA

November

210-229

Muscat Region, Oman
Fukuoka, Japan
Kangaroo Island, Australia
East Sussex, England
Southern Lakes, New Zealand/Aotearoa
Bangkok, Thailand
Grand Canyon, USA
Yucatán, Mexico
Valletta, Malta
Vientiane, Laos
Marrakesh, Morocco
Churchill, Canada
Uttar Pradesh, India
New Zealand/Aotearoa
Schloss Neuschwanstein, Germany
Aswan, Egypt
Tokyo, Japan
Joshua Tree National Park, USA
Cappadocia, Türkiye
Galápagos Islands, Ecuador
Plymouth, USA
Chiang Mai, Thailand
Cayman Islands
Dubai, United Arab Emirates
Central Highlands, Guatemala

December

230-249

Rarotonga, Cook Islands
Rio di Janeiro, Brazil
Northland, New Zealand/Aotearoa
Port Arthur, Australia
South Coast, Sri Lanka
St-Martin
Dolomites, Italy
San Antonio, USA
Hong Kong, China
London, England
Ranthambhore National Park, India
South Coast, Uruguay
Kraków, Poland
Plettenberg Bay, South Africa
Jamaica
Mombasa, Kenya
Barbados
Copenhagen, Denmark
Île aux Aigrettes, Mauritius
Oamaru, New Zealand/Aotearoa
The Pampas, Argentina
Sydney, Australia
Salzburg, Austria
Oʻahu North Shore, Hawaiʻi
Cancún, Mexico

5

Introduction

→ 'Are we there yet?'
'I'm hungry!'
'This so sooo boring...'

Anyone who's taken a trip with kids will be familiar with the refrains of family-holiday discontent – even those who navigate adults-only vacation planning like a pro. Travelling with children is a whole new ballgame, and one that requires a lot more thought, organisation and know-how to get right.

Acing the practicalities of family travel – from perfect packing to conquering long journeys with sanity intact – is one thing, but finding a destination that everyone can enjoy is much more difficult. When you do hit the child-friendly-trip sweet spot, though, there's nothing like it. What could be more rewarding than watching toddler toes take their very first paddle on the calm Caribbean beaches of Guadeloupe's Îles des Saintes? Or seeing dino buffs delight in following the actual (fossilised) footsteps of dinosaurs in Spain's La Rioja, and budding Ariels learn to swim with a fishtail at Maui's Mermaid School?

This book gives essential pointers that will help you find the right trip for your family. The 12 chapters – one for each month – cover 300 destinations across the globe. As well as touching on all-important basics (from kid-friendly snacks to finding a playground), every entry outlines what makes that country, region, island or city perfect for family travel at that moment – whether it's beating the heat on a January safari around Chobe National Park, or boating through Peruvian Amazon rainforests (without the rain) in July.

As school holidays vary so much around the world, we've applied an equal-opportunity vacation policy to each month, but we've also taken into account that some places do become uncomfortably busy at specific times. So in August, when most of Europe takes its summer break, our suggestion is

© NavinTar / Shutterstock

to swerve sardine-like Spanish beaches in favour of breezy Brittany, or head further north to watch baby puffins fledge from Icelandic cliffs. We also reveal the quietest times to visit Orlando's theme parks and Sri Lanka's surf schools (both May, since you ask), and when to catch unique events like watching whale mums nurse newborn calves from Warrnambool's beachside lookouts in Australia, or seeing the Northern Lights from a heated seat in Canada's Yellowknife.

But one thing's for sure: every family is unique, and there's no one-size-fits-all approach to travel with kids. So this book is designed to give you an abundance of options – and perhaps inspire you to consider places you've never thought of visiting before. Each chapter starts with a flowchart: answer the questions and follow the strands to find the trip you and your family want. There are also monthly charts detailing family-friendly festivals and events, and the value and age-appropriateness of each destination – all tools designed to ignite wanderlust in children and adults alike, and help those doing the planning make informed decisions to answer that most important of questions: where to go when with kids?

(L) The Wizarding World of Harry Potter at Universal Orlando, Florida; (R) Spot giraffes on safari; (B) Learn to surf in Sri Lanka

January

WHERE TO GO WHEN WITH KIDS

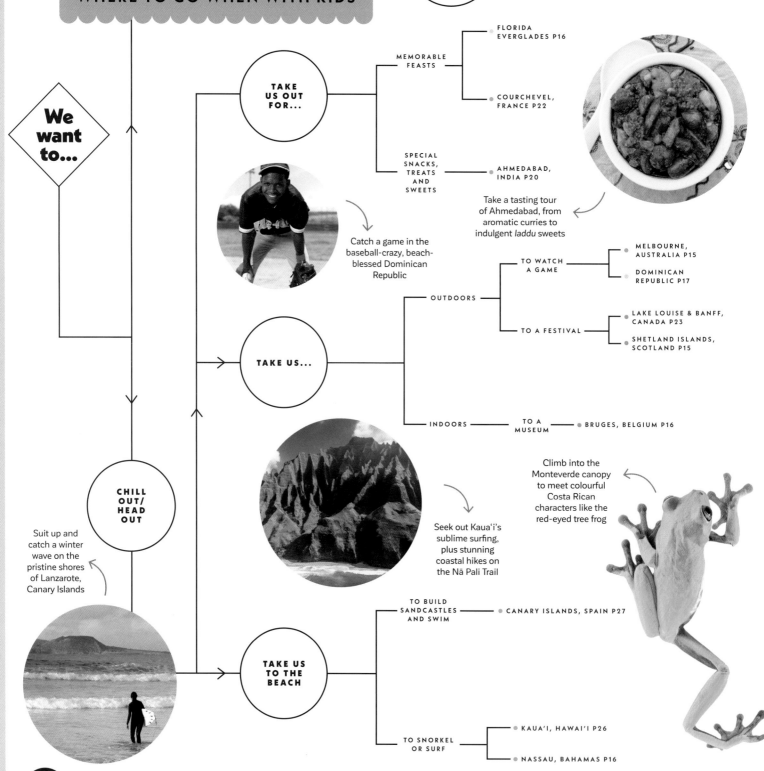

HAVE AN ADVENTURE

We want to...

TAKE US OUT FOR...

MEMORABLE FEASTS
- FLORIDA EVERGLADES P16
- COURCHEVEL, FRANCE P22

SPECIAL SNACKS, TREATS AND SWEETS
- AHMEDABAD, INDIA P20

Take a tasting tour of Ahmedabad, from aromatic curries to indulgent *laddu* sweets

Catch a game in the baseball-crazy, beach-blessed Dominican Republic

TAKE US...

OUTDOORS

TO WATCH A GAME
- MELBOURNE, AUSTRALIA P15
- DOMINICAN REPUBLIC P17

TO A FESTIVAL
- LAKE LOUISE & BANFF, CANADA P23
- SHETLAND ISLANDS, SCOTLAND P15

INDOORS

TO A MUSEUM
- BRUGES, BELGIUM P16

Climb into the Monteverde canopy to meet colourful Costa Rican characters like the red-eyed tree frog

Seek out Kaua'i's sublime surfing, plus stunning coastal hikes on the Nā Pali Trail

CHILL OUT/ HEAD OUT

Suit up and catch a winter wave on the pristine shores of Lanzarote, Canary Islands

TAKE US TO THE BEACH

TO BUILD SANDCASTLES AND SWIM
- CANARY ISLANDS, SPAIN P27

TO SNORKEL OR SURF
- KAUA'I, HAWAI'I P26
- NASSAU, BAHAMAS P16

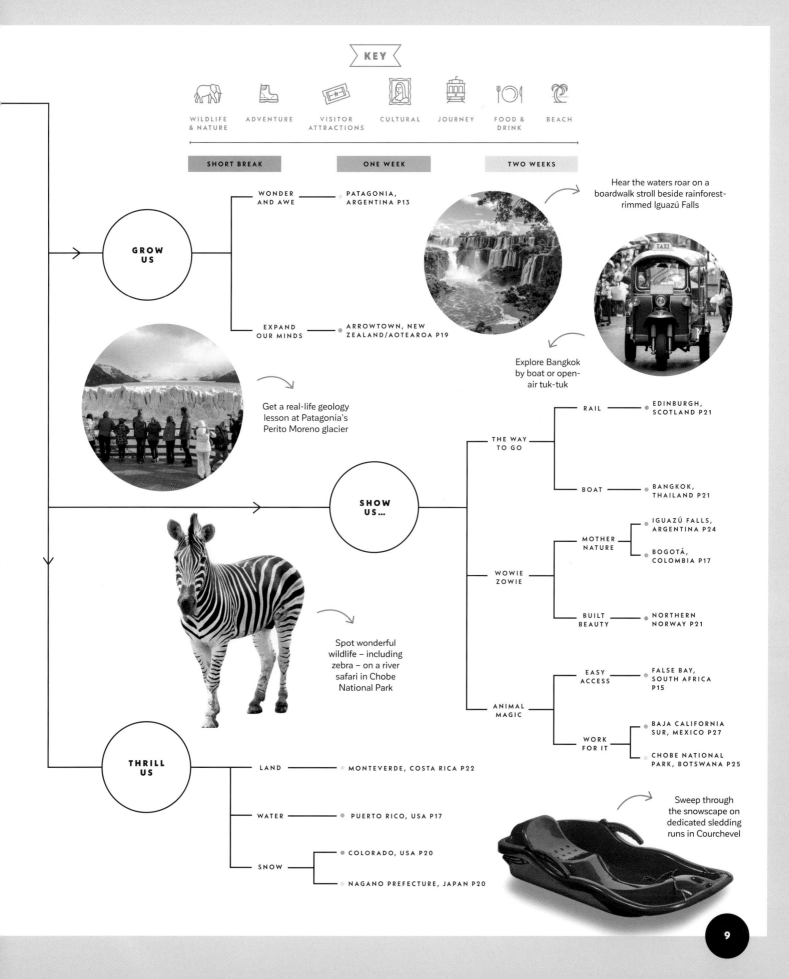

KEY

WILDLIFE & NATURE   ADVENTURE   VISITOR ATTRACTIONS   CULTURAL   JOURNEY   FOOD & DRINK   BEACH

SHORT BREAK   ONE WEEK   TWO WEEKS

GROW US

WONDER AND AWE ——— PATAGONIA, ARGENTINA P13

EXPAND OUR MINDS ——— ARROWTOWN, NEW ZEALAND/AOTEAROA P19

Hear the waters roar on a boardwalk stroll beside rainforest-rimmed Iguazú Falls

Get a real-life geology lesson at Patagonia's Perito Moreno glacier

Explore Bangkok by boat or open-air tuk-tuk

SHOW US...

THE WAY TO GO
- RAIL ——— EDINBURGH, SCOTLAND P21
- BOAT ——— BANGKOK, THAILAND P21

WOWIE ZOWIE
- MOTHER NATURE ——— IGUAZÚ FALLS, ARGENTINA P24
  - BOGOTÁ, COLOMBIA P17
- BUILT BEAUTY ——— NORTHERN NORWAY P21

ANIMAL MAGIC
- EASY ACCESS ——— FALSE BAY, SOUTH AFRICA P15
- WORK FOR IT ——— BAJA CALIFORNIA SUR, MEXICO P27
  - CHOBE NATIONAL PARK, BOTSWANA P25

Spot wonderful wildlife – including zebra – on a river safari in Chobe National Park

THRILL US

LAND ——— MONTEVERDE, COSTA RICA P22

WATER ——— PUERTO RICO, USA P17

SNOW ——— COLORADO, USA P20
    ——— NAGANO PREFECTURE, JAPAN P20

Sweep through the snowscape on dedicated sledding runs in Courchevel

9

Events in January

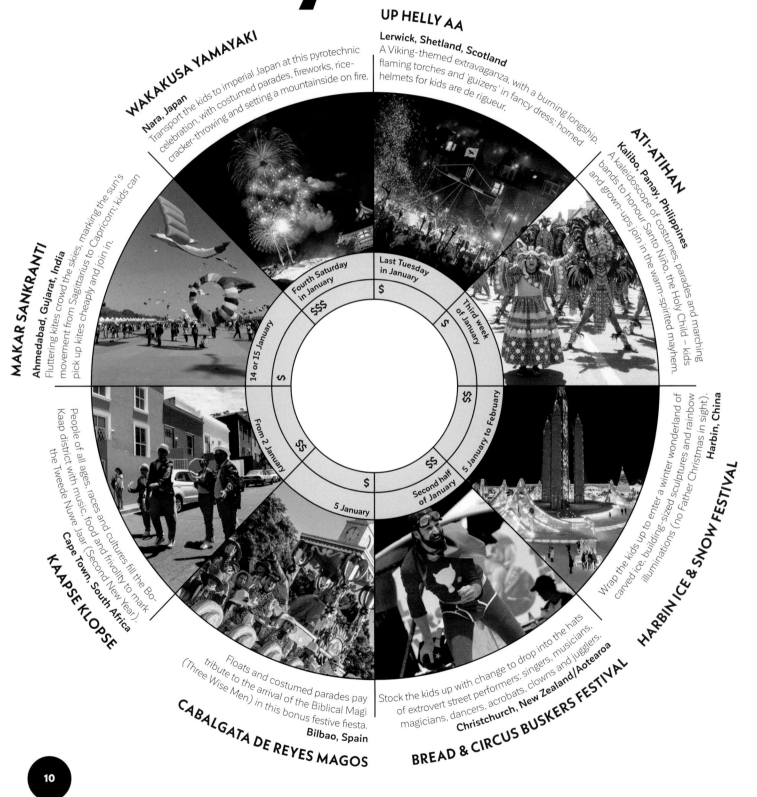

WAKAKUSA YAMAYAKI
Nara, Japan
Transport the kids to imperial Japan at this pyrotechnic celebration, with costumed parades, fireworks, rice-cracker-throwing and setting a mountainside on fire.

UP HELLY AA
Lerwick, Shetland, Scotland
A Viking-themed extravaganza, with a burning longship, flaming torches and 'guizers' in fancy dress: horned helmets for kids are de rigueur.

ATI-ATIHAN
Kalibo, Panay, Philippines
A kaleidoscope of costumes, parades and marching bands to honour Santo Niño, the Holy Child – kids and grown-ups join in the warm-spirited mayhem.

MAKAR SANKRANTI
Ahmedabad, Gujarat, India
Fluttering kites crowd the skies, marking the sun's movement from Sagittarius to Capricorn; kids can pick up kites cheaply and join in.

KAAPSE KLOPSE
Cape Town, South Africa
People of all ages, races and cultures fill the Bo-Kaap district with music, food and frivolity to mark the Tweede Nuwe Jaar (Second New Year).

HARBIN ICE & SNOW FESTIVAL
Harbin, China
Wrap the kids up to enter a winter wonderland of carved ice, building-sized sculptures and rainbow illuminations (no Father Christmas in sight).

CABALGATA DE REYES MAGOS
Bilbao, Spain
Floats and costumed parades pay tribute to the arrival of the Biblical Magi (Three Wise Men) in this bonus festive fiesta.

BREAD & CIRCUS BUSKERS FESTIVAL
Christchurch, New Zealand/Aotearoa
Stock the kids up with change to drop into the hats of extrovert street performers: singers, musicians, magicians, dancers, acrobats, clowns and jugglers.

Fourth Saturday in January — $$$

Last Tuesday in January — $

Third week of January — $

14 or 15 January — $

5 January to February — $$

From 2 January — $$

Second half of January — $$

5 January — $

10

● MELBOURNE, AUSTRALIA

Pirates no more: the pink Parliament buildings of Nassau in the Bahamas

● NASSAU, BAHAMAS

Spend a night in an icy (but comfortable) igloo in Norway

● NORTHERN NORWAY

Play on snowboards, skies and snowshoes in wintry Colorado

● COLORADO, USA

● BANGKOK, THAILAND

Go fly a kite at Ahmedabad's kite festival

● FALSE BAY, SOUTH AFRICA

● CANARY ISLANDS, SPAIN

● EDINBURGH, SCOTLAND

Chocolate is on the menu in Bruges

● DOMINICAN REPUBLIC

● ARROWTOWN, NEW ZEALAND/AOTEAROA

Spot some residents of the Boulders penguin colony in South Africa

● AHMEDABAD, INDIA

● LAKE LOUISE & BANFF, CANADA

● BRUGES, BELGIUM

● IGUAZÚ FALLS, ARGENTINA

A violet sabrewing surveys Monteverde's cloud forest

● COURCHEVEL, FRANCE

● NAGANO PREFECTURE, JAPAN

An African skimmer bird swoops over Chobe River in Botswana

Follow tobogganing at Courcheval with rosti and raclette

● PATAGONIA, ARGENTINA

● CHOBE NATIONAL PARK, BOTSWANA

● MONTEVERDE, COSTA RICA

● FLORIDA EVERGLADES, USA

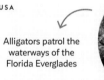

Alligators patrol the waterways of the Florida Everglades

● SHETLAND ISLANDS, SCOTLAND

● KAUA'I, HAWAI'I

● BOGOTÁ, COLOMBIA

● PUERTO RICO, USA

● BAJA CALIFORNIA SUR, MEXICO

Up Helly Aa is the fiery end of the Yule season in the Shetlands

PATAGONIA
ARGENTINA

5-16 **Why now?** Discover an otherworldly landscape of jagged peaks, cerulean lakes and sparkling glaciers.

Thrill-seeking families have a ball in Parque Nacional Los Glaciares, a vast outdoor playground of nature's best climbing structures and most spectacular scenery. Summiting iconic peaks such as Fitz Roy and Cerro Torre are all-day adventures (feasible for active, older kids), but there are plenty of more moderate routes to glacial lakes and stunning viewpoints. Give your kids a real-world geology lesson at the massive Perito Moreno, one of the planet's few remaining stable glaciers. The 70m-high (230ft) facade is a sight to behold, especially when it calves, sending big chunks of ice into the water and waves across the lake. When legs get tired, opt for a horseback trek through the Patagonian steppe, a cruise on lovely Lago Argentina or whitewater rafting on Río de las Vueltas.

Trip plan: The gateway to Los Glaciares is El Calafate, which has airport access and many excursions available, including boat trips to Perito Moreno. A 3hr drive north, El Chaltén is the main base for hiking, so it's worth spending some time in both locations.

Need to know: Layer up! Patagonia's weather is entirely unpredictable, so be prepared for wind, rain and cold, even if daytime temperatures usually hit 10°C to 15°C (50°F to 60°F).

Other months: Dec-Feb – peak season, long days, mild but windy weather, sometimes crowded trails; Mar-Apr & Nov – cooler temperatures, light crowds, lower prices; May-Oct – low season, most tourist-oriented businesses close.

(L) The view to Fitz Roy on a hike from El Chaltén; (R) Perito Moreno

(A) Penguins on
Boulders Beach,
South Africa;
(L) Up Helly Aa
guizers in Lerwick,
Shetland Islands;
(R) Melbourne's
Luna Park, Australia

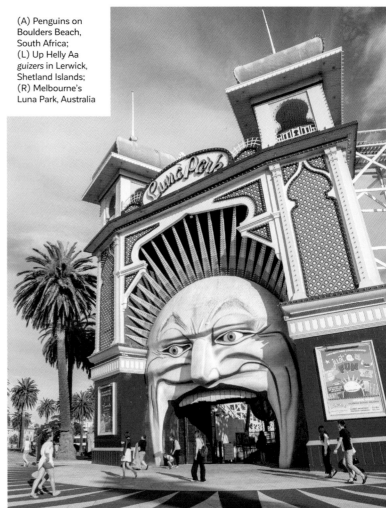

FALSE BAY
SOUTH AFRICA

5-16 Why now? The southern summer brings throngs of penguins to Boulders Beach.

South Africa's lions, rhinos and elephants grab the headlines, but children – particularly toddlers and younger kids – may get more from close encounters with the cute, pocket-sized African penguins at Boulders Beach near Simon's Town, on the sand-lined coast of False Bay. These pint-sized waddlers are remarkably unfazed by the presence of humans (even small humans), and you'll discover a calmer vision of South Africa, away from the noise and bustle of central Cape Town, with family-friendly hotels and guesthouses, and inviting sprays of golden sand (the beaches at Muizenberg, Simon's Town and sheltered Fish Hoek are shark-netted and lifeguard-patrolled). Mix up spotting penguins among the giant rocks at Boulders Beach with days on the sand, beginner surf lessons, café lunches (fruit plates, French toast, burgers, pizzas, smoothies and ice cream are easy to find), seaside strolls and splashing in the tidal pools at St James and Dalebrook.

Trip plan: False Bay is easily accessible from downtown Cape Town by rental car, taxi or commuter train. Muizenberg, Kalk Bay, Fish Hoek and Simon's Town are all cosy bases for exploring.

Need to know: January is moulting season, drawing large numbers of juvenile African penguins to Boulders Beach.

Other months: Nov-Feb – warm, sunny, lots on the cultural calendar; Mar-Jun – crisp, clear, good for hiking; Jul-Sep – whale-watching season.

SHETLAND ISLANDS
SCOTLAND

5-16 Why now? The sight of a Viking ship ablaze beneath a crisp January night sky is a childhood memory that will last a lifetime.

The tradition of Up Helly Aa (literally 'Up Holy Day All') isn't unique to Lerwick, but Shetland's capital hosts the biggest version of the fire festival seen across the Scottish archipelago. The last act of local Yule-time celebrations, the festival happens on the last Tuesday in January, when a thousand torch-wielding 'guizers' march through Lerwick, led by the 'Jarl', before hurling their flaming sticks into a replica Viking longship that is lovingly created each year. Although Up Helly Aa harks back to Shetland's millennia-old Viking heritage, the modern tradition began in the 1880s. Only locals can participate, but visitors are welcome to watch the spectacular event. Look out, too, for the 'Mirrie Dancers' (Northern Lights), which sometimes light up Shetland's skies in winter, and take coastal walks to spot seals, otters, porpoises and even orcas.

Trip plan: The NorthLink ferry from Aberdeen and Kirkwall docks at Lerwick; Sumburgh Airport is 39km (24 miles) south of town. Take taxis, buses, or hire a car to explore the Shetland Mainland, or the inter-island ferry to reach other inhabited islands.

Need to know: Lerwick's average temperature in January is 4°C (39.5°F); days are short (sunset is around 4pm) and nights are long. Take a good torch and lots of layers.

Other months: Mar-May – spring, seabirds return (including puffins), Shetland Folk Festival; Jun-Aug – summer sun, long days, pufflings; Sep-Nov – autumn bird migration.

MELBOURNE
AUSTRALIA

5-16 Why now? Find family-friendly fun in a city abuzz with the Australian Tennis Open.

Known as the 'happy slam' for good reason, the Australian Open (AO) has totally zoned in on families, offering an unbelievable experience for kids that is far from just watching tennis balls fly back and forth. The AO Ballpark on the north bank of the Yarra River, between Federation Sq and the courts at Melbourne Park, is a hotspot for youngsters, with a splash zone, zipline, obstacle course, tennis playground and much more – it's literally all fun and games in the Melbourne sun. Other family-friendly draws include unlimited rides in the CBD's free tram zone, or taking a tram to St Kilda, home of the 1912-built Luna Park. This old-style amusement park kicks off with creepy Mr Moon's gaping mouth swallowing you up as you enter, and its heritage-listed wooden roller coaster is the oldest of its kind in the world. You can even try surfing in the city at UrbnSurf, Melbourne's artificial wave park.

Trip plan: January means summer school holidays in Australia, so there'll be plenty of families on the move. Book Melbourne accommodation early, especially if you're hoping to be near the tennis.

Need to know: Free trams run from the CBD to the AO's Garden Square Entrance. An AO ground pass will be all you need to keep most kids happy and entertained; you'll need a stadium seat to watch the top players.

Other months: Nov-Mar – warm, potentially extremely hot in midsummer; Apr-Oct – the cooler months.

NASSAU
BAHAMAS

5-16 **Why now?** Avast! January brings blue skies, fair winds, calm water and wildlife sightings.

With 700 islands scattered across the azure Atlantic, the Bahamas delights travelling families seeking sun-splashed beaches, remote bays and quiet cays – but in days of yore these same features attracted very different visitors. In the early 18th century the capital, Nassau, was home to a real-life Pirates Republic. Under a skull-and-crossbones flag, it was run by renegade sea-captains Benjamin Hornigold and Henry Jennings, whose combined crew included Edward Teach (better known as Blackbeard), John 'Calico Jack' Rackham, 'Black Sam' Bellamy, Charles Vane, Stede Bonnet and the famous female buccaneers Anne Bonny and Mary Read. They were collectively known as the Flying Gang, and their dastardly deeds defined the 'Golden Age' of piracy – as you'll discover at the interactive Pirates of Nassau museum in the heart of the city. January is also a good time to head to the coast, with settled weather and good conditions for spotting sea creatures (turtles, sharks, rays, dolphins, sea lions), and exploring beaches across the archipelago, where sunken 'treasure' includes a surreal underwater sculpture garden and snorkelling site in Clifton Heritage National Park.

Trip plan: Get around on jitneys (local buses), water taxis and ferries.

Need to know: Avoid cruise-ship crowds by exploring the Bahamas' 14 national parks.

Other months: Mid-Dec to Apr – ideal weather; May to mid-Dec – quieter, hurricane season Jun-Dec.

BRUGES
BELGIUM

0-16 **Why now?** Step back in time during the city's delightfully sleepy winter season.

With its glorious medieval architecture, cosy cafes and scenic canal cruises, Bruges is a beautiful city for a short break. Trouble is, that point hasn't gone unnoticed: more than eight million visitors cram its cobbled streets in the busiest years. The trick is in the timing. January may be chilly, but it's usually dry, and much less crowded. Wrap up warm and stroll those ancient alleys around the historic Markt and Burg squares, appreciate the Flemish masters in Groeningemuseum's galleries, and climb the Belfort tower for incredible views without being jostled. Once you've reached your sightseeing limit, the absorbing Choco-Story museum provides the backstory to the fine chocolates you've seen in the city's tempting window displays. You can learn about the history of chocolate, watch a video about cocoa production, and even sample a praline made in front of you (the last demonstration is at 4.45pm). The Volkskundemuseum (Folk Museum) has a floor dedicated to the life of children, and puts on sweet-making sessions on the first and third Thursday of each month.

Trip plan: Allow at least two days to explore. Bruges is 1hr by train from Brussels, with good connections Europe-wide.

Need to know: City museums are free for children under 18; there's a fee for the Belfry and for private museums.

Other months: Feb-Mar – cold, quieter; Apr-May – spring, warming; Jun-Aug – busiest; Sep-Nov – cooler, still popular; Dec – cold, busy during Christmas markets.

FLORIDA
EVERGLADES USA

0-16 **Why now?** Hike among cypress trees, kayak the mangroves and count gators during the dry season in this unique ecosystem.

The Florida Everglades is a vast wilderness that includes several diverse habitats and an enormous number of alligators. (Keep a running count throughout your trip and see if you can hit triple digits.) During the dry season, the landscape becomes much more accessible for hikers, and it's also easier to spot wildlife, as the animals congregate around central waterholes. The 1.3km (0.8-mile) Anhinga Trail from Royal Palm Visitor Center is a favourite for families, with a good chance of turtle and bird sightings. At the Shark Valley Visitor Center, you can rent a bike or take a tram tour along a 24km (15-mile) paved loop, spotting otters, turtles, wading birds and alligators along the way. Season aside, it's wonderful to explore the Everglades from the water: paddle through the mangroves or catch fish from your kayak. After you've worked up an appetite you can feast on fresh stone crabs – an Everglades speciality.

Trip plan: There are various camping and lodging options in Flamingo and Everglades City. You can even rent a houseboat at Flamingo Lodge and cruise around Whitewater Bay in your lodging. (You're welcome, kids.)

Need to know: There is little shade in the Everglades, so sun hats and sunblock are a must. There are also lots of mosquitoes – insect repellent is also a must.

Other months: Nov-Apr – less rain and fewer mosquitoes; May-Oct – very hot and humid, daily afternoon thunderstorms.

DOMINICAN REPUBLIC

5-16 Why now? Catch a Dominican League baseball game, then head to the beaches and waterfalls.

Baseball – or pelota – is both national pastime and national passion in the DR, home of Major League Baseball players like David Ortiz and Albert Pujols. The season runs from October to January, making this Caribbean island the perfect winter getaway for baseball fans suffering from withdrawal back home. Of the six teams in the Dominican League, two of the best play in Santo Domingo. Cheer them on at Estadio Quisqueya – and don't miss the post-game party, when fans take to the streets for music and dancing. Come to the DR for the baseball, but stay for the beaches. East of Santo Domingo, there's a string of white-sand beauties – most famously, Boca Chica, with tranquil waters and decent snorkelling. While in Boca Chica, don't miss the baseball exhibit at BHD Bank, displaying memorabilia from Dominican players. Other fun family adventures include swimming under the waterfalls at Salto Socoa; exploring caves at Parque Los Tres Ojos; and taking a catamaran tour to Isla Saona.

Trip plan: As an alternative to Santo Domingo, you might also stay in Punta Cana (see a baseball game in La Romana), or Puerto Plata (games in Santiago de los Caballeros).

Need to know: It's usually easy to get game tickets at stadiums, even on the day; local agencies also offer tours (including transport and refreshments).

Other months: Dec-Mar – dry season, with mild temperatures and light rain; Apr-Oct – hot, hot, hot; Nov – peak rainy season.

BOGOTÁ
COLOMBIA

5-16 Why now? See Bogotá lit up by lights and hummingbirds.

Bogotá might sound like an out-there family destination, but the Colombian capital is great for museum visits, rainforest tours and close encounters with tropical wildlife – and the twinkling lights on Cerro de Monserrate in January elevate the holiday mood. Start by diving into the historic streets of La Candelaria, then let the kids practise their haggling skills in the artisan markets of Usaquén. When you're ready to roam beyond the centre, take a morning mountain hike on the bird-filled trails of the Cerros Orientales, or drop into the Observatorio de Colibries, around 9km (5.5 miles) west of Bogotá, where 14 species of hummingbirds zip about like levitating jewels. To see more of Colombia, reward the kids with some time on the glorious beaches of Parque Nacional Natural Tayrona near Santa Marta, a 90-minute flight from Bogotá.

Trip plan: Bogotá is a busy international hub, and domestic flights on Avianca and LATAM Colombia run daily to Santa Marta and other cities. In Bogotá, base yourself in La Candelaria for easy access to the sights and the Cerro de Monserrate funicular train.

Need to know: With older kids, the Amazon Basin makes for a wild side-trip; boat tours from Leticia (two hours by air from Bogotá) roam deep into the rainforest in search of jaguars, monkeys and macaws.

Other months: Dec-Feb & Jun-Aug – hot and bright; Mar-May & Sep-Nov – hot and rainy.

PUERTO RICO
USA

12-16 Why now? Combine outdoor adventure with festival fun and cultural immersion on a colourful Caribbean island.

Swap screens for screams (of excitement) by taking teenagers on canyoning, tubing and hiking adventures along Rio Tanamá to Mukaro Cave, exploring caverns, underground rivers and (optional) plunge spots en route. Winter also offers perfect paddling and swimming in Puerto Rico's bioluminescent bays (permit required – go with a licensed tour operator), where each oar stoke or movement provokes the ignition of an otherworldly underwater light show, produced by glowing dinoflagellate plankton. Book the family on to a night-kayaking tour on Laguna Grande, near San Juan; or head towards Puerto Rico's southwestern tip where – uniquely – you can swim amid the blue bioluminescence in the La Parguera 'bio bay'.

Trip plan: Puerto Rico is just 160km (100 miles) long and 56km (35 miles) wide, but with a wild Atlantic-facing shore and a calmer Caribbean coast (not to mention a magnificent mountainous hinterland), there's a lot to explore; renting a 4WD is the best way to get around.

Need to know: Puerto Rico is an unincorporated territory of the USA, with the same visa requirements. January is holiday and festival season, from Three Kings Day on the 6th to Las Octavitas (14-17 January) and the multiday Fiestas de la Calle San Sebastián (from the third Thursday in January) in Old San Juan; it's busy but fun.

Other months: Mar-May – good beach weather, breezy with some showers; Jun-Aug – swelteringly hot; Aug-Nov – hurricane season.

ARROWTOWN
NEW ZEALAND/ AOTEAROA

5-16 **Why now? Summer light provides perfect conditions for gold panning in Otago.**

For any kid on the planet, spotting something gleaming as you pan the riverbed for gold is guaranteed to spark a surge of excitement. Just 25 minutes' drive from Queenstown, historic Arrowtown was settled during the Otago Gold Rush of 1862, when the first glinting particles were discovered in the burbling Arrow River. Today, it's a scenic hub for country walks, immersive history, and gold panning on a river that produced hundreds of kilograms of gold in the first year of operations. The good news? You don't need to be a grizzled prospector to give it a go. Gold pans can be rented from shops in town (ask staff for tips) and the river is just minutes from the centre. Make gold panning the focus of a long weekend of walks, river paddling and museum visits, plus detours to *Lord of the Rings* filming locations and to the old encampment used by Chinese prospectors.

Trip plan: Get here from Queenstown by rental car or on the Orbus shuttle bus. Arrowtown has plenty of hotels and guesthouses, or you can bring a tent or RV to the town campground.

Need to know: Set aside a day to explore one of Arrowtown's 15 walking routes – the Big Hills Trail scores highly for views.

Other months: Feb – warm and summery; Mar-May – cooler, unpredictable weather; Jun-Sep – snowy and cold; Oct-Dec – brightening skies.

Old-fashioned shopfronts on Buckingham St in Arrowtown

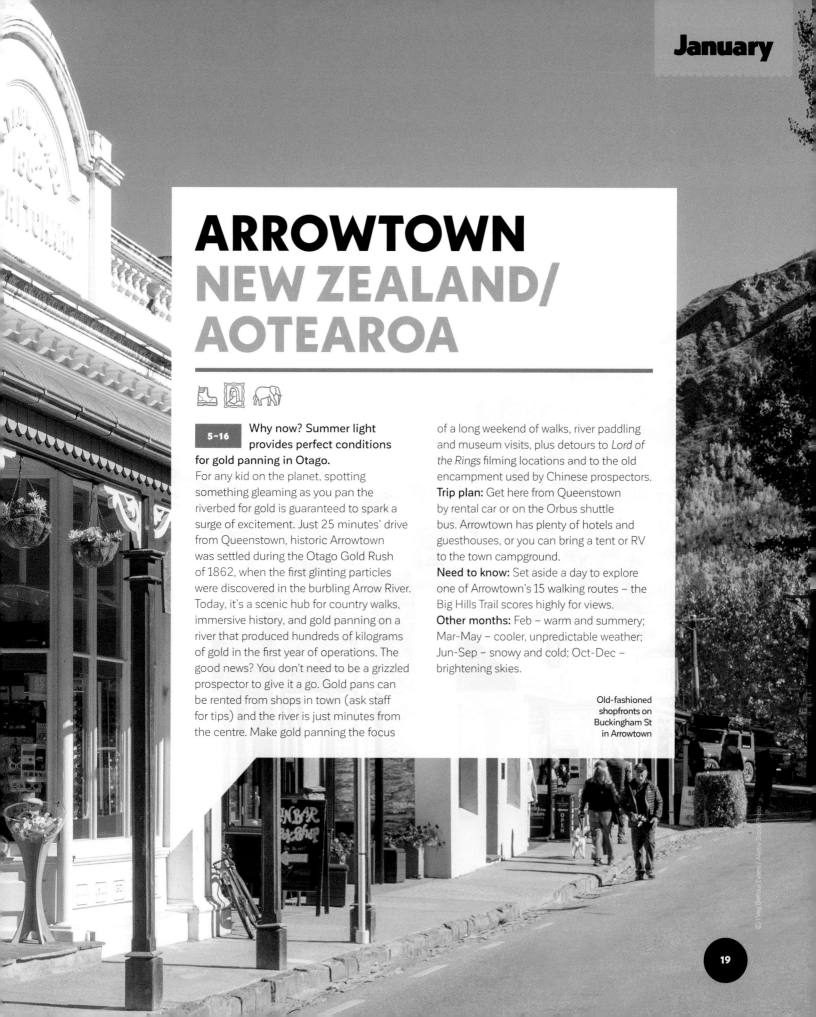

COLORADO
USA

5-16 Why now? Winter sports, hot springs and ice festivals.

There are two tricks to surviving (and thriving) in winter: snow sports and winter warmups. This is well understood in Colorado. Downhill skiing and snowboarding are the clear favourites in 'America's skiing capital', but there's also snow-tubing, snowshoeing, snow forts, ice skating, ice fishing and ice climbing. The point is that winter is not just for adrenaline junkies, it's for everyone. January festivals such as Alamosa's Rio Frio Ice Fest, Wintersköl in Aspen and Ouray Ice Festival celebrate all aspects of the winter season. Even ski-hub Breckenridge holds a world-famous snow-sculpting competition, resulting in amazing, hand-carved artworks that decorate the town until spring. Winter warmups also come in many forms, but geothermal springs and pools are a Colorado speciality. There's no better way to recover from a day of winter fun than soaking in a steaming bath, heated by Mother Nature.

Trip plan: Several Colorado towns – Steamboat Springs, Pagosa Springs and Glenwood Springs – have hot springs and (smallish) ski resorts. Vail and Aspen are less than 1hr from Glenwood Springs; from Telluride, it's about 1hr to Ouray.

Need to know: Some hot-springs resorts have age restrictions (for certain pools and facilities, or for the whole resort). Check what your kids will and won't have access to.

Other months: Nov-Mar – peak winter sports season; Apr-May – low season, low prices, muddy/snowy trails; Jun-Oct – prime hiking season, mild, sunny skies.

NAGANO PREFECTURE
JAPAN

5-16 Why now? Explore Nagano after the New Year holidays, when crowds thin and the snow is deep.

With abundant snow sports, steaming hot springs, cultural wonders, traditional villages and even 'snow monkeys', this slice of central Honshū is a winter playground for families. Nagano hosted the 1998 Winter Olympics, and skiers and snowboarders will be in heaven amid the deep snow at resorts such as Hakuba, Shiga Kōgen and Nozawa Onsen; après-ski options include *onsen* hot springs and lots of tasty Japanese cuisine. If your family isn't already completely satiated, take time out to visit the famous 'snow monkeys', who soak in an *onsen* surrounded by snow at Yudanaka. On the cultural side, prefectural capital Nagano City is home to Zenkō-ji, one of Japan's oldest Buddhist temples, a surreal and atmospheric experience. Nicknamed 'Crow Castle', Matsumoto-jō in Matsumoto City is the country's oldest original wooden castle; youngsters might enjoy its museum of weapons, firearms, swords and armour – some items are over 400 years old.

Trip plan: Allow plenty of time in Nagano, at least a week if you're on a winter-sports holiday; Nagano City is best reached by Shinkansen train from Tokyo in 1hr 30min.

Need to know: All the resorts offer excellent accommodation, from inexpensive budget options (some with dorm-style rooms) right through to big hotels. For a traditional experience, book a Japanese-style place and sleep on a futon on the floor.

Other months: Dec-Mar – winter sports; Apr – cherry blossoms; Jun-Sep – mild summer; Oct – autumn colours.

AHMEDABAD
INDIA

5-16 Why now? The skies above Ahmedabad are kaleidoscopic with kites in combat during Uttarayan.

The Hindu festival of Makara Sankranti – triggered by the sun's mid-January transit to Capricorn, signalling winter's end – is celebrated differently across India, but in the Gujarat city of Ahmedabad, where the event is called Uttarayan, it's marked with the incredible International Kite Festival. In the lead up, killer kites are conjured from paper, bamboo and *manja* (a spool of special string coated in glue and shards of glass). Then, for two days, the blue sky is crowded with whirling, swirling kites, surfing breezes and battling for space and aerial supremacy, as skilled pilots attempt to cut the strings of their rivals' creations while crowds of excited spectators cheer through mouthfuls of sweet treats like *laddu* and *surti jamun*. Held in the heavens above Ahmedabad since 1989, the festival's fame has grown internationally and now, alongside the nimble *tukkal* design favoured by local participants, you'll see Chinese flying dragons, Japanese *rokkaku* (fighting kites) Malaysian wau-balang (moon-kites), graceful Indonesian *layang-layang*, Italian sculptural kites, and giant American banner kites. After dark, bright white kites are sent aloft, illuminated by the moonlight with strings of lit lanterns, while rooftop parties are staged across the city.

Trip plan: Be sure to explore Ahmedabad's mosques, mausoleums and the city's maze-like Old Quarter.

Need to know: Ahmedabad (India's first UNESCO Urban World Heritage Site) has sensational street food.

Other months: Nov-Feb – dry, cool, breezy; Mar-Jun – searing heat; Jun-Sep – monsoonal.

NORTHERN NORWAY

5-16 Why now? Shelter from the Nordic winter in a cosy Norwegian igloo.

Sweden's famous Icehotel may be a little too (ahem) cool for families with boisterous kids in tow. Pop over to neighbouring Norway though, and you'll be spoiled for choice when it comes to igloo hotels. Kids can sleep in ice-built domes or toastily heated glass pods, enveloped by ice and snow and basking under skies illuminated by a tiara of stars or the Northern Lights. Book in for a few days at the Tromsø Ice Domes or Snowhotel Kirkenes and you'll get the full igloo experience, with stays in ice-block domes and activities such as dogsledding, snowshoe hikes and snowmobile tours on tap. If sleeping on a block of ice on a reindeer skin feels like too much adventure for your kids, trade the igloos for a cosy glass dome at Lyngen North, east of Tromsø near Rotsund.

Trip plan: With the icy terrain and a limited road network, it pays to fly to an airstrip close to where you are staying. The Tromsø and Kirkenes airports receive local and international flights, with easy bus transfers to the resorts.

Need to know: With temperatures dipping to -5°C (23°F), bank on spending lots of time indoors between excursions: bring games, pens and paper, or family films and tech to play them on.

Other months: Nov-Apr – icy cold, Northern Lights; May-Aug – warmer weather, good for walking; Sep-Oct – often damp.

EDINBURGH
SCOTLAND

5-16 Why now? See Edinburgh at its best between Hogmanay and Burns Night.

Edinburgh during Hogmanay can be a bit too boisterous for youngsters; come a week or two later and the crowds thin, prices drop and general noise levels fall (with the notable exception of busking bagpipers). Make your journey part of the destination by booking overnight berths on the Caledonian Sleeper train, arriving in Edinburgh at breakfast time, rested and ready to see the sights. Focus your attention on Edinburgh Castle, the family galleries at the National Museum and the ever-popular Museum of Childhood. Older kids will enjoy the echoing boom of the castle's One O'Clock Gun, and spooky but fun tours of the reputedly haunted vaults under South Bridge.

Trip plan: The Caledonian Sleeper leaves London's Euston Station at 10.30pm, reaching Edinburgh Waverley at 7.30am; book a family ticket and you'll get a discount of up to 33% (under-4s ride free). Staying in Edinburgh's Old Town puts you close to the sights, reducing the need for long walks in the cold.

Need to know: Look out for special Burns Night suppers at hotels and restaurants on or around 25 January. The haggis part is optional, and you can get youngsters in the mood with the nonsense poem *First Catch your Haggis!* by Brenda Williams.

Other months: Dec-Feb – cold, some rain, occasional snow; Mar-May & Sep-Nov – cool, grey, quieter; Jun-Aug – warm, brighter.

BANGKOK
THAILAND

5-16 Why now? Warm, dry days are perfect for exploring Bangkok by boat.

Meandering *khlongs* (canals) and the mighty Chao Phraya River offer a fascinating, kid-friendly way to explore Bangkok, away from the honking traffic. For a family temple trip, board the Chao Phraya Express Boat at Phra Arthit, then hopscotch along the river to Tha Chang (to visit the Temple of the Emerald Buddha, Wat Pho and the Royal Palace) and Ratchawong Pier (to browse Chinatown's markets and see the Wat Traimit Golden Buddha). Keep pint-sized shopaholics entertained on the Khlong Saen Saep Express Boat: disembark at Pratunam for teen-oriented malls and Sukhumvit for pocket-money-priced souvenirs. Alternatively, charter a longtail boat and buzz along the canals in a fountain of spray. Wherever you go, graze on street food; cafes and food stalls abound near ferry stops, and most kids love satay skewers and pad thai fried noodles.

Trip plan: On a Bangkok city break, devote one day to exploring temples and palaces on the Chao Phraya Express Boat, and another to canal-side stops on the Khlong Saen Saep Express Boat. With more time to spare, take the river ferry north for gentle walks on the leafy, pottery-making island of Ko Kret.

Need to know: Bangkok ferries only stop for moments at each pier, so move into position early and be ready to grab the kids and leap ashore at short notice.

Other months: Nov-Feb – cooler, drier weather; Mar-Apr – hot and humid; May-Oct – hot and rainy.

COURCHEVEL
FRANCE

5-16 Why now? Plenty of snow for tobogganing down the slopes at Courchevel.

Not everyone was born standing up on skis like alpine ace Mikaela Shiffrin, and that's where tobogganing comes in – it's easy, safe and accessible to everyone from tots to teens. And Courchevel is one of the top spots to barrel down the slopes, with dedicated sledding areas for kids at Courchevel 1850 and Courchevel La Tania – ideal for first-time tobogganers. Once the kids have got the hang of turning and stopping, families can take on more ambitious runs, like the 2km (1.2-mile) course from Courchevel 1850 to Courchevel village. With teens in tow, up the ante on the 3km (2-mile) racing run at Courchevel Moriond. It's just one source of snowy fun in a resort that's packed with kids' ski schools, babysitting services and family-friendly places to stay and eat. On which note, rosti (potato cakes) and raclette (melted cheese) will quickly become family favourites.

Trip plan: Book into a family-focused ski lodge at Courchevel – Hôtel Barrière Les Neiges, Hotel des Trois Vallées and L'Apogée have good reputations – and take advantage of kid-oriented features such as magnetic safety vests for children on the ski lifts.

Need to know: The Courchevel toboggan runs are open from 9am to 7.30pm and floodlit at night; rent or buy sleds at local ski shops.

Other months: Dec-Apr – ski and tobogganing season; May-Jun & Sep-Nov – damp, often soggy; Jul-Aug – good for summer mountain biking, hiking and rock climbing.

MONTEVERDE
COSTA RICA

12-16 Why now? January is the coolest time to climb into the canopy of Costa Rica's incredible cloud forests.

Cloaked in ephemeral mist and populated by a bedazzlingly rich biodiversity of tropical creatures, Monteverde's hazy, humid cloud forests are home to some 425 species of birds, 120 different mammals, 60 amphibians and 101 kinds of reptile. Here, where the verdant peaks of the Cordillera de Tilarán meet the sky and the treetops tickle the clouds, the best way to explore the fecund forests is by clambering up into the canopy amid the branches of the Biological Preserve. Helpfully, the ficus – a strangler fig that encircles and eventually kills its host tree, which then decays – offers a ladder to the clouds; safely harnessed up, teenagers can climb inside or outside these extraordinary trees to reach viewing platforms. After-dark adventures are also possible, during which you ascend a 40m-high (131ft) internally illuminated ficus to meet Monteverde's nocturnal wildlife.

Trip plan: Sandwiched between the Caribbean Sea and the Pacific Ocean, Costa Rica offers everything from beautiful beaches and towering volcanoes to wild outdoor pursuits. Guided snorkelling excursions in Caño Island Biological Reserve and rafting on the Savegre River are perfect family-friendly adventures.

Need to know: Prepare to embrace the national spirit of *pura vida* (pure life), but note: it's illegal to feed or take selfies with wild animals in Costa Rica.

Other months: Late Nov to mid-Jan – windy, misty season; mid-Jan to Apr – dry season; May-Nov – rainy season, hurricanes possible Sep-Nov.

Crossing over the canopy in Monteverde, Costa Rica

Ice sculpture at
Lake Louise, Canada

LAKE LOUISE & BANFF
CANADA

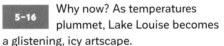

5-16 **Why now? As temperatures plummet, Lake Louise becomes a glistening, icy artscape.**

During midwinter in Alberta, you don't have to wait long for the sun to set – and once evening arrives, extraordinary things happen beneath the stars on the frozen expanse of Lake Louise. Throughout January, artists armed with chisels and chainsaws create the coolest sculptures on Earth as they prepare their extravagant entries for the Ice Magic Festival, held annually around Fairmont Chateau hotel. The world's best H20 carvers have 30 hours to transform a colossal ice cube into an ephemeral masterpiece – maybe a monster or mythical beast, depending on the theme – before it melts back into the landscape. While you're here, take the kids ice-skating on the lake (sensationally surrounded by snow-topped mountains),

experience a horse-drawn sleigh ride or grab some snowshoes and explore more of the great white wintry wonderland of Banff National Park.

Trip plan: Fly into Calgary, the nearest international airport, 187km (116 miles) from Lake Louise. The Rocky Mountaineer train runs from here to Banff between April and October; in January you'll need to arrange a shuttle bus.

Need to know: Winter (December to March) temperatures range from -10°C to -30°C (14°F to -22°F); wrap up in thermals, fleeces, bobble hats, gloves and puffer jackets. If you're not staying at Fairmont Chateau, tickets to Ice Magic must be pre-purchased.

Other months: Apr-Jun – nature awakes (along with bears); Jun-Aug – warm and sunny weather, ideal for outdoor adventures; Sep-Nov – kaleidoscopic autumn colours.

© GEOPIX Photography / Shutterstock

© Scott Clarence / Shutterstock

IGUAZÚ FALLS ARGENTINA

Walkways along the
waters at Iguazú Falls

0-16 **Why now? Full falls bring ultimate drama at one of the planet's most awe-inspiring sights.**
You'll hear the falls before you see them. A visceral roar builds until it vibrates the air, then there they are, the Iguazú Falls – a rainforest-rimmed chain of hundreds of waterfalls, nearly 3km (1.85 miles) in extension. Clouds of mist hover in the January humidity, and ahead of you condors float on the warm air currents. The falls lie split between Brazil and Argentina in a large expanse of national park, much of it rainforest teeming with unique flora and fauna. The Argentine side arguably gives the best experience, with walkways that take you above the falls or descend to the river. The Brazil side requires at least another day for full panoramic views of the cascades

and, just outside the national park gates, the Parque das Aves (Bird Park), with walk-through aviaries that house toucans, macaws and other birds rescued from the wildlife trade.

Trip plan: Iguazú is a 16hr bus ride from São Paulo, or 24hr from Buenos Aires, so most people fly into Argentina's Cataratas del Iguazú (2hr from Buenos Aires), or Foz do Iguaçu Airport in Brazil (1hr 45min from Rio de Janeiro).

Need to know: January can get busy, so visit early in the morning; midweek is quieter than weekends. The trail paths are flat and accessible.

Other months: Nov-Mar – hot and humid, Feb and Easter bring holidaying locals; Apr-Jun – dry season; Aug-Sep – dry, cooler, great for bike rides.

Bathtime fun in the
Chobe River, Botswana

CHOBE NATIONAL
PARK BOTSWANA

5-16 Why now? Embark on green-season river cruises to marvel at migrating birds.

Botswana's wet season brings heat, with temperatures reaching between 35°C and 40°C (95°F to 104°F), along with heavy rainfall. But as sultry mornings give way to afternoon thunderstorms, the air is refreshed and the bush transformed into a lush, vibrant green. During this time, there are fewer visitors, lower prices and a park teeming with life and drama. January is the best time to spot migratory birds, including the black-and-white long-toed lapwing and the African skimmer, with its bright orange bill. While other wildlife tends to be more dispersed, you can still expect to see large herds of zebra and antelope (and their predators) as well as the occasional newborn. Most visits centre on the Chobe River, a major tributary of the Zambezi that flows gently through the park's northeast. A cruise along its serene waters is the perfect way to get close to wildlife in safety and comfort – and a great way for families to avoid long, hot days on a jeep safari.

Trip plan: There's plenty to fill two to three days at Chobe; most people visit as part of a longer (12-14 day) trip into Botswana. Kasana is the main gateway by road; it's also possible to fly into the park.

Need to know: By law, lodges here are small and low-impact, which also means fewer beds and higher prices than other safari destinations.

Other months: Nov-May – green season, birds, cheaper; Jun-Sep – peak season, best for big animals; Aug-Oct – dry winter season, elephant herds at waterholes.

© THP Creative / Shutterstock

Heading to
the breaks for
bodyboarding
on Kaua'i

KAUA'I HAWAI'I

0-16 Why now? Seek out surfing, snorkelling and whale-watching during Kaua'i's shoulder season.

There are few experiences in the animal kingdom that are quite as awesome as witnessing a massive humpback breaching, but even the less acrobatic manoeuvres of these majestic marine giants are impressive. From December to April, Hawai'i is home to the densest population of humpback whales in the North Pacific. Indeed, you're likely to spot whales from the shore, but you'll see more (and see them better) from a whale-watching boat. Back on land, Kaua'i is a stunner, with jaw-dropping coastal scenery at every turn. Plan a hike along the kid-friendly Maha'ulepu Heritage Trail or the more challenging Nā Pali Coastal Trail. And don't skimp on dedicated beach time: kids can snorkel in the protected lagoons at Po'ipū Beach Park and learn to surf on the gentle waves in Hanalei Bay. January is ideal because weather is mild and the holiday crowds have dispersed.

Trip plan: Kaua'i is small enough that you can see the entire island from one home base (though you'll need to rent a car). Your longest drive won't be more than 1hr 30min.

Need to know: Kaua'i is an island of microclimates, which means that weather fluctuates even from one side of the island to another. If skies are stormy or the surf is dangerous in the north (as can be the case in January), head to the south shore.

Other months: Apr-Oct – consistently sunny skies; Apr-Jun & Sep-Dec – reduced prices during off-peak months.

© FatCamera / Getty Images

Canaries contrasts:
(R) Fuerteventura;
(B) Timanfaya,
Lanzarote

CANARY ISLANDS
SPAIN

0-16 Why now? Warm 'winter' climes mean beachtime, watersports and lava-field hikes.

When most of Europe is dragging itself through the wet and cold of winter, the Canaries are an oasis of sunshine. Each island has its own unique identity, some more heavily touristed than others, but if it's beaches you are after, then Fuerteventura has the best. In the far south, Parque Natural de Jandía is a golden desert-scape, its dunes crumbling down towards the sea and flattening out into Atlantic-washed playa. On the northeast corner, the Grandes Playas de Corralejo (literally, the 'big beaches') are protected as the Parque Natural de Corralejo and remain utterly pristine. From Fuerteventura, it's just a 45-minute ferry hop over to neighbouring Lanzarote, where volcanic cones and eerie blackened lava fields form an otherworldly playground.

Scramble up volcanic calderas on the fringes of lava-moulded Parque Nacional de Timanfaya for views across Lanzarote. The island's wide, open coastline is brilliant for watersports – from snorkelling to kayaking, paddleboarding, windsurfing and kitesurfing.

Trip plan: Fly into Fuerteventura or Lanzarote; a ferry connects the two. Tenerife is easier for US travellers; take ferries to reach Fuerteventura (7hr) or Lanzarote (9hr), or connect via short flights.

Need to know: Some areas of Fuerteventura have strong currents and swimming is dangerous. Stick to beaches with lifeguards.

Other months: Feb-Mar & Jul-Aug – peak seasons, very hot; May-Jun & Sep-Nov – off-season, still hot, cooler nights, quieter.

BAJA CALIFORNIA SUR MEXICO

0-16 Why now? Enjoy wild and magical marine-life encounters.

It's called 'Lower' California, but this 1200km-long (746-mile) peninsula that drops down off the bottom of California is actually part of Mexico. Once your kids learn that little geography lesson, they are ready to discover this sunshine paradise, where the desert meets the sea. The weather is warm and dry all year round in this desert climate; and in winter, Baja California Sur offers incredible opportunities to get up close and personal with marine life. The bays and

lagoons along the Pacific coast are mating and birthing grounds for several species of whales, including greys and humpbacks. These whales are not going anywhere, so it's often possible to enjoy extended, up-close observation of these magnificent creatures. Meanwhile, on the east coast, the Sea of Cortez provides the chance to snorkel with sea lions at Isla Espíritu Santo and swim with whale sharks in the Bay of La Paz. Encountering these massive creatures in their natural habitat is an exhilarating experience at any age.

Trip plan: At Baja California Sur's southern tip, Cabo San Lucas is the peninsula's more famous, more glamorous destination, but La Paz is a more affordable, low-key choice for families. Rent a car for maximum flexibility.

Need to know: Animal encounters are strictly regulated to minimise the impact on the wildlife. Seasonal restrictions are rigidly enforced, as are prohibitions on feeding and baiting.

Other months: Nov-Apr – coolest temperatures; May-Oct – hot weather, hurricanes possible Jul & Sep.

February

WHERE TO GO WHEN WITH KIDS

We want to...

HAVE AN ADVENTURE

TAKE US OUT FOR...

MEMORABLE FEASTS
- ● ROME, ITALY P35
- ● NICE, FRANCE P46

SPECIAL SNACKS, TREATS AND SWEETS
- ● ANTIGUA & ATITLÁN, GUATEMALA P43

See off Rome's winter chill with perfect pizzas and warming hot chocolate

Watch epic (mock) battles at York's Jorvik Viking Festival

TAKE US...

OUTDOORS

FOR MAGICAL NIGHT SKIES
- ● YELLOWKNIFE, CANADA P40
- ● SOUTH DOWNS, ENGLAND P34

TO A FESTIVAL
- ● YORK, ENGLAND P35
- ● TRINIDAD & TOBAGO P39

INDOORS

FOR SOME KID-FRIENDLY FUN
- ● LOS ANGELES, USA P45

TO A MUSEUM
- ● CHICAGO, USA P36
- ● DUBLIN, IRELAND P47

Doze with the dinos on a sleepover at Chicago's Field Museum

CHILL OUT/ HEAD OUT

Bask in winter sun on Imsouane's beaches

TAKE US TO THE BEACH

TO BUILD SANDCASTLES AND SWIM
- ● ÎLES DES SAINTES, GUADELOUPE P33

TO SNORKEL OR SURF
- ● IMSOUANE, MOROCCO P44

Soak up some Hollywood glamour on an awards-season tour around LA

KEANU REEVES

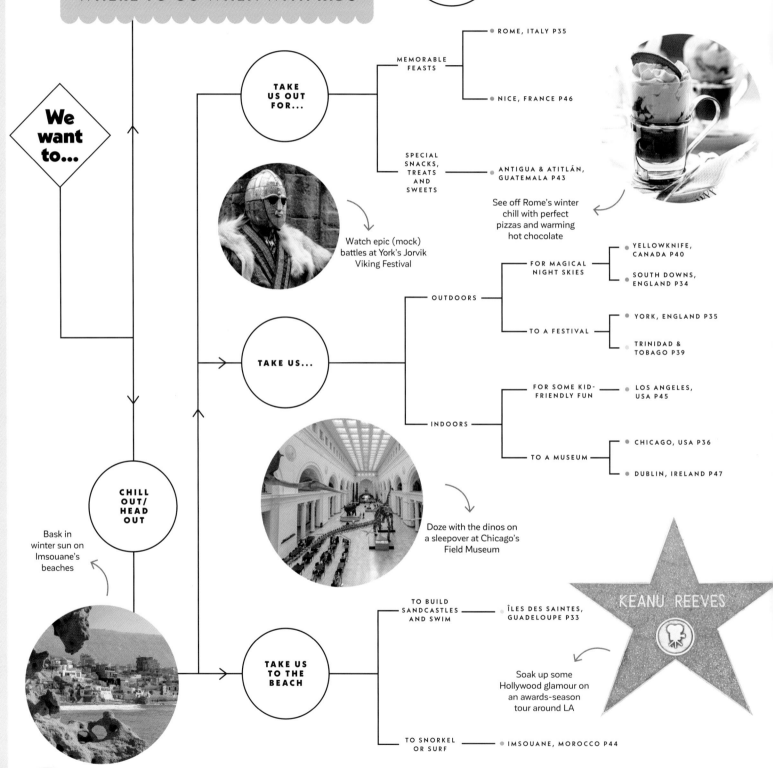

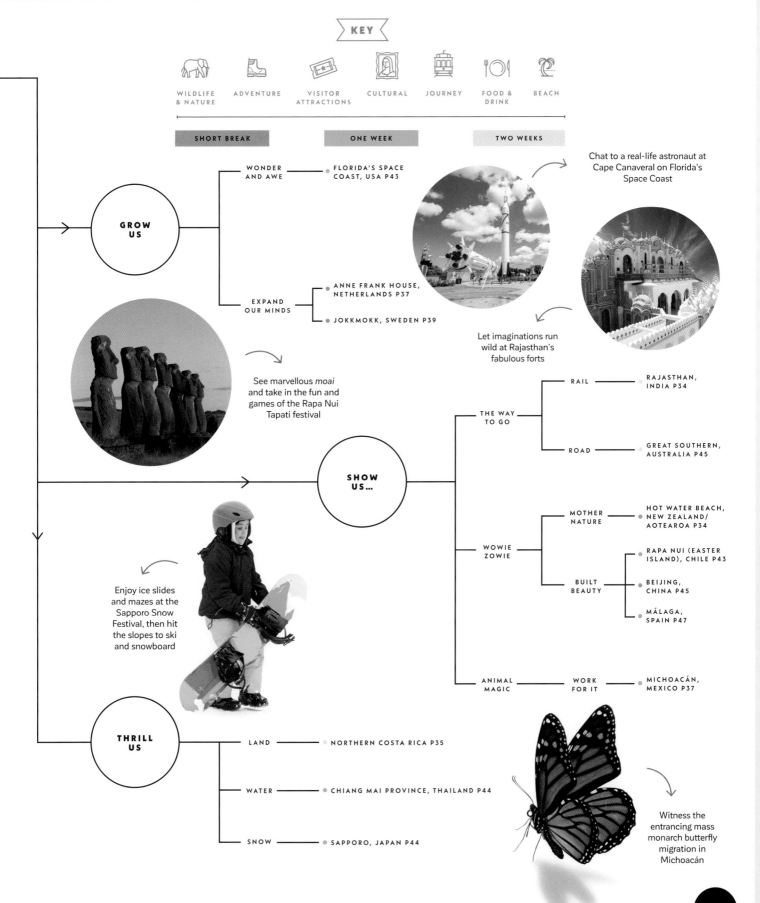

KEY

WILDLIFE & NATURE ADVENTURE VISITOR ATTRACTIONS CULTURAL JOURNEY FOOD & DRINK BEACH

| SHORT BREAK | ONE WEEK | TWO WEEKS |

GROW US

WONDER AND AWE —— ● FLORIDA'S SPACE COAST, USA P43

Chat to a real-life astronaut at Cape Canaveral on Florida's Space Coast

EXPAND OUR MINDS —— ● ANNE FRANK HOUSE, NETHERLANDS P37

● JOKKMOKK, SWEDEN P39

Let imaginations run wild at Rajasthan's fabulous forts

See marvellous *moai* and take in the fun and games of the Rapa Nui Tapati festival

SHOW US…

THE WAY TO GO —— RAIL —— RAJASTHAN, INDIA P34

ROAD —— GREAT SOUTHERN, AUSTRALIA P45

WOWIE ZOWIE —— MOTHER NATURE —— ● HOT WATER BEACH, NEW ZEALAND/ AOTEAROA P34

BUILT BEAUTY —— ● RAPA NUI (EASTER ISLAND), CHILE P43

● BEIJING, CHINA P45

● MÁLAGA, SPAIN P47

ANIMAL MAGIC —— WORK FOR IT —— ● MICHOACÁN, MEXICO P37

Enjoy ice slides and mazes at the Sapporo Snow Festival, then hit the slopes to ski and snowboard

THRILL US

LAND —— ● NORTHERN COSTA RICA P35

WATER —— ● CHIANG MAI PROVINCE, THAILAND P44

SNOW —— ● SAPPORO, JAPAN P44

Witness the entrancing mass monarch butterfly migration in Michoacán

Events in February

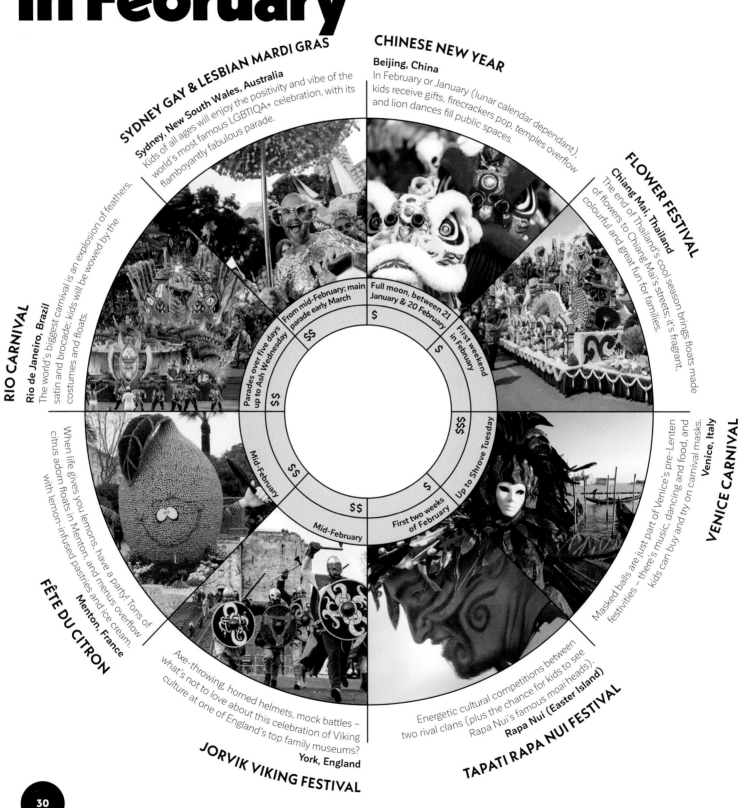

SYDNEY GAY & LESBIAN MARDI GRAS
Sydney, New South Wales, Australia
Kids of all ages will enjoy the positivity and vibe of the world's most famous LGBTIQA+ celebration, with its flamboyantly fabulous parade.

CHINESE NEW YEAR
Beijing, China
In February or January (lunar calendar dependant), kids receive gifts, firecrackers pop, temples overflow and lion dances fill public spaces.

FLOWER FESTIVAL
Chiang Mai, Thailand
The end of Thailand's cool season brings floats made of flowers to Chiang Mai's streets; it's fragrant, colourful and great fun for families.

RIO CARNIVAL
Rio de Janeiro, Brazil
The world's biggest carnival is an explosion of feathers, satin and brocade; kids will be wowed by the costumes and floats.

FÊTE DU CITRON
Menton, France
When life gives you lemons, have a party! Tons of citrus adorn floats in Menton, and menus overflow with lemon-infused pastries and ice cream.

JORVIK VIKING FESTIVAL
York, England
Axe-throwing, horned helmets, mock battles – what's not to love about this celebration of Viking culture at one of England's top family museums?

TAPATI RAPA NUI FESTIVAL
Rapa Nui (Easter Island)
Energetic cultural competitions between two rival clans (plus the chance for kids to see Rapa Nui's famous moai heads).

VENICE CARNIVAL
Venice, Italy
Masked balls are just part of Venice's pre-Lenten festivities – there's music, dancing and food, and kids can buy and try on carnival masks.

Inner wheel labels:
- From mid-February; main parade early March — $$
- Parades over five days up to Ash Wednesday — $$
- Full moon, between 21 January & 20 February — $
- First weekend in February — $
- First two weeks of February — $
- Up to Shrove Tuesday — $$$
- Mid-February — $$
- Mid-February — $$

Snack until your stomach is content in Rome

● ÎLES DES SAINTES, GUADELOUPE

Discover York's Viking history this month

● CHICAGO, USA

Inspire the dreams of future astronauts in Florida's Kennedy Space Center

Check out technicolour carnival costumes in Trinidad

● ROME, ITALY

● YORK, ENGLAND

Soak in hot springs in northern Thailand

● FLORIDA'S SPACE COAST, USA

● CHIANG MAI PROVINCE, THAILAND

There's something for parents to sample in Dublin

● HOT WATER BEACH, NEW ZEALAND/AOTEAROA

● SAPPORO, JAPAN

● TRINIDAD & TOBAGO

● MÁLAGA, SPAIN

● NICE, FRANCE

● DUBLIN, IRELAND

● BEIJING, CHINA

● SOUTH DOWNS, ENGLAND

● RAJASTHAN, INDIA

Explore Hollywood on a star-spotting trip to Los Angeles

Hunt historic dragons in Beijing, China

A volcanic backdrop to Guatemala's Lake Atitlán

● NORTHERN COSTA RICA

● ANTIGUA & ATITLÁN, GUATEMALA

● JOKKMOKK, SWEDEN

● GREAT SOUTHERN, AUSTRALA

Is that a little fluffy cloud or a sheep on England's South Downs?

● MICHOACÁN, MEXICO

● LOS ANGELES, USA

Borrow some bicycles to explore Amsterdam

● YELLOWKNIFE, CANADA

Do the Tree Top Walk in Australia's Valley of the Giants

● IMSOUANE, MOROCCO

● RAPA NUI (EASTER ISLAND), CHILE

● ANNE FRANK HOUSE, NETHERLANDS

ÎLES DES SAINTES
GUADELOUPE

0-16

Why now? Sunbathing, snorkelling and meeting goats on the beach.

Les Saintes are a group of nine mountain-peaked islands off the coast of Guadeloupe. Terre-de-Haut is the ultimate Caribbean getaway – an island off the coast of an island – where days revolve around beach outings, leisurely lunches and island explorations, all at your own pace. You might visit a different beach every day, each more idyllic than the last, some dotted with grazing goats. The waters are calm and crystalline blue – perfect for little swimmers. Best of all, several beaches have the coral reef right offshore, so you can snorkel from the beach to see extravagant fish lurking just below the surface. If and when your family needs a break from the beach, there are centuries-old forts to explore, mini mountains to climb, and fabulous vistas at every turn. Don't miss indulging in the

local speciality pastry, *tourment d'amour*, a crunchy tart with a fruit filling.

Trip plan: Many people come to Terre-de-Haut for a day trip, but it's a perfect destination for a relaxing weekend or even a week away. Ferries run from Point-à-Pitre (50min) several times a day. Don't forget the travel sickness meds – the crossing can be rough.

Need to know: Terre-de-Haut is small enough that you can visit the entire island without a car. If your kids get tired of walking, consider renting scooters or e-bikes.

Other months: Dec-Apr – sunny and dry, peak tourist season; Nov & May – shoulder season; Jun-Oct – humid and rainy, hurricane season Aug-Sep.

Terre-de-Haut harbour, Îles des Saintes

33

SOUTH DOWNS
ENGLAND

0-16 Why now? For a dive into Sussex's past and the South Downs Dark Skies Festival.

England's South Downs undulate between Winchester and Eastbourne, its fields and woods scattered across chalkland carved over millennia. As the winter sun sets, shadows lengthen, and the cosmic cloud of the Milky Way sprinkles across the night sky. The light-free conditions here are increasingly rare, and in 2016 the South Downs National Park was designated as the world's 13th International Dark Sky Reserve (IDSR). Each February, the park hosts the nine-day South Downs Dark Skies Festival; highlights of the indoor and outdoor activities have included a 'Walk the Planets' trail, with the planets laid out to scale; stargazing talks and demos; guided tours of nocturnal wildlife at Queen Elizabeth and Seven Sisters Country Parks; and Star Parties on Brighton seafront, Goodwood and at Hogmoor Inclosure in Bordon, with telescopes laid on. You can also explore Sussex's Earthly past at Singleton's Weald & Downland Living Museum, just north of Chichester, which recreates rural life in a Sussex village, with a watermill and bakehouse, plus farm animals and games to keep smaller visitors entertained.

Trip plan: Brighton and Chichester are good bets for overnights; the South Downs website (southdowns.gov.uk) has local info.

Need to know: Star Parties can attract up to 500 people!

Other months: Jan & Mar – cold, wet; Apr-May – bluebells; Jun-Aug – busiest; Sep-Nov – cooler, getting wetter; Dec – cold.

HOT WATER BEACH
NEW ZEALAND/ AOTEAROA

0-16 Why now? Fewer crowds and settled summer weather.

The name Hot Water Beach says it all – there aren't many places where you can rent a spade and fashion your own family hotpool just metres from the waves, or dig your toes into hot water oozing up through the sand from underground thermal springs. Needless to say, most children absolutely love it, and with Kiwi kids back in school, February is a perfect time to hit this 'bucket list' beach on the eastern Pacific Ocean coast of the Coromandel Peninsula. There are a few caveats: arrive within two hours either side of low tide – check tide times online – or you'll be frustrated at having to wait; and before jumping in to your private pool, test the water with a finger or toe to avoid scalding your kids and totally wrecking your day. After a thermal wallow, a refreshing ocean dip is on the cards, but keep an eye on kids as there can be strong undertows that make swimming out dangerous. That said, Hot Water Beach is a unique and unmissable Kiwi experience, and its thermal waters ensure the kids will have fun even if the weather isn't great.

Trip plan: Hot Water Beach is 32km (20 miles) southwest of the beach town of Whitianga, and a 173km (107-mile) drive from Auckland.

Need to know: There are cafes, galleries, spades for rent, plus 'wash off' showers and toilets at the car park.

Other months: Oct-Apr – warm summer weather; May-Sep – winter, cooler.

RAJASTHAN
INDIA

5-16 Why now? Take advantage of dry, cool days to explore Rajasthan's evocative forts.

While India throws up a few challenges for small explorers, the desert forts of Rajasthan are the closest thing you'll find to Disney's *Aladdin* in real life, and a perfect family adventure. Behind the towering walls of famous fortifications such as Amber Fort near Jaipur and the Mehrangarh in Jodhpur, you'll find extravagantly decorated royal chambers, elegant gardens, mural-covered pavilions, armouries stuffed with jewel-encrusted swords and gateways bristling with spikes to deter battle elephants – plus welcome respite from India's teeming traffic. Plot a route from Jaipur (with stops at Amber, the City Palace and the Jantar Mantar, Jai Singh II's royal observatory) to Jodhpur (home to the mighty Mehrangarh), returning via the sand-coloured desert fortress in Jaisalmer, where you can take a bonus camel ride through the dunes.

Trip plan: Trains are the most family-friendly way to get around – comfy 2-Tier AC class is ideal for kids. It's a 5hr journey from Jaipur to Jodhpur and 5-6hr from Jodhpur to Jaisalmer; the 12hr trip from Jaisalmer to Jaipur is best tackled on an overnight sleeper train – an adventure in itself.

Need to know: The Rajasthani desert is cooler than you might expect in winter – pack for mild days that peak at around 22°C (72°F), and cool nights and mornings, when you'll need a coat.

Other months: Dec-Jan – cooler, drier and busier; Mar-May & Oct-Nov – warmer and quieter; Jun-Sep – the soggy monsoon.

© ChameleonsEye / Shutterstock

YORK
ENGLAND

5-16 Why now? York's storied streets throng with axe-wielding warriors and wide-eyed berserkers during the Jorvik Viking Festival.

Ambling through the twisty, narrow, atmospheric alleyways of the Shambles in mid-February, every second person you meet has a beard and a blade. Fear not, though – the weapons, shields and ferocious frowns are all for show at this time of the year, when York celebrates Britain's biggest Viking-themed event and stages epic re-enactments of battles between Anglo-Saxons and rampaging Norsemen. Jórvík is the Norse name for this wall-encircled city, which starred in multiple historical dramas, from the Roman occupation to the War of the Roses, and saw several pivotal Viking-era events. This history is boisterously celebrated with this annual festival of (mock) fighting, featuring characters with names like Sigurd Snake-in-the-Eye, Ivar the Boneless, Sweyn Forkbeard and Eric Bloodaxe – flaxen-haired hardmen who fought for real here 1000 years ago. There's something for everyone, though, including Scandinavian crafting sessions; and Jorvik Viking Centre is open year-round.

Trip plan: York is well serviced by trains and buses. The nearest airport is Leeds Bradford. The best way to explore is by walking the medieval walls that surround the city – don't miss the castle (Clifford's Tower) and the grimacing gargoyles of York Minster.

Need to know: Northern England is chilly in February – bring a hat (but not a horned one; real Vikings didn't wear them).

Other months: Apr-May – daffodils around the castle mound and walls; Jun-Aug – very busy; Sep-Nov – autumn colours along the River Ouse.

NORTHERN COSTA RICA

5-16 Why now? For sunny, rain-free days and jungle fun.

Costa Rica is one of the few places in the world where wildlife is both accessible and well-protected. For families with younger children, the national parks are full of animal surprises, while older kids will thrive with activities like rafting and ziplining. It's hard to beat a wildlife tour of Parque Nacional Tortuguero. Often called the 'mini-Amazon', this coastal, canal-swathed park is home to more than 400 bird species and 60 known species of frog, plus monkeys and threatened West Indian manatees. Wildlife here is observed through leisurely boat rides, perfect for explorers of all ages. Laid-back adventure can also be found in Monteverde, where the beautiful cloud forest reserve can be visited on foot, horseback, or from a suspension bridge through the canopy. If your family has ziplining on their must-do list, swoop along the circuits – some over 750m (2460ft) long – in Monteverde and at the Arenal Volcano (minimum age is five), while kids aged eight or over can tackle whitewater rafting on the Pacuare or Sarapiquí Rivers, within the Parque Nacional Braulio Carrillo.

Trip plan: Allow at least five days to visit Tortuguero and Monteverde, more to fit in activities in Bralio Carrillo and beyond. The closest airport is in San José; car rental is available. Dedicated tourist shuttle services run between popular destinations.

Need to know: Visitor numbers are limited at the Monteverde reserve; get there before the gates open.

Other months: Sep-Oct – rainy season; Jul-Oct – nesting green turtles at Tortuguero.

ROME
ITALY

5-16 Why now? Smaller crowds and shorter queues for Rome's famous pizzas.

Foodies are torn over which Italian city produces the best pizzas – Rome or Naples? For our money, Rome's pizzas come out top for tots: they're thin, crispy and not too stodgy, so kids won't be too full for an afternoon of serious sightseeing. There's also less mess (Neapolitan pizzas stay moist, maximising the chances of sauce dribbles). On a January visit to Rome, you can wrap up to explore the Colosseum, the Forum and the Vatican Museums, then warm up in pizzerias made cosy by the heat radiating from the pizza oven. Top stops for pizza pilgrims include Pizzeria Alle Carrette near the Forum, or Emma Pizzeria south of the Pantheon; away from the centre, seek out Seu Pizza Illuminati in the Trastevere neighbourhood, or Pizzeria Remo in Testaccio – both districts also have lots of authentic *gelaterie*.

Trip plan: Rome is best tackled neighbourhood by neighbourhood. Stay centrally and spend a busy few days around Campo di Fiori and the Vatican, Pantheon, Forum and Colosseum, followed by more relaxed days exploring residential quarters such as Testaccio and Trastevere.

Need to know: Work out how to reach any destination in Rome on public transport using the ATAC website (atac.roma.it) and the Moovit app; buy tickets on your phone using TicketAppy.

Other months: Nov-Mar – cool, smaller crowds; Apr-May & Oct-Nov – warmer but still calm; Jun-Sep – hot, humid and busy.

Hanging with the animals at Chicago's Field Museum

CHICAGO USA

5-16 Why now? Winter is the perfect time to take in some culture in the Windy City.

Winter comes in hard on the shores of Lake Michigan, but Chicago is jammed with indoor things to see and do. Kids can have a ball in the dinosaur-stuffed Field Museum of Natural History even when it's blowing a blizzard. In February, bring *Night at the Museum* to life at the museum's Dozin' with the Dinos event, open to kids aged six to 12, with science-based activities and tours by torchlight. Extra events are held in January, March, April and November. Continue the education at the Art Institute of Chicago and the Museum of Science & Industry, then drop into the respected zoo at Lincoln Park (special arrangements are made for the animals in winter). For a change of pace, get dizzying views of the city from the 360 Chicago and Willis Tower viewing decks, then break for a cheese-drenched Chicago pizza at Vito & Nick's on South Pulaski Rd.

Trip plan: Chicago's O'Hare and Midway airports receive flights from everywhere; get around town by bus, taxi or by the elevated trains of the 'L'. Lincoln Park, River North and South Loop are convenient bases for families.

Need to know: Chicago's Windy City nickname may refer to boastful politicians, but the wind-chill effect of the lake can be severe: bring scarves, hats and earmuffs for the kids.

Other months: Dec-Jan – cold and icy; Mar-May & Sep-Nov – mild, some rain; Jun-Aug – hot, humid.

Monarch butterflies in Michoacán's Mariposa Reserve

© JHVEPhoto / Shutterstock

ANNE FRANK HOUSE
NETHERLANDS

12-16 Why now? Read and reflect in peace during Amsterdam's low season, when you'll have more time slots to choose from.

Visit the house and annexe where, in July 1942, 13-year-old Jewish schoolgirl Anne Frank went into hiding from the Nazis, along with her parents, sister Margo and two other families. Two years later they were discovered and taken to Auschwitz. Anne and Margo were subsequently transferred to the Bergen-Belsen concentration camp, where they caught typhus and died within weeks of each other, less than three months before Germany surrendered and the camps were liberated. While young people (and parents) will inevitably find this experience upsetting and confronting, it's also highly educational, helping teenagers to empathise with Anne's life while she was in hiding. Anne's original diary is displayed at the museum. Her account of the experience, first published in 1947 as *Het Achterhuis* (*The Secret Annexe*), has been translated into 70 languages and continues to serve as a powerful and poignant reminder of the dangers of discrimination and hatred. Visiting the house where the family hid brings the horror of the Holocaust into even clearer focus.

Trip plan: Rent bikes and explore the canals and side streets of Amsterdam via dedicated cycling lanes.

Need to know: The Anne Frank House Museum is open daily (9am-10pm), but you must buy a ticket online (annefrank.org) in advance, for a specific time slot.

Other months: Mar-May – tulips; Jun-Sep – warm weather, festivals, crowds, queues.

MICHOACÁN MEXICO

5-16 Why now? See butterflies take flight from the mountains near Mexico City.

The mercury can hit 25°C (77°F) in Mexico City in February, providing welcome respite from the harsh winter further north in the Americas. Millions of monarch butterflies have the same idea, fluttering south from Canada and the United States for a warmer winter in the forested hills of the Reserva de la Biósfera Santuario Mariposa Monarca, 100km (62 miles) west of the capital. Bring the family in winter and you can graze on tacos and quesadillas, climb the gargantuan Teotihuacán pyramids, take in a *lucha libre* (wrestling) match and keep the kids entertained at museum-crammed Bosque de Chapultepec, before heading out to see monarch butterflies filling the forests like flying confetti. The most accessible sections of the biosphere reserve are Sierra Chincua and El Rosario near Angangueo and Piedra Herrada near Valle de Bravo – reach the sanctuary trailheads by taxi then explore on foot or on horseback.

Trip plan: Mexico City is Central America's biggest air hub, and buses run regularly from the city's Poniente Bus Terminal to Angangueo and Valle de Bravo. On arrival, join a guided walk or horseback trek to reach the best monarch-viewing sites.

Need to know: Day tours are a hassle-free butterfly-spotting option, leaving from Mexico City and Morelia (1hr from Mexico City by air).

Other months: Nov-Feb – dry, slightly cooler; Mar-Apr – warmest days; May-Oct – humid, stormy.

Reindeer and Sámi herders at the Jokkmokk Winter Market

JOKKMOKK
SWEDEN

5-16 Why now? Experience Sámi culture and Arctic excitement during Jokkmokk's Winter Market.

Don't expect much sunshine during your visit to the far north in February – Jokkmokk, the capital of Sámi culture, is north of the Arctic Circle – but there may well be the opportunity to see the dancing green lights of the Aurora Borealis in the night sky. Held annually since 1606, the fabulous Winter Market starts on the first Thursday in February and lasts for three intense days, with intriguing activities, going on from early to late, that will fascinate youngsters. It's like a yearly party for Sámi, who come from far and wide to see extended family, old friends and to make new contacts. Expect to see Sámi in colourful traditional clothing, plenty of reindeer and food stalls selling local delicacies. Visitors are most welcome and can splurge on the widest array of Sámi *duodji* (handcrafts) to be seen anywhere. While Jokkmokk has a population of only 3000, well over ten times that number turn up for the market. Regular accommodation gets booked out quickly, but Jokkmokk residents open their homes to market visitors and, somehow, everything seems to work out.

Trip plan: The nearest airports are in Gällivare, Arvidsjaur and Luleå. Either take a bus or pick up a rental car and drive to Jokkmokk.

Need to know: It can get very cold! Ensure everyone has warm clothing and shoes, a hat that covers the ears, and good gloves or mittens.

Other months: Nov-Mar – Aurora Borealis; Jun-Jul – Midnight Sun; May-Sep – summer outdoor activities.

Carnival parade in Port of Spain, Trinidad

TRINIDAD & TOBAGO

5-16 Why now? Kiddie's Carnival delivers all the glitz but none of the debauchery of the main event.

Trinidad's epic Caribbean Carnival is famous for its danceable music, eye-popping costumes and all-night parties. This celebration of Trinbagonian heritage is an incredible feast for the senses – but too bacchanalian for the younger set. Fortunately, Trinidad engages and educates the youngsters with a dedicated Kiddie's Carnival – and it's a big deal. Kids from small to tall prepare for months, creating costumes and learning choreography for their own jubilant 'mas' (masquerade); the parade lasts several hours, the music jams and the costumes are out of this world. To recover from the revelries, head north to Maracas Beach, a gorgeous stretch of sand with a backdrop of rainforest-swathed hills. And don't leave Trinidad without visiting some of the island's nature preserves and bird sanctuaries. Budding birders can see an incredible spectacle at Caroni Sanctuary, where thousands of scarlet ibis return to roost every evening. Chaguaramas National Heritage Park is a gem, with rainforest trails, howler monkeys and waterfall swims.

Trip plan: Stay in Port of Spain and explore the capital, then rent a car for easy access to nature and beaches out of the city.

Need to know: Kiddie's Carnival takes place on the Saturday before the main (pre-Lenten) Carnival weekend; if you plan your trip carefully, you can avoid the highest Carnival-season prices.

Other months: Jan-May – sunny skies; Jun-Dec – daily showers (hurricanes rare).

© Herve Gyssels / Getty Images

YELLOWKNIFE
CANADA

5-16 **Why now? The best of times for aurora-watching.**

With wide-open skies and little light pollution, Yellowknife has been dubbed the 'aurora capital of North America' – and it's a top spot to introduce your family to the spectacular Northern Lights, which can be seen here on around 240 nights of the year. On the northern shore of Great Slave Lake, about 400km (250 miles) south of the Arctic Circle, the capital of Canada's Northwest Territories was named after the 'Yellowknife Indians', known today as the Yellowknives Dene First Nation. Book ahead for an evening tour at Indigenous-owned Aurora Village, and hang out in atmospheric teepees with a warm wood stove, games and hot drinks to keep kids happy while waiting for the aurora to appear. Even better, there are heated bathrooms and, once the natural light show begins, unobstructed views and swivelling heated outdoor viewing seats. If your family is up for more action during the day, consider a dogsledding adventure.

Trip plan: Yellowknife is surprisingly accessible, with daily direct flights to and from major Canadian cities. Plan to stay at least three nights to maximise your chances of seeing the aurora.

Need to know: Aurora-viewing on winter nights in northern Canada means you need to prepare for the cold. Bring your own gear, or rent from local outfitters in Yellowknife. The town has lots of warm places to stay, eat and hang out.

Other months: Mid-Nov to early April & mid-Aug to Sep – peak aurora season; Jun-Aug – pleasant summer weather.

The Northern Lights dance over Aurora Village, Yellowknife

(A) Saturn V rocket at Florida's Kennedy Space Center, USA; (L) Volcano-ringed Antigua, Guatemala; (R) *Moai* on Rapa Nui, Chile

FLORIDA'S SPACE COAST
USA

5-16 **Why now?** Visit the USA's gateway to the galaxy and enjoy the best of the Sunshine State with fewer crowds (and no twisters).

Seeing a real-life spaceport is a mind-blowing experience for young travellers. Cape Canaveral is where space shuttles once launched and rockets still race away from Earth's atmosphere, hurtling towards infinity. Located on Merritt Island, NASA's Kennedy Space Center exhibits space tech – including the actual flown-in-space shuttle *Atlantis* – and offers visitors the chance to chat to a real astronaut, before entering a futuristic spaceport and embarking on an immersive (virtual) adventure to distant worlds. Nearby, Cape Canaveral Space Force Station is where rockets blast off (many pioneering space flights have begun here, including one carrying the first ever US astronaut). Also home to the US Air Force Space Command's 45th Space Wing, it's closed to the public; only US citizens are allowed to tour the lighthouse here, but everyone can visit the fascinating (and free) Sands Space History Center, just outside the south gate.

Trip plan: Fly to Orlando and get a shuttle bus to Port Canaveral (45min). Hire a car to enjoy more fantastic Florida experiences: December to February is the best time to swim with manatees at West Palm Beach and explore extraordinary Everglades National Park.

Need to know: Sands Space History Center is closed Mondays. Unfortunately, real rocket launches are rare and often delayed.

Other months: Nov-Jan – cooler, drier; Mar-May – comfortable heat, quite dry; Jun-Aug – hot, wet, busy; Sep-Oct – humidity drops, hurricanes/tornadoes possible.

ANTIGUA & ATITLÁN
GUATEMALA

0-16 **Why now?** Candy-coloured charm, volcano hikes and lake cruises during the dry season.

Ringed by a trio of volcanoes and with its grid of historic streets lined with pastel-painted facades and romantic baroque ruins, the multicoloured city of Antigua is a charmer. Kids can freely explore the courtyards and ruins of the Convento de Capuchinas; make (and eat) chocolate at the ChocoMuseo; and roam the whimsical sculpture gardens at Santo Domingo del Cerro. Active and adventurous families might summit nearby Volcán Pacaya, an easy 5km (3-mile) hike. (You can hire horses for the trek up if you're not sure your kids will make it.) A special treat awaits at the top: marshmallows, roasted over hot lava. End your trip at Lago de Atitlán, a scenic crater lake surrounded by volcanic peaks. Book the kids on a weaving lesson at the famous women's textile cooperatives in mellow San Juan La Laguna, and hop on a boat or hire a tuk-tuk to visit the other picturesque Maya towns lined up along the shore.

Trip plan: Start in Antigua, then book a tour or hire a driver for the 1hr trip to Volcán Pacaya. Take a shared shuttle bus to Panajachel, a convenient base for exploring Lago Atitlán.

Need to know: A guide is obligatory for the Pacaya hike. Book a guided tour (with transportation) from Antigua, or hire a local guide (often Spanish-speaking only) at the trailhead.

Other months: Nov-Mar – dry season, chilly at night; Apr-May & Sep-Oct – rainy season; Jun-Aug – hot weather, afternoon showers.

RAPA NUI (EASTER ISLAND)
CHILE

5-16 **Why now?** Experience the unique annual Rapa Nui Tapati festival.

Calling Rapa Nui remote and isolated doesn't even come close: this volcanic speck lies adrift in the Pacific over 3600km (2237 miles) west of mainland Chile. No wonder its culture, seeded by Polynesian settlers in the first millennium CE, evolved a series of unique traditions – most famously, hundreds of colossal, mysterious *moai* (carved stone heads), looming up to 10m (33ft) tall. Centuries of clan strife, colonisation, assimilation and ecological collapse wreaked havoc on that heritage – but today, it's celebrated once more during the Rapa Nui Tapati festival at the start of February, a hot, dry month that's also prime time for exploring the island. Get teenagers involved plotting your route around key sites – Orongo Ceremonial Village; the Rano Raraku volcano, from which part-quarried *moai* sprout; the monumental platform of Ahu Tongariki – making time at the festival to cheer on the horse-racing, running, swimming and boat-paddling competitions, the music and dance, and the final crowning of the Ariki (Queen) Tapati.

Trip plan: Rapa Nui is accessible by plane from Santiago, Chile – consider combining your visit with a trip around Chile. Allow at least three or four nights on the island to explore fully. Book flights and accommodation well in advance if planning to attend the Rapa Nui Tapati festival.

Need to know: Mosquitoes sometimes carry dengue fever and Zika virus on Rapa Nui – cover up and bring insect repellent.

Other months: Nov-Mar – hot, driest, busiest; Apr-Oct – cooler, wetter (May is the rainiest month).

SAPPORO
JAPAN

0-16 **Why now?** Combine a family ski adventure with the Sapporo Snow Festival.

The truly spectacular week-long Sapporo Yuki Matsuri (Snow Festival) seems to get bigger and better every year. It's a total extravaganza – renowned as one of Japan's top festivals – with everything from entire frozen stages for visiting musical acts to ice slides and ice mazes for the kids, plus a huge ice sculpture competition with teams turning up from all over the planet. Throw in countless bowls of steaming Sapporo miso-ramen, plenty of iconic Sapporo beer for the adults, illuminations of Hello Kitty ice statues once it's dark, and you've got endless entertainment for the whole family. The region hosted the 1972 Winter Olympics; Sapporo Teine ski area, home to many of the events, is only a short distance west. The 'Bus Pack' is ideal for families, as it includes return transfers from downtown Sapporo hotels, and a lift pass, for a surprisingly good rate. If you want to head further afield, Niseko famously receives over 15m (50ft) of the fluffy white stuff each winter, while Furano Ski Resort, in central Hokkaidō, offers free lift passes for kids aged 12 and under.

Trip plan: Fly into New Chitose Airport, the main entry point to Hokkaidō, 45km (28 miles) southeast of Sapporo, then take a train into the city.

Need to know: Book Sapporo accommodation well in advance around the Snow Festival.

Other months: Dec-Apr – ski season; Apr – cherry blossoms; Jun-Sep – mild summer; Oct – autumn colours.

CHIANG MAI PROVINCE
THAILAND

5-16 **Why now?** Trade the northern hemisphere winter for Thailand's hot springs.

Basking in a hot spring in the steamy tropics might seem like one high-temperature experience too far, but the jungle-cloaked hills around Chiang Mai are dotted with thermal resorts that will thrill young adventurers. At San Kamphaeng, Doi Saket and Pong Arng near Chiang Dao, plumes of steam rise above rainforest glades and clear mountain streams mingle with hot spring water, creating fantasy bathing pools – some toddler-friendly and others best reserved for old-timers with heatproof skin (it's a good idea to test the waters before you dive in with little ones). In between splashing and chasing butterflies and lizards between the steam vents, kids can buy baskets of eggs to boil in undiluted hot pools for an impromptu picnic lunch. Don't worry about overheating – in Chiang Mai province, you're never far from a waterfall delivering cool water from the mountaintops into natural splash pools.

Trip plan: Charter a *rod daeng* (pick-up truck) in Chiang Mai for leisurely day trips to San Kamphaeng, Doi Saket and Pong Arng (conveniently close to the waterfall at Sri Sangwan). At the end of the day, it's an easy drive back to town to indulge in some of Asia's best street food.

Need to know: If the kids turn up their noses at thermally heated eggs, all the hot springs have food stalls selling sticky rice and other kid-friendly snacks.

Other months: Nov-Mar – dry, warm not scorching; Apr-May – hot, hot, hot; Jun-Oct – deeply damp.

IMSOUANE
MOROCCO

12-16 **Why now?** For mellow surf and winter sun without the summer crowds.

Once a haven for backpackers and adventurous surf travellers, the coastal fishing village of Imsouane may no longer be a well-kept secret, but it's still easy to avoid the crowds if you visit during the European winter. Dubbed 'Magic Bay' for its spectacular setting – towering sandstone cliffs frame the ocean, while blue-and-white fishing boats line the harbour – Imsouane is a great spot for older kids to progress their surfing. The beautiful peeling right-hand wave here usually breaks gently, even during winter storms, as the harbour wall takes the punch out of the Atlantic swell, and the relaxed waves attract relaxed surfers, so the vibe in the water is friendly. Imsouane is also a good base for day trips up the coast to the towns of Sidi Kaouki and Essaouira, or sandboarding at nearby Tamri and hiking in the Atlas Mountains.

Trip plan: Fly to Agadir for the shortest transfer, then take the Souk to Surf bus or a private transfer to Imsouane.

Need to know: The water isn't tropical, but it isn't cold – spring wetsuits should work even in February for older kids, though younger children will need a 4/3. The sun usually shines, even in winter, with February temperatures averaging around 20°C (68°F), though take jumpers as it can get cold at night.

Other months: Dec-Jun – good surf, with waves getting smaller towards summer; Jul-Aug – flat surf and very crowded with summer tourists; Sep-Nov – the best waves, main surf-tourist season.

BEIJING
CHINA

5-16 Why now? Hunt dragons in a less-crowded, fabulously frosty Forbidden City.

Enclosed by 3.5km (2 miles) of citadel walls and a moat, the mere name of this epic 600-year-old palace excites young ears. Built by Ming emperor Yongle, its construction involved a million workers, and only the emperor's inner circle had access to what was originally named Zijincheng (Purple Forbidden City). Now officially called Gùgōng Bówùguǎn (Palace Museum), Mao's picture hangs over a gate that 16 million visitors stream through each year – but February is refreshingly quiet. The scale is bamboozling nonetheless. Besides courtyards capable of holding 100,000 people, there are, apparently, 9,999½ rooms (to avoid, legend says, upsetting the God of Heaven, whose palace has 10,000 rooms). Of the Three Great Halls, most important is the Hall of Supreme Harmony, containing the ornately decorated Dragon Throne – seat of power for 24 rulers of the Ming and Qing dynasties until Puyi, China's last emperor, was evicted in 1924. There's much to see, and lots of walking; smart families limit trips to a few hours and ask guides to focus on things kids are interested in (like dragons). To see the whole Forbidden City, take in the view from Jingshan Park.

Trip plan: Take Subway Line 1 to Tiananmen West and walk through Tiananmen Square to the Forbidden City.

Need to know: The site is closed on Mondays. If Chinese New Year and the Lantern Festival fall in February, the Forbidden City will be busier (but more interesting) than normal.

Other months: Apr-May & Sep-Oct – good weather; Jul-Aug – peak season, busy.

GREAT SOUTHERN
AUSTRALIA

5-16 Why now? Road-trip WA to chill on beautiful beaches, ride waves and watch huge pods of orca.

Australia's most beautiful beaches aren't around Sydney or on Queensland's tropical islands, but strung like a set of gleaming pearls along the south coast of Western Australia, between Albany and Esperance. Yet this region is relatively quiet – and in February, after schools restart but while the mercury still hovers at a balmy 24°C (75°F) or so, it's the perfect time to enjoy that soft sand by yourselves. There's also lots to do beyond the beaches. Take a nerve-jangling canopy walk amid towering tingle trees in the Valley of the Giants; explore the child-friendly hiking trails at Stirling Range and Fitzgerald River National Parks; and join family-oriented surf classes at Albany and around the southern coast. This is also the perfect time of year to gasp at killer whales (orca) gathering in large numbers in Bremer Bay to snaffle squid and fish. Follow their cue and try some of the region's beautifully fresh fish and chips.

Trip plan: Fly (1hr) or drive (4hr 30min) from Perth to Albany, then steer east to Esperance – allow a week to explore Bremer Bay, Fitzgerald River National Park and the succession of golden-sand beaches en route.

Need to know: Public transport in this region is limited – you'll want a vehicle to get around.

Other months: Jan & Mar-Apr – warm, sunny, orca in Bremer Bay; May-Jun – cool, quiet; Jul-Nov – cooler, southern right whales calving; Dec – hot, busier.

LOS ANGELES
USA

5-16 Why now? The glitz and glamour of awards season hits fever pitch.

To weave into the magic of Hollywood on a family trip to LA, begin with a Warner Bros Studio tour of the sets from favourite films and TV shows; kids will also gain insights into the technology and skill of movie-making. Next, before you wander along the Walk of Fame on Hollywood Blvd, create a DIY celebrity bingo card and see how many stars the kids can spot (hint: start outside the TCL Chinese Theatre). The Academy Museum of Motion Pictures has an unparalleled collection of memorabilia that will delight burgeoning film buffs, plus a calendar of films, talks and Oscar-week festivities, and the chance to simulate accepting your own golden statue. To further fuel career aspirations, book a celebrity homes tour that takes in the high-walled mansions and manicured gardens of Beverly Hills, as well as other LA landmarks such as Sunset Strip and Rodeo Dr. Next day, take the family on the 10km (6.5-mile) hike to the Hollywood sign along the Brush Canyon Trail, or try your luck spotting local silver-screen stars keeping fit at Runyon Canyon. Finally, satisfy any lasting yearning for celebrity sightings at Madame Tussauds Hollywood.

Trip plan: Hire a car or take Big Bus hop-on hop-off tours to many of the sights above.

Need to know: Prebook tours and scour the internet for fan tickets to red carpet events in February.

Other months: Sep-Jan – winter, mild, some rain; Mar-Apr – crowds around spring break; May-Aug – warm, dry.

NICE
FRANCE

0-16 Why now? Festival time on the Côte d'Azur, with multitudes of local lemons fashioned into hugely elaborate sculptures.

In a tradition dating back to the 19th century, Nice comes alive with colour for two weeks in February when the gleefully ostentatious Carnaval de Nice rolls into town. With comically large floats, large crowds and busy stalls offering lavender, fabrics and street food, it's quite a spectacle. This is also peak citrus season, and Nice's popular Cours Saleya market has stalls piled with oranges and Menton lemons. Wander the produce-packed aisles for supplies and souvenirs; there are plenty of street snacks and pastries to munch on as you browse. The season's zesty heroes are celebrated in typically extravagant style in nearby Menton. This pastel-coloured seaside town is the last stop on the Côte d'Azur before Italy, and makes for a lovely day trip; the Fête du Citron parades (from mid-February) feature huge designs painstakingly fashioned from thousands of lemons.

Trip plan: With good transport links, Nice is a great base for exploring the Riviera. The closest airport is Nice Cote d'Azur; Menton is a 40min drive away.

Need to know: Both the Carnaval de Nice (nicecarnaval.com) and the parade at the Fête du Citron (fete-du-citron.com) are ticketed; book in advance.

Other months: Nov-Jan – colder, quiet, Christmas markets in Dec; Mar – the Festin des Cougourdons celebrates Niçois culture; Apr-Jun – warmer weather, busy, Cannes Film Festival and Monaco Grand Prix; Jul – Bastille celebrations, busier; Aug – hot, busy, Assumption Day fireworks; Sep-Oct – glorious.

Menton's Fête du Citron, Cote d'Azur

DUBLIN
IRELAND

5-12 **Why now?** Wintry weather means smaller crowds and more rainbows – ideal conditions for discovering this crock of gold.

People visit Dublin to immerse themselves in the history, culture and stories that swirl around this tale-drenched city, and for children, an adventure into Ireland's mysterious Tír na nÓg – a Celtic Otherworld inhabited by spirits and supernatural beings – is utterly spellbinding. According to Irish folklore, only a handful of humans have entered this fantastical realm (typically through ancient burial mounds or caves), but kids aged six and up can gain access via the National Leprechaun Museum, where skilled storytellers guide wide-eyed explorers on a beguiling journey into a timeless place that's been talked about for millennia. Despite the museum's ultra-touristy title, this experience involves much more than a fleeting meeting with Ireland's legendary little people – Celtic mythology is every bit as rich as the Nordic Sagas and stories of Ancient Greece. There's something here for everyone (including an after-dark tour of the more twisted side of Ireland's underworld that only parents are allowed access to).

Trip plan: See the city's other sights on an exciting Viking Splash Dublin tour, aboard an amphibious 6WD vehicle.

Need to know: Visitors to the Leprechaun Museum need to be at least six years old. Tours last 45min; storytelling is in English.

Other months: Oct-Jan – inclement conditions; Mar – St Patrick's Day celebrations (and crowds); Apr-Jun – variable conditions, come prepared for anything; Jul-Sep – busy, better weather for outdoor exploring.

MÁLAGA
SPAIN

5-16 **Why now?** For vibrant off-season city life, Picasso, history – and the beach.

Most people pass through Málaga on their way somewhere else, but it's a great destination in its own right. Loaded with history and brimming with a youthful vigour, the city that gave the world Picasso has great art galleries to visit – including an unmissable museum dedicated to the artist – and a creative district called Soho, adorned with street art that might capture the interest of older kids; the smart port area has plenty of restaurants overlooking the boats, too. While this is very much a city to wander aimlessly, there are also plenty of sights. Children might enjoy the kid-specific audio tour of Málaga's cathedral, which will have them studying artworks and looking for clues in stained-glass windows. No time to visit Granada's Alhambra? Then Málaga's evocative Alcazaba can provide a taster. Another remnant of Málaga's Islamic past is the Castillo de Gibralfaro, spectacularly located high on the hill overlooking the city. And of course there's always the beach, gloriously empty off season.

Trip plan: Málaga Airport is well connected to Europe. The city itself can be explored largely on foot, but there's a great bus and train network.

Need to know: Málaga's stone streets can get slippery in the rain, so pack some shoes with a bit of grip.

Other months: Nov-Jan – more rain, cooler; Mar-May – some rain, but starting to warm up; Jun-Aug – temps around 28°C (98°F), very busy; Sep-Oct – still very warm, prices fall.

March

WHERE TO GO WHEN WITH KIDS

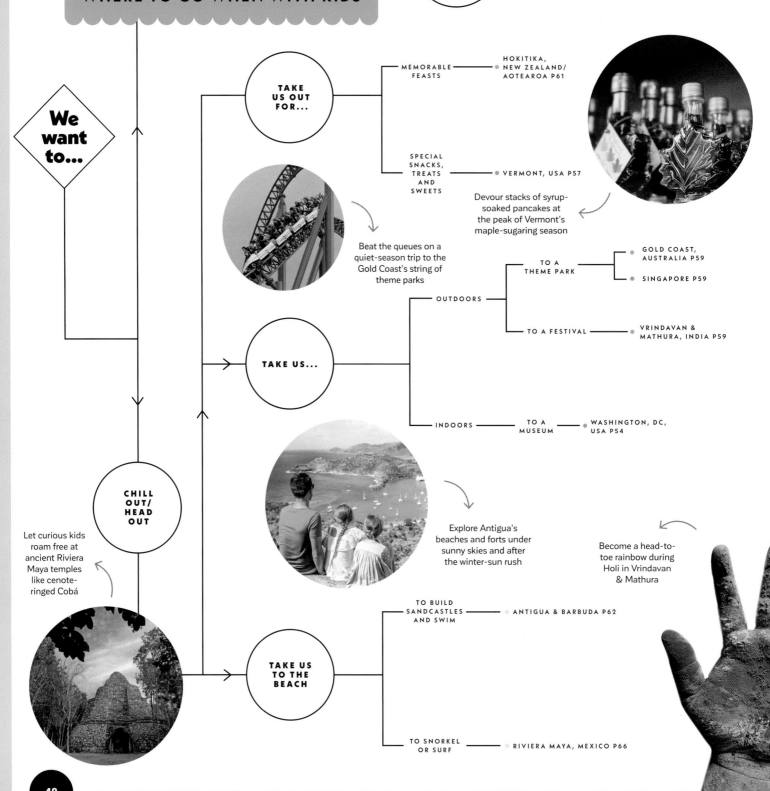

READY FOR ADVENTURE

We want to...

TAKE US OUT FOR...

MEMORABLE FEASTS ● HOKITIKA, NEW ZEALAND/ AOTEAROA P61

SPECIAL SNACKS, TREATS AND SWEETS ● VERMONT, USA P57

Devour stacks of syrup-soaked pancakes at the peak of Vermont's maple-sugaring season

Beat the queues on a quiet-season trip to the Gold Coast's string of theme parks

TAKE US...

OUTDOORS

TO A THEME PARK
● GOLD COAST, AUSTRALIA P59
● SINGAPORE P59

TO A FESTIVAL ● VRINDAVAN & MATHURA, INDIA P59

INDOORS

TO A MUSEUM ● WASHINGTON, DC, USA P54

Explore Antigua's beaches and forts under sunny skies and after the winter-sun rush

Become a head-to-toe rainbow during Holi in Vrindavan & Mathura

CHILL OUT/ HEAD OUT

Let curious kids roam free at ancient Riviera Maya temples like cenote-ringed Cobá

TAKE US TO THE BEACH

TO BUILD SANDCASTLES AND SWIM ● ANTIGUA & BARBUDA P62

TO SNORKEL OR SURF ● RIVIERA MAYA, MEXICO P66

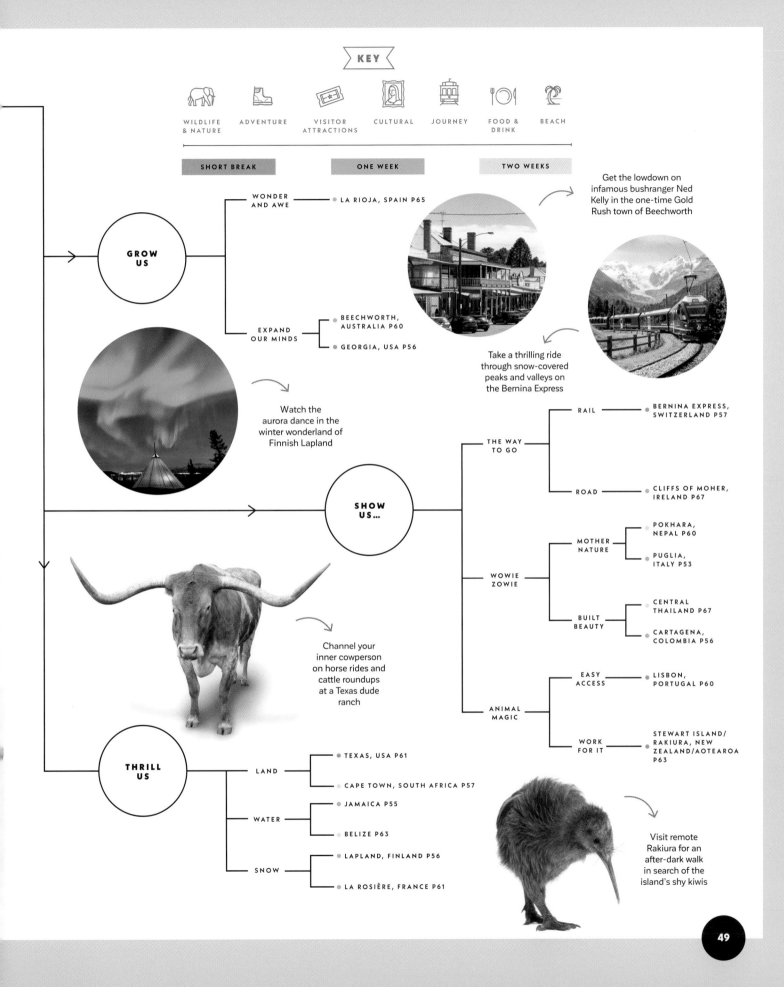

KEY

WILDLIFE & NATURE | ADVENTURE | VISITOR ATTRACTIONS | CULTURAL | JOURNEY | FOOD & DRINK | BEACH

SHORT BREAK | ONE WEEK | TWO WEEKS

GROW US

WONDER AND AWE — LA RIOJA, SPAIN P65

EXPAND OUR MINDS — BEECHWORTH, AUSTRALIA P60 — GEORGIA, USA P56

Get the lowdown on infamous bushranger Ned Kelly in the one-time Gold Rush town of Beechworth

Take a thrilling ride through snow-covered peaks and valleys on the Bernina Express

Watch the aurora dance in the winter wonderland of Finnish Lapland

SHOW US…

THE WAY TO GO
RAIL — BERNINA EXPRESS, SWITZERLAND P57
ROAD — CLIFFS OF MOHER, IRELAND P67

WOWIE ZOWIE
MOTHER NATURE — POKHARA, NEPAL P60 — PUGLIA, ITALY P53
BUILT BEAUTY — CENTRAL THAILAND P67 — CARTAGENA, COLOMBIA P56

ANIMAL MAGIC
EASY ACCESS — LISBON, PORTUGAL P60
WORK FOR IT — STEWART ISLAND/ RAKIURA, NEW ZEALAND/AOTEAROA P63

Channel your inner cowperson on horse rides and cattle roundups at a Texas dude ranch

THRILL US

LAND — TEXAS, USA P61 — CAPE TOWN, SOUTH AFRICA P57
WATER — JAMAICA P55 — BELIZE P63
SNOW — LAPLAND, FINLAND P56 — LA ROSIÈRE, FRANCE P61

Visit remote Rakiura for an after-dark walk in search of the island's shy kiwis

49

Events in March

WAFFLE DAY
Gothenburg, Sweden
Like pancake day in 3D, Sweden's waffle day is an excuse for youngsters to indulge in jam- and cream-topped delights.

HOLI
Mathura & Vrindavan, Uttar Pradesh, India
This vibrant Hindu festival sees coloured powder hurled at anyone within reach – dress kids in cheap white clothes and see outfits transform into rainbows.

SPRING EQUINOX
Chichén Itzá, Yucatán, Mexico
The mythical serpent that appears to descend the steps of Il Castillo pyramid will fascinate kids who visit Mexico's most famous Mayan site.

NYEPI
Bali, Indonesia
Bali's Day of Silence is quiet and contemplative, but kids will love the before-and-after parades of demons, and the feasts of festival food.

CHERRY BLOSSOM SEASON
Japan
The arrival of the spring sakura (cherry blossom) brings picnics, promenades and photo ops to cities all over Japan (perfect for aspiring Instagrammers).

LAS FALLAS
Valencia, Spain
Floats, fireworks, parties and parades, and the building and burning of giant effigies – what kid wouldn't be captivated by Las Fallas?

PACIFIKA
Auckland, New Zealand/Aotearoa
Get the kids to practise their haka – vigorous dancing and drumming take centre stage at this huge festival of Pacific Island culture.

ST PATRICK'S DAY
Belfast, Northern Ireland
Even those too young to like Guinness will enjoy the craic (fun): join the parades, then stay on for the Belfast Children's Festival.

25 March
$$

Mid- or late March
$

March to May
$

Early March
$$

March (sometimes February)
$

Around 21 March
$$

1-19 March
$$

17 March
$$

● SINGAPORE

Saddle up for a Texas horse-riding trip

Soak up the spring's cherry blossom in Washington, DC

● LISBON, PORTUGAL

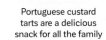

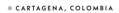

Splash down in the Gold Coast's Wet'n'Wild water park

● GOLD COAST, AUSTRALIA

Portuguese custard tarts are a delicious snack for all the family

● WASHINGTON, DC, USA

Admire New Zealand's greenstone crafts

● CARTAGENA, COLOMBIA

● VRINDAVAN & MATHURA, INDIA

Vrindavan & Mathura is the homeland of the deity Krishna

● TEXAS, USA

● CENTRAL THAILAND

● JAMAICA

● HOKITIKA, NEW ZEALAND/AOTEAROA

● RIVIERA MAYA, MEXICO

● CLIFFS OF MOHER, IRELAND

EXPENSIVE BUT WORTH IT

GOOD VALUE

● GEORGIA, USA

● PUGLIA, ITALY

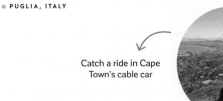

Catch a ride in Cape Town's cable car

● VERMONT, USA

The Forsyth Park fountain in Savannah, Georgia

● CAPE TOWN, SOUTH AFRICA

● LA RIOJA, SPAIN

● LA ROSIÈRE, FRANCE

● LAPLAND, FINLAND

● POKHARA, NEPAL

● BERNINA EXPRESS, SWITZERLAND

The sun shines over Antigua & Barbuda

● BEECHWORTH, AUSTRALIA

Wombats can be spotted around the town of Beechworth in Australia

Check out the conical houses in Alberobello, Puglia

● STEWART ISLAND/RAKIURA, NEW ZEALAND/AOTEAROA

The Bernina Express takes a scenic route through Switzerland

● ANTIGUA & BARBUDA

● BELIZE

PUGLIA ITALY

0-16 **Why now?** For dinosaurs and spectacular stalactites, plus *trulli* and city sights.

Beautiful Puglia has some of Italy's most picturesque beaches, but in summer the heat can mean families struggle to do much more than head for the coast. In March, though, the region will be nudging its way out of winter, with drier days and temperatures averaging around 15°C (59°F) – all the better for taking in the city sights of Taranto or Bari, with their cobbled roads and Ancient Greek ruins, and the towns and villages of the countryside.

You can take your time wandering around Alberobello's cone-shaped *trulli*, houses that date back to the 14th century and are unique to the region. Dinosaur fans should stop at the Museo Paleontologico e Parco dei Dinosauri, deep within the Parco Nazionale del Gargano at the village of San Marco in Lamis. Or for something more adventurous, take a guided tour of the Grotte di Castellana, an extensive series of caves that are sure to awe all young explorers.

Trip plan: There are two international airports serving Puglia: Brindisi and Bari. Car rental is available at both. It's also easy to get around the region by train.

Need to know: The Trenitalia app allows you to check routes and timetables as well as purchase tickets. Children under four are free, up to 15 years half price. Most museums and activities also offer reduced tickets for kids.

Other months: Apr-Jun – Easter celebrations, weather warming; Jul-Aug – high season, festivals, summer heat; Sep-Oct – harvest, still warm, fewer visitors; Nov-Feb – cool, rain, carnival season.

Traditional Puglian *trulli* in Alberobello

WASHINGTON, DC
USA

(A) Cherry blossom
blooms at DC's
Jefferson Memorial;
(R) Climbing Dunn's
River Falls, Jamaica

5–16 **Why now? Cherry blossoms abloom, plus free museums.**

DC's Tidal Basin is ringed with some 2500 cherry trees, a gift of friendship from Japan to the American people. It's a gift that keeps on giving in spring, when the trees burst into bloom and their branches hang heavy with sweet-smelling blossoms. If your kids aren't impressed by flowers, there's also the various shenanigans of the National Cherry Blossom Festival, from parades, fireworks and a Japanese street festival to a kite-flying event and the all-ages activities of 'Petalpalooza'. Cherry blossom festivities aside, you can't come to DC without taking advantage of the incredible (free!) collections of the Smithsonian Institute. The Museum of Natural History and the Air & Space Museum are the traditional kid favourites, but you'll find exhibits to engage younger people at the art and history museums too.

Trip plan: You can easily fill a long weekend without ever leaving the National Mall. Choose a museum or two to explore on your first day, then spend your second admiring the monuments and catching special events. If you have a third day, tour the US Capitol or add on an additional museum. Nearby, the Yards is a great destination to take a break and cool off in the fun water features.

Need to know: The cherries generally bloom for several weeks between mid-May and mid-April. The Cherry Blossom Festival website predicts the 'peak' dates.

Other months: Dec-Feb – cold, lighter crowds, lower prices; Apr-May & Sep-Oct – mild temperatures, sunny skies; Jun-Aug – hot, humid, crowded.

JAMAICA

5-16 **Why now?** Cool off in a Caribbean waterfall as the weather hits perfection.

Splashing in a waterfall is even more exhilarating than it looks in the holiday brochures and shampoo ads; the roar of the water, the billowing spray and the power of the flow create a bathing experience kids will remember for years. March is a great weather window in the Caribbean – not too hot, not too wet, not too windy. For the full 'waterfall in a rainforest glade' experience, point your compass at the island of Jamaica. At Cool Blue Hole near Ocho Rios, leaping into the plunge pool at the base of the cascade is the main attraction, while nearby Dunn's River Falls is great for photo ops in fountaining white spray as you climb from the bottom to the top. For more peace while you splash, try the quieter cascades of Reach Falls, YS Falls or Mayfield Falls. Mix up trips to the falls with forest walks, horse-riding, visits to waterparks and beach time at Ocho Rios, Negril and Montego Bay.

Trip plan: Jamaica's most accessible – and busiest – falls are close to the resort of Ocho Rios on the north coast, which also has fine beaches and watersports to keep kids amused. To reach inland waterfalls, rent a car and hike.

Need to know: Hit the falls early in the morning to beat the crowds. Bring grippy shoes and be careful on the slippery rocks around the water's edge.

Other months: Nov-Apr – warm, drier, busy; May-Oct – hot, wet, quieter.

GEORGIA
USA

 0–16 Why now? Unique museums, blooming azaleas and plenty of Southern charm.

Savannah, Georgia is the quintessential Southern city, decked out in antebellum architecture and ostentatious azaleas. Younger kids can play all day at two playgrounds in Forsythe Park or at the fantastic Children's Museum, located on the grounds of the former railway repair facility (so perfect for train buffs). With older kids, take a golf-cart tour of beautiful Bonaventure Cemetery and visit the Owens-Thomas House and Slave Quarters for a poignant history lesson. Tours showcase the art, architecture and history of the house, all through the lens of the institution that supported it: enslavement. Take a break from the city with a day (or longer) at Tybee Island. It might be too cold to swim, but it's perfect weather for hiking, kayaking or dolphin-spotting tours. And whatever you do, don't leave town without catching the Savannah Bananas in a game of banana ball (basically baseball, plus stunts, breakdancing and lots of laughs).

Trip plan: Spend a weekend exploring the Savannah sights, with a day (or longer) at the beach on Tybee Island. A free shuttle bus circles Savannah's historic district, but you'll need a car to get to Tybee.

Need to know: Most kids love this city's homestyle Southern cooking. Don't miss the famous fried chicken from Mrs Wilkes Dining Room, a Savannah staple since 1943.

Other months: Apr–Jun – peak season, warm, blooming flowers; Jul–Aug – hot, humid; Sep–Nov – mild, many special events; Dec–Feb – cooler, few crowds.

LAPLAND
FINLAND

5–16 Why now? Dogsled rides and dancing lights amid a snowbound wilderness.

Santa has hung up his hat for another year, the queues have disappeared, and Lapland's vast, untouched white wonderland unfurls. The Arctic Circle in March is magical: the ringing silence of frozen fells, the snow-daubed taiga forests, the remote Sámi *lavvu* tents. And the magical Northern Lights are quite likely to dance: according to the Finnish Meteorological Institute, the best time to look for aurora is February to March and September to October. This is a great time for families to get into the great outdoors. Though still chilly, temperatures start to rise this month, and wilderness lodges offer full programmes of activities. Pallas-Yllästunturi National Park in Lapland's western wilds is a particularly lovely spot. Straddling seven fells and sprinkled with traditional Lappish villages, the park is perfect for holing up in a log cabin and playing in the snow: possible pursuits include dogsledding and reindeer-sleigh rides, as well as snowmobiling, snowshoeing and ice fishing – the whole winter-wonder shebang.

Trip plan: Fly to Kittilä for Pallas-Yllästunturi; the airports in Rovaniemi and Ivalo offer access to Finland's north. Spend four or more nights at a wilderness lodge to maximise chances of seeing the aurora, and to pack in plenty of snowy fun.

Need to know: Many lodges offer 'aurora alerts' – a wake-up call if the lights emerge.

Other months: Dec–Feb & Apr – snow activities, aurora; May–Aug – long days, warmest; Sep–Nov – brief autumn, cooling.

CARTAGENA
COLOMBIA

5–16 Why now? Clamber around castle ramparts to battle (imaginary) buccaneers.

In the midst of dry season along Colombia's Caribbean coast, March is perfect for patrolling the tunnels, bunkers, batteries and parapets of Cartagena's Castillo de san Felipe de Barajas, and scanning the waves for approaching ships; it's an experience that delights young (and young-at-heart) travellers. Built atop San Lázaro hill in the 16th century, to protect this port city from the real pirates of the Caribbean, this fantastic fortress was constructed by Spanish Conquistadors (although enslaved Africans did the hard labour). Not quite impregnable – it was taken by the French privateer Bernard Desjean (Baron de Pointis) and his gang of bounty-seeking buccaneers in 1697 – the fortress repelled numerous attacks and saw action in several conflicts, including the War of Jenkins' Ear between Britain and Spain. The entrance is stunning, and there's a catacomb of cool tunnels to explore beneath the castle.

Trip plan: Fly to Rafael Núñez International Airport and take a taxi or bus 5.5km (3.5 miles) to Cartagena. Wander around Cartagena's wonderful walled Old Town (don't miss the scary Palace of the Inquisition) and walk to the fortress over the bridge from Getsemaní. Head to Parque Nacional Natural Tayrona to chill on rainforest-fringed Caribbean beaches.

Need to know: The fortress (along with Cartagena's historic centre) is a UNESCO-listed World Heritage Site. Guided castle tours are a good investment – on-site signage is poor.

Other months: Dec–April – dry season (and high season); May–Nov – rainy season (especially wet Sep to Nov).

VERMONT
USA

0–16 Why now? Skiing the slopes and tapping the trees.

Winter in Vermont is bitterly cold – but it is sweetened by the tantalising sap of the maple tree. When the nights are still cool but days start to warm, Vermonters tap their sugar maples to catch the sap that runs from the trees. Maple-sugar season usually starts in late February and can run through April. Sugarmakers collect buckets and buckets of sticky sap, then boil it down until it morphs into a thick, rich sticky syrup. At farms around the state, you can observe and even assist the process – or do the important job of devouring pancakes doused in maple syrup. If it sounds decadent, it is. Fortunately, Vermont offers plenty of chances to burn off calories at downhill and cross-country ski resorts.

Trip plan: Any Vermont ski resort has a sugar shack nearby. From Sugarbush or Mad River Glen, check out Morse Farm in Montpelier. From Killington, Baird Farm in North Chittenden has tours and a store. And in Jay's Peak – home of some of the gnarliest skiing in the east – head for Little Charlie's Sugarbush, also in Jay.

Need to know: Sugarhouses around the state invite visitors in to see their operations during the Maple Open House Weekend on the last weekend in March (but many offer tours and demonstrations throughout the season).

Other months: Dec-Feb – cold, dark, skiing is tops; Apr-Jun – shoulder season, mild, muddy trails (St Albans' Vermont Maple Festival in Apr); Jun-Oct – peak season, good weather, busy; Nov – cold, grey, bleak.

BERNINA EXPRESS
SWITZERLAND

0–16 Why now? Snowy scenery and fewer visitors before the crowds of summer.

One of the world's great train journeys – with its route declared a UNESCO World Heritage Site in 2008 – the legendary Bernina Express offers a fun family expedition. The tracks climb up the Bernina Valley from St Moritz, at 1775m (5823ft), reaching the highest point at 2353m (7720ft) Ospizio Bernina, then descend south into Val Poschiavo before crossing into Italy just before Tirano, at a mere 429m (1407ft) above sea level. The Alpine scenery is simply stupendous, especially when the peaks and valleys glisten under a covering of snow; and the Brusio Viaduct, where the line makes a full 360-degree spiral, is a highlight that will have kids on the edge of their seats. The link between St Moritz and Tirano takes two hours and 20 minutes direct, but it's possible to make stops along the way. Hop off at Bernina Diavolezza, then ride the Diavolezza cable car to its top station at 2973m (9754ft), where there's a *berghaus* with a restaurant, and incredible views over the Morteratsch Glacier and of 4049m (13,284ft) Piz Bernina, the highest mountain in the eastern Alps.

Trip plan: You can also catch the Bernina Express from Chur in Switzerland to Tirano; in summer, a Bernina Express bus continues on from Tirano to Lugano in Switzerland.

Need to know: The Bernina Express is free with a Swiss Travel Pass (though there's a fee for seat reservations).

Other months: Nov-Apr – winter, lots of snow; Jul-Aug – busy summer season.

CAPE TOWN
SOUTH AFRICA

5–16 Why now? Cool dry days for exploring Table Mountain.

March is the tail end of summer in Cape Town, but the crowds are thinning out and peak temperatures are starting to dip – optimum conditions for hiking on Table Mountain. With younger kids along for the hike, take the cable car up, gawp at the eye-popping views, then walk down – or stick to the gentler trails on top of the plateau, such as the mostly level, hour-long tramp from the cable car station to Maclear's Beacon. For a more ambitious family hike, descend from the plateau via the Platteklip Gorge, following stone steps through a rocky cleft lined with fynbos vegetation. Incentivise less enthusiastic hikers with promises of a few days on the sparkling beaches southwest of Cape Town at Clifton, Camps Bay and Llandudno.

Trip plan: Free MyCiTi buses run to the lower station for the Table Mountain cable car from Kloof Nek (with onward connections to Camps Bay), or you can take the City Sightseeing hop-on, hop-off bus from downtown. To reach the beaches from the centre, take the shuttle bus from Victoria Waterfront.

Need to know: Queues for the Table Mountain cable car build quickly; aim to get there before the desk opens at 8am, or pay extra for the Fast Track ticket.

Other months: Dec-Feb – warm and dry days, crowds; Apr-Sep – cooler and wetter, whale season; Sep-Nov – warming days, wildflowers.

(A) Surfers Paradise on Australia's Gold Coast; (L) Sentosa Island's Universal Studios theme park, Singapore; (R) Colourful holi revelry in Mathura, India

GOLD COAST
AUSTRALIA

`0-16` **Why now?** Make the most of the Gold Coast after the summer peak.

Can it get any better than 52km (32 miles) of pristine sand with epic surf breaks, blissful water temperatures and 300 sunny days a year? With its gloriously long stretch of sand, ready availability of spacious apartments and kid-friendly eating options, families flock in to the Gold Coast resort of Surfers Paradise. And with so much to do nearby, there's not really a bad time to turn up – except when everybody else does. So come in March, after Aussie kids return to school, to enjoy some seriously dizzying action on the gravity-defying rollercoasters and water slides at Warner Bros Movie World, Wet'n'Wild and Dreamworld. The Paradise Country 'Aussie Farm Experience' is particularly good for younger kids, with native species, farm animals and other furry cuties; while Currumbin Wildlife Sanctuary includes Australia's biggest rainforest aviary, where you can hand-feed a technicolour blur of rainbow lorikeets, plus kangaroo and crocodile feeding, photo ops with koalas, reptile shows and a treetop ropes course.

Trip plan: Gold Coast Airport is 21km (13 miles) south of Surfers Paradise, at Coolangatta; Brisbane Airport is 84km (52 miles) northwest and accessible by train. Both receive international flights. G-link is a useful light-rail service connecting points along the Gold Coast.

Need to know: There are good accommodation options for families across the length of the Gold Coast.

Other months: Dec-Jan – Aussie school summer holidays; Apr, Jul & Sep-Oct – more school holidays; May-Sep – winter, cooler air and water temperatures.

VRINDAVAN & MATHURA
INDIA

`5-16` **Why now?** See India in vivid colour during the festival of Holi in Uttar Pradesh.

Pack clothes that you don't mind spoiling if you travel to India during Holi – the famous festival of colours sees astonishing quantities of water and rainbow-hued gulal powder thrown over anyone within reach. Celebrating the victory of good over evil, it's a blast for travellers of all ages, but you will end up looking like an explosion in a tie-dye factory! For maximum festival fun, kit the kids out with cheap white t-shirts and swimming goggles (to keep eyes powder-free) and head to the twin towns of Vrindavan and Mathura – set in the ancestral homeland of the Hindu god Krishna. Stock up on powder at streetside stalls and join in the madcap hurling at sacred sites such as Vrindavan's Banke Bihari Temple, Mathura's Shri Dwarkadhish Temple and the village of Barsana – birthplace of Krishna's consort, Radha.

Trip plan: Vrindavan and Mathura are easily reached by train from Delhi, making for an easy detour off the popular Golden Triangle circuit, linking Delhi, Agra and Jaipur. Trains are thronged at festival time, so with family in tow it may be easier to travel by chartered taxi.

Need to know: The date of Holi moves with the Hindu lunar calendar, falling on the full moon in the Indian month of Phalguna – usually in March.

Other months: Dec-Feb – mild temperatures, dry days; Apr-May & Oct-Nov – hot, fewer tourists; Jun-Sep – skies open for the monsoon.

SINGAPORE

`0-16` **Why now?** The least rain, the lowest humidity and the most sunshine.

Singapore's location, just a smidge over one degree from the equator, means it has a perpetual tropical vibe. Exploring this island republic with kids is a joy: child-friendly attractions abound and nearly all offer kid-centric tours, child-focused exhibitions or play parks. As a bonus, many outdoor attractions have free water-play areas, perfect for a quick cool down. For wildlife encounters, a plethora of parks await: Singapore Zoo features orangutans and the slides, swings, pony rides and farmyard animals of Kidzworld. Get a combined ticket for the zoo, River Wonders, Bird Paradise and the Night Safari experience. Sentosa Island caters to older thrill-seekers with attractions such as Universal Studios, while young kids will enjoy splashing around at the island's family-friendly beach clubs. Food is one of Singapore's greatest loves and you'll easily find nosh that will satisfy even the pickiest little foodies. Kiddie favourites include chicken rice, Chinese-style dumplings and roti canai (fluffy, fried South Indian flatbreads).

Trip plan: Singapore is worth a visit in itself (allow three or four days for a good look around), but many use it as a layover on trips to or from Europe or other parts of Asia. Singapore Changi Airport is one of the region's largest transportation hubs.

Need to know: Considering Singapore's hot and humid weather, pack a sun hat, insect repellent, rain gear and an insulated water bottle for each tiny traveller.

Other months: Dec-Jan – monsoon rain; Jun-Jul – summer holidays and high temperatures.

LISBON
PORTUGAL

 Why now? For trams, custard tarts and an amazing aquarium amid crowd-free calm.

With average temperatures of 18°C (64°F), and tourist season yet to take off, March is a great time to really sink yourselves into the city, taking your time to get to know its cobbled streets. Lisbon is surprisingly easy with younger kids. While the steepest hills can be a challenge with a pushchair, the metro system is good, and few small people can resist the charm of the city's brightly coloured antique trams, or the excitement of a funicular cranking its way up a hill. One of Portugal's great culinary wonders, the cinnamon-dusted *pastel de nata* (custard tart), will bring calm when you most need it. The Antiga Confeitaria de Belém is the site of pastry pilgrimages, but you'll find counters packed with trays of warm *pastel de nata* everywhere. Just outside the city centre, and easily accessed by train or bus, the Oceanário de Lisboa aquarium will blow minds. With 8000 marine creatures splashing in vast wraparound seawater tanks, no amount of hyperbole does it justice.

Trip plan: Fly into Lisbon Airport, 7km (4 miles) from the city. Lisbon is a perfect long-weekend destination; hire a car (or take the train) for forays to the coast as part of a longer break.

Need to know: Keep an eye on the Easter calendar, as this is a busy time in Lisbon.

Other months: Dec-Feb – cool, but least expensive; Apr-May & Sep-Oct – warm without the crowds; Jun-Aug – hot, with summer festivals and outdoor events.

BEECHWORTH
AUSTRALIA

Why now? Cooler nights at the tail end of summer make for a magical time in northeast Victoria.

In the foothills of the Victorian Alps, the one-time Gold Rush town of Beechworth has retained its handsome heritage buildings, and its Burke Museum is a great place for kids to discover the region's history, from prospecting to the infamous 'bushranger' Ned Kelly. Learn about the Kelly Trials at the nearby Courthouse, and send messages across the world using morse code at the Telegraph Station. Beechworth is on the eastern reaches of Yorta Yorta Country, and you can hike to centuries-old cave paintings at Yeddonba Aboriginal Cultural Site in nearby Chiltern-Mt Pilot National Park. Other active pursuits include cycling to the Ovens Valley (and back) on a former railway line; cooling off with canoeing on Lake Sambell; river kayaking from Myrtleford; or dipping into the swimming holes at Bright. Older kids might be up for the challenge of an abseiling and rock-climbing tour of the cliffs and granite boulders in the Mt Buffalo National Park. For a more leisurely day in the park's high plains, pack a picnic and walk the wildflower meadows and meandering plateau trails.

Trip plan: Beechworth is walkable and bikes can be rented for the rail trail; you'll need a car to get further afield.

Need to know: Campgrounds make for family-friendly stays, but there are plenty of purpose-built cottages for a bit more luxury.

Other months: Oct-Feb – summer heat; Apr-Jun – autumn colour, cool nights; Jul-Sep – winter, snow possible.

POKHARA
NEPAL

Why now? Enjoy post-monsoon hikes in Nepal's gentle Middle Hills.

Not every child has the energy or inclination for a two-week trek to Everest Base Camp, but don't write off a family holiday to Nepal. Short, easy walking trails crisscross the green, serene foothills, offering a taste of the Himalayan high life that even small kids can enjoy. Come in March for warm, dry days, and base yourself in Pokhara – a lively traveller hub on the shores of Phewa Tal, blessed by views of the perfect pyramid of 6993m-high (22,943ft) Mt Machhapuchhre. Starting from the lakeshore, low-stress day-hikes climb to Himalayan viewpoints such as Sarangkot and the ridgetop Peace Pagoda, while easy multiday hikes visit Poon Hill, Ghandruk and Ghorepani for even closer mountain views. In between, kids can enjoy medieval temples, boat rides, mountain biking, ziplining and other thrilling adventure sports.

Trip plan: It takes a day by tourist bus (or a 30min flight) to reach Pokhara from Kathmandu. Local trekking agencies can arrange permits, guides and porters for family treks to Poon Hill, Ghorepani and Ghandruk; the trails to Sarangkot and the Peace Pagoda are easy to follow without a guide.

Need to know: If kids are reluctant to hike all the way to Sarangkot, take the Annapurna Cable Car uphill and hike down.

Other months: Dec-Feb – cold, with a risk of snow; Apr & Oct-Nov – warm and dry, good hiking weather; May-Sep – muggy, monsoon rain.

HOKITIKA
NEW ZEALAND/ AOTEAROA

0-16 Why now? Adventurous Kiwi cuisine at the Hokitika Wildfoods Festival.

It's a bit like the 'Wild West' over here on the South Island's west coast – more or less anything goes at this now legendary event. While youngsters may be keen to start out simple with popular local delicacies such as a whitebait sandwich or a venison sausage, there's also the opportunity to test themselves – and for you to instil some adventurous eating habits – on possum pies, 'mountain oysters' (sheep testicles), 'nipples on a stick' (pigs' nipples) or the grubs of the large local huhu beetle. The list of totally mind-boggling cuisine gets longer each year. Needless to say, there are plenty of colourful locals on display, many sporting the latest in 'Feral Fashion'. While the Wildfoods Festival attracts all sorts, there's a lot more to do on the west coast. Hokitika is a pounamu (greenstone) hotspot and there are numerous galleries and workshops in town. There's excellent hiking nearby in the Hokitika Gorge, while Pancake Rocks and its blowholes aren't far north. Glacier Country, home to the Franz Josef and Fox Glaciers, isn't far south. Carry on through to Wanaka and Queenstown.

Trip plan: While you can fly into Hokitika from Christchurch, it's much more fun to drive across Arthur's Pass or take the TranzAlpine scenic train over to Greymouth; pick up a rental car there, then drive south and return it in Queenstown.

Need to know: The festival is an extremely popular event; book accommodation early.

Other months: Oct-Apr – warm; May-Sep – cold and wet.

LA ROSIÈRE
FRANCE

5-16 Why now? For max family fun on and off the slopes.

The French Alps are full of sublime ski resorts, but few are as well suited to families as La Rosière, with great beginner areas, wide and gentle sun-facing slopes (which encourage progression) and fun forest trails with St Bernard-themed obstacles, a nod to the resort's canine mascot. For older kids who have mastered the easier runs, there is the tantalising prospect of skiing to Italy via the remote-feeling Petit St-Bernard Pass, feasting on incredible pizza and ice cream for lunch, then skiing back. Known as the balcony of the Tarentaise for its dreamy 180-degree views down the valley, La Rosière has an excellent snow record and, thanks to its lofty 1850m (6070ft) altitude, the white stuff hangs around for a long time. And March is a lovely time to visit, for fun spring skiing under blue skies, without the deep chill of winter.

Trip plan: Get the train (from London, Paris or Lyon) to Bourg-Saint-Maurice, then a bus or taxi to the resort, 20km (12 miles) away.

Need to know: La Rosière scores high for off-slope family fun: kids can go ice skating and dogsledding, try snake-gliss (a sled convoy piloted by a professional), hit the climbing wall, go snowshoeing, watch the local Tigres Blanc ice hockey team, or play bubblefoot (football in a giant inflatable bubble).

Other months: Dec – short days, snow is less reliable; Feb – good snow, beware busy school holidays; Apr – fun, slushy snow time.

TEXAS
USA

5-16 Why now? Horseback riding, rodeos and campfires under the stars.

In the midst of Texas Hill Country, northwest of San Antonio, the town of Bandera has earned its title as 'Cowboy Capital of the World'. In the late 1800s, it was the staging ground for the region's last great cattle drives; nowadays, it's home to a handful of dude-ranch resorts, where kids can summon their inner cowperson during horseback treks and hayrides, cattle roundups and campfires. But even if you don't stay on an actual dude ranch, your kids can still experience the cowboy lifestyle. A vast territory of canyons, plateaus and – in March – fields of delicate bluebonnets (the Texas state flower), Hill Country State Natural Area is an ideal setting for hiking and horseback riding. Back in town, a bronze monument honours the many rodeo champions that hailed from Bandera. See their successors in action at the Bandera Ham Rodeo (hogs instead of cows) or the Tejas Rodeo in nearby Bulverde. There's lots more to learn and do at the Frontier Times Museum, including a monthly cowboy jamboree. Yeehaw!

Trip plan: Fly into Austin or San Antonio. Most dude-ranch resorts are all-inclusive, with meals and loads of activities included. Independent travellers will need a vehicle to get around.

Need to know: Popular Bandera lodgings include horse-focused Hill Country Equestrian Lodge, and the more traditional Mayan Dude Ranch.

Other months: Nov-Feb – mild; Apr-May – warm, sunny, bluebonnets; Jun-Aug – humid, very hot; Sep-Oct – cooler, cheaper.

Zip through the canopy in Antigua's forest-swathed interior

ANTIGUA & BARBUDA

0-16 Why now? Bright Caribbean sunshine and cool breezes in the perfect season.

Antigua has a beach for every day of the year – or so the legend goes. Whether or not there are 365 separate stretches of sand on the island, it's true that you won't want for a patch of soft, golden-tinted shoreline on which to play. March sees a lull in tourist arrivals after the midwinter peak and before Easter, but the weather is still dry and hurricane-free. With calm, warm waters ringed by colourful coral reefs, Antigua is great for snorkelling. Most people stick to the beach, but there's plenty more to delight the kids, from hikes in the wildlife-rich, rainforested interior to flying through the canopy on a zipline tour. Venture to Nelson's Dockyard or the atmospheric 18th-century Fort James for absorbing maritime history (and cannons!), or hire kayaks and take a gentle paddle around the island's mangrove sanctuary.

Trip plan: International flights serve VC Bird Airport in Antigua's north, near the capital, St John's; the dual coves and historic sites of Falmouth Harbour and English Harbour in the south make a good base. With its compact 21km (13-mile) length and beaches all around the island, it's easy to access all parts of Antigua.

Need to know: March is towards the end of the mating season for frigate birds – look for the red throat sacs of courting males at Codrington Lagoon on neighbouring island Barbuda.

Other months: Dec-Feb & Apr – driest; May & Jun – hot; Jul-Nov – showers, Carnival in Jul.

Beautiful Belize:
(R) Snorkelling
Ambergris Caye;
(B) Xunantunich

BELIZE

12-16 **Why now?** Water-based fun and Maya monuments amid dry and sunny weather.

Diminutive Belize packs a big punch. Only about 290km (180 miles) long, and with English the official language, it's easy to hop between its ancient Maya ruins, wildlife-rich tropical forests, living Maya communities and the cays and atolls of the world's second-longest barrier reef, which offers gorgeous beaches and fabulous snorkelling. One of the most exciting ways to explore is by canoe. The Belize River runs through the centre of the country, or try the Moho River out to the Caribbean sea; both are enveloped in rainforest, and glide past villages that are far away from tourist hubs. Choose a trip with a local guide who can tell you all about the communities – and the wildlife – that you'll paddle past. Enhance your river adventure with trips to

relatively little-visited, jungle-set temples in the north, from Xunantunich (access is via a fun hand-cranked cable ferry) and Lamanai. Today, the descendants of the ancient Maya who built these monuments live in villages around Toledo, where they welcome visitors to immersive homestays.

Trip plan: From Belize City, head west to Lamanai and Xunantunich, then go south to join the Belize River at San Ignacio and visit Toledo, and to snorkel, dive and chill on Glover's Reef and Ambergris Caye.

Need to know: Using public water taxis to get to the cays is fun and cost-efficient.

Other months: Dec-May – relatively dry and warm, whale sharks arrive Apr; Jun-Nov – wetter, still warm.

STEWART ISLAND/RAKIURA NEW ZEALAND/AOTEAROA

12-16 **Why now?** Relatively stable weather on this far-flung, windswept island off the south coast of the South Island.

Its Māori name means 'glowing skies' (after the Aurora Australis), and with its pristine wilderness and lack of light pollution, Rakiura is a prime stargazing destination year-round. It's also home to that iconic Aotearoa native: the kiwi. These shy, flightless birds were put at risk by introduced rats, possums and cats, but hard work by the islanders has protected some kiwi habitats, and plans are underway

to make Rakiura predator-free once more. (There's an important life lesson for young people: community working together can make things better.) After a day spent hiking in the lush rainforest and sailing or kayaking (look out for seabirds, dolphins and seals), book a small-group tour to spot kiwis by night. Guides brief on responsible kiwi-spotting, and issue red-light torches to protect the birds' eyes while listening out for them in the dark. Hopefully somewhere along the shore, someone will spot a kiwi furrowing for insects in the sand. With

shaggy feathers that comically contrast with their long, slender bills, they have an almost fairy-tale quality. Seeing kiwis under a canopy of stars, with waves crashing on the beach nearby, only adds to the dreaminess of the experience.

Trip plan: Take the ferry from Bluff to Oban (1hr), or fly from a city further north.

Need to know: Holiday accommodation is scarce on Rakiura – book well ahead.

Other months: Dec-Feb – summer, but mild; Apr-Sep – wild and wintry; Oct-Nov – wind and rain.

LA RIOJA SPAIN

5–16 Why now? Blue-sky roadtripping along the 'Route of the dinosaurs'.

Following fossilised footprints (ichnites) across the mountainous landscape of La Rioja in northern Spain is a family-thrilling escapade. Scientists have identified thousands of footprints spread over 110 Riojan sites (originally attributed to the Apostle James' horse) as having been left by different dinosaurs around 140–110 million years ago, in the late Jurassic and the Cretaceous periods. Start in Munilla and explore nearby sites including Barranco de la Canal, where there's a 27m-long (89ft) iguanodon trail, and Peñaportillo, where you'll see footprints left by carnivorous dinosaurs, plus prints and tail-marks made by a stegosaurus. Head south to Enciso to discover life-sized model dinosaurs and thousands more footprints, as well as visiting the informative Centro Paleontológico. Here kids can also explore El Barranco Perdido (The Lost Canyon), a paleontology-themed adventure park, where educational dinosaur exhibits are paired with activities ranging from hiking to rock climbing and archery; its Playa Cretácica (Cretaceous Beach) pool area features slides, geysers and a solarium.

Trip plan: There are more tracks to trace beyond El Barranco Perdido; continue your journey through Spain's 'Jurassic Park' in Poyales and Cuesta de Andorra, before finishing by an extraordinary 11m (36ft) fossilised conifer tree near Igea's Chapel of the Virgin of Villar.

Need to know: Besides child-delighting dinosaurs, La Rioja has more than 500 parent-pleasing wineries (and in June, Haro hosts a hilarious wine war, when combatants soak each other in vino).

Other months: Dec-Feb – chilly; Jun-Aug – hot, wine battle; Sep-Nov – grape harvest, good weather, busy with wine tourists.

(L) Dino displays dot the landscape near Enciso; (R) Fossilised footprints aplenty

Seaside temple at
Tulum, Riviera Maya

RIVIERA MAYA
MEXICO

5-16 **Why now?** Swimming, snorkelling, cenotes and the mysterious ancient Maya. Also, tacos.

The Riviera Maya – the coastline south of Cancún – has so much to offer curious kids. Countless beaches beckon for swimming and sandcastle-building, while the protected waters of gorgeous Laguna Yal-kú promise snorkelling with tropical fish. Or you could take a boat tour at Reserva Sian Ka'an, and explore the mysterious cenotes of Dos Ojos or Chukum-Ha. Best of all, the remains of the ancient Maya are all around – intriguing and explorable. Besides the spectacular seaside ruins at Tulum, there are other lesser-known sites that are more enticing for active kids. At both Cobá and Ek' Balam, you can roam freely through the rainforest and climb the pyramids. It's a long haul to Chichén Itzá, but it's worth it to see the feathered serpent on El Castillo – aka the Pyramid of Kukulcán – around the spring equinox (between 19 and 23 March), when the sun's shadow creates an incredible illusion of a serpent slithering down its slope.

Trip plan: Skip the resorts and stay in one of the delightful coastal towns south of Cancún. Renting a car will give you optimum flexibility.

Need to know: Chichén Itzá's equinox phenomenon occurs in the late afternoon for a few days around the spring equinox. Most come to see it on equinox day; visit a day or two before to avoid the crowds.

Other months: Dec-Feb – perfect weather, busy, high prices; Apr-May & Nov – shoulder season, fewer crowds, lower prices; Jun-Oct – hot, rainy (dry spell in Jul, autumn equinox at Chichén Itzá in Sep).

CLIFFS OF MOHER
IRELAND

5-16 **Why now?** Take a Wild Atlantic road trip for great views, with no queues.

Ireland's west coast is magical in spring, with wildflowers and hares going mad in green fields, and westerly winds sending white horses charging into dramatic cliffs. Rearing over 200m (700ft) straight out of the Atlantic, and extending 14km (8 miles) around County Clare's curvaceous coastline, the Cliffs of Moher stand tall on Europe's extreme western edge, where the beautiful, barren-looking Burren region meets the blue ocean. Views across Galway Bay to the Aran Islands are breathtaking, especially around sunrise and sunset. Stories swirl around this myth-soaked site, and at the Visitor Centre, youngsters can learn about the Mermaid of Moher, the Aill na Searrach (Leap of the Foals), the legendary Celtic warrior Cú Chulainn (who leapt from the cliffs to escape a love-struck witch) and a lost city beneath the waves. Older kids get a buzz traversing the footpaths above the vertiginous drop, listening to 30,000 breeding pairs of noisy nesting seabirds and the boom of wild water thumping into the cliffs far below, where a reef break creates a mighty swell known to big-wave surfers as Aileen's. This monster is strictly for pros, but 30 minutes' drive south, Lahinch Beach offers family-friendly surf.

Trip plan: Fly to Shannon airport. Hire a car to reach the cliffs and explore the Wild Atlantic Way.

Need to know: Book online for reduced admission prices.

Other months: Dec-Feb – cold; Jun-Aug – good weather but busy; Sep-Nov – often wet and windy.

Ruined temples at Ayuthaya's Wat Mahathat, Thailand

© Preto Perola / Shutterstock

CENTRAL THAILAND

5-12 **Why now?** Thailand's golden temples sparkle under dry skies.

March is sunny and bright in central Thailand – a perfect time to dive into a mystical world of golden Buddhas, long-fanged giants, Naga serpents and religious rituals that will captivate small travellers. Kick off with a few days of temple hopping in Bangkok – visit Wat Pho, centred on a 46m-long (151ft) reclining Buddha with toes as tall as a toddler; boggle at the gold and mosaics inside Wat Phra Kaew; gasp at the pottery-encased *prangs* (towers) of Wat Arun, guarded by giant *yaksha* demons. It's only an hour north by train to the ruined temples at Ayuthaya; an hour's ride west will take you to the 120m-tall (394ft) *chedi* (stupa) at Nakhon Pathom. Older kids will be amazed at the sight of devotees being tattooed with intricate designs at Wat Bang Phra, a 30-minute trip northwest from Bangkok; grab some seasonal mangoes and rose apples to munch on the train.

Trip plan: Bangkok's Suvarnabhumi Airport receives flights from everywhere, and taxis, buses, ferries and mass transit trains will whisk you around downtown. Trains to Ayuthaya leave from Bangkok's Hua Lamphong Station; trains to Nakhon Pathom leave from Thon Buri Station.

Need to know: Most religious sites have offering stations where kids can buy flower offerings and gold leaf to apply to Buddha statues, and exchange banknotes for small coins to drop into donation bowls.

Other months: Jan-Apr – dry, hot; May-Oct – hot, humid; Nov-Dec – drier, cooler.

April

WHERE TO GO WHEN WITH KIDS

READY FOR ADVENTURE

Kick off a fun-filled Seoul sojourn by riding the Namsan Mountain cable car

We want to...

TAKE US OUT FOR...

MEMORABLE FEASTS
● ATHENS, GREECE P81

SPECIAL SNACKS, TREATS AND SWEETS
● LONDON, ENGLAND P81

Visit vibrant food markets in Athens

TAKE US...

OUTDOORS

FOR SOME KID-FRIENDLY FUN
● SEOUL, SOUTH KOREA P81
● DORDOGNE, FRANCE P74

TO GO HIKING OR BIKING
● CENTRAL OTAGO, NEW ZEALAND/ AOTEAROA P75
● DUIN- EN BOLLENSTREEK, NETHERLANDS P82

TO A FESTIVAL
● THAILAND P78
● MASSACHUSETTS, USA P77

INDOORS

TO A MUSEUM
● MEXICO CITY, MEXICO P75

Cycle repurposed train tracks on the Otago Central Rail Trail

Range around parklands and absorbing museums in Mexico City's Bosque de Chapultepec

CHILL OUT/ HEAD OUT

Learn to surf on gentle spring-season waves in the Algarve

TAKE US TO THE BEACH

TO LEARN TO SURF
● ALGARVE, PORTUGAL P87

68

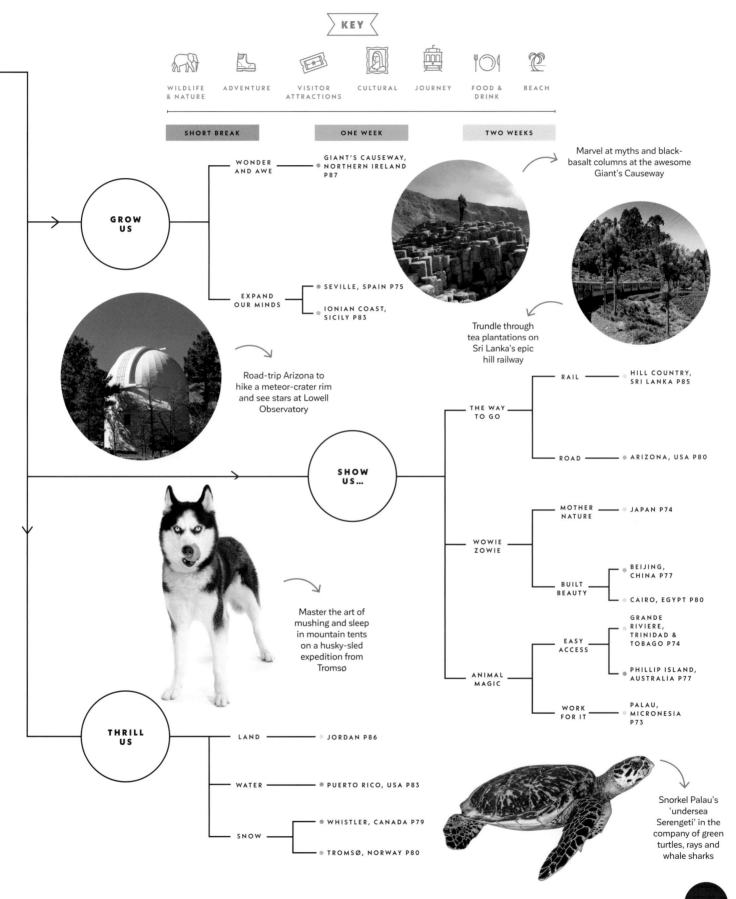

KEY

WILDLIFE & NATURE · ADVENTURE · VISITOR ATTRACTIONS · CULTURAL · JOURNEY · FOOD & DRINK · BEACH

SHORT BREAK · ONE WEEK · TWO WEEKS

GROW US

WONDER AND AWE — GIANT'S CAUSEWAY, NORTHERN IRELAND P87

EXPAND OUR MINDS — SEVILLE, SPAIN P75 / IONIAN COAST, SICILY P83

Marvel at myths and black-basalt columns at the awesome Giant's Causeway

Trundle through tea plantations on Sri Lanka's epic hill railway

Road-trip Arizona to hike a meteor-crater rim and see stars at Lowell Observatory

SHOW US...

THE WAY TO GO
- RAIL — HILL COUNTRY, SRI LANKA P85
- ROAD — ARIZONA, USA P80

WOWIE ZOWIE
- MOTHER NATURE — JAPAN P74
- BUILT BEAUTY — BEIJING, CHINA P77 / CAIRO, EGYPT P80

ANIMAL MAGIC
- EASY ACCESS — GRANDE RIVIERE, TRINIDAD & TOBAGO P74 / PHILLIP ISLAND, AUSTRALIA P77
- WORK FOR IT — PALAU, MICRONESIA P73

Master the art of mushing and sleep in mountain tents on a husky-sled expedition from Tromsø

THRILL US

LAND — JORDAN P86

WATER — PUERTO RICO, USA P83

SNOW — WHISTLER, CANADA P79 / TROMSØ, NORWAY P80

Snorkel Palau's 'undersea Serengeti' in the company of green turtles, rays and whale sharks

Events in April

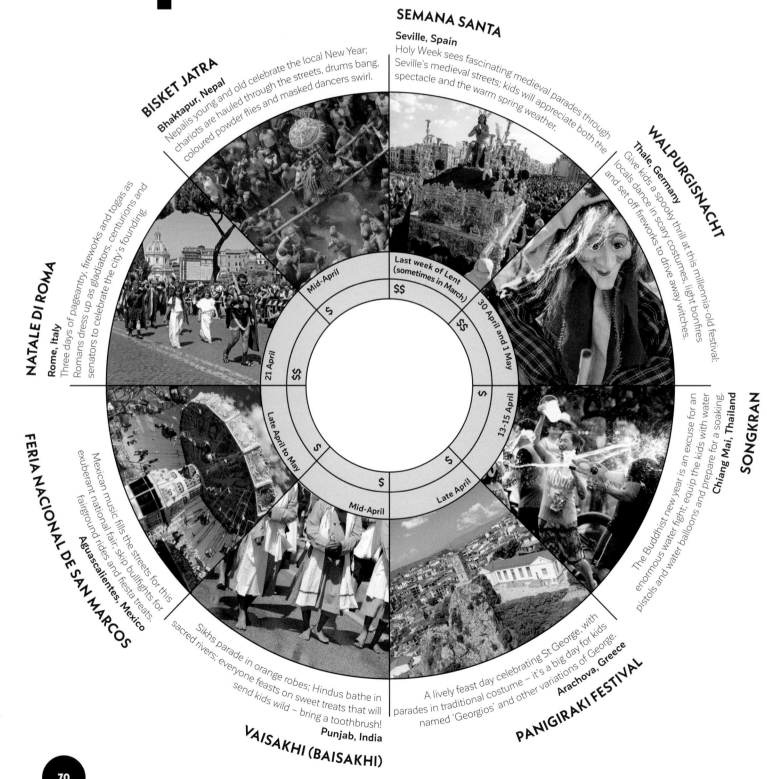

BISKET JATRA
Bhaktapur, Nepal
Nepalis young and old celebrate the local New Year; chariots are hauled through the streets, drums bang, coloured powder flies and masked dancers swirl.

SEMANA SANTA
Seville, Spain
Holy Week sees fascinating medieval parades through Seville's medieval streets; kids will appreciate both the spectacle and the warm spring weather.

WALPURGISNACHT
Thale, Germany
Give kids a spooky thrill at this millennia-old festival: locals dance in scary costumes, light bonfires and set off fireworks to drive away witches.

NATALE DI ROMA
Rome, Italy
Three days of pageantry, fireworks and togas as Romans dress up as gladiators, centurions and senators to celebrate the city's founding.

SONGKRAN
Chiang Mai, Thailand
The Buddhist new year is an excuse for an enormous water fight; equip the kids with water pistols and water balloons and prepare for a soaking.

FERIA NACIONAL DE SAN MARCOS
Aguascalientes, Mexico
Mexican music fills the streets for this exuberant national fair; skip bullfights for fairground rides and fiesta treats.

PANIGIRAKI FESTIVAL
Arachova, Greece
A lively feast day celebrating St George, with parades in traditional costume – it's a big day for kids named 'Georgios' and other variations of George.

VAISAKHI (BAISAKHI)
Punjab, India
Sikhs parade in orange robes; Hindus bathe in sacred rivers; everyone feasts on sweet treats that will send kids wild – bring a toothbrush!

Last week of Lent (sometimes in March)

$$

Mid-April

$

21 April

$$

$$

30 April and 1 May

$$

$

13-15 April

Late April to May

$

$

$

Mid-April

Late April

$

● PHILLIP ISLAND, AUSTRALIA

● LONDON, ENGLAND

Get soaked
at Thailand's
Songkran festival

Hike along a stretch
of the Great Wall
of China

Take a family bike
ride on Central Otago's
rail trails

Learn about
cocoa pods and
baby turtles in
Trinidad & Tobago

Follow blooming
cherry trees
through Japan

● GRANDE RIVIERE,
TRINIDAD & TOBAGO

● IONIAN COAST, SICILY

● THAILAND

● MASSACHUSETTS, USA

● CENTRAL OTAGO, NEW
ZEALAND/AOTEAROA

Root for the Red
Sox at Fenway
Park, Boston

● JAPAN

● BEIJING, CHINA

● SEOUL, SOUTH KOREA

EXPENSIVE
BUT WORTH IT

GOOD
VALUE

● ARIZONA, USA

● DORDOGNE, FRANCE

● WHISTLER, CANADA

● CAIRO, EGYPT

The weather is cool
for contemplating
the Acropolis

Bedouin guides
lead visitors into Wadi
Rum, Jordan

● SEVILLE, SPAIN

Ride some late-
season snow in
Whistler

● DUIN- EN BOLLENSTREEK,
NETHERLANDS

● GIANT'S CAUSEWAY,
NORTHERN IRELAND

Flower
power strikes
Netherlands in
spring

● ATHENS, GREECE

● HILL COUNTRY, SRI LANKA

Cairo's classic
sights are at
their best in this
month

Follow the pack on a
dogsledding trip in
northern Norway

● PUERTO RICO, USA

● JORDAN

● MEXICO CITY,
MEXICO

● TROMSØ, NORWAY

● PALAU, MICRONESIA

● ALGARVE, PORTUGAL

PALAU MICRONESIA

12-16 Why now? Take to the seas in the calmest and clearest of conditions.

A picture-perfect archipelago in the western Pacific Ocean, Palau (also known as Belau) is a legendary snorkelling and diving destination. While it looks spectacular above the water – a sprinkling of 300 lush-green limestone islands, sheltered lagoons, white sands and blindingly turquoise seas – it's under the water where things become truly mesmerising. This is the undersea version of the Serengeti, with some 1500 fish species gliding around soft corals and sea fans, sheer drop-offs and WWII wrecks. Palau is balmy, with year-round water temperatures of 28°C (82°F) and visibility up to 100m (328ft). There's no really bad time to visit, though April sees calmer and clearer seas. You're more likely to spot whale sharks and manta rays January to April, and green and hawksbill turtles from April to July. The cherry on the top? Jellyfish Lake, a lagoon pulsating with

a million harmless, golden, translucent, stingless jellies – a snorkelling experience extraordinaire. You'll want to make sure that your teenagers are competent swimmers and snorkellers – or have PADI certification if diving – before making the lengthy trip to this remote, pristine Pacific paradise.

Trip plan: Keen diver families should consider a liveaboard trip, to maximise dive opportunities and ease access to the best sites (including Blue Corner and German Channel).

Need to know: Palau International Airport is on Babeldaob Island; it's a 1hr 30min flight from Guam (which has US connections), 4hr from Tokyo.

Other months: Nov-Mar – drier, best diving; May-Oct – wetter, typhoons a little more likely.

Paradisical Palau
from above

JAPAN

0-16 Why now? It's cherry blossom season!

Turn up at cherry-blossom time in Japan and, on top of that intriguing Japanese culture that's all around you, there's extra excitement for the whole family. The sheer beauty of a stroll in a park, beneath clouds of pink and white blossoms, is matched only by the antics of enthusiastic locals enjoying *hanami* (flower-viewing) parties. The *sakura-zensen* (cherry-blossom front) swings up the country from south to north – from late March in Kyūshū to early April in Tokyo and late April in Hokkaidō – with a couple of weeks of blossoms after the initial opening (keep an eye on blossom forecasts). Yoshino in Nara Prefecture has been Japan's most famous blossom-viewing spot for centuries; the mountain here features 30,000 cherry trees. The grounds around some of Japan's top castles are also renowned for *hanami* – Matsumoto, Osaka, Himeji, Matsuyama and Kumamoto among others. There are more than 1000 cherry trees in Shinjuku Gyoen, one of Tokyo's largest and most popular parks, while the Path of Philosophy (Tetsugaku-no-Michi) in Kyoto is a glorious stroll when the cherries are in flower.

Trip plan: Fly to Tokyo's Haneda or Narita Airports, or Osaka's Kansai.

Need to know: Although the exact date for the best cherry-blossom viewing isn't predictable, you're reasonably safe if you turn up in Tokyo during the first 10 days of April.

Other months: Nov-Mar – winter turning to spring; Jun-Sep – hot, humid; Oct – autumn colours.

DORDOGNE
FRANCE

5-12 Why now? Spring flowers, camping and cave art.

The Dordogne is warming up nicely by April, with mild days and bounteous spring blooms. By the middle of the month, camping is back on the menu, along with kayak and canoe trips on the Dordogne and Vézère Rivers. Base yourself in charming Sarlat-la-Canéda, where kid-friendly activities range from châteaux tours and picnicking on early-season strawberries to admiring paintings daubed by cavemen (and cavewomen) artists more than 17,000 years ago. The famous painted cave at Lascaux closed to visitors in 1963, but the nearby International Centre of Parietal Art contains a convincing facsimile of the entire cave system, with murals reproduced using the same pigments deployed by ancient painters. You can also see original Neolithic art in situ at Grotte de Rouffignac, reached via an underground train ride. Drum up enthusiasm for prehistoric creativity by screening the *Ice Age* and *Croods* movies before you set off.

Trip plan: Bergerac is the region's main air hub, but it's just as easy to get to the Dordogne by train, with regular services to Sarlat-la-Canéda via Bergerac or Bordeaux. Sarlat is ringed by campsites, and has plenty of rental apartments too; hire a car on arrival for easy exploring.

Need to know: If the kids tire of history and green spaces, head for Quercyland near Souillac, open from mid-April and with pools, slides and high-ropes activities.

Other months: Dec-Mar – cold, grey; May & Oct-Nov – mild, sun and rain; Jun-Sep – warm, sunny.

GRAND RIVIERE
TRINIDAD & TOBAGO

5-16 Why now? Egg-laying turtles, waterfalls and plunge pools, handmade chocolate.

Visitors to Trinidad's gorgeous Grande Riviere Beach on the Caribbean island's northeast coast revel in the idyllic surrounds, with the curving beach framed by forested headlands and backed by a river-fed lagoon – but many must wonder why eggshells are scattered across the yolk-coloured sand. In April, all is revealed, as hundreds of female leatherback turtles haul themselves up the beach after sunset, choose a nesting spot, lay dozens of eggs, flipper sand over them and slip back into the night. This is one of the world's busiest leatherback nesting sites, where 400 of the impressively enormous animals can arrive in one night, each depositing up to 115 eggs that hatch later in the season (July to August). Leatherbacks are endangered, and great care must be taken to avoid disrupting them, but a community owned tourism group runs responsible, family-friendly tours to observe this incredible event. By day, kids enjoy river swimming, waterfall hikes and delicious bars of dark delight from Grande Riviere's small-scale chocolate company, right behind the beach (tip: do a bean-to-bar tour).

Trip plan: Reach the beach via a turnoff from the coast road, between Sans Souci and Matelot.

Need to know: Permits are required to visit the beach after dark (included in the tour price); guides will send alerts to your hotel when turtles are spotted – and they sometimes nest during the day, too. Avoid sea swimming November–April, when waves are powerful.

Other months: Dec-Mar – high (busy) season, ideal weather, Carnival; May-Nov – wet season.

CENTRAL OTAGO
NEW ZEALAND/ AOTEAROA

5-16 Why now? Good weather for family bike rides amid autumn colour.

Put active kids on bikes in Central Otago in autumn and it may be hard to keep up with them. It's a great time to hit the cycle trails of 'Central': temperatures are mild and there are fewer bikers out there. The 152km (94-mile) Otago Central Rail Trail, linking Clyde and Middlemarch, follows the route of the former Otago Central Railway, which closed in 1990. Tracks and sleepers were pulled up, tunnels and viaducts upgraded, and an unpaved rail trail opened in 2000; as steam trains could only manage a 1:50 gradient, it's easy riding with no steep spots – perfect for youngsters. Sleepy towns along the route suddenly roared back to life, catering to hungry, thirsty, tired riders, many of them families, who needed refreshments and a bed – everything you need is out there for a full-on family adventure. Bigger kids with strong cycling experience will revel in the 41km (25-mile) Lake Dunstan Trail between Cromwell and Clyde, with cantilevered boardwalks attached to almost sheer rock walls along the lake, an 86m-long (282ft) suspension bridge, plenty of steeper riding and a floating trailside cafe.

Trip plan: Clyde, only an hour away from the Southern Lakes resorts of Queenstown and Wanaka, is a biking boom town with a number of bike-rental outlets offering lots of options.

Need to know: 'Rental bike & shuttle transport' options mean you only have to bike the trails one way.

Other months: Oct-Mar – perfect weather for biking; May-Sep – winter.

SEVILLE
SPAIN

5-16 Why now? Experience an Easter like no other in Seville.

You can rely on a Catholic city like Seville to make Easter an experience to remember. In place of bunnies and chocolate eggs, the citizens of Andalucía don extravagant costumes and take to the streets, filling Seville's historic heart with incense, chanting and magic. Semana Santa – the week running up to the Easter weekend – is famed for the sculpture-topped floats known as *pasos*, paraded to Seville Cathedral by enthusiastic city residents, accompanied by processions of *nazarenos* in strange, wizard-like robes with pointy hoods. It's an arcane tradition dating back to at least the 16th century and the spectacle will fill young minds with questions. Use the celebrations as an anchor for a week of tapas lunches, park picnics and riverside walks.

Trip plan: Book ahead to find affordable family accommodation in Seville for Semana Santa, but the sacred celebrations are just the beginning. The warm, dry spring weather is great for exploring incense-perfumed basilicas, mind-expanding museums, an above-average aquarium and some of the most charming public parks in Andalucía. For a full-on day out, head for the white-knuckle rides and waterpark at Isla Mágica, just northwest of the centre in La Cartuja.

Need to know: There's no Easter egg tradition in Seville, but the treats known as *torrijas* are a good consolation – milk-soaked, citrus-infused toast, fried and topped with cinnamon and sugar.

Other months: Nov-Feb – cool, damp; Mar-May & Oct – warm, bright; Jun-Sep – hot.

MEXICO CITY
MEXICO

0-16 Why now? Clear, mild days are ideal for outdoor activities.

Begin your Mexico City explorations in the vast parklands of Bosque de Chapultepec. First stop here should be the Museo Nacional de Antropología, where artefacts from the Aztec, Olmec and Maya civilizations include the incredible Piedra del Sol (Aztec sun stone). Across the road, Chapultepec Zoo has animals from around the globe, and is free to visit. Rent paddleboats on the park's lake, have lunch at the food vendors nearby, then head up to the Castillo de Chapultepec for expansive views of the city. Chapultepec also promises Mexican history at the Museo Nacional de Historia, and interactive, child-centred exhibits at Papalote Museo del Niño; round off the evening by riding the rollercoaster and giant Ferris wheel at Aztlán Parque Urbano. The next day, take a relaxed wander around the Plaza de la Constitución (the Zócalo), then cruise the Xochimilco Canals aboard a colourful *trajinera* boat. Next, make your way to the Coyoacán neighbourhood, where you can visit the vibrantly colourful Museo Frida Kahlo (prebook tickets online), and spend a leisurely afternoon in the area's artisan markets and parks. Other must-dos include a day-tour to Teotihuacan (an hour away), and a fun-filled *lucha libre* (Mexican wrestling) show.

Trip plan: Mexico City is vast, but public transport is excellent and taxis easy to find.

Need to know: Pickpockets are highly skilled, and distracted parents can be a target. Keep valuables hidden.

Other months: Oct-Mar – cooler, dry; May – hottest; Jun-Sep – rainy season.

(A) Patriots' Day parade in Concord, Massachusetts; (L) Watch fairy penguins on Phillip Island, Australia; (R) The Great Wall near Badaling, China

MASSACHUSETTS
USA

5-16 Why now? Battle re-enactments, patriotic parades and a historic road race.

On 19 April 1775, British regulars marched west from Boston and confronted the rebellious colonial 'Minutemen' in Lexington and Concord. These were the first battles in the American Revolutionary War – a conflict that would launch a new nation. Nowadays, Massachusetts celebrates Patriots' Day on the third Monday in April, commemorating these momentous events with a packed calendar of events in Lexington and Concord. Kids can witness history unfolding before them, as local enthusiasts re-enact the battles, honour the fallen soldiers and march in patriotic parades. Meanwhile, back in Boston, a festive spirit pervades the city, with more parades and patriotic festivities. Later in the day, thousands of spectators come out to root for the Red Sox at Fenway Park, or cheer on the throngs of runners in the Boston Marathon.

Trip plan: Stay west of the city for easy access to the action in Lexington and Concord, as well as the beginning of the marathon route. Boston-area lodgings get booked way in advance, so plan ahead.

Need to know: The main events take place on Patriots' Day itself, but there are many (less crowded) historic re-enactments, walking tours and battle demonstrations throughout the weekend at the Minute Man National Historical Park in Lincoln, between Lexington and Concord.

Other months: Nov-Mar – cold weather and muddy (or frozen) trails; May-Jun – spring rains and mild temperatures; Jul-Aug – hot, humid and sunny; Sep-Oct – cool, crisp autumn days attract lots of tourists.

BEIJING
CHINA

5-16 Why now? Enjoy the Great Wall of China with less company.

Standing on top of the Great Wall of China is one of those everyone-should-do-it-once-in-a-lifetime experiences, so why not start the kids young? Strolling between ancient watchtowers, surrounded by tumbling hills that once sheltered invading Mongol armies, is endlessly evocative, and easy to achieve on a family trip to Beijing. The touristy sections of wall at Badaling and Mutianyu have bonus family amusements such as cable cars and toboggan rides; quieter Jinshanling, Huanghuacheng and Simatai offer wilder adventures. To fill out a fun-packed week, take a day trip to the Ming Tombs, 50km (31 miles) north of Beijing; the vertiginous Shilinxia Glass Viewing Platform, 70km (43 miles) northwest; or the timeless stone alleyways in the village of Cuandixia, 90km (56 miles) west.

Trip plan: With a week in Beijing, devote half your time to family-friendly sights inside the city (such as the Forbidden City, the Beihai and Chaoyang parks and the hutong alleyways) and the other half to day trips. It takes 1hr 30min to 2hr to reach the Great Wall, the Ming Tombs and Shilinxia, and 2hr to 3hr to reach Cuandixia.

Need to know: Buses or local trains run from Beijing to various sections of the Great Wall and other day-trip destinations – Mubus (beijingmubus.com) has a handy direct bus service from central Beijing to Mutianyu, or you can arrange a rideshare taxi using the DiDi app.

Other months: Nov-Mar – dry but chilly, cold winds; May & Sep-Oct – mild temperatures; Jun-Aug – hot and muggy.

PHILLIP ISLAND
AUSTRALIA

5-16 Why now? Penguins, seals and excited squeals, without a late night.

Connected to the Victorian mainland via San Remo bridge, Phillip Island is a family-friendly holiday destination and popular surfing spot that has become internationally famous thanks to a natural nightly phenomenon known as the Penguin Parade. Each evening, around dusk, thousands of little fairy penguins come ashore at Summerland Bay, near the island's western tip. Having spent all day braving the waves (and some super-toothy predators), these charismatic creatures – the planet's smallest penguins – gather together to form rafts before making landfall. Once on the sand, they huddle in the surf, plucking up courage before dashing across the exposed beach to reach their burrows. Humans huddle too, on viewing platforms, overseen by rangers who ensure no-one interferes with the wild animals. The penguins won't emerge from the ocean until nightfall, making April (Aussie autumn) a good time to visit with kids, because the sun sets around 6pm and it's not too cold.

Trip plan: Phillip Island is a 1hr 30min drive from Melbourne; take a tour or hire a car and explore the island independently. Don't miss the Nobbies Boardwalk, near the Penguin Parade, from where you'll spot fur seals and, at the Nobbies Centre, learn about the great white sharks that prey on them (and snack on penguins).

Need to know: Flash photography is strictly prohibited. Take a blanket.

Other months: Dec-Mar – summer, large crowds, late sunsets; Jun-Aug – winter, surprisingly cold conditions.

Wet and wild
Songkran fun
in Chiang Mai

THAILAND

5-16 Why now? Grab a water gun and join a joy-drenched Songkran street party.

A five-day fun-infused festival that explodes across Thailand in mid-April's blistering heat, Songkran is a traditional Lunar New Year celebration (according to the Buddhist calendar), when the old year is symbolically washed away with water. The event is celebrated differently around the country, ranging from relatively conservative traditional events to utterly anarchic, good-natured street parties where everyone – locals and visitors, strangers and friends, young and old – soak one another with complete abandon. Kids of all ages can revel in the colourful chaos surrounding this event, as locals paint their faces with white paste and a huge amount of H2O is hurled around, fired from powerful pump-action

water guns and hoses, lobbed in balloon bombs and poured from buckets. On the streets of Bangkok, epic aquatic battles are complemented by beauty pageants, live music, food fairs and foam parties. However, for a mix of culture and water-fighting fun, head to the foodie hotspot of Chiang Mai, where spiritual rituals and traditional art performances are punctuated by wonderfully wet and wild melees.

Trip plan: In Bangkok, visit Khao San Rd, Silom Rd and Phra Padaeng; in Chiang Mai, try Tha Pae Gate, Wat Phra Singh and along the Ping River.

Need to know: Don't wear revealing or expensive clothes – you will get drenched (and probably paste-splattered). Book travel and accommodation well in advance.

Other months: Nov-Feb – dry and 'cool' (perfect); May-Oct – wet season.

Powder perfection on
the slopes in Whistler

WHISTLER
CANADA

0-16 **Why now?** Spring skiing at
one of North America's top
winter-sports resorts.

Take your family to Whistler, renowned for
having one of the longest and most reliable
snow seasons on the planet. Combining two
mountains – Whistler and Blackcomb – with
a purpose-built, strikingly attractive alpine
village that hosted events during the 2010
Winter Olympics, Whistler is the blueprint
for successful ski resorts. Want some
action? Snowboard over car-size bumps
on Whistler Bowl. After some quiet family
time? Go cross-country skiing in Callaghan
Country before sinking into a giant whirlpool
bath in a Creekside resort. On a budget?
Go snowshoeing and be selective when
it comes to choosing dates. A mere 90
minutes north of Vancouver, Whistler was
named for its furry marmots that whistle like
deflating balloons. Families will find it a kid-
friendly place with plenty of energy. Besides
family zones on the slopes, there's ice-
skating, tubing, snowmobiling, playgrounds
and more. Resort transit options mean it's
easy to get around – kids aged 12 and under
ride for free on the BC Transit System. The
variety and quality of facilities is staggering,
and your family is likely to head home
beaming after a week in Whistler.

Trip plan: While most visitors arrive by
car from Vancouver via Hwy 99, there are
regular buses from the city and some from
Vancouver Airport.

Need to know: Whistler World Ski &
Snowboard Festival is held in early to
mid-April; the resort will be busy with a
week of non-stop events and action, on
and off the slopes.

Other months: Dec-May – winter sports;
Jun-Oct – summer alpine activities.

© stockstudioX / Getty Images

ARIZONA
USA

5–16 Why now? Space kicks on Route 66.

In Winslow, northern Arizona, near the ravines of Canyon Diablo and the ghost town of Two Guns, Meteor Crater is a dent in the desert that's 170m (560ft) deep and 1.2km (0.7 miles) across. Created 50,000 years ago by a massive meteor smashing into Earth with the force of 150 atomic bombs, it's an extraordinary place to explore. Hike around the perimeter rim (there's no access into the crater) before relaxing in air-conditioned observation rooms in the Barringer Space Museum (despite being a Natural Landmark, the crater is privately owned by the Barringer family). Here you can see an Apollo 11 space capsule, used for training by NASA at the crater before the 1969 moon-landing voyage, and join an immersive planet-saving mission in a 4D Experience Room. Night skies are spectacular in Arizona, and Lowell Observatory in nearby Flagstaff is where the now-relegated non-planet of Pluto was first spotted in 1930; with a solar scope and high-powered telescopes, it's worth visiting day or night, and kids can stroll the Pluto Walk, a paved path through a built-to-scale solar system.

Trip plan: The crater is just off I-40/Route 66. Go west to explore the nearby fossil-rich Painted Desert within the badlands of Petrified Forest National Park.

Need to know: Days are warm and nights cold in the desert, where cacti and wildflowers start to bloom during spring.

Other months: Dec-Feb – snow season; Jun-Aug – brutally hot; Sep-Nov – comfortable temperatures, fall colours.

© Nikolas_jkd / Shutterstock

CAIRO
EGYPT

5–16 Why now? See the pyramids on camelback before the summer heat rises.

On a busy day in Cairo during winter, you can barely see the pyramids for sightseers, while the city turns into a furnace from June to September, but spring is the sweet spot, particularly with kids along for the camel ride. Cairo's sights are pleasantly uncrowded and daytime temperatures stay on the right side of 30°C (86°F) – prime conditions for exploring the pyramids on a rocking dromedary (Arabian camel). Arrive at sunrise to beat the crowds and you'll feel like an early Egyptologist discovering Giza for the very first time. Rolling past the Great Pyramid of Khufu and the Sphinx on camelback is just the start – set aside time for paddleboard trips on the Nile, haggling for souvenirs in the Khan el-Khalili Bazaar and marvelling at King Tut's death mask in the Grand Egyptian Museum (due to finally open to the public in 2024).

Trip plan: On a Cairo city break, block out at least a day to admire the mesmerising monuments of Giza, a day or two for the museums and Islamic quarter, and another for bazaar shopping and chilling by the hotel pool.

Need to know: Shade is in short supply at Giza, so bring sunglasses, sunscreen, loose-fitting trousers, long-sleeved tops and a hat or sun umbrella for every member of the family.

Other months: Dec-Feb – cool, dry and crowded; Mar-May & Oct-Nov – warmer but quieter; Jun-Sep – scorching.

TROMSØ
NORWAY

12–16 Why now? Sparkling spring weather for week-long dogsledding trips.

Led by Active Tromsø, this guided adventure into the pristine Arctic wilderness offers an incredible opportunity for adventurous families to skim through the stunning scenery of northern Norway, Sweden and Finland by dogsled, mushing by day and sleeping each night in high-altitude mountain tents. The trip starts in Tromsø, 350km (217 miles) north of the Arctic Circle, and finishes near Kiruna, Sweden, from where you'll bus back to Tromsø. Once you've learned how to look after the dogs and to give mushing instructions, you'll get your own team of highly intelligent huskies for the duration of the expedition, each clever dog with its own individual character. The following days are all different once the trip begins, sledding through varying terrain – through wooded valleys, over mountain passes and past frozen lakes, all the while keeping alert for Arctic wildlife such as reindeer and moose. There's endless gleaming snow during the day, a star-studded sky at night and, if you can keep your eyes open after a tiring day of dogsledding, the chance of seeing the Northern Lights.

Trip plan: Trips start and finish in Tromsø. There are direct flights to Tromsø from Oslo and a number of major European cities.

Need to know: This arduous, week-long trip is for adventurous families only; discuss with Active Tromsø if you're not sure whether your kids are up to it. If uncertain, book a one-day or overnight trip instead.

Other months: Nov-Mar – dogsledding trips, Northern Lights; May-Sep – kayaking, hiking, husky walks.

SEOUL
SOUTH KOREA

5-16 Why now? Kid-friendly fun amid mild temperatures, low humidity and cherry blossoms.

Start your Seoul family adventure by riding the cable car up Namsan Mountain for city views from iconic N Seoul Tower, then head to Seoul Children's Grand Park for the zoo, botanic gardens, playgrounds, picnic areas, walking trails and, on its east side, interactive activities focused on science, tech and creativity at Seoul Children's Museum (pre-booked tickets required). Then it's time for cherry-blossom viewing, play-friendly fountains and a glasshouse insect garden at Seoul Forest. Zaha Hadid's Dongdaemun Design Plaza is a neofuturistic knockout of a building, and has the toddler-focused DiKi DiKi playground; with older kids, head to the Trick Eye Museum to muck about with 3D optical illusions. Gyeongbokgung Palace offers a more cultural experience. The changing of the guard is impressive for kids of all ages, and there's lots to learn about Korean history and culture at the Children's Museum of the National Folk Museum (don't miss the Mythological Animal playground); teens might want to stay for a Starlight Tour of the palace complex at sunset. Finally, hit the food courts or the city's hotpot restaurants or buffet-style all-you-can-eat Korean barbecue joints for an authentic South Korean 'mukbang' (your kids can explain more).

Trip plan: Public transport, including the subway, buses and cycle-share schemes, is efficient and affordable.

Need to know: Although Seoul is very family-friendly, it's generally expected that children are not too noisy or disruptive.

Other months: Oct-Mar – cold, potential snow; May-Jun & Sep– perfectly warm; Jul-Aug – high humidity.

LONDON
ENGLAND

5-12 Why now? London is the capital of chocolate-egg-hunting at Easter.

England's Easter celebrations are a guaranteed hit with the kids, and believing in an egg-delivering magical bunny is entirely optional. Many of London's top tourist attractions lay on Easter egg hunts for kids, but every supermarket stocks ready-to-hide chocolate eggs, so it's easy to improvise your own hunt in any green space in the city. London Zoo's Zoonormous Egg Hunt has an educational angle; Hampton Court Palace litters its gorgeous Tudor gardens with Lindt chocolate bunnies; and 17th-century Ham House in Richmond and Kenwood House on Hampstead Heath back up their egg hunts with games in their grounds. If you're looking for a perfect space for a homemade hunt, the Royal Parks (particularly Hyde Park and Regents Park) and the greenhouses at Kew Gardens are hard to beat.

Trip plan: Easter brings four days off work for most Brits, from Good Friday to Bank Holiday Monday. Set aside Sunday for an Easter egg hunt and use the rest of the long weekend to visit the Kensington museums, the British Museum, the Thames riverbanks and London's Royal Parks.

Need to know: The long weekend brings heavy traffic – use the Tube and commuter trains to explore, and book seats ahead for trains into and out of the city.

Other months: Nov-Feb – cool, often rainy; May & Sep-Oct – warming days, spring flowers, autumn leaves; Jun-Aug – warm and dry.

ATHENS
GREECE

5-16 Why now? Quieter times, before the summer heat and crowds.

There's lots to keep kids entertained in Athens. Most children understand that they're somewhere special when walking up the hill to explore the Acropolis, though you'll want to head up early on a weekday to avoid crowds and the midday heat. Children who are into sports should enjoy visiting the stunning Panathenaic Stadium, built in the 4th century BCE, then restored to be the main site for the first modern Olympic Games in 1896. It seats 70,000 and hosted various events during the 2004 Athens Olympics. The hourly changing of the guard before the parliament building on Plateia Syntagmatos is another kid-friendly highlight, with the guards marching in exquisite historic uniforms; on Sundays at 11am, a whole platoon marches, accompanied by a band. The meat section at Varvakios Agora may (or may not!) be a highlight, but Athens' Central Market is a vibrant, colourful place to explore, with an incredible range of fruit and vegetables, olives, spices, cheese and deli treats. Not too far away, the vintage wares of Monastiraki Flea Market might pique the interest of teens.

Trip plan: Allow three or four days to explore Athens; consider taking a ferry from the port at Piraeus to continue your trip with some island-hopping through the Aegean Sea.

Need to know: Athens is reasonably safe, but you'll want to take care of your possessions. Drink plenty of water if temperatures rise.

Other months: Nov-Mar – cooler, wet; Jun-Aug – hot, dry, high season.

Blooming tulip fields
in the Netherlands

DUIN- EN BOLLENSTREEK
NETHERLANDS

5-12 Why now? Cycle through Dutch flower fields ablaze with brilliant colour.

Duin- en Bollenstreek literally means 'dune and bulb region' – an unpoetic name for the gorgeous, garden-backed beaches of the Netherlands coast. Flat as a Dutch pancake, this is perfect cycling country, even for smaller riders, so pick a base – the towns of Lisse and Noordwijk are handy hubs – and explore by pedal power. Flowers have been cultivated here since the 17th century, when the country was gripped by tulip fever, and cycle paths meander between friendly beach towns and endless fields of tulips, daffodils and hyacinths, which paint the landscape in rainbow-coloured stripes each spring. It's not all about flowers – boat tours cruise the canals, watersports abound on the Kaag Lakes, and Linnaeushof near Heemstede is Europe's largest outdoor playground, with indoor and outdoor sections.

Trip plan: Trains and planes connect Amsterdam to cities across Europe, or you can come by car ferry via Rotterdam, IJmuiden or the Hook of Holland. From March to May, Keukenhof Express buses run to Bollenstreek from Amsterdam, Rotterdam and Den Haag. Bikes can be rented in Lisse, Noordwijkerhout, Noordwijk, Katwijk Beach and Keukenhof, and at Hillegom Train Station.

Need to know: Time your trip to coincide with the Bloemencorso Bollenstreek festival in late April, when extravagant floral floats are paraded from Noordwijk to Haarlem.

Other months: Dec-Feb – cold, sometimes snowy; Mar-May – warming weather, flower season; Jun-Sep – warm and humid; Oct-Nov – milder, greyer.

© frans lemmens / Alamy Stock Photo

Sicilian splendour:
(R) Isola Bella;
(B) Teatro Greco,
Taormina

© Gary Yeowell / Getty Images

IONIAN COAST
SICILY

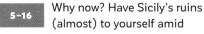

5-16 **Why now?** Have Sicily's ruins (almost) to yourself amid balmy spring days.

Before the summertime crowds arrive, the Ionian Coast of Sicily is Mediterranean perfection: agreeably mild, sunny but not scorching, adorned with spring flowers and blissfully calm, except over the Easter weekend. If your kids love making a drama of things, build your trip around the ancient theatres in Taormina and Syracuse, which hosted Greek tragedies and comedies as early as the 3rd century BCE – kids can put on spontaneous performances for parents watching from the ancient stone stalls. Mix up the ancient sites with beach days, gelato stops, pizza lunches, boat trips on the bay and a hike on the slopes of Mt Etna, where the Funivia dell'Etna cable-car swoops to a station at 2500m (8202ft) up the volcano's ash-strewn flank. Set aside time,

too, for a family picnic on pretty Isola Bella, accessible on foot at low tide from the beach below Taormina.

Trip plan: Book a villa or Airbnb on the east coast and get around by hire car or train. Taormina is the ideal family hub, dotted with ancient ruins and kid-friendly restaurants, and ringed by sand and pebble beaches; it's 50min by road to Catania (for trips up Mt Etna), and 1hr 30min to Syracuse.

Need to know: For your best chances of an empty amphitheatre stage, visit ancient ruins when they open at around 9am.

Other months: Nov-Mar – cool, sometimes rainy or overcast; May & Sep-Oct – rising temperatures, more sunshine; Jun-Sep – hot, crowded, more expensive.

© Arts Illustrated Studios / Shutterstock

PUERTO RICO USA

 Why now? Rainforest hikes, bioluminescent bays and historic forts.

Sunny skies and sandy beaches might be the main draw, but Puerto Rico is blessed with natural and cultural attractions that will keep your family entertained, for as much time as you've got to spend. San Juan is one of the oldest cities in the western hemisphere, and the historic district – Old San Juan – is a museum of colourful period architecture and cobblestone streets, not to mention the imposing 500-year-old fortress,

Castillo San Felipe del Morro, which is open for exploration; its surrounding fields are popular with picnickers and kite flyers, with food stalls set up to cater to visitors. Outside the city, adventures await. It's a 45-minute drive to El Yunque National Forest, where rainforest trails lead to waterfalls, swimming holes, cliff jumps, vine swings and natural water slides. Other options include cycling the coastal boardwalks of the Paseo Piñones Trail, or an illuminating outing to kayak in Laguna Grande, a bioluminescent bay that will blow your kids away!

Trip plan: Stay in Old San Juan or on the beach in Isla Verde or Ocean Park. Rent a car or book a tour for trips out of the city (tours are mandatory to kayak at Laguna Grande).

Need to know: Save your bathing suit and flip-flops for the rainforest and beach. Even kids should be appropriately dressed on the streets of San Juan, especially in the evenings.

Other months: Dec-Mar – high season, sunny skies crowded sights; May – shoulder season; Jun-Nov – low season, lower prices, lots of rain, hurricanes possible.

HILL COUNTRY
SRI LANKA

 Why now? Quieter days in Sri Lanka's green, gorgeous Hill Country.

The luscious beaches of the 'Pearl of the Indian Ocean' lure families in droves, but that's just the start of the Sri Lanka experience. Inland lie the lush, green highlands of the Hill Country, where sprawling tea plantations paint the landscape in fingerprint-like swirls. Visit in April and you'll get warm, mostly dry days on the coast, and refreshingly cool temperatures inland as compensation for leaving the sand. Sweeten the deal for kids with a ride in the observation car on the famous hill railway from Colombo to the hill-country village of Ella, where you can rest up in laid-back homestays and take gentle forest hikes to temples, waterfalls and viewpoints. Book a tour of the Uva Halpewaththa tea plantation to learn where a cup of tea comes from; bonus family fun awaits at nearby Uda Walawe National Park, where encounters with elephants are pretty much guaranteed.

Trip plan: The best beaches near Colombo are at laid-back Negombo, Bentota and Hikkaduwa. Book tickets for trains from Colombo to the Hill Country in advance, particularly for the observation car. Tuk-tuks provide easy transport to sights around Ella; take a tour to reach Uda Walawe.

Need to know: Hill hikes abound around Ella; kids will likely prefer the easy tramp to Little Adam's Peak over the steep uphill trek to Ella Rock.

Other months: Dec-Mar – hot by the sea, cooler in the hills; May-Sep – warm but more rain on the west coast; Oct-Nov – soggy in the highlands.

Trundling through emerald hills on the Colombo to Ella train

Petra's rock-cut
Treasury (Al
Khazneh), Jordan

JORDAN

12-16 Why now? For desert adventures in the kindest temperatures.

Compact Jordan is a great destination to explore with older kids. In April you can travel with ease – humidity and rainfall are low and temperatures loiter at a mild 20°C to 23°C (68°F to 73°F), perfect for squeezing as much as you can into a full week, or an easy two weeks. You certainly won't be short of things to do. Ancient wonders? Visit the 2000-year-old rock-hewn city of Petra, or Karak's hilltop Crusader castle. City sights? Try Roman ruins in Jerash or the souks of Amman. Jaw-dropping landscapes? Camp or roll down the dunes in the otherworldly deserts of Wadi Rum. Activities? Cycle and walk among the strawberry trees and rock roses of Ajloun Forest. Wildlife? The Shaumari Reserve is one of the few places in the world where you can still see the Arabian oryx, and very likely the only place where you can cycle among these long-horned ruminants as they graze. Beach? Pick between the salty Dead Sea or snorkel-friendly Red Sea.

Trip plan: From Amman, nip north to Jerash and Ajloun (which has cool forest lodges for nature watching) before veering east to Shaumari, returning west for the Dead Sea, and south for Petra and Wadi Rum.

Need to know: The Khamsin (hot, sandy wind) can hit Jordan in spring. The Dead Sea is better suited to older kids, as getting water in your eyes is incredibly painful.

Other months: Nov-Feb – cold in many areas; Mar-May – springlike, ideal; Jun-Sep – very hot; Oct – fleeting autumn, pleasant.

ALGARVE
PORTUGAL

5-16 Why now? For spring surf lessons on beautiful beaches.

The golden, cliff-backed beaches of the Algarve rank among the loveliest in Europe, with great surfing, kayaking and other aquatic activities. In April the days are warm and sunny, but there's a fraction of the summer's visitors. Plus, winter waves are making way for calmer seas, ideal for learner surfers; and there's always a protected bay somewhere that will be suitable for beginners. The ideal first stop for new surfers is an easy hop from the Algarve's capital, Faro. Navigate your way through the flamingo-stalked saltmarshes of the Parque Natural da Ria Formosa to reach Praia de Faro. This 5km (3-mile) strand is blessed with a series of shifting sandbanks that produce some of the Algarve's most beginner-friendly waves. Alternatively, Sagres and the Costa Vicentina have famous surf breaks, and learners are well served by numerous surf schools. Heading up the coast, Arrifana is hallowed ground in the learn-to-surf world. As the Atlantic swell slackens off, the beach here becomes a hubbub of surf camps and surf schools.

Trip plan: Sagres is 120km (75 miles) west of Faro airport. It's easiest to get there and to Arrifana by car; or you can take the train from Faro to Lagos, then a bus.

Need to know: Easter in April typically marks the end of the off-season; processions add excitement, as does Liberation Day (25 April), with fireworks and parades in some towns.

Other months: Oct-Dec & Feb-Mar – mild climes, big waves; May-Sep – warm to hot (heat and crowds peak Jul-Aug).

Dive in to Celtic mythology at Antrim's legendary Giant's Causeway

© Umomos / Shutterstock

GIANT'S CAUSEWAY NORTHERN IRELAND

5-16 Why now? Dramatic seas, spellbinding mythology and rock legends (minus giant crowds).

On the awesome Antrim coast, where the Atlantic Ocean crashes into the Irish Sea, the enigmatic Giant's Causeway leads out into the waves. Some 40,000 columns of black basalt erupt from the beach here, each one perfectly polygonal, and some – like the Giant's Boot and the Wishing Chair – sculpted by the elements into formations that have acquired their own stories. But what caused this phenomenon? The sciency answers are explained in the National Trust's award-winning Visitor Experience, but according to Celtic mythology the causeway was created by an Irish giant, Fionn Mac Cumhaill (aka Finn McCool), so he could reach Scotland and fight his rival Benandonner. Arriving to find his enemy more enormous than he'd expected, Fionn ran home. The Scottish giant came after him, but when he arrived Fionn was asleep. Oonagh, Fionn's quick-witted wife, told Benandonner that the snoozing giant was her son, and his much-bigger dad would soon be home. Terrified, Benandonner scarpered back to Scotland, bashing up the causeway behind him.

Trip plan: Visit via bus from Belfast, or drive and explore the epic Causeway Coast, testing the family mettle on a crossing of the wobbly Carrick-a-Rede Rope Bridge.

Need to know: Beyond the rocks you might spot bottlenose dolphins, porpoises, minke whales and basking sharks.

Other months: Oct-Mar – wild; May-Sep – beautiful, busy.

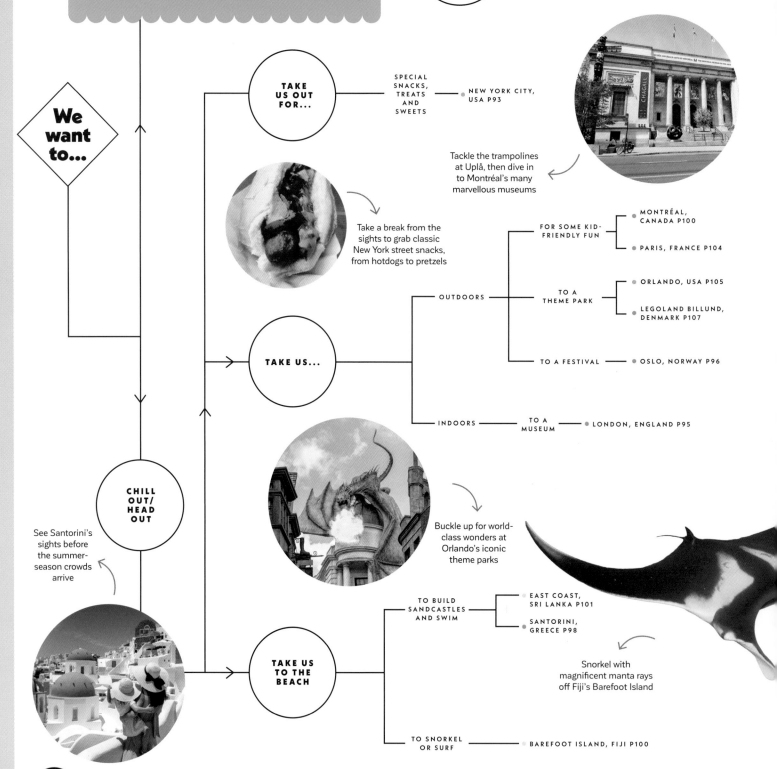

May

WHERE TO GO WHEN WITH KIDS

HAVE AN ADVENTURE

We want to...

TAKE US OUT FOR...

SPECIAL SNACKS, TREATS AND SWEETS — ● NEW YORK CITY, USA P93

Tackle the trampolines at Uplå, then dive in to Montréal's many marvellous museums

Take a break from the sights to grab classic New York street snacks, from hotdogs to pretzels

TAKE US...

OUTDOORS

FOR SOME KID-FRIENDLY FUN
- ● MONTRÉAL, CANADA P100
- ● PARIS, FRANCE P104

TO A THEME PARK
- ● ORLANDO, USA P105
- ● LEGOLAND BILLUND, DENMARK P107

TO A FESTIVAL — ● OSLO, NORWAY P96

INDOORS — TO A MUSEUM — ● LONDON, ENGLAND P95

CHILL OUT/ HEAD OUT

See Santorini's sights before the summer-season crowds arrive

Buckle up for world-class wonders at Orlando's iconic theme parks

TAKE US TO THE BEACH

TO BUILD SANDCASTLES AND SWIM
- ● EAST COAST, SRI LANKA P101
- ● SANTORINI, GREECE P98

Snorkel with magnificent manta rays off Fiji's Barefoot Island

TO SNORKEL OR SURF — ● BAREFOOT ISLAND, FIJI P100

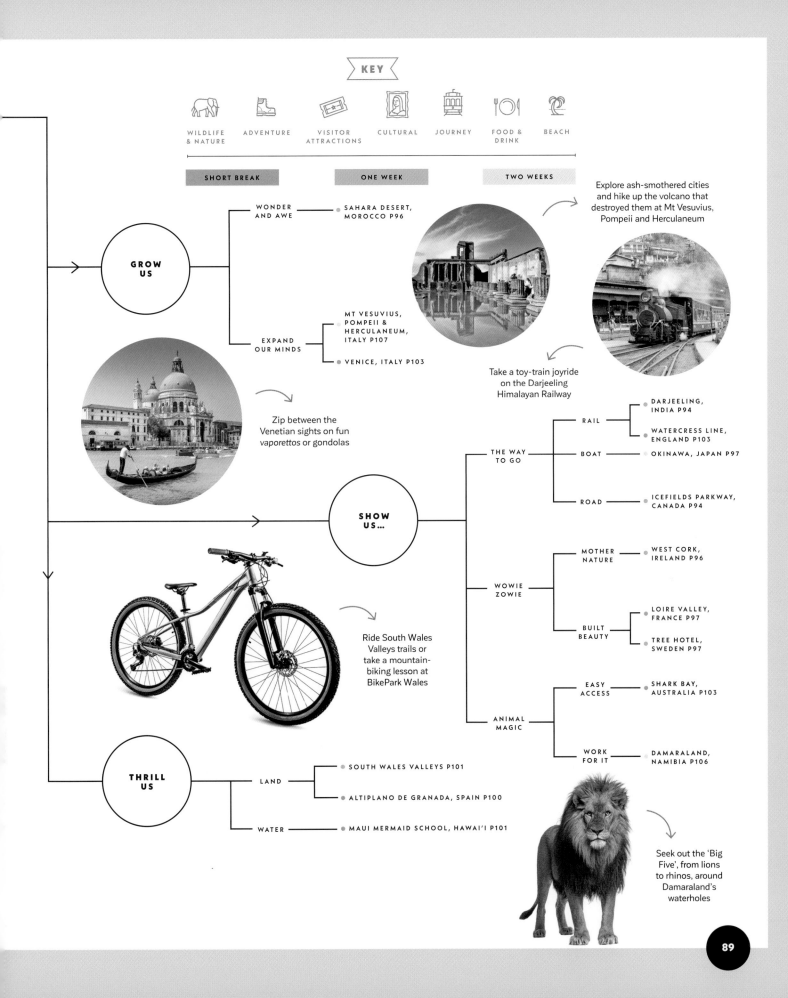

WILDLIFE & NATURE

ADVENTURE

VISITOR ATTRACTIONS

CULTURAL

JOURNEY

FOOD & DRINK

BEACH

SHORT BREAK

ONE WEEK

TWO WEEKS

Explore ash-smothered cities and hike up the volcano that destroyed them at Mt Vesuvius, Pompeii and Herculaneum

GROW US

WONDER AND AWE — SAHARA DESERT, MOROCCO P96

EXPAND OUR MINDS — MT VESUVIUS, POMPEII & HERCULANEUM, ITALY P107

VENICE, ITALY P103

Take a toy-train joyride on the Darjeeling Himalayan Railway

Zip between the Venetian sights on fun *vaporettos* or gondolas

SHOW US...

THE WAY TO GO

RAIL — DARJEELING, INDIA P94

WATERCRESS LINE, ENGLAND P103

BOAT — OKINAWA, JAPAN P97

ROAD — ICEFIELDS PARKWAY, CANADA P94

WOWIE ZOWIE

MOTHER NATURE — WEST CORK, IRELAND P96

BUILT BEAUTY — LOIRE VALLEY, FRANCE P97

TREE HOTEL, SWEDEN P97

ANIMAL MAGIC

EASY ACCESS — SHARK BAY, AUSTRALIA P103

WORK FOR IT — DAMARALAND, NAMIBIA P106

Ride South Wales Valleys trails or take a mountain-biking lesson at BikePark Wales

THRILL US

LAND — SOUTH WALES VALLEYS P101

ALTIPLANO DE GRANADA, SPAIN P100

WATER — MAUI MERMAID SCHOOL, HAWAI'I P101

Seek out the 'Big Five', from lions to rhinos, around Damaraland's waterholes

Events in May

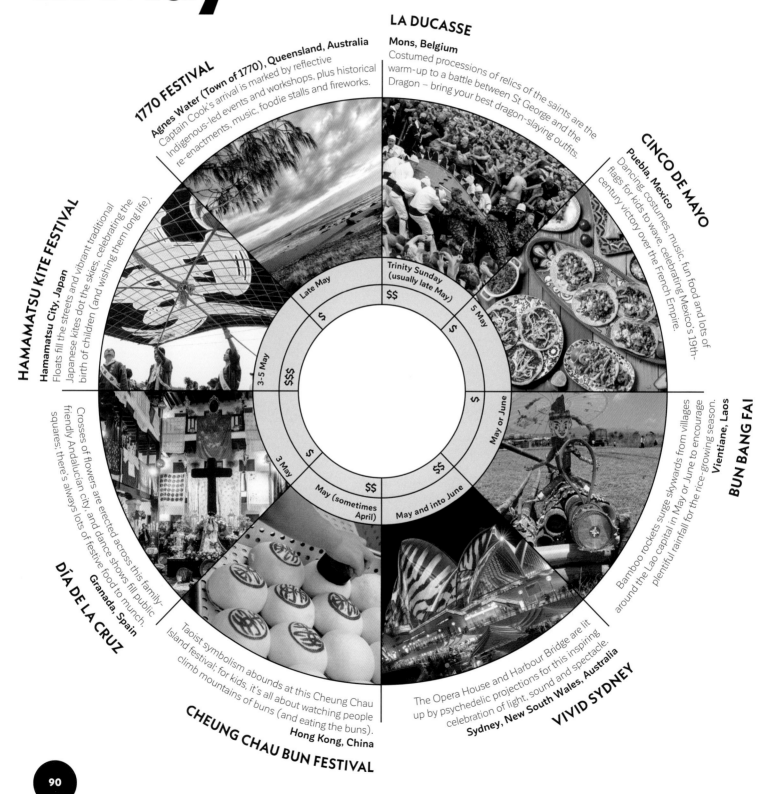

LA DUCASSE

Mons, Belgium
Costumed processions of relics of the saints are the warm-up to a battle between St George and the Dragon – bring your best dragon-slaying outfits.

1770 FESTIVAL

Agnes Water (Town of 1770), Queensland, Australia
Captain Cook's arrival is marked by reflective Indigenous-led events and workshops, plus historical re-enactments, music, foodie stalls and fireworks.

CINCO DE MAYO

Puebla, Mexico
Dancing, costumes, music, fun food and lots of flags for kids to wave, celebrating Mexico's 19th-century victory over the French Empire.

HAMAMATSU KITE FESTIVAL

Hamamatsu City, Japan
Floats fill the streets and vibrant traditional Japanese kites dot the skies, celebrating the birth of children (and wishing them long life).

BUN BANG FAI

Vientiane, Laos
Bamboo rockets surge skywards from villages around the Lao capital in May or June to encourage plentiful rainfall for the rice-growing season.

DÍA DE LA CRUZ

Granada, Spain
Crosses of flowers are erected across this family-friendly Andalucian city, and dance shows fill public squares; there's always lots of festive food to munch.

CHEUNG CHAU BUN FESTIVAL

Hong Kong, China
Taoist symbolism abounds at this Cheung Chau Island festival; for kids, it's all about watching people climb mountains of buns (and eating the buns).

VIVID SYDNEY

Sydney, New South Wales, Australia
The Opera House and Harbour Bridge are lit up by psychedelic projections for this inspiring celebration of light, sound and spectacle.

Late May — $

Trinity Sunday (usually late May) — $$

5 May — $

3-5 May — $$$

May or June — $

3 May — $

May (sometimes April) — $$

May and into June — $$

● LEGOLAND BILLUND, DENMARK

Watch a play in Shakespeare's Globe theatre in London

Fall in love with art at the Louvre in Paris

● WATERCRESS LINE, ENGLAND

● TREE HOTEL, SWEDEN

Thrills and spills at Universal Studios in Orlando, Florida

A trip to family-friendly Montréal in Canada

Meet lots of Lego characters, such as this traveller, in Billund, Denmark

● ORLANDO, USA

● OSLO, NORWAY

● MONTRÉAL, CANADA

● LONDON, ENGLAND

● LOIRE VALLEY, FRANCE

● DARJEELING, INDIA

● ICEFIELDS PARKWAY, CANADA

Fresh tea leaves are picked and dried in Darjeeling, India

● PARIS, FRANCE

● MAUI MERMAID SCHOOL, HAWAI'I

● SANTORINI, GREECE

● BAREFOOT ISLAND, FIJI

● EAST COAST, SRI LANKA

● NEW YORK CITY, USA

● SHARK BAY, AUSTRALIA

Climbing Mt Vesuvius in Italy

Dolphins surf off Fijian islands

● VENICE, ITALY

Don't forget a helmet when mountain biking in Wales

● ALTIPLANO DE GRANADA, SPAIN

Namibia's Damaraland is one of the few places where rare black rhinos live

● MT VESUVIUS, POMPEII & HERCULANEUM, ITALY

Look for Shisa statues throughout Okinawa

Explore Eyeries on the Ring of Beara in Ireland

● OKINAWA, JAPAN

● DAMARALAND, NAMIBIA

● SOUTH WALES VALLEYS

● SAHARA DESERT, MOROCCO

● WEST CORK, IRELAND

NEW YORK CITY
USA

`0-16` **Why now? Come before summer brings crowds and baking streets.**

Begin your NYC trip in Central Park with its excellent playgrounds, waterfalls and roller-skating circle near Strawberry Fields. Most young kids love the dino skeletons and planetarium at the American Museum of Natural History; the more art-inspired take in the Metropolitan Museum of Art. Now hit the bright lights of Downtown: in Times Square, grab quintessential NYC street snacks: pretzels, pizza slices or hotdogs (expect to be dragged into M&M's New York, Hershey's Chocolate World or the Krispy Kreme store, too). Get last-minute tickets to a Broadway show at TKTS Times Square, then head to Rockefeller Plaza for a behind-the-scenes NBC Studios tour. The next day, hop on a ferry from Battery Park to the moving Ellis Island Museum of Immigration and the Statue of Liberty (you need special tickets to visit her crown). On your return to Manhattan, wander up Wall St, past the inspiring *Charging Bull* statue and Trinity Church (*Hamilton* fans take note!), to visit the astonishing September 11 Memorial and the adjacent Memorial Museum. Round off with a stroll on the 2.4km-long (1.5-mile) High Line, admiring sculptures and gardens along this reclaimed freight line.

Trip plan: The subway will be your main transport; note that kids under 112cm (44in) tall can ride for free.

Need to know: Ticket touts are everywhere, in person and online; only purchase tickets directly from venues or licensed outlets.

Other months: Jan-Apr – fewer tourists; Jun & Sep-Oct – best sightseeing weather; Jul-Aug – hot; Nov-Dec – festive delights.

Metro magic in New York's Times Square

DARJEELING
INDIA

5-16 Why now? Mild temperatures and great views from the toy train to Darjeeling.

With the mercury soaring on the Indian plains, it's time to head to the hills – more specifically Darjeeling, where kids can gawp at the Himalayas, tour tea plantations and ride one of the world's most charming miniature railways. The first trains on the Darjeeling Himalayan Railway trundled uphill in 1881, and diminutive steam engines still haul carriages on 'joy ride' services from Darjeeling to Ghum – a more enjoyable excursion for pint-sized rail enthusiasts than the line's long diesel-powered journey from New Jalpaiguri station to Darjeeling. But on the way up and en route to Ghum, you'll trundle slowly past dizzying views and coil around the legendary Batasia Loop, where the train completes a full 360-degree turn. It's the perfect warm-up for several relaxing days of tea tours, hill hikes and spectacular views of Khangchendzonga, the world's third-highest mountain.

Trip plan: The gateway to Darjeeling is New Jalpaiguri, itself an all-day or overnight train ride from Kolkata. Change here for the Darjeeling toy train (a 7hr trip), or reach the hills in half the time by shared 4WD and enjoy the hill railway on a joy ride to Ghum.

Need to know: Motion sickness is a risk whether reaching Darjeeling by road or rail; ply kids with plenty of drinking water and let them have the window seats.

Other months: Dec-Feb – cold, foggy; Oct-Nov & Mar-Apr – mild, great for views; Jun-Sep – views vanish behind monsoon rainclouds.

ICEFIELDS PARKWAY
CANADA

0-16 Why now? The Parkway is best in spring, before the summer crowds.

There are amazing road trips – and then there's the Icefields Parkway. This 232km (144-mile) ribbon of asphalt parallels the Continental Divide between Lake Louise and Jasper in the Canadian Rockies of Alberta. It's the lone sign of human influence in an otherwise pristine wilderness – there are two types of sights here: static (lakes, glaciers and mountains) and moving (elk, bears, moose and more). If you don't see at least one wild animal you'll be very unlucky. This isn't a long drive that's going to put the kids to sleep: you'll be keeping an eye out for animals and stopping a lot. Peyto Lake's incredibly vibrant blue can be seen in countless publicity shots, but there's nothing like gazing at the real thing. The vast Columbia Icefield, covering an area the size of Vancouver and feeding eight glaciers, is stunning. The tongue of the Athabasca Glacier can be visited on foot or in an all-terrain vehicle. And at the end of the line is Jasper, an unpretentious mountain town with more wilderness on its doorstep.

Trip plan: Drive the Parkway in either (or both!) directions; the resort town of Banff is 57km (35 miles) from the southern end near Lake Louise; Jasper is at the Parkway's northern end. There are places to stay along the way, but book ahead.

Need to know: The route is open year-round; rogue snowfalls can occur in May, so keep an eye on weather forecasts.

Other months: Oct-Apr – quieter, snowy; Jun-Sep – busy.

Peyto Lake, just one of the mind-blowing sights along the Icefields Parkway

LONDON
ENGLAND

The Hintze Hall blue
whale skeleton at
London's Natural
History Museum

5-16 **Why now? London's mood lifts the moment the sun comes out.**

There are many ways into London, no matter what kids are interested in. History? Science? Museums? Tick, tick and tick. For starters, take a day each at the British Museum and the Natural History and Science Museums. Then there's the Postal Museum with its underground mail train; the London Transport Museum and its vintage trains and buses; and the National Maritime Museum and Museum of London Docklands for local history. For iconic sights with a family-friendly feel, book tickets to the Tower of London and a behind-the-scenes tour of Shakespeare's Globe theatre; for older kids, the London Dungeon is often a big (and surprisingly educational) hit. If they're bored of 'old stuff', check out family activities at Tate Britain and Tate Modern or the National Portrait Gallery; the cable car across the Thames at North Greenwich is an inexpensive alternative to the London Eye. *Harry Potter* fans should make a pilgrimage to the fabled Platform 9¾ at King's Cross Station, but do budget for Warner Bros Studio Tour: The Making of Harry Potter – it's worth it. London is also filled with expansive parks to unwind in, some with epic playgrounds they'll never forget.

Trip plan: London is vast, but children under 11 ride on public transport for free.

Need to know: Public toilets can be hard to find and are often subpar; make a beeline for the nearest museum or art gallery.

Other months: Jan-Mar – cold, grey days; Apr – spring flowers; Jun-Aug – summer warmth; Sep-Dec – winter, festive vibes.

OSLO
NORWAY

0-12 Why now? Experience an event where kids are at the forefront.
Children's Day, on 17 May, offers a special insight to Norwegian national pride and the reverence in which childhood is held here. A mix of parades, traditional games, marching bands and kid-friendly festive foods make it a memorable and joyous experience for children. As soon as you land, get yourself a Norwegian flag (a paper one is fine); this is also Norway's Constitution Day, and flag-waving is very much a part of the festivities. Children from about 100 schools, some in traditional Norwegian dress, lead the Barnetoget parade from the main gate of Akershus Fortress at 10am. Paraders are greeted by the royal family from the balcony of the Royal Palace on their march around central Oslo; stages with choirs, dance troupes and bands are also set up in public spaces around the city. When you're ready to escape, head up to the broad lawns of Frognerparken, where you'll find families picnicking and playing traditional games like sack races and tug-of-war. As well as typical Norwegian foods such as *smørbrød* (open sandwiches), there are loads of kid favourites – hotdogs, ice-cream, waffles and cakes – to be enjoyed.
Trip plan: Frognerparken is a long uphill walk for tired children; check the Ruter app for when tram services resume after the parade.
Need to know: Bring plenty of water but be aware there may be queues for public toilets in parks and shopping centres.
Other months: Oct-Mar – cold, dark, snowy; Apr – longer days; Jun-Sep – summer, longest days.

WEST CORK
IRELAND

12-16 Why now? Adventure amid wonderful wild landscapes, with no one else around.
West Cork is stacked with outdoor adventure possibilities for families with older kids. And if you come in May, you can dodge the school crowds and enjoy long, light days, and a lower chance of rainfall than in the summer months. Start by surfing at Garretstown, a pretty stretch of sand with a surf school run from a camper van on the beach. Next, go west along the Wild Atlantic Way – a 2575km (1600-mile) coastal route from nearby Kinsale to Donegal – to the Sheep's Head Peninsula, where you can hike spectacular coastal trails like the Lighthouse Loop, with its steep rocky paths and vertiginous sea cliffs. A sunrise kayak at Glengarriff Bay in the Beara Peninsula, between the low Caha Mountains and the sea, is a must: sightings of harbour seals, white-tailed eagles, grey herons and oystercatchers are highly likely at this time of year. Finish with a folklore e-bike tour in Union Hall, enjoying a 19km (12-mile) ride through rolling hills and ancient forest, while learning about local myths and legends.
Trip plan: Driving is the best way to get around. Rent a car at Cork Airport and head west along the Wild Atlantic Way.
Need to know: With sporty kids in tow, consider catching a game of Gaelic Football (GAA), which is hugely popular in County Cork. Most parishes have a team: ask around for details of upcoming matches.
Other months: Nov-Feb – cold; Mar-Apr – rainy; Jun-Aug – warmest but peak season; Sep-Oct – cooler, fairly dry.

SAHARA DESERT
MOROCCO

12-16 Why now? Drive through the desert before it gets too hot.
This week-long family road trip takes you out of Marrakesh and out into the Sahara. First stop is Ouarzazate, 193km (119 miles) away. Often called the 'Hollywood of North Africa', the town has served as a stand-in for various locations in films such as *Gladiator*, but older teens might recognise it from the TV series *Game of Thrones*; Atlas Studio provides a desert tour of the discarded film sets. From Merzouga, 368km (229 miles) on from Ouarzazate, it's possible to arrange camel treks into the cinematic desert dunes of Erg Chebbi. Kids will find bedding down for the night in a Berber-style desert camp hugely atmospheric – watch as the sunset turns the dunes stunning shades of orange, pink and purple. After breakfast at camp, drive 195km (121 miles) on towards Tinerhir. The road passes green *palmeraies* (palm groves) and Berber villages until, 15km (9 miles) along, high walls of pink and grey rock close in around the tarmac at the Todra Gorge, a 300m-deep (984ft) fault that's ripe for rock climbing and treks. Return to Marrakesh via another *Game of Thrones* location, the mudbrick fortified village of Aït Ben Haddou, 200km (124 miles) from Todra.
Trip plan: Hire a car at Marrakesh Airport, and spend at least a day here (park outside the Medina) before heading to the desert. Local operators can also arrange family-friendly Sahara itineraries.
Need to know: Temperatures in the Sahara can drop by 20°C (68°F) at night.
Other months: Nov-Mar – cool; Apr & Sep-Oct – warm, pleasant; Jun-Aug – hot.

© Nigel Jarvis / Shutterstock

LOIRE VALLEY
FRANCE

5-12 **Why now?** Seek out *Sleeping Beauty* inspiration in a sensational château as the Loire Valley awakens in spring.

Step straight into a scene from a fairy tale while visiting the stunning 15th-century Château d'Ussé, overlooking the River Indre in the lush Loire Valley of central France. Known as 'Sleeping Beauty Castle', this multi-turreted, mind-bogglingly opulent mansion apparently inspired the story collector Charles Perrault to pen his adaption of *La Belle au Bois Dormant* in the 17th century, a traditional tale about a slumbering spellbound princess condemned by an evil fairy to spend a century asleep in a remote castle, until cured of her curse by a prince. (Perrault's plot is several degrees darker than the Disney rendition, through which the yarn is known to most children.) The Château's octagonal Knights' Dungeon is dedicated to the tale, with various (fairly chintzy) waxworks portraying scenes from the story – younger children enjoy this, while older kids and parents can drink in the sheer splendour of the place, once a fancy family abode, with its own drawbridge and vault.

Trip plan: A short train ride or drive from Paris, the Loire Valley is famed for wine and lined with châteaux and feudal castles from the pre-revolutionary era – explore the cities of Orléans, Blois, Tours and Angers.

Need to know: Many Loire Valley châteaux close in winter. The Château d'Ussé opens mid-February to mid-November.

Other months: Dec-Jan – châteaux typically closed; Feb-Apr & Sep-Nov – cooler and quieter; Jun-Aug – hot weather, peak-season busy.

TREE HOTEL
SWEDEN

5-16 **Why now?** It's early summer, perfect weather for sleeping in a tree house.

With long warm days here in the small village of Harads, just 50km (31 miles) south of the Arctic Circle, the Tree Hotel makes a top base for exploring remote, rural Norrbotten, Sweden's northernmost county. With eight unique 'rooms' built high into the canopy of a pine forest, each designed by a different architect, this place is both quirky and fun, bound to capture the attention of both of kids and kids-at-heart. Stay in the Bird's Nest, reached by climbing a near-vertical ladder high into the trees, or the UFO room, resembling a hovering spacecraft. The Dragonfly room blends seamlessly into the trees, while access to Biosphere is via a suspended bridge, and Mirrorcube reflects the surrounding forest and is hard to spot up there in the treetops. There's lots to do in the area, from meeting a moose to visiting a reindeer herder, plus hiking, river kayaking and lake paddling under the Midnight Sun (starting at 10.30pm). The Tree Hotel's restaurant serves all kinds of Swedish delicacies, from wild game to hand-picked berries.

Trip plan: Open year-round, the Tree Hotel is just outside Harads, on Rte 97, 80km (50 miles) northwest of Luleå and 88km (54 miles) southeast of Jokkmokk. There's an airport at Luleå.

Need to know: Sweden's National Day is 6 June, but Midsummer is when Swedes truly celebrate. It changes by the year but it's around 21 June, the longest day of the year.

Other months: Nov-Mar – cold, dark; Jun-Sep – light, warm.

OKINAWA
JAPAN

12-16 **Why now?** Avoid the heat, humidity and potential typhoons of summer.

Didn't know you could go on a family island-hopping adventure in Japan? Take the troops on an off-the-beaten-track ferry expedition southwest from Kagoshima City, in southern Kyūshū, to Naha, capital of Okinawa Prefecture. This trip is well off the radar of most visitors, and offers an incredibly rewarding journey through parts of the country that see few foreign tourists. Get teenagers involved in planning and logistics, studying ferry timetables, accommodation options and things to do on each of the fascinating islands – Amami Ōshima, Tokunoshima, Okinoerabu-jima and Yoron – where you can make a layover along the way. Ferries leave Kagoshima City at 6pm daily, run by two companies – Marix Line and Marue Ferry – on alternating days. The ferry arrives in Naha the following day at 7pm, but purchase a very reasonable Marue Ferry 'Yui Ticket' to get a 21-day unlimited-ride pass allowing you to stop over at any of the islands in between.

Trip plan: The departure port is in Kagoshima City at the southern end of Japan's Shinkansen (bullet train) line; Kagoshima Airport is 30km (18 miles) northeast of the city. Naha Airport is 4km (2.5 miles) west of central Naha, with regular flights back to mainland cities. This trip can be done in either direction.

Need to know: June to October is typhoon season; typhoons can affect ferry schedules, especially if they pass over or near Okinawa.

Other months: Nov-Mar – cooler, but still warm; Jun-Sep – hot, humid.

SANTORINI GREECE

`0-16`

Why now? Get there before everybody else does.

Santorini is spectacular, but it's best visited before the heat and crowds of the European summer holiday period. With multicoloured cliffs soaring above a sea-drowned caldera, the island resembles a giant slab of layered cake, with white Cycladic buildings lining the clifftops like a generous topping of icing sugar. It's a 'take your breath away' sight, especially when arriving by ferry. Even better, there's plenty to keep your family intrigued for a three- or four-day visit. The vibrant, bustling main town of Fira offers a warren of narrow streets for exploring, full of shops and restaurants, plus views that actually look better than the postcards. A walk along the caldera rim is another top family experience: head out from Fira and enjoy stunning vistas en route to Oia, on Santorini's northern tip, renowned for its world-class sunsets. For beach time,

seaside tavernas and budget family-friendly accommodation (without caldera views), try black-sand Perissa Beach in the southeast. And get out onto the water via a small-boat day cruise in the caldera that includes a stop at the rocky islet of Nea Kameni, where you can swim into lukewarm springs in the sea. Back on Santorini, take in a family movie under the stars at open-air CineKamari.

Trip plan: Santorini Airport receives direct flights from numerous European cities; ferries arrive from Athens, via the Cyclades, and from Crete.

Need to know: You'll pay a premium for accommodation with caldera views.

Other months: Nov-Apr – winter, quiet; Oct – shoulder season; Jun-Sep – hot and busy.

Stroll Santorini's caldera rim to stunning Oia

BAREFOOT ISLAND
FIJI

5-16 Why now? Sleep by the beach and snorkel with manta rays.

Fiji is a famously family-friendly destination, but many people head to touristy spots like the Mamanuca Islands. For a less manicured and more interesting experience, go a little further and explore the Yasawa Group, 20 paradisical punctuation points in the Pacific. Here you can still enjoy a tropical vacation – sleeping in beachside *bures* (thatch-roofed huts), hanging in hammocks, snorkelling in lemonade-clear fish-filled lagoons and coconut bowling in the evening. But in places like Drawaqa (home to the Barefoot Manta Island Resort), you can also go sea kayaking, caving, trekking around volcanic peaks, scuba diving on kaleidoscopic reefs and snorkelling with manta rays, magnificent giants of the deep that frequent a channel on the island's northern tip from April to October. Plus, it's possible to visit local villages. Older kids might be inspired by the island's conservation programme, learning about the rays and reef farming from the resident marine biologist. Some may even return on voluntourism programmes run by Vinaka Fiji, to teach in island schools.

Trip plan: Fly to Nadi International Airport on the main island of Viti Levu. Awesome Adventures ferries leave from Port Denarau in Nadi and island-hop around the Mamanucas and Yasawas.

Need to know: Attending open-air Sunday-morning church services offers a wonderful window into local life.

Other months: Nov-Apr – wet season, tropical cyclones possible; Jun-Sep – peak season, busy; Oct – festival season.

ALTIPLANO DE GRANADA
SPAIN

5-16 Why now? For horse riding in the green of late spring.

This corner of Granada and Jaen provinces is home to lesser-visited towns and some of Spain's most beautiful inland scenery. The dramatic rock formations and lush forests of the Altiplano de Granada encompass two natural parks – Sierra de Baza and Sierra de Castril – attracting adventure-seekers keen to explore its limestone slopes and kayak its turquoise reservoirs. It's a particularly fun region to explore on horseback. Guides will lead you and your entourage on four-legged explorations through cool pine forests, where the needle-strewn floor muffles each hoof step, across rock-strewn gorges where your movements echo across walls, and past richly hued rivers and streams. The historic white village of Castril, perched on the side of the Sierra de Castril, makes a good base, with local operators who can organise riding for your family (age eight and up); alternatively El Geco Verde, a classic Altiplanto hotel in Campo Cebas, 13km (8 miles) west of Castril, will arrange activities on your behalf, including kayaking (age five and above), canyoning (age 12 and above) and biking.

Trip plan: The nearest airport to Castril is Granada-Jaén. You can take a bus from Málaga-Costa del Sol Airport to Castril (5hr 40min). A car is needed to explore the area.

Need to know: Granada – with its churches, old-school tapas bars and street art – is a 1hr 40min drive from Castril, or a 2hr 30min train journey via Guadix.

Other months: Dec-Mar – mild; Apr-Jun – sunny, warm; Jul-Aug – hot, busy; Sep-Nov – mild, quiet.

MONTRÉAL
CANADA

0-16 Why now? Enjoy spring weather and light crowds at Montréal's museums and parks.

Picture this: a series of nets hovering 6m (20ft) above ground, suspended from the treetops in the Mont Saint-Grégoire Forest. The nets connect a series of ramps and slides, tunnels and trampolines, giving the possibility of bounding through the treetops. This is Uplå, the continent's largest outdoor trampoline park. Come by day for sunshine and fresh air; come by night for a futuristic, colorific light display; come in May to beat the summer-vacation crowds and enjoy cooler temperatures. Trampolines are not recommended for kids under three, but little ones are welcome to explore the treetop village, with seven treehouses connected by bridges and slides. Uplå is bound to be a highlight of the weekend, but Montréal is also home to a slew of cool museums, such as the Biodôme (five ecosystems and hundreds of plant and animal species) and the Insectarium (with 3000 species of creepy crawlies). On a sunny spring day, Parc du Mont-Royal is a required destination for playgrounds, walking trails and fabulous views from the top.

Trip plan: If you're staying in Montréal, you'll need a car to get to Uplå, which is 48km (30 miles) east of the city.

Need to know: Uplå is open year-round (daily in summer, weekends only September to June), with daytime sessions (2hr) and night-time experiences (1hr 30min); the treetop village is closed after dark.

Other months: Nov-Apr – cold, dark, dreary; Jun-Sep – long days, warm temperatures and sunny skies; Oct – pleasant weather, autumn foliage.

SOUTH WALES VALLEYS

12-16 Why now? Ride the UK's best mountain-bike park before the summer crowds descend.

After years of industrial decline, the South Wales Valleys have been reborn as a top mountain-biking destination – and BikePark Wales is the region's jewel in the crown. Nestled in a forested valley with views of Bannau Brycheiniog (the Brecon Beacons), it was founded by two passionate pro mountain bikers in 2013, inspired by French ski resorts where riders put their bikes on chairlifts and ride downhill on dirt trails; here you board a bus with a bike trailer to reach the top. Start kids (especially those new to downhill mountain biking) on the Kermit, a gentle, swooping 5km (3-mile) trail with plenty of rest spots; move them on to the easiest blue trails if they need more of a challenge. Or book beginners on a four-hour Ticket to Ride taster session, where a guide will teach them how to tackle the trails safely and skilfully. More experienced riders can test themselves on the harder blue and red trails (the blacks and purples are for experts only).

Trip plan: Spend at least two days here to make the most of the trails.

Need to know: Bring your own bike or hire one (plus a helmet, pads and body armour). The park is closed on Tuesdays and Wednesdays except during UK school holidays; book gear hire and uplift tickets in advance.

Other months: Nov-Feb – chilly, wet; Mar-Apr – driest, spring flowers; Jun-Aug – warmest, school holidays mid-Jul & Aug; Sep-Oct – cooler, autumn colours.

MAUI MERMAID SCHOOL
HAWAI'I

5-16 Why now? Maui is magical in May, with perfect spring weather, fewer tourists and lower costs.

Tales involving tailed beings that are part human and part sea creature date back centuries, and feature in the folkloric and storytelling traditions of many coast-blessed countries, from selkies in Celtic culture to the sirens of Ancient Greece. Hans Christian Andersen wrote *Den lille havfrue* (*The Little Sea Maid*) in 1837, and in modern times Hollywood, Disney and Netflix have dramatically deepened children's interest in such magical marine characters. Many young minds dream of morphing into a mer-creature, and on the idyllic Hawaiian island of Maui, kids aged over six (and, indeed, parents) can do exactly that, by enrolling in the Mermaid University and learning to swim with a very realistic looking fin. More than simply discovering your inner Ariel, the course (run by professional mermaids) teaches aspirant aquafolk all about mermaid mythology and imparts the skills required to move through water with a tail. The classroom is an ocean cove, rich with wildlife and surrounded by magical views of Maui's neighbouring volcanic islands, including Molokini and Kaho'olawe.

Trip plan: Fly to Kahului Airport and rent a car (book well in advance). Be sure to explore the volcano-scape of nearby Haleakalā National Park.

Need to know: Courses take place in Makena Bay. Participants must be aged over six and be comfortable in the sea.

Other months: Jan-Mar – ocean swells, surfing; Apr: settled, quiet; Jun-Sep – warm, dry, busy; Oct-Nov – quieter.

EAST COAST
SRI LANKA

5-16 Why now? For between-season quiet and chilled surf beaches.

Timing is everything in Sri Lanka, where monsoons hit the southwest and northeast over different months. May, nestled between these rain-drenched seasons, is a peaceful month to explore. With the southwest monsoon just underway, head to the unspoiled beaches on the eastern coast, where you'll find warm sunshine and temperatures averaging 25°C (77°F). Nilaveli's 4km (2.5-mile) stretch of sand is considered one of Sri Lanka's best, and with its paradise-island remoteness, swaying palms and golden tinge to the shore, it's easy to see why. As such, it's a surprise that it is so little-frequented. A few modest resorts are tucked above the shoreline, and Pigeon Island, which offers great snorkelling opportunities, is a short boat-ride away.

In Weligama, well-established surf camps are available for kids eager to learn to 'hang ten', while the long crescent of sand at Arugam Bay has several surf schools and board-rental spots.

Trip plan: From Colombo, it's a 5hr drive to Nilaveli; break it up by spending a night in Kandy and another at Habarana to explore Sigiriya. Or, take the busy but atmospheric train from Colombo Fort Station to Trincomalee (8hr), a 14km (9-mile) taxi hop from Nilaveli. Internal flights to locations over the east coast take 50min.

Need to know: During May's two-day Vesak Poya festival, coloured lights adorn every Buddhist home, shop and temple.

Other months: Nov-Feb – driest, peak season; Mar-Oct – heavy rains in the southwest, dry in the north and east.

© Pubudini / Shutterstock

101

(A) Artist Lorenzo Quinn's *Support* for Venice's 2017 Biennale; (L) Dolphins at Shark Bay Marine Park; (R) Thomas Day on the Watercress Line

© Pete Seaward / Lonely Planet

VENICE
ITALY

5-16 Why now? Explore Venice in spring and discover all-ages appeal at the Biennale.

It might be aimed at serious fans and professionals, but the Venice Biennale has plenty to wow children, including teens looking for career inspiration. If you miss out on tickets to educational workshops, fear not: contemporary art – from immersive sculptural pieces to video projections – has incredible pulling power for kids of all ages. If it's an architecture year, pavilions with interactive installations and large-scale models can captivate young imaginations. And without the fear of cars or speeding cyclists, Venice itself is a pleasure to travel with children (just watch them near water, of course). From the Giardini della Biennale, head to the nearby Naval Museum of Venice to learn about the city's fascinating maritime history and peruse the model ships and maritime artefacts. Jump on the *vaporetto* back to Santa Maria del Giglio ferry terminal to wander in Piazza San Marco and climb the Campanile (the bell tower of Basilica di San Marco) for views of the city and water below. Other kid-friendly options include gondola rides, watching glass-blowers on Murano Island, and escaping to the beach Lido di Jesolo. And did we mention gelato?

Trip plan: You'll be walking a lot, over uneven pavements and bridges with stairs; make use of ferries as much as possible.

Need to know: Italians are generally very family-focused – expect plenty of cheek-squeezing and fussing over little ones.

Other months: Nov-Mar – foggy, cold, no crowds; Apr & Sep-Oct – sunny, smaller crowds; Jun-Jul – hot, packed (avoid).

WATERCRESS LINE
ENGLAND

0-16 Why now? For nostalgic train journeys through green countryside and flower-decked stations.

Young children have always found steam trains captivating: the jewel-coloured engines, the chug and whistle as the carriages work their way along the track, and the formal, smart uniforms of the station staff. A day out at the Watercress Line will tick all those boxes. Named after the crop that the line used to carry, it's a beautifully realised slice of nostalgia, with steam trains carrying passengers through 16km (10 miles) of Hampshire countryside and stopping at charming restored stations along the way; in May, station planters and hanging baskets will be in full colourful bloom. You can board the train at either end of the line: at the picturesque Georgian town of Alresford, 11km (7 miles) from Winchester, or at the market town of Alton. The main bulk of activities are at Ropley, including a playground, a young engineer's trail and (on select days) a miniature railway. Fans of the books and TV series will love the line's Thomas the Tank Engine days, featuring full-size steam trains decked in full Thomas regalia.

Trip plan: Fares give you all-day travel, so you can visit all four of the line's heritage stations, as well as Alresford and Alton.

Need to know: Separate tickets may be needed for special events, including dining trains, Thomas days and festive-season rides; check online (watercressline.co.uk).

Other months: Dec-Feb – train illuminations & Father Christmas; Mar-Apr – Easter-themed rides; Jun-Aug – summer, busy weekends and school holidays; Oct-Nov – Halloween-themed rides.

SHARK BAY
AUSTRALIA

5-16 Why now? Meet wild dolphins in calmer conditions.

Shark Bay might sound scary, but friendly finned aquatic animals have long been attracting travellers to this corner of Western Australia's Coral Coast. Just past Denham, on a peninsula poking into the bay, is Monkey Mia Conservation Park, where there are no apes, but you can definitely have an up-close encounter with wild dolphins. For decades, small groups of bottlenose dolphins (always females, sometimes with calves) have visited the beach here, swimming into knee-deep water to interact with humans every morning. The tradition began when a local fisherman started feeding the dolphins during the 1960s. The area is now part of Shark Bay Marine Park, and rangers strictly control encounters: only five dolphins are fed, and the food is limited to 10% of their daily dietary intake so they don't become reliant. Swimming isn't permitted in the dolphin area, but the snorkelling nearby is sensational. Aside from dolphins, you might spot dugongs, rays, turtles and...sharks. The area is rich in Indigenous culture and birdlife too; walk the Wulyibidi Yaninyina Trail, a short loop through red dunes and along the beach.

Trip plan: Monkey Mia is a 10hr drive from Perth. Discover stromatolites – aka 'living fossils' – in nearby Hamelin Pool.

Need to know: May is less windy and humid than summer, with smaller crowds (so a better chance of being picked to hand-feed the dolphins). Arrive early. Touching the animals is strictly forbidden.

Other months: Nov-Mar – hot, windy and busy; Jun-Oct – chilly nights and mornings, wildflowers.

PARIS
FRANCE

 Why now? Take a toon-tastic tour of Paris in the glowing late-spring light.

For fans of the cartoon series *Miraculous: Tales of Ladybug & Cat Noir*, spring is a great time to discover its Paris locations in person. First, pick out the landmarks you'll be seeing during your adventure from the top of the Eiffel Tower, then head across the Seine to the Jardins du Trocadéro (a popular *Miraculous* hangout), and on to Place de la Concorde, where Ladybug cut the tip off the Luxor Obelisk to save Paris. Take a rest stop in the blooming Jardin des Tuileries and ride its famous carousel; next door is the Louvre, where villain Copycat stole the *Mona Lisa*. On day two, zip around Paris on the Metro to other *Miraculous* locations. Begin at manicured Place des Vosges (where Marinette first spies Adrien Agreste doing a photoshoot), then it's on to Blvd Malesherbes, where Lycée Carnot is the model for the characters' Françoise Dupont High School. Fontaine du Palmier on Place du Châtelet is where Ladybug (Marinette) kisses Cat Noir (Adrien); then tick off the Arc de Triomphe, Pont des Arts, Hôtel Plaza Athénée, Hôtel de Ville and, of course, Notre Dame. Finally, scoff delectable goodies at Boris Lume Patisserie Boulangerie in Montmartre, the inspiration for Marinette's family bakery.

Trip plan: Foldable scooters can help kids on walks between sights.

Need to know: Prebook tickets for the Eiffel Tower and the Louvre.

Other months: Oct-Mar – cold, more local life; Apr, Jun & Sep –sunshine, fewer crowds; Jul-Aug – heat, crowds.

Track iconic *Miraculous* sites through the streets of Paris

Make a splash in Universal's Volcano Bay water park

ORLANDO USA

0–16 **Why now? A quieter time for the magic of Orlando attractions.**

Walt Disney World is one of those places where the peak season lasts all year (almost). May is one of the few narrow windows of calm – or at least calm-er – between the madness of winter and summer vacations. So if your kids are hankering to meet Anna and Elsa or fly the *Millennium Falcon*, this is the time to do it. The same is true of Universal Studios. Spend less time waiting in line, and more time riding the *Hogwarts Express*, choosing a wand at Ollivander's and experiencing the Wizarding World of Harry Potter. Both parks have a lot to offer, but generally speaking, Disney has more rides and attractions for small children, while Universal has more thrill-rides for older kids and teens. Both are built around their own characters, movies and brands, so ultimately your decision probably depends on your kids' tastes. No matter which theme park you choose, be sure to save a day for a waterpark. Whether Blizzard Beach or Typhoon Lagoon (both at Disney), or Volcano Bay (at Universal), the water parks offer welcome relief from the heat.

Trip plan: Unless you have an extremely high tolerance for amusement parks, choose either Disney or Universal: don't try to do both in one Florida trip.

Need to know: Hotel rates and Disney ticket prices fluctuate according to demand; both are more affordable when crowds are lighter.

Other months: Nov-Mar – busiest, highest prices; Apr & Sep-Oct – shoulder season, lighter crowds; Jun-Aug – summer crowds.

Giraffes roam
Damaraland's
desertscape
wilderness

DAMARALAND
NAMIBIA

12-16 **Why now? See local wildlife on warm days in green wilderness.**

Even in a country as sparse as Namibia –
the second least-populated place on Earth
– Damaraland stands out as especially
empty. Sprawling across north-central
Namibia, this fascinating wilderness
of craggy mountains and dry riverbeds
supports desert-adapted wildlife, including
elephants, rhinos and lions. In May, the
days are warm and dry and the landscape
is still tinged green. It's a great time for
families to seek out animals as they gather
around waterholes; you can see a multitude
of wildlife in one place, and avoid hot, tiring
treks. Better still, the country is a pioneer in
community-driven ecotourism, with large
areas run as communal conservancies that
empower local people. Damaraland has
several award-winning, community-run
camps that use solar energy, recycle water
and employ former poachers as rangers
and guides. The stars of the show are rare
black rhinos and the region's famous desert
elephants, and the experience of watching
them drink together is something you'll not
forget in a hurry.

Trip plan: Southern Damaraland is around
560km (348 miles) from the capital,
Windhoek (6hr drive); you can also fly
in to some lodges. Allow at least three or
four days in the area; combine it with the
Atlantic coast and Etosha National Park.

Need to know: Full-day drives past endless
sandy landscapes may be unappealing,
so plan routes and rest days carefully. The
concentration of wildlife at Etosha might
suit younger kids.

Other months: Jan-Apr – peak rains, hot;
Jun – dry, greener, cheaper; Jul-Sep – dry,
peak season; Oct-Dec – hot, early rains.

(R) Heading in to Legoland Billund; (B) Block-built heaven at Billund

© LEGOLAND Billund

LEGOLAND BILLUND
DENMARK

5-16 Why now? Enjoy an epic block party (without too many gatecrashers).

Few toys have delighted successive generations like Lego, going strong since its plastic bricks were launched in 1949. May is a relatively quiet time to visit, but there will still likely be as many excited parents as amped-up kids in the entry queue for Legoland Billund, and for good reason. Built beside the original Lego factory, it has multiple themed areas (Wild West, Knights' Kingdom, Pirate Land) with rides and experiences, plus the mind-blowing Miniland, featuring famous cities and movie scenes made from some 20 million bricks. Nearby, in central Billund, is Lego House, a multistorey 'Experience Centre' engineered to look like a stack of 21 massive Lego bricks, built around the impressive 15m-high (49ft) Tree of Creativity, itself made from

6.3 million bricks. Strewn across the various zones are a further 25 million bricks to make into whatever you (sorry, your kids) want to. You'll also find displays about the history and learn-through-play philosophy of Lego (the brand's Lego-acy), plus eating places, rooftop terraces and – of course – a shop.

Trip plan: Billund Airport is beside Legoland. If brick boredom sets in, head to the adjacent Aquadome to zoom down waterslides and float along a river.

Need to know: Tickets for Legoland and Lego House (combis available) are cheaper bought online in advance. Saturdays are quietest; Tuesdays and Wednesdays busiest.

Other months: Sep-Feb – chilly; Jul-Aug – local school holidays, very busy.

© LEGOLAND Billund

MT VESUVIUS, POMPEII & HERCULANEUM ITALY

5-16 Why now? See the almost-intact ruins of ancient towns, amid cooler weather and lighter crowds.

In 79 CE, Mt Vesuvius erupted for the first time in centuries, spewing ash, rock and lava high into the air, and blanketing the nearby towns of Pompeii and Herculaneum in volcanic debris. Preserved by the ash and mud, the two towns are now amazing museums of art, architecture and daily life in Ancient Rome. Kids can wander around historic houses and courtyards, replete with mosaics and murals. Don't miss Pompeii's

Cave Canem (Beware of the Dog) mosaic outside the Casa del Poeta Tragico (House of the Tragic Poet), or the intriguing (and creepy) plaster reproductions of volcano victims at the moment of their death. After a day of exploring the ruins of Pompeii and/or Herculaneum, the logical next stop is the fiery mountain itself. It's an invigorating 1.6km (1-mile) hike from the parking area to the summit of Mt Vesuvius and part way around the crater. The volcano is now quiet, but it's wild to see the source of the destruction, still smoking.

Trip plan: Stay in Sorrento and visit Vesuvius, Pompeii and Herculaneum as part of a longer trip to the Amalfi Coast. Circumvesuviana trains connect all three towns; catch the Vesuvio Express bus from Herculaneum (Ercolo) to the mountain.

Need to know: Although Pompeii is more famous, Herculaneum is actually better preserved. It's also smaller, easier to navigate and generally less crowded.

Other months: Nov-Mar – low season, cooler, fewer crowds; Apr & Sep-Oct – shoulder season; Jun-Aug – peak season.

June

WHERE TO GO WHEN WITH KIDS

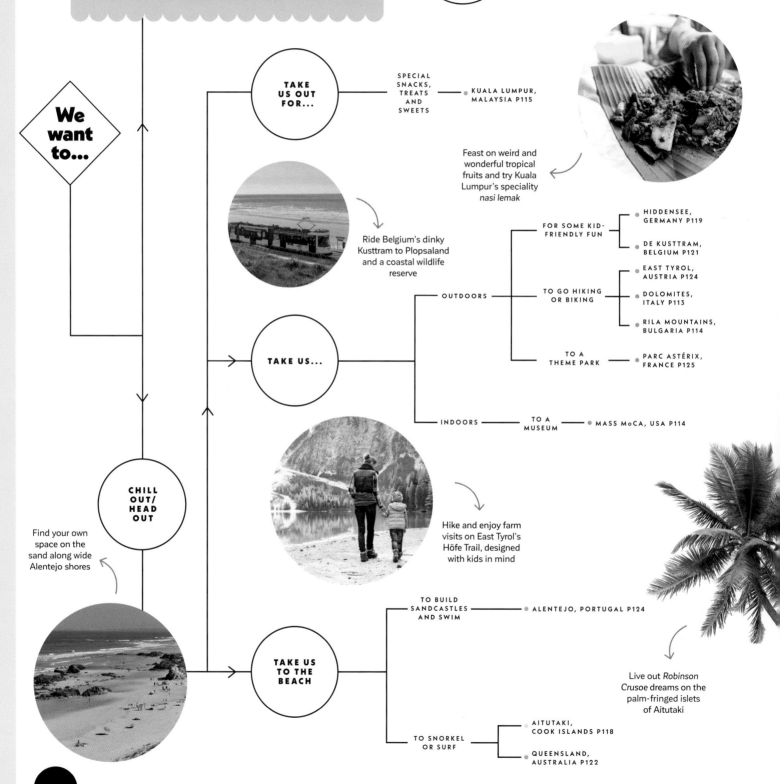

We want to...

HAVE AN ADVENTURE

TAKE US OUT FOR... — SPECIAL SNACKS, TREATS AND SWEETS → ● KUALA LUMPUR, MALAYSIA P115

Feast on weird and wonderful tropical fruits and try Kuala Lumpur's speciality *nasi lemak*

Ride Belgium's dinky Kusttram to Plopsaland and a coastal wildlife reserve

TAKE US...

OUTDOORS
- FOR SOME KID-FRIENDLY FUN
  - ● HIDDENSEE, GERMANY P119
  - ● DE KUSTTRAM, BELGIUM P121
- TO GO HIKING OR BIKING
  - ● EAST TYROL, AUSTRIA P124
  - ● DOLOMITES, ITALY P113
  - ● RILA MOUNTAINS, BULGARIA P114
- TO A THEME PARK — ● PARC ASTÉRIX, FRANCE P125

INDOORS — TO A MUSEUM — ● MASS MoCA, USA P114

Hike and enjoy farm visits on East Tyrol's Höfe Trail, designed with kids in mind

CHILL OUT/ HEAD OUT

Find your own space on the sand along wide Alentejo shores

TAKE US TO THE BEACH

TO BUILD SANDCASTLES AND SWIM — ● ALENTEJO, PORTUGAL P124

Live out *Robinson Crusoe* dreams on the palm-fringed islets of Aitutaki

TO SNORKEL OR SURF
- ● AITUTAKI, COOK ISLANDS P118
- ● QUEENSLAND, AUSTRALIA P122

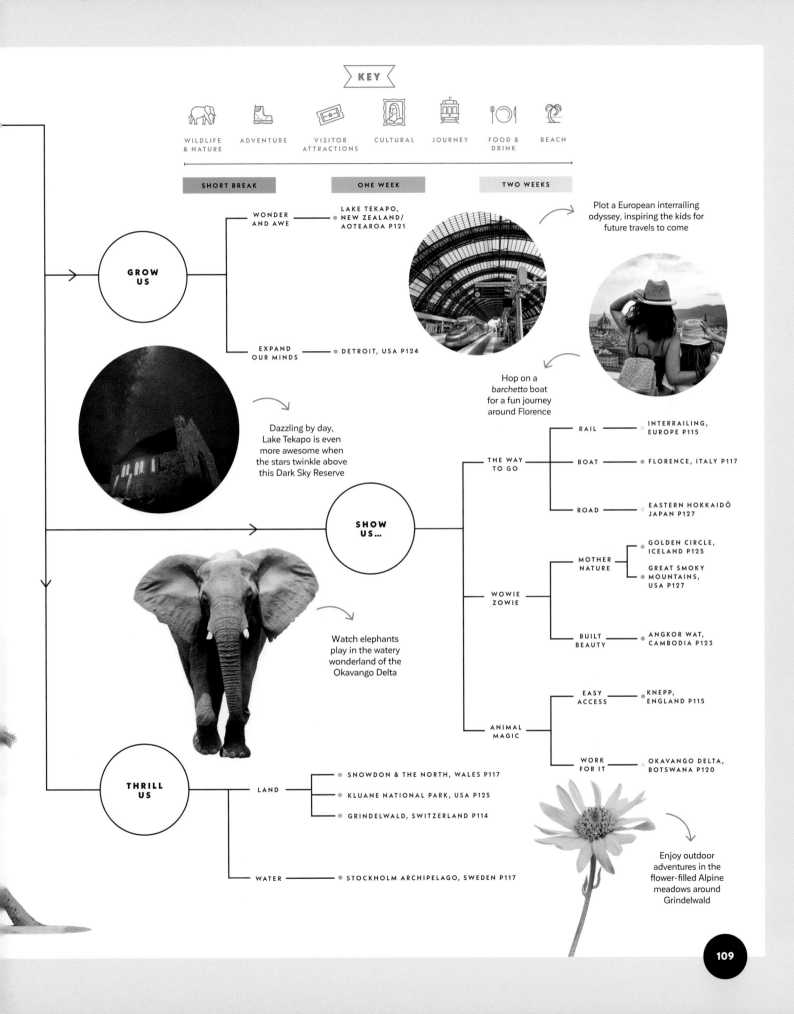

KEY

WILDLIFE & NATURE   ADVENTURE   VISITOR ATTRACTIONS   CULTURAL   JOURNEY   FOOD & DRINK   BEACH

SHORT BREAK   **ONE WEEK**   **TWO WEEKS**

GROW US

WONDER AND AWE ── LAKE TEKAPO, NEW ZEALAND/ AOTEAROA P121

EXPAND OUR MINDS ── DETROIT, USA P124

Plot a European interrailing odyssey, inspiring the kids for future travels to come

Hop on a *barchetto* boat for a fun journey around Florence

Dazzling by day, Lake Tekapo is even more awesome when the stars twinkle above this Dark Sky Reserve

SHOW US...

THE WAY TO GO ┬── RAIL ── INTERRAILING, EUROPE P115
├── BOAT ── FLORENCE, ITALY P117
└── ROAD ── EASTERN HOKKAIDŌ JAPAN P127

WOWIE ZOWIE ┬── MOTHER NATURE ┬── GOLDEN CIRCLE, ICELAND P125
│   └── GREAT SMOKY MOUNTAINS, USA P127
└── BUILT BEAUTY ── ANGKOR WAT, CAMBODIA P123

ANIMAL MAGIC ┬── EASY ACCESS ── KNEPP, ENGLAND P115
└── WORK FOR IT ── OKAVANGO DELTA, BOTSWANA P120

Watch elephants play in the watery wonderland of the Okavango Delta

THRILL US

LAND ┬── SNOWDON & THE NORTH, WALES P117
├── KLUANE NATIONAL PARK, USA P125
└── GRINDELWALD, SWITZERLAND P114

WATER ── STOCKHOLM ARCHIPELAGO, SWEDEN P117

Enjoy outdoor adventures in the flower-filled Alpine meadows around Grindelwald

109

Events in June

SYNCHRONOUS FIREFLIES
Great Smoky Mountains National Park, USA
Nature puts on a lightshow of its own every summer in the Smoky Mountains – kids will have a ball chasing lightning bugs around the campground.

MIDSUMMER
Sweden
This summer party sees Swedish youngsters don flower garlands, dance around maypoles and picnic in nature – bring a blanket and join the fun!

SUMMER SOLSTICE
Stonehenge, England
The solstice sees a spirited revamp of pagan rituals at Stonehenge: it's a great chance for kids to get close to the standing stones.

NATIONAL ARTS FESTIVAL
Makhanda, South Africa
Ten fun-filled days of dance, theatre, comedy and music exploring the culture of a continent, with loads of young performers showing off amazing skills.

INTI RAYMI
Sacsaywamán, Peru
Read the Tintin book *Prisoners of the Sun* as a primer for this centuries-old Inca tribute to the Sun God in the ruins outside Cuzco.

QUEENSTOWN WINTER FESTIVALS
Queenstown, New Zealand/Aotearoa
Come for snow sports but stay for music, comedy shows, fireworks, fun family activities and a party vibe at Queenstown's string of winter bashes.

DRAGON BOAT FESTIVAL
Hong Kong, China
Sticky-rice dumplings and enthusiastic dragon-boat races will keep kids gripped at this festival honouring 4th-century BCE Chinese poet Qu Yuan.

GAWAI DAYAK FESTIVAL
Sarawak, Malaysia
Flamboyant costumes, tribal rituals, intriguing musical traditions and 'dare to try' foods feature in this tribute to Sarawak's Indigenous peoples.

Early to mid-June — $$
Second half of June — $$
Second half of June — $$
20 or 21 June — $
24 June — $
June or July — $$
1 June — $
All month — $$

TOTS TO PRE-TWEENS

EXPENSIVE BUT WORTH IT

GOOD VALUE

OLDER KIDS AND TEENS

INTERRAILING, EUROPE

Get around Magnetic Island, Queensland by bicycle or bus

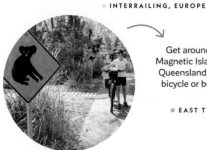

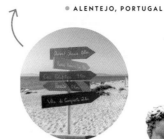

EAST TYROL, AUSTRIA

Have an alpine adventure in Grindelwald, Switzerland

QUEENSLAND, AUSTRALIA

Red-crowned cranes call Hokkaidō home

LAKE TEKAPO, NEW ZEALAND/AOTEAROA

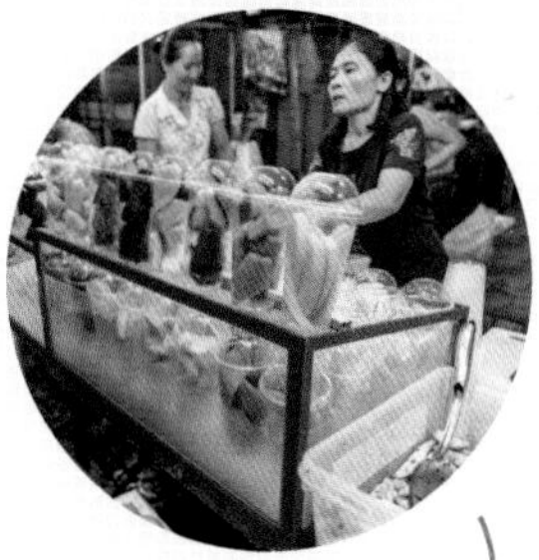

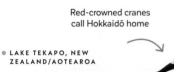

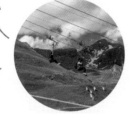

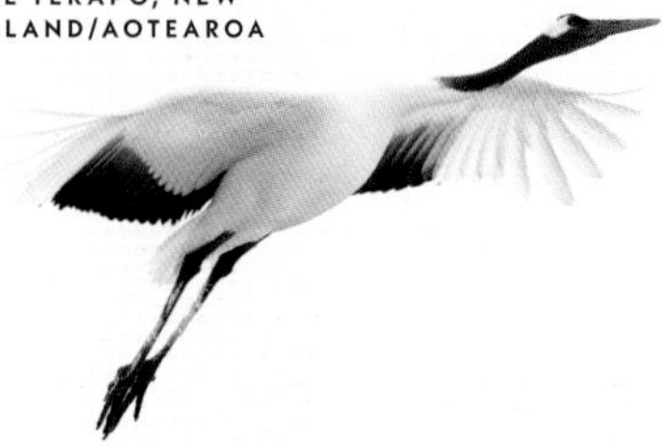

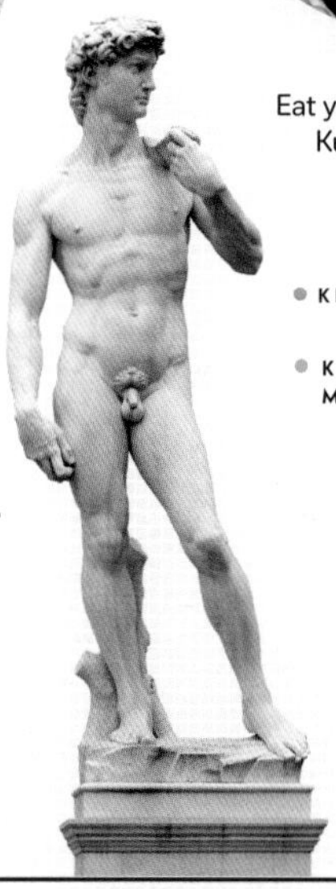

GRINDELWALD, SWITZERLAND

EASTERN HOKKAIDŌ, JAPAN

PARC ASTÉRIX, FRANCE

DE KUSTTRAM, BELGIUM

HIDDENSEE, GERMANY

Soak up the laid-back surf scene in Portugal's Algarve

ALENTEJO, PORTUGAL

Eat your way around Kuala Lumpur

FLORENCE, ITALY

KNEPP, ENGLAND

MASS MoCA, USA

KUALA LUMPUR MALAYSIA

Seek out Michelangelo's *David* in Florence

AITUTAKI, COOK ISLANDS

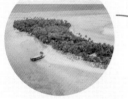

An aerial view of Aitutaki's islands

Meet a real-life Pumbaa, a warthog, in the Okavango Delta

GOLDEN CIRCLE, ICELAND

Stokkur is one of several geysers in Iceland's Golden Circle

OKAVANGO DELTA, BOTSWANA

KLUANE NATIONAL PARK, CANADA

DOLOMITES, ITALY

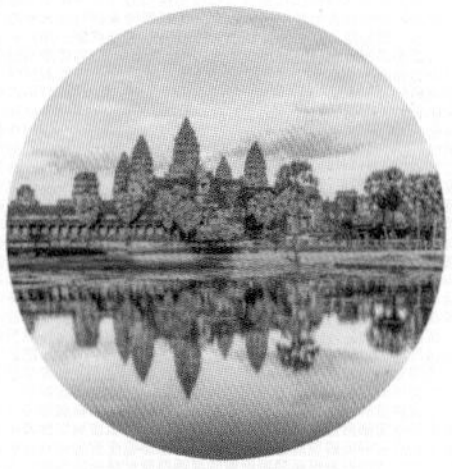

The ruins of Siem Reap inspire all ages

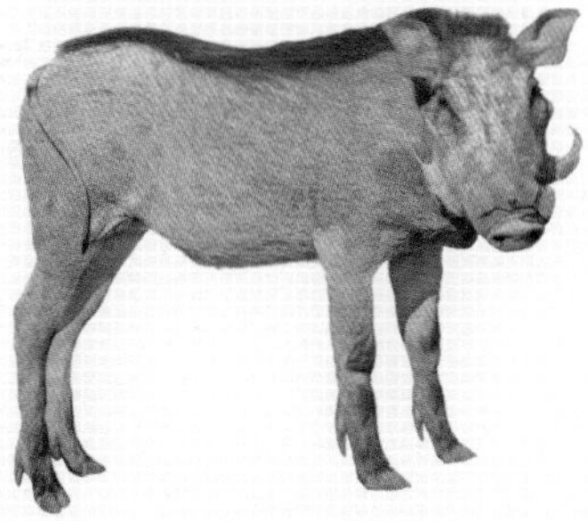

SNOWDON & THE NORTH, WALES

ANGKOR WAT, CAMBODIA

GREAT SMOKY MOUNTAINS, USA

Millions of fireflies put on a show in the Great Smoky Mountains

RILA MOUNTAINS BULGARIA

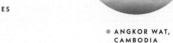

DETROIT, USA

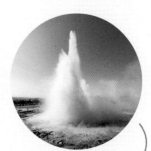

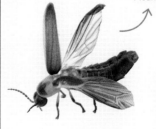

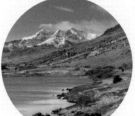

Experience early summer in Snowdonia

STOCKHOLM ARCHIPELAGO, SWEDEN

DOLOMITES ITALY

5–16 **Why now? Great weather and Dolomites Bike Day.**

The spectacular sawtoothed Dolomite mountain range offers stunning scenery year-round and, through the summer, the chance to partake in fun family activities. The course for Dolomites Bike Day, a 51km (32-mile) traffic-free loop, is on the same roads as the Giro d'Italia and Maratona dles Dolomites cycle races – it's a rare opportunity for youngsters to cycle on these famous roads, and e-bikes have the thumbs up. The 105km (65-mile) Pustertal cycle path is ideal for families; most use rental bikes and ride it over three days. The path runs east from Mühlbach in Italy to Lienz, Austria, with bike-friendly hotels along the way. Best of all, if youngsters become tired, you can just stop and take the train back. Ready for a family adventure that's even more challenging? The Dolomites are a hiking and rock-climbing paradise, dotted with via ferrata – 'iron paths' of cables and ladders that were originally installed during WWI (and have been since updated!). Take your kids on a course that starts on easier routes, then gets more challenging once they've gained some experience.

Trip plan: The Dolomites are in northeastern Italy, close to the Austrian border. Fly to a nearby airport (Bolzano, Venice, Treviso, Verona, Innsbruck, Milan or Munich), then rent a car to get around.

Need to know: Residents of the Dolomites speak Italian, German and, in five of the valleys here, the ancient Rhaeto-Roman Ladin language.

Other months: Dec-Apr – winter sports; Jul-Aug – busy summer holiday period.

(L) Mountain-biking bliss in the Dolomites; (R) Dolomites peaks

MASS MoCA
USA

`5-16` **Why now?** Music, art and family-friendly festival fun.

MASS MoCA is a sprawling contemporary art museum, housed in the buildings of the former Sprague Electric Co, in the gritty Massachusetts city of North Adams. It's a cool, post-industrial setting for some mind-opening art, often incorporating sound, video or other interactive elements. Kids are sure to get a kick out of the unconventional artworks – such as Gunnar Schonbeck's funky musical instruments (that they can actually play) and James Turrell's *CAVU*, a freestanding cylindrical building – one of his *Skyscape* installations – with an open upward-facing window. Plus, budding artists are invited to create their own masterpieces in a dedicated Kidspace. In June, MASS MoCA is the setting for Wilco's Solid Sound Music Festival, three days of fantastic Indie music – and a slew of shows and activities for kids. In past years, the lineup has included performances from the likes of Bread and Puppet (a radical puppet-theatre company) and Story Pirates (a troupe that invents skits and songs based on children's stories).

Trip plan: Albany is the closest airport to North Adams; Boston and New York are both about a 3hr drive away. There is camping on site, as well as lodgings in North Adams and nearby Williamstown.

Need to know: Solid Sound is a three-day festival, but most of the events for families are scheduled on the Saturday. MASS MoCA is open year-round.

Other months: Nov-Mar – winter, cold, dark; Apr-May – volatile weather, no crowds; Jul-Oct – sunny, biggest crowds.

GRINDELWALD
SWITZERLAND

`0-16` **Why now?** Pristine mountains before the crowds of summer.

Sitting in the valley, more or less right underneath the north face of the legendary 3967m-high (13,015ft) Eiger, Grindelwald is an absolute joy for families in the summer. You can take trains up to Jungfraujoch (the 'Top of Europe'), on a saddle between the Jungfrau and Mönch peaks, and there are plenty of enthralling outdoor adventures to tire kids out. From Grindelwald – itself at an altitude of 1034m (3392ft) – riding the aerial gondola up to the adventure hotspot of First, at 2166m (7106ft), sets you up for a number of family-friendly activities. The 360-degree First View platform, perched out over the valley, is a stunner, staring straight out at the Eiger; the First Cliff Walk suspension bridge, attached to a sheer wall of rock, will test any teen's mettle. There's also a relatively gentle hike with stupendous views to the alpine lake of Bachalpsee; with little ones in tow, head for the playground at Bort, one of the gondola stations. The descent to Grindelwald from First throws up a plethora of options: take your pick of flying fox, all-terrain mountain carts or trottibike (an easy-to-ride mashup of bike and scooter).

Trip plan: Stay for multiple nights in Grindelwald and use it as a base to explore the Bernese Oberland region by train and bus, easy with a Swiss Pass.

Need to know: Grindelwald is a full-on resort village, 45min from Interlaken by train, and busiest in winter as a ski destination.

Other months: Dec-Apr – ski season; Jul-Aug – busy summer season.

RILA MOUNTAINS
BULGARIA

`12-16` **Why now?** Clear days and warmer weather for hiking by mountain lakes.

Just two hours from Bulgaria's capital, Sofia, the jewel-like glacial lakes that dot the Rila Mountains make for a super-scenic family day-hike. The route starts with a chairlift ride from the Pionerska ski resort, ascending over towering trees to a 2100m (6890ft) elevation among Alpine meadows encircled by granite rocks. The first of the seven lakes soon comes into view, and over the next 14km (9 miles), you follow a well-marked path past another six shimmery lakes of different shapes and sizes (there are shorter routes back if anyone is flagging). Admire the epic views, spy wildflowers among the granite outcrops, and golden eagles and peregrine falcons above. After you're done hiking, reward the family with an afternoon (or a whole day if time allows) soaking in the geothermal waters of nearby Sapareva Banya. Here pools of varying temperatures make for a family-friendly experience: teens might enjoy the monkey bars over the water, while younger kids can splash in a shallower child-friendly pool (and parents can opt for steam rooms, Jacuzzis and massages). There's another family-friendly diversion nearby: a short forest walk to admire the Goritsa Waterfall.

Trip plan: While the hike is possible on a day-long tour from Sofia, 90km (55 miles) north, it's more relaxing to stay nearby and enjoy your time here.

Need to know: Arrive early to avoid the chairlift queue on weekends. Bring your own food, water and sunscreen.

Other months: Oct-Mar – ski season; Apr-May – snow still possible; Jul-Sep – summer weather.

KUALA LUMPUR
MALAYSIA

5-16 Why now? Drier days for exploring and feasting on weird and wonderful tropical fruits.

The Malaysian capital of Kuala Lumpur is an easy Southeast Asia option for families – stresses are few, public transport is efficient, air-conditioning is ubiquitous, every meal is a banquet and tropical jungles creep into the city centre, full of scuttling monitor lizards, birds and butterflies. Keep kids sweet while you explore temples, museums, malls and gardens by sustaining them with a non-stop buffet of tropical fruit: rambutans, langsats, longans, rose apples, star fruit, mangosteens and – if you feel brave – pongy durians. Essential family stops include the Chow Kit and Jalan Petaling markets, the science-focused Petrosains Discovery Centre and the soaring viewdeck atop the rocket-like Petronas Towers. Set aside one day for wild encounters in the KL Forest Eco Park (with rope bridges through the canopy), KL Bird Park (species include big-beaked hornbills) or the excellent, animal-welfare-conscious Zoo Negara; and another day to dive into Malaysian spirituality in the temple-filled Batu Caves.

Trip plan: Kuala Lumpur is a major air hub (and the main base for discount carrier Air Asia), but you can also get here by train or bus from elsewhere in Malaysia or from Singapore. Stay in Chinatown or Bukit Bintang, and use the monorail and commuter trains to explore.

Need to know: June is one of the drier months, but be ready for tropical showers with umbrellas or lightweight raincoats.

Other months: Jan-Feb & Jul-Aug – drier, but still hot and humid; Mar-May & Sep-Dec – hot, humid, often rainy.

KNEPP
ENGLAND

0-16 Why now? Witness a rewilding success story in action, and Britain's first colony of breeding storks in over 600 years.

Twenty years ago, Knepp was a struggling farm – but then its owners decided to do something radical: nothing. By letting wildlife reclaim the land, they embarked on an experiment that has since become known as rewilding. Today this savannah-like estate in West Sussex has become a hotbed of biodiversity, attracting a host of endangered animals and birds. It has also reintroduced some key species, including beavers, but has had particular success with white storks. In June, you can observe these long-legged visitors as they tend their enormous nests, perched perilously atop ancient oak trees. Footpaths are free and a great way to dip into the park (reptiles and birds are at their busiest now); for older kids, Knepp's prebooked themed walks and drives – or safaris – take you on the trail of everything from free-roaming longhorn cattle and Tamworth pigs to butterflies and bats.

Trip plan: Enjoy a morning walk followed by a visit to the excellent cafe, or a weekend camp (in stunning surroundings) to really experience the Knepp ethos. Closest train stations are Billingshurst, 13km (8 miles) northwest, and Horsham or Christ's Hospital, both around 14km (9 miles) north.

Need to know: Knepp has a strict over-12s policy for safaris and all camping options; book well ahead (via knepp.co.uk).

Other months: Apr-May – prime dawn chorus; late Jun to Jul – bats, moths, butterflies; mid- to end-Oct – deer rut.

INTERRAILING
EUROPE

5-16 Why now? Long sunlit days and warm summer weather.

A family interrailing adventure has a lot of pluses: you can take your own food and drinks on board; you'll be free to give kids lots of attention; and toddlers can move around the carriages when they need to. Begin a low-carbon route around Western Europe in Paris, with its iconic sights and its Disneyland (loved by kids of all ages). Head to Brussels for a Belgian chocolate tasting tour; Germany for Munich's Schloss Nymphenburg; or Lucerne for horizon-expanding views from Mt Pilatus. In Italy, kids can explore Milan's interactive Leonardo da Vinci Museum, and the *vaporettos* and traffic-free streets of Venice. Florence is a dream for art lovers, but children might be more interested in roaming free in parks and squares (ideally with a gelato in hand). Finish up in the most recognisable city for kids: Rome. There's the Colosseum (sign them up to the Gladiator School!), the Trevi Fountain (who doesn't want to make a wish?), plus multiple museums, galleries and parks to explore. And the finale – the Capitoline Museums, where paintings and statues of Greek gods and mythical beasts will capture the hearts of *Percy Jackson* readers.

Trip plan: A multiday Interrail ticket allows you to traverse Europe with ease.

Need to know: Book (and pay for) sleeper-train cabins in advance.

Other months: Jan-Apr – cold, short days; May – mild; Jul-Aug – peak summer holidays; Sep-Nov – crisp nights; Dec – Christmas markets.

(A) Lakeside in Snowdonia, Wales; (L) Cool down with gelato in Florence, Italy; (R) Paddling between islands in Sweden's Stockholm Archipelago

116

SNOWDON & THE NORTH
WALES

5–16 Why now? Wales is always lush and green, but June brings longer days and less chance of rain.
Summiting Yr Wyddfa (Snowdon) is on many a bucket list, but the arduous 15km (9.3-mile) walk up this 1085m-high (3560ft) mountain is too much to ask of little ones. Instead, opt for a round-trip ride aboard the heritage Snowdon Mountain Railway from Llanberis; teens might be up to the walk (with optional wild swimming at Llyn Padarn at the end), but pick a clear day, or the views may be shrouded in clouds. Next, challenge the family with more outdoorsy thrills at Zip World: the Betws-y-Coed centre has tree-top rope circuits and the toboggan/rollercoaster Fforest Coaster; the speedy zipline at Zip World Penrhyn Quarry flies you over a stark slate quarry. Then soak up Welsh history and culture with a visit to medieval Caernarfon Castle, followed by Conwy's UNESCO-listed castle (and the town's Smallest House in Great Britain), with a detour to take selfies at the longest-name-in-Wales signboard at Llanfair PG's train station. Finally, soak up the spirit-of-yesteryear vibes by the seaside in Llandudno. Ride the Great Orme Tramway for ocean views, then ramble back down before exploring the beach, the Victorian pier and the amusement arcades.
Trip plan: With winding roads and remote activities, a car is pretty essential to get around in Wales.
Need to know: Always expect rain: take waterproof boots, raincoats and umbrellas, even if the sun is shining.
Other months: Dec-Mar – dark winters; Apr-May – light returns; Jul-Aug – warm(ish); Sep-Oct – autumn colour.

STOCKHOLM ARCHIPELAGO
SWEDEN

12–16 Why now? The best weather for paddling and wild-camping on scattered, sun-splattered treasure islands.
Stockholm is surrounded by upwards of 24,000 islands, rocks and skerries, collectively known as the Skärgården, which splays across the Baltic Sea in a giant arc from Sweden's capital. Passenger ferries go hither and thither between larger islands, around 150 of which are inhabited, but in summer, island-hopping around this awesome archipelago in a sea kayak or canoe is a great adventure for families with older kids. Set your own itinerary, perhaps paddling kayaks to Grinda to enjoy the island's idyllic beaches, or Möja for hiking trails and scenic views. Around Husarö you can discover a shipwreck. Canoeists are encouraged to remain within the tranquil waters of the inner archipelago, where you can explore the nature reserve of Bogesundslandet. The Scandinavian philosophy of Allemansrätten (Every Man's Right) means you can roam, paddle and pitch almost anywhere – though ensure you 'leave no trace'. Find an island, make camp and cook freshly caught fish over a firepit.
Trip plan: Outfitters such as Skärgårdens Kanotcenter offer guided day-long and multiday kayaking and canoeing trips; confident paddlers can rent single or tandem boats and go exploring independently.
Need to know: Midges can be annoying in Sweden during summer; Stockholm is typically fine, and numbers are lower early in the season, but bring repellent and long sleeves/trousers.
Other months: Dec-Feb – possible ice-skating around the Skärgården (weather permitting; go with a guide); Jul-Oct – great weather, festivals.

FLORENCE
ITALY

0–16 Why now? For glorious weather and gentle days with gelato aboard characterful *barchetto* boats.
You could easily fill a week in Florence's historic centre just visiting its world-class museums, churches and galleries. In June you'll avoid the worst of the summer's crowds and queues, but attempting to take it all in can be overwhelming just the same. The river offers one of the city's most atmospheric escapes. From May to September you can join a Renaioli *barchetto* cruise aboard a traditional wooden boat, and drift gently through the city – and under the 14th-century Ponte Vecchio – from the relative peace of the water. Florence is the home of gelato, and with June temperatures potentially reaching 30°C (86°F), there will be ample opportunity to visit the city's many *gelaterie*: opt for artisanal scoops at Sbrino, La Sorbettiera or Gelateria della Passera.
Trip plan: A week gives plenty of time to take in big-hitters like the Uffizi, Galleria dell'Accademia and Il Duomo, as well as the city's ornamental gardens. The first Renaioli *barchetto* cruise (renaioli.it) starts at 10am, the last at 8pm; trips last 1hr and prices vary.
Need to know: The popular Calcio Storico tournament is held in Piazza Santa Croce over three weekends in June. A brutal mashup of rugby, football and boxing, the tournaments bring crowds, but also pageantry; it all adds an interesting angle to a visit, though the tournament itself is really only suitable for hardier, older children.
Other months: Mar-May – wisteria, iris blooms at the Giardino dell'Iris; Jul & Aug – hot, touristy; Sep-Nov – quiet; Dec – festive lights and markets.

AITUTAKI
COOK ISLANDS

5-16 **Why now? The best time of year on the Pacific's most mesmerising lagoon.**

One look at an image of Aitutaki from the air will probably be enough to have you ready to click on the 'book now' button for the perfect family getaway. Lonely Planet founder Tony Wheeler nominated Aitutaki as the 'world's most beautiful island' – and he's visited a lot of islands! Just 45 minutes by plane from the Cook Islands capital of Rarotonga, this place has lagoon lovers drooling. While the main island of Aitutaki (pop 1800) is home base for accommodation and eating options, it's the stunning turquoise lagoon, brimming with marine life and ringed with 15 uninhabited, palm-covered *motu* (islets), that is a South Pacific treasure. Take a lagoon cruise for a day to check things out. Tapuaeta'i (One Foot Island) is the best known *motu*, fringed by white beaches and divided from its neighbour, Tekopua, by a deep channel that teems with tropical fish. In the west of the lagoon, Honeymoon Island is a stunner – consider getting your family dropped off on this deserted island for the day by a taxi-boat, and don't forget to bring snorkelling gear. Aitutaki's lagoon is also a top spot to learn to kite-surf, a great experience for teenagers.

Trip plan: Combine your visit to Aitutaki with some time in Rarotonga, the international gateway to the Cook Islands.

Need to know: The Cook Islands uses New Zealand currency; ensure you carry some cash.

Other months: Nov-Apr – hot, humid, South Pacific cyclone season; May-Oct – cool, busy tourist season.

Above and below the water in the Cook Islands

Public transport on car-free Hiddensee

© Pawel Kazmierczak / Shutterstock

HIDDENSEE GERMANY

0-16 **Why now?** Horses, bikes and children rule on this idyllic island in the Baltic Sea.

Trotting along pine-forest trails, cantering across sand dunes and taking your horse for a cool-down dip at the end of your ride – it's fair to say the German island of Hiddensee is a paradise for equine-loving kids. But alongside cycling and walking, riding a horse – or being pulled by one in a wagon – is not just a fun pastime but a primary means of transport on this car-free island. Shaped like a seahorse and covering just under 19 sq km (7.3 sq miles), Hiddensee sits off the west coast of Rügen Island in the Baltic Sea. Locals call it *söten länneken* (the 'sweet little country'), and it's this gentle mindset, along with its raw natural beauty and plentiful children's activities, that make

it a great choice for families, especially on long, light-filled June days. Along with horse riding and cycling (hiring bikes is easy), there are football pitches, volleyball courts and themed playgrounds – Jonah and the Whale, Grimms' Fairy Tales – all around the island, plus kids' films in a tent cinema and beach treasure hunts.

Trip plan: Ferries to Hiddensee run from Stralsund on the mainland, which has rail links from across Germany.

Need to know: Hiddensee's 14km-long (8.5 mile) beach – all fine white sand and crystal-clear water – has many designated swimming areas, lifeguarded mid-May to mid-September.

Other months: Apr-May – spring, pleasant, sea cold; Jul-Aug – warm, long days; Sep – cooling, sea is warmest; Oct-Nov – chillier.

119

Spot big cats –
including leopard
– in Botswana's
Okavango Delta

OKAVANGO DELTA
BOTSWANA

12-16 Why now? The dry season delivers easy-to-spot wildlife congregations across the Okavango Delta floodplains.

The vast Okavango Delta spreads out over thousands of square kilometres in the interior of Botswana, as a result of seasonal flooding. Heavy rainfall occurs in the highlands from January to February, causing a surge in the Okavango River; the waters drain downstream and flood the Delta over the following months. By the time the weather dries out in June, the Okavango is a watery wonderland of swelling rivers and flooded plains. During the dry season, this unusual geography attracts animals from far and wide. Your list of spotted species will be long, perhaps including the Big Five (lion, leopard, buffalo, elephant and rhino) and many more. If you have time, Chobe National Park is a natural add-on: cruise down the Chobe River to spy the world's largest concentration of African elephants, as well as big cats, buffalo, giraffe and zebra. These are animals at their wildest, but they're still up-close and easily accessible – guaranteed to thrill the family (even the teens).

Trip plan: Starting in Maun or Kasane, you can fly into a lodge to live it up in wild luxury. Or spend more time and less money on a driving-and-camping 'mobile safari' through Chobe.

Need to know: Botswana's tourism strategy is to maximise value and minimise volume, thus limiting the industry's ecological impact. Expect light crowds, customised service and high price tags.

Other months: Dec-Mar – green season, rain, mud; Apr-May & Nov – shoulder season, unpredictable weather, lower prices; Jul-Oct – dry season, best wildlife watching.

DE KUSTTRAM
BELGIUM

5-16 Why now? Ride a tram along the Belgian coast for theme-park fun and birdlife.

Since 1885, the 68-stop De Kusttram (coastal tram) has connected De Panne on the French border with Knokke near the Netherlands. Hopping aboard, with stops at Belgium's popular Plopsaland and at Knokke for the Zwin Natuur Park, makes for a fun and varied weekend – because what child wouldn't want to visit somewhere called Plopsaland? Based around Belgian TV character Plop the gnome and his friends, this family attraction has themed rides and a good selection of rollercoasters. Continue on to Knokke, a pretty seaside town with wide sandy beaches for swimming and play. The mudflats, salt marshes and scrub forest at nearby Zwin make a nice contrast to all that theme-park noise and colour. The Visitor Centre has interactive exhibits aimed at kids, exploring avian biology, the science behind flight and the incredible journeys made by migratory birds.

Trip plan: The complete Kusttram journey takes 2hr 30min, but you can jump off at any beach town that takes your fancy. Ride to Plopsaland station for the park; Zwin lies 12km (7.5 miles) east of Knokke station in the small city of Knokke-Heist. Bus line 12 provides handy access. The reserve is also easily reached by bike, with dedicated cycle lanes from town.

Need to know: Zwin's Visitor Centre and walking trail are both wheelchair- and pram-accessible.

Other months: Nov-Dec – Christmas markets; Jan-Feb – cold, cheaper prices; Mar-May – warming up; Jul-Aug – busier beaches; Sep-Oct – mild weather, quieter.

The Milky Way lights up the night over Lake Tekapo

© MawardiBahar / Shutterstock

LAKE TEKAPO NEW ZEALAND/AOTEAROA

0-16 Why now? Midwinter stargazing at a Dark Sky Reserve.

Aotearoa is serious about the stars – the Southern Cross features on the national flag, while Matariki, the country's newest national holiday, marks the beginning of the new year in the Māori lunar calendar. First celebrated in 2022, Matariki is observed nationwide in late June, and there's no better place to check out the stars in winter than in the remote South Island town of Lake Tekapo – this place is seriously serious about stars. Picturesque by day and positively dazzling by night, Lake Tekapo has little in the way of light pollution – there are no big cities nearby and local ordinances restrict outdoor lighting so that none can be emitted horizontally or upwards. The upside? Stargazing extraordinaire. Thanks to innovative locals who saw the benefits of sustainable tourism, the area was originally awarded Dark Sky Reserve status in 2012; it later became the world's first with gold-star status, and Aoraki Mackenzie International Dark Sky Reserve is still the largest such reserve in the world. This is *the* place to go for family stargazing – check out all the options online at Dark Sky Project. Bonus for kids: the hot pools and Aqua Play area at Tekapo Springs, open year-round.

Trip plan: From Queenstown and Christchurch (both with international airports), it's a 3hr drive to Lake Tekapo.

Need to know: This is a mountain setting; warm clothing and sturdy footwear are essential, especially in winter.

Other months: Oct-Apr – shorter nights; May-Sep – longer, darker nights.

© Klara Zamourilova / Shutterstock

QUEENSLAND AUSTRALIA

Sandy shores beckon
on Queensland's
Magnetic Island

5-16 Why now? Explore Townsville and Magnetic Island amid mild climes and low humidity (and before the winter-sun crowds).

Un-touristy Townsville brims with child-friendly experiences. South of town, you can snap a selfie with a koala and learn about Australia's unique birds, mammals and crocs at Billabong Sanctuary. Back in Townsville, hike 3.5km (2 miles) up the 286m-high (938ft) Castle Hill for views of Magnetic Island in a cerulean sea, then cool off at the free splash park on the Strand; older kids will prefer the huge Riverway Lagoons lido complex by the lush banks of the Ross River. Next, book a tour to the Museum of Underwater Art (MOUA), two hours away by boat at the John Brewer Reef, where the art installations are just as mesmerising as the technicolour marine life. The *Ocean Sentinels* and *Coral Greenhouse* sculptures can be viewed from above by snorkellers, or fully explored by divers. On your return, check out Townsville's *Ocean Siren* sculpture – it changes colour based on water temperature data (raising awareness of the effects of global warming locally), and gazes out over the sea to your next destination, laid-back Magnetic Island. Spend a few days enjoying pristine swimming beaches, nature walks and spotting adorable rock wallabies.

Trip plan: A car is useful in Townsville; ferries connect to Magnetic Island, where you can get around on foot and by bus.

Need to know: Take seasickness tablets for boat journeys, as seas can get rough.

Other months: Jan-May – wet, warm; Jul-Aug – dry season, low humidity; Sep-Dec – hot, rain likely.

Tree roots thread
through the ruins at
Angkor's atmospheric
Tar Som

ANGKOR WAT
CAMBODIA

5–16 **Why now?** Smaller crowds at Asia's most spectacular ancient ruins.

The rains are building over northern Cambodia in June, but the afternoon showers bring down temperatures, making for cooler nights – something you'll appreciate after steamy days exploring the carving-covered temples of glorious Angkor Wat. With a three-day pass (free for under-12s), there's no need to rush around these spectacular Hindu and Buddhist ruins; pace yourself, visiting early in the morning, then retreat to Siem Reap for a dunk in the hotel pool. Younger kids will be wowed by the giant faces of Avalokiteshvara on the Bayon temple, and the carved demon armies marching along the walls of Angkor Wat; get older kids in the mood by casually mentioning that Angkor Wat was a setting for *Lara Croft: Tomb Raider*. Even the most travel-jaded youngster will likely be impressed by the ruins of Ta Prohm, a temple torn apart by the tentacle-like roots of giant jungle trees.

Trip plan: From Siem Reap, it's just a 10min taxi or tuk-tuk ride, or a 25min cycle ride, to the ruins of Angkor. Four days in Siem Reap is time enough to explore Angkor, browse the markets, swim in the Kulen Waterfalls and take a cruise around the floating villages of Tonlé Sap Lake.

Need to know: For an unforgettable family experience, set an early alarm to watch sunrise over Angkor Wat; the temple opens from 5am.

Other months: Nov-Mar – dry, sunny, cooler; Apr-May – hot, humid; Jul-Oct – rain mixed with bright spells

DETROIT
USA

0-12 **Why now?** See Detroit's past, present and future at parks, outdoor exhibits and a summer-opening history museum.

Journey through time to experience 19th-century American life at Greenfield Village, about 20km (12 miles) west of Detroit. This is hands-on history, where children can ride in a horse-drawn carriage or a Ford Model T, tour an old-fashioned working farm and visit Thomas Edison's laboratory; kids who are loco for locos can also traverse the village on a vintage steam train; and on weekends you can catch a game of 'base ball', played with 1867 rules and equipment. While you're in the Detroit area, take a look at how the Motor City is moving into the future. Spend a day at Belle Isle, an urban escape with an aquarium, beaches, bike routes and kayaking, not to mention the Giant Slide. Then stroll along the Southwest Greenway to admire alfresco art at the Yard Graffiti Museum, and check out Michigan Central – once Detroit's most famous urban ruin, now a symbol of the city's resilience, with exhibits about its history as a train depot and its new role as Ford Motors' innovation hub.

Trip plan: Whether you stay in downtown Detroit or in Dearborn near Greenfield Village, you'll need a car to explore the Motor City. Obviously.

Need to know: Attached to Greenfield Village, the Henry Ford Museum of Innovation is also excellent.

Other months: Jan-Apr – winter, Greenfield Village closes (the museum stays open); May-Oct – warmer, events and activities; Nov-Dec – short days, cold, festive events.

ALENTEJO
PORTUGAL

0-16 **Why now?** For space on sparkling beaches, plus walking and cycling trails through wild Portugal.

The Alentejo – a region of sprawling wild beaches and scenic biking and hiking routes – is a favourite holiday spot for the Portuguese, and in June you'll mix with weekend visitors before the summer season begins. Vila Nova de Milfontes is one of its most charming coastal towns, with an attractive whitewashed centre, a lovely sand-edged limb of estuary and a laid-back population. June days move at a slow and easy pace, with beaches like Praia das Furnas at their relative busiest early in the morning and in the golden glow of late afternoon, when beachgoers return after leisurely seafood lunches. The sandbars at Furnas are ideal for gentle play in the waves, perfect for little ones experiencing the sea for the first time; families with older children might opt for walking or cycling local sections of the Fishermen's Trail. Part of the Rota Vicentina network, this 226km (140-mile) trail winds along the Algarve coast, through slumberous fishing villages, cork-oak forests and pristine beaches where egrets forage, all situated in the heart of the beautiful Parque Natural do Sudoeste Alentejano e Costa Vicentina.

Trip plan: Fly to Lisbon, from where it's a 2hr drive to Vila Nova de Milfontes.

Need to know: In August, Milfontes is packed, with up to 50,000 surfers and sun-seekers descending on the town.

Other months: Nov-Feb – cooler, wetter, quieter; Apr-May – pleasantly warm; Jul-Aug – hot, coast busy; Sep-Oct – mellow.

EAST TYROL
AUSTRIA

5-12 **Why now?** Farm-to-farm hiking that will delight younger children.

Churning butter, collecting berries, making cheese and baking bread are just some of the real-life farm experiences children can have on the Höfe Trail, Austria's first long-distance hiking route designed with families in mind. Because if you want your kids to enjoy hiking, it pays to start along gentle paths on long, sunny June days – and make it as fun as possible, with ample distractions and food stops along the way. Tracking through the Osttirol (East Tyrol) between the spectacular peaks of the Lienz Dolomites and the Carnic Alps, the Höfe Trail can be hiked in single short stages or across a few days, overnighting in mountain huts. It's designed to be open to the whole family, from five-year-olds to grandparents. As well as learning farming lore, kids can run free through flower meadows and shaded forests, throw sticks in fast-flowing streams, and generally immerse in this unspoiled mountain landscape.

Trip plan: You can hike the Höfe Trail independently (there's plenty of route info online), but book farm experiences and accommodation in advance through a local operator. The route starts from Sillian Train Station and finishes in the Lesachtal Valley, from where shuttle buses (or taxis) connect to the train stations in Oberdrauburg or Kötschach-Mauthen.

Need to know: A night watchman has patrolled the streets of Obertilliach, on the Höfe Trail, since the 14th century; he makes his singing, storytelling rounds on Tuesdays and Fridays.

Other months: Jul-Aug – warmest months; Sep-Oct – hiking possible until the first snow arrives.

PARC ASTÉRIX
FRANCE

5-16 **Why now?** Enjoy historical high-jinks in early summer heat, before peak-season hordes arrive.

Disneyland Paris might be bigger and brasher, but to experience an authentically French theme park, spend a day exploring Parc Astérix, where all rides and attractions are based on the exploits of Astérix, tiny titular hero of the *Astérix le Gaulois* comic books by Albert Uderzo and René Goscinny. In the history-bending series, the diminutive Astérix and his behemoth big buddy Obelix lead a band of Gaulish warriors on magic-potion-powered adventures to thwart the invading forces of Julius Caesar's Roman Republic. Beloved by French children, the stories have been popularised internationally by films and a TV series. The park takes squealing visitors on a Gallic gallivant around an imaginative rendition of late-Bronze Age and Roman-era France, on rides such as Romus et Rapidus (a scenic river-rapids experience), La Galère (a swinging ship), Pégase Express (a rollercoaster that reverses direction halfway around), the Menhir Express (a menhir-themed log flume), Le Défi de César (a 'Madhouse' ride) and the country's fastest and tallest rollercoaster, Toutatis.

Trip plan: Parc Astérix is 35km (22 miles) north of Paris; it's a 40min drive on the A1 motorway towards Lille (the turnoff is signed). Buses run to and from Paris Gare du Nord.

Need to know: Though the motorway is free, parking at Parc Astérix costs €20.

Other months: Dec-Mar – park only opens for special events; Apr-May & Sep-Nov – limited opening hours; Jul-Aug – peak season, busy, park open 10am–7pm daily.

KLUANE NATIONAL PARK
CANADA

5-16 **Why now?** Camping fun under the Midnight Sun in the Yukon.

In southwest Yukon, just beneath the Arctic Circle, the sun barely sets over the snowcapped peaks of Kluane National Park around the summer solstice in June. Home to the Southern Tutchone First Nations, this is an epically remote place of massive mountains and valleys, translucent-green glacial lakes and boreal forests populated by bears, beavers, caribou, wolves, wolverines, moose and marmots. It's idyllic backpacking terrain with endless amounts of wilderness to explore, but you don't have to hike deep into the backcountry to have a life-defining adventure. Try trekking around (or canoeing across) sparkling Mät'àtäna Män (Kathleen Lake), and pitching a tent in the 38-site campground, with water, firewood, toilets and bear-proof food-storage lockers (very important!). For an extra challenge, do the 5km (3-mile) King's Throne Trail to reach an alpine cirque (natural amphitheatre). Most kids love sitting around campfires and staying up late, and here – beneath the Midnight Sun – they won't even need a torch.

Trip plan: Kluane is 160km (100 miles) west of Whitehorse. Drive towards Haines Junction on the Alaska Hwy (Hwy 1). Mät'àtäna Män/Kathleen Lake is one of two places from where you can drive into the park.

Need to know: Park entry fees are payable for adults, under-18s adventure for free. Don't forget bear spray (and bug repellent), and obey 'bare campsite' safety rules.

Other months: Oct to mid-Apr – dark, winter, ice and snow, Northern Lights; mid-May to mid-Sep – camping season.

GOLDEN CIRCLE
ICELAND

5-16 **Why now?** Endless nights mean more time for Iceland's geological wonders.

When you reach that inevitable day when the kids have to build a model volcano at school, you've hit the sweet spot for a trip to Iceland. In summer, the Midnight Sun shines for up to 22 hours per day here, meaning you can take your time exploring real-life volcanoes, bathtub-warm geothermal springs, thundering waterfalls and gleaming glaciers and icebergs (yep, even in June). Starting from Reykjavík, the Golden Circle circuit takes in the meeting point of two tectonic plates at Þingvellir National Park; the surging double cascades of Gulfoss waterfall; and the Geysir geyser (after which all such hot-water plumes are named), which blows its top every 8-10 minutes. Before flying home, it's almost mandatory to visit the ice-covered Snæfellsjökull volcano north of Reykjavík, and soak in the volcanically heated waters of the Blue Lagoon, near the airport at Keflavík.

Trip plan: Tours run from Reykjavík to the Golden Circle, Snæfellsjökull and the Blue Lagoon, but hiring a car means you can tack on little detours, such as a trip to the natural hot springs at Hrunalaug, near Flúðir. Allow at least five days to explore, with one day blocked out to visit the Snæfellsjökull volcano and glacier.

Need to know: Kids may struggle to sleep during the bright nights of Iceland in June – bring eye masks for small travellers.

Other months: Dec-Mar – cold, snowy and dark; Apr-May & Oct-Nov – warmer, but only just; Jul-Sep – mild to warm, light at night.

125

Surveying the scene in the Great Smoky Mountains National Park

GREAT SMOKY MOUNTAINS USA

0–16 **Why now?** An ostentatious display of fireflies lights up the forest.

Every year, armies of *Photinus carolinus* put on a fantastic fireworks show in the Great Smoky Mountains National Park. These beetles, better known as synchronous fireflies, are one of the few species that synchronise their flashing pattern. When the sun sets and the forest is dark, the fireflies begin their mating ritual, letting their little light shine bright and bold. All at once, the forest is alive with the twinkling of hundreds of thousands of lightning bugs. The Smokies are one of only a few places on the planet where you can see this incredible light show, and this nightlife is the park's main draw in June, but there are plenty of daytime activities to keep the troops entertained. Hike to waterfalls, raft through rapids, and cycle around the 19km (11-mile) Cades Cove Loop Rd (closed to car traffic on Wednesdays). If your kids get tired of the great outdoors, nearby towns have more civilised attractions, including waterparks, mini-golf and, in Pigeon Forge, a huge Titanic Museum.

Trip plan: Book well in advance for 'frontcountry' (car-accessible) campgrounds in the national park. Otherwise, there are some excellent lodges and glamping possibilities just outside its boundaries.

Need to know: The NPS limits the number of people admitted to see the synchronous fireflies. Check the website (nps.gov) in April to learn the viewing dates and enter the lottery for admission tickets.

Other months: Nov-Feb – cooler temperatures, winter sports; Mar-May – spring flowers, light crowds; Jul-Oct – peak season for summer fun, then fall foliage.

Red-crowned cranes in Kushiro Shitsugen, Hokkaidō

© Auttapon Nunti / Shutterstock

EASTERN HOKKAIDŌ JAPAN

5–16 **Why now?** Hokkaidō basks in warm sunshine.

The advent of multilingual sat-nav systems has made driving in Japan a breeze, especially in Hokkaidō, which has 20% of the country's land area, but only 5% of its population. This is a place to explore with your family on a road trip, especially in the east of the island, where there are lots of wildlife-viewing options. *Higuma* (brown bears) can be seen at UNESCO-listed Shiretoko National Park, a finger peninsula poking northeast into the Sea of Okhotsk; at Sakura-no-taki (Cherry Falls), thousands of salmon try to jump up a 3.7m-high (12ft) waterfall on their journey upriver to spawn. The wetlands of Kushiro Shitsugen National Park are a habitat for red-crowned cranes, a symbol of longevity in Japan (and the inspiration for the logo on the tails of Japan Airlines aircraft). On the cultural side, visit the Ainu *kotan* (village) in Akan Mashū National Park, a modern-day community of Ainu, the Indigenous people of Hokkaidō. Throw in some great hikes, outdoor *onsen* (hot springs) and tasty Japanese cuisine, and the whole family will be well entertained.

Trip plan: Fly into New Chitose Airport, Hokkaidō's main gateway, and pick up a rental car; book in advance online (most rental outfits have an English-language option on their websites).

Need to know: Drive on the left and be careful of speed limits – rules are not made to be broken in Japan.

Other months: Dec-Apr – winter skiing, cherry blossoms mid-Apr; Jul-Aug – summer, busy; late Sep – fall colour starts.

July

WHERE TO GO WHEN WITH KIDS

HAVE AN ADVENTURE

We want to...

TAKE US OUT FOR...

SPECIAL TREATS AND MEMORABLE FEASTS

INNSBRUCK, AUSTRIA P141

Walk Innsbruck's Bee Trail, then tuck in to kid-friendly Tyrolean specialities

Enjoy costumes and conga drums at Santiago de Cuba's colourful Carnival

TAKE US...

OUTDOORS

FOR SOME KID-FRIENDLY FUN

FASTA ÅLAND, FINLAND P137

MACKINAC ISLAND, USA P139

RĪGA, LATVIA P141

TO GO HIKING OR BIKING

ÎLE DE RÉ, FRANCE P133

VAL D'AZUN, FRANCE P143

TO A FESTIVAL

THE BERKSHIRES, USA P137

SANTIAGO DE CUBA, CUBA P137

APPALACHIAN TRAIL - SOUTH

OLD SUMMIT ROAD TR

FOOT ONLY

DAY USE PARKING ONLY

Enjoy car-free summer bliss, exploring Mackinac Island by bike or horse-drawn carriage

CHILL OUT/ HEAD OUT

Take a family cycling holiday along the gentle trails of Île de Ré

Follow in the footsteps of famed fossil-finder Mary Anning, combing the Jurassic Coast for ammonites

TAKE US TO THE BEACH

TO BUILD SANDCASTLES AND SWIM

JURASSIC COAST, ENGLAND P142

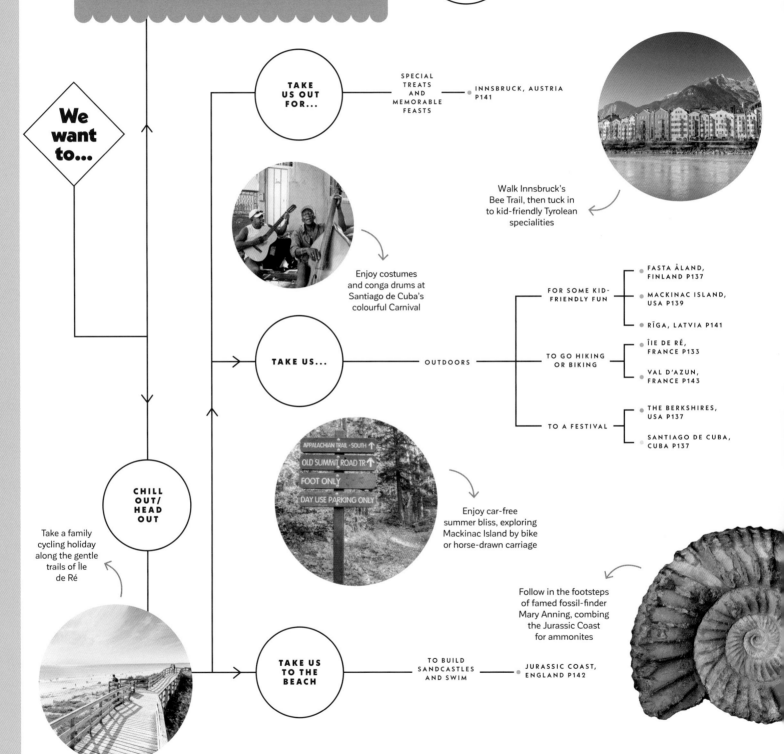

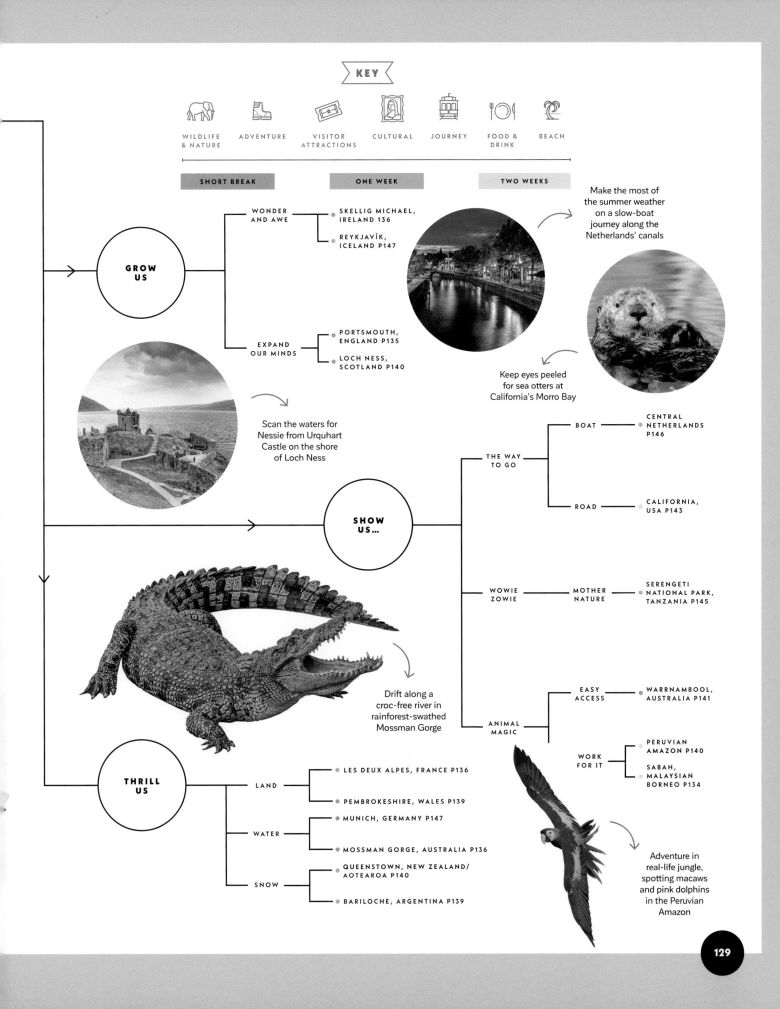

WILDLIFE & NATURE ADVENTURE VISITOR ATTRACTIONS CULTURAL JOURNEY FOOD & DRINK BEACH

SHORT BREAK   ONE WEEK   TWO WEEKS

Make the most of the summer weather on a slow-boat journey along the Netherlands' canals

GROW US

WONDER AND AWE
- SKELLIG MICHAEL, IRELAND 136
- REYKJAVÍK, ICELAND P147

EXPAND OUR MINDS
- PORTSMOUTH, ENGLAND P135
- LOCH NESS, SCOTLAND P140

Keep eyes peeled for sea otters at California's Morro Bay

Scan the waters for Nessie from Urquhart Castle on the shore of Loch Ness

SHOW US...

THE WAY TO GO
- BOAT — CENTRAL NETHERLANDS P146
- ROAD — CALIFORNIA, USA P143

WOWIE ZOWIE — MOTHER NATURE — SERENGETI NATIONAL PARK, TANZANIA P145

ANIMAL MAGIC
- EASY ACCESS — WARRNAMBOOL, AUSTRALIA P141
- WORK FOR IT — PERUVIAN AMAZON P140 / SABAH, MALAYSIAN BORNEO P134

Drift along a croc-free river in rainforest-swathed Mossman Gorge

THRILL US

LAND
- LES DEUX ALPES, FRANCE P136
- PEMBROKESHIRE, WALES P139

WATER
- MUNICH, GERMANY P147
- MOSSMAN GORGE, AUSTRALIA P136

SNOW
- QUEENSTOWN, NEW ZEALAND/ AOTEAROA P140
- BARILOCHE, ARGENTINA P139

Adventure in real-life jungle, spotting macaws and pink dolphins in the Peruvian Amazon

Events in July

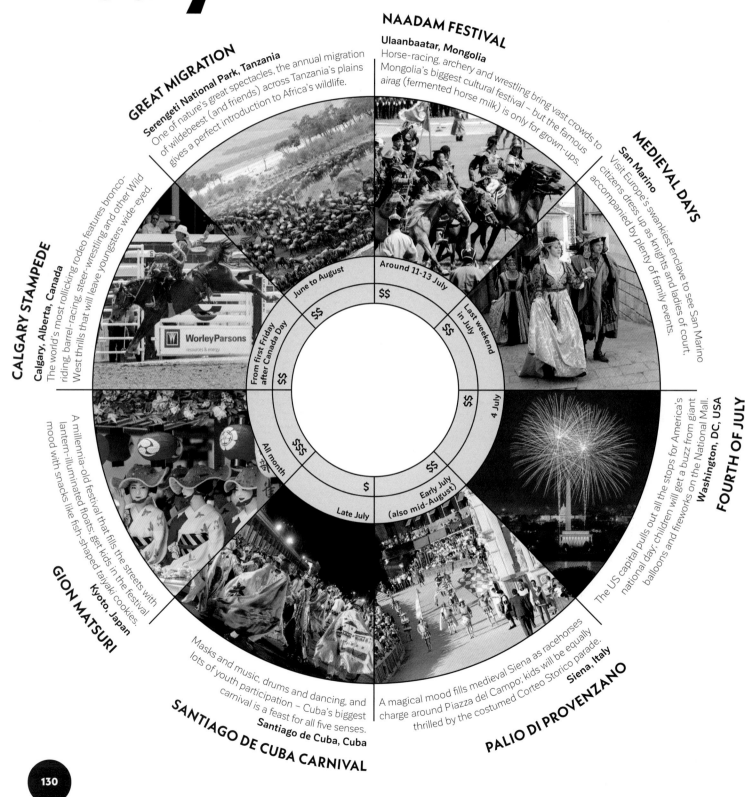

GREAT MIGRATION
Serengeti National Park, Tanzania
One of nature's great spectacles, the annual migration of wildebeest (and friends) across Tanzania's plains gives a perfect introduction to Africa's wildlife.

NAADAM FESTIVAL
Ulaanbaatar, Mongolia
Horse-racing, archery and wrestling bring vast crowds to Mongolia's biggest cultural festival – but the famous airag (fermented horse milk) is only for grown-ups.

MEDIEVAL DAYS
San Marino
Visit Europe's swankiest enclave to see San Marino citizens dress up as knights and ladies of court, accompanied by plenty of family events.

CALGARY STAMPEDE
Calgary, Alberta, Canada
The world's most rollicking rodeo features bronco-riding, barrel-racing, steer-wrestling and other Wild West thrills that will leave youngsters wide-eyed.

GION MATSURI
Kyoto, Japan
A millennia-old festival that fills the streets with lantern-illuminated floats; get kids in the festival mood with snacks like fish-shaped taiyaki cookies.

SANTIAGO DE CUBA CARNIVAL
Santiago de Cuba, Cuba
Masks and music, drums and dancing, and lots of youth participation – Cuba's biggest carnival is a feast for all five senses.

PALIO DI PROVENZANO
Siena, Italy
A magical mood fills medieval Siena as racehorses charge around Piazza del Campo; kids will be equally thrilled by the costumed Corteo Storico parade.

FOURTH OF JULY
Washington, DC, USA
The US capital pulls out all the stops for America's national day: children will get a buzz from giant balloons and fireworks on the National Mall.

Inner wheel labels:
- June to August — $$
- Around 11-13 July — $$
- Last weekend in July — $$
- July 4 — $$
- Early July (also mid-August) — $$
- Late July — $
- All month — $$$
- From first Friday after Canada Day — $$

● REYKJAVÍK, ICELAND

● JURASSIC COAST,
ENGLAND

● RĪGA, LATVIA

Relax under
summery skies
in Reykjavík

Pick your own
summer soft fruit
in Finland

● CALIFORNIA, USA

Commune with
orangutans in
Malaysian Borneo

Watch whales
raise their young
from the shores of
Warrnambool

● FASTA ÅLAND,
FINLAND

● WARRNAMBOOL,
AUSTRALIA

● ÎLE DE RÉ, FRANCE

● PORTSMOUTH, ENGLAND

● MACKINAC
ISLAND, USA

From sequoia
cones, big
trees grow in
California

● SABAH, MALAYSIAN
BORNEO

● SANTIAGO DE CUBA, CUBA

Get around
France's Île de Ré
by bicycle

● INNSBRUCK, AUSTRIA

● THE BERKSHIRES, USA

● MOSSMAN GORGE, AUSTRALIA

● SERENGETI NATIONAL
PARK, TANZANIA

Embrace the mysteries
of Skellig Michael

● MUNICH, GERMANY

Stay in an airy lodge
in the Queensland
rainforest of
Mossman Gorge

Take to some
cross-country
skis in Bariloche,
Argentina

● LOCH NESS, SCOTLAND

● CENTRAL
NETHERLANDS

● PEMBROKESHIRE, WALES

● VAL D'AZUN, FRANCE

Munich is
BMW's base
for car fans of
all ages

● SKELLIG MICHAEL
IRELAND

Queenstown is the capital
of southern hemisphere
winter sports

Hit the bike trails
of Les Deux
Alpes, France

● BARILOCHE, ARGENTINA

● QUEENSTOWN, NEW
ZEALAND/AOTEAROA

● PERUVIAN AMAZON

● LES DEUX ALPES, FRANCE

ÎLE DE RÉ FRANCE

5-16 **Why now? It's the closest you'll get to family holiday cycling heaven.**

Holidaying in Île de Ré during summer, it's all about the bike – but cycling here is a civilised family affair. Forget the Lycra, tracking apps and big-budget bikes; you'll be riding upright cycles with wicker baskets, wearing normal clothes, and your kids will be merrily pedalling along with you (or being towed on a tagalong or trailer). This classy, photogenic island is only 30km by 5km (19 miles by 3 miles), but it's blessed with 100km (68 miles) of well-maintained cycle paths, most off-road or segregated. You'll ride past salt pans and oyster farms, a lighthouse and a historic fort, through pine forests, vineyards and marshland, and alongside many a wooden fishing boat bobbing in the glistening sea. Load up on bread, cheese, charcuterie and fruit at outdoor markets for regular picnic stops; the pretty port town of St-Martin-de-Ré holds the best ice-cream parlour on the island, perfect for keeping little legs pedalling. Most younger children will also love the local funfairs, while older kids can surf, bodyboard and jump into waves at beaches on the south of the island.

Trip plan: Riding a 22km (14-mile) loop from La Flotte will cover much of the island, including St-Martin-de-Ré and La Couarde-sur-Mer; alternatively, there are plenty of shorter options.

Need to know: There are bike-hire places all over, including at many campsites, and the routes around the island are clearly signposted.

Other months: Nov-Mar – cold, wet; Apr-May & Oct – unreliable weather; Jun-Sep – hot, sunny, warm seas.

(L) Lunchtime shopping on Île de Ré;
(R) Island oysters for sale

133

SABAH MALAYSIAN BORNEO

Snacking at Sabah's
Sepilok Orangutan
Rehabilitation Centre

5-16 **Why now?** See orangutans during the dry season.

August and September are the peak months to visit Malaysian Borneo, but July is calmer, and fallen fruit from rainforest trees lures orangutans, proboscis monkeys and other primates down from the canopy. With its steamy heat, dense jungles and fascinating tribal traditions, Sabah makes for a proper family adventure, but infrastructure is well developed, so even younger kids can enjoy the experience. Flying into Kota Kinabalu, fill the days with mangrove cruises, reef snorkelling, mountain hikes, walks in bird-filled tropical gardens and street-market shopping, or goggle at the wild wildlife in Sabah's nature parks and reserves (head to the Kinabatangan Wildlife Sanctuary to spy crocs, pygmy elephants, proboscis monkeys and hornbills). Kids can see the 'old man

of the forest' up close at Sepilok Orangutan Rehabilitation Centre, established to protect orphaned orangutans and one of Asia's top wildlife experiences; the babies lark around at feeding time, just like human youngsters.

Trip plan: Flights from across Asia land at Kota Kinabalu, the best base for exploring Sabah; take buses and taxis to sights in and around the city. To reach Sandakan (for Sepilok), take the bus from Kota. Get to Kinabalu Park (for Mt Kinabalu hikes) by minivan or shared taxi.

Need to know: To escape the heat and humidity in Kota Kinabalu, hit the beach: Tanjung Aru is the best beach downtown, while Tunku Abdul Rahman Marine Park – a 20min ferry ride offshore – has fine sand and snorkelling.

Other months: Oct-Mar – hot, humid, rainy; Apr-Sep – hot, humid, less rain.

HMS *Victory*,
flagship vessel of
the Portsmouth
Historic Dockyard

PORTSMOUTH
ENGLAND

5–16 **Why now? Tour England's mightiest warships in balmy t-shirt weather.**

Three of the Royal Navy's most celebrated warships are found at the fascinating Portsmouth Historic Dockyard. The ships span 400 years of naval history, from Tudor times to the 19th century, offering children an intriguing insight into life at sea during the age of sail. Built in the Portsmouth docks in 1510–11, the *Mary Rose* was Henry VIII's flagship during wars with France and Scotland, but in 1545 the king watched his beloved carrack sink just off Portsmouth, during the Battle of the Solent; 437 years later the wreck was raised and is now on permanent display. HMS *Victory* is the most famous of the three, thanks to its role as England's flagship at the 1805 Battle of Trafalgar, when the Royal Navy defeated the combined fleets of France and Spain, but England's greatest naval hero, Horatio Nelson, was killed (the spot where he fell is marked on the deck). Built in 1859–61, the *Warrior* is a 40-gun frigate powered by steam and sail; one of the first armour-plated iron-hulled warships, it never saw action.

Trip plan: Trains run regularly to Portsmouth Harbour from London Waterloo. After you've walked around the ships, it's worth touring the historic harbour by waterbus, visiting the Submarine Museum and the brilliantly named Explosion Museum of Naval Firepower.

Need to know: HMS *Victory* was never decommissioned, making it the world's oldest navy ship still in service.

Other months: Oct–Mar – colder, wetter weather and shorter days; Apr–Sep – warm, more time aboard.

SKELLIG MICHAEL
IRELAND

12-16 Why now? Find your inner Jedi on 'Star Wars Island'.

The Skelligs – two tiny islands off the coast of County Kerry in the wild west of Ireland – have been UNESCO World Heritage-listed since 1996, but after the larger isle, Skellig Michael, scored a starring role in the final *Star Wars* films (*The Force Awakens* and *The Last Jedi*), it started attracting younger travellers. The location is as dramatic as it appears in the movies, with angry Atlantic waves walloping the rocks, twin craggy peaks stabbing the clouds and some 27,000 pairs of gannets creating a cacophonous soundtrack. Puffins arrive in late spring and pufflings hatch in early summer. May the force be with you during the climb – it's steep, with 618 stone steps that are slippery when wet (often); junior Jedis require careful supervision. Higher up, you'll find stone-built beehive huts (habitation cells), a ruined church and graveyard; higher, just below the south peak, is a hermitage. These are the remains of a monastery occupied between the 6th and 12th centuries, which suffered several Viking attacks.

Trip plan: Between 12 May and 2 October, boats run from Portmagee, 77km (48 miles) southwest of Kerry, and land on Skellig Michael (weather permitting); the crossing takes around 50min. From mid-March (weather dependent), there are also non-landing eco-tours around Skellig Michael and its neighbouring island of Little Skellig (2hr 30min).

Need to know: Wear shoes with good grip. There's no toilet on Skellig Michael, nor on the boats.

Other months: Oct to mid-May – no boats.

© fieguiluz / Getty Images

MOSSMAN GORGE
AUSTRALIA

5-16 Why now? Perfect weather for drifting through a tropical rainforest along a croc-free river.

Many visitors to North Queensland do walking tours through the Daintree Rainforest along Mossman Gorge – a fantastic way to learn about the region's Indigenous culture and wonderful wildlife – but there's another, super-exciting way of exploring this 135-million-year-old forest. During family-friendly river-drift escapades, you join small guided groups – where everyone is wetsuit-clad and armed with a 'river sled' – to float along the Mossman River on a voyage of discovery through a rainforest that buzzes with activity and offers endless fascination for children. Iridescent kingfishers dart between branches and brilliant butterflies flutter above the water. You'll likely see tropical river fish, green tree frogs, saw-shelled turtles and spotted eels; if you're lucky, a platypus might swim past. It's an education, too, with guides explaining how nutrients and nitrogen from the rainforest flow into the Coral Sea and sustain the Great Barrier Reef by providing food for coral polyps. Afterwards, take a snorkelling tour out to the reef and explore the other half of this amazing ecosystem.

Trip plan: Tours are run by Back Country Bliss. Port Douglas – gateway to the reef, rainforest and gorge – is a 1hr drive from Cairns.

Need to know: Never enter creeks, rivers or waterholes in North Queensland without a qualified guide – enormous estuarine crocodiles can really ruin your day.

Other months: Nov-Apr – the humid Wet, 'stingers' in the sea; May-Oct – the Dry, ideal for exploring.

LES DEUX ALPES
FRANCE

12-16 Why now? Summer in the Alps means family-friendly adventure.

The pull of ski resorts in winter is obvious – but the summer appeal of these majestic mountain landscapes is equally strong, especially for adventurous families. In Les Deux Alpes, an atmospheric village at the foot of the Parc National des Écrins peaks, give children their first taste of climbing vertical rockfaces on La Balade des Lutins (The Elves' Walk). Specifically tailored for younger climbers and first-timers, the route is a mellow via ferrata, where you'll climb while clipped into iron cables that are pre-fixed to the mountain for safety. Another day, take them mountain biking on the resort's extensive 96km (60-mile) network of trails, many of which are ski pistes in winter. Start with the mini ramps-and-pump track at the Easy 2 Ride Park at the bottom of the slopes, then head up the mountain to try the 5km (3-mile) Vallée Blanche green run, building up to red- and blue-rated routes depending on their level.

Trip plan: You don't need a car here, as all the activities are within walking distance. Take the bus from Grenoble train station; journey time is just over 1hr.

Need to know: La Balade des Lutins takes 2hr 30min to complete, and guided tours are available in the morning and afternoon (book in advance). For downhill mountain biking, hire a guide through Ecole MCF, the state-run school.

Other months: Dec-May – winter, ski season; mid-Jun to mid-Aug – summer season.

FASTA ÅLAND
FINLAND

5-16 Why now? Long, light-filled days, perfect for biking and exploring an enticing northern isle.

The Åland islands are a Finnish-owned, Swedish-speaking autonomous archipelago in the Gulf of Bothnia. Getting there by ferry – from Stockholm or Turku – is part of the fun: the latter route is especially scenic, meandering through the Turku archipelago to Åland. On the largest island, Fasta Åland, Mariehamn is the capital of the Åland archipelago, and has long been a centre of seafaring and boat-building. Kids can climb aboard the good ship *Pommern* and check out an extensive collection of vessels at the Sjöfartsmuseum (Marine Museum), and see boats under construction at the Mariehamn Maritime Quarter. Outside town, Fasta Åland is peppered with immersive historic sites, such as the medieval castle at Kastelholm and the adjacent Jan Karlsgårdens outdoor museum. On the eastern edge of the island, ruined Bomarsund is a beautifully situated and totally climbable 19th-century Russian fortification. Signposted biking routes crisscross the island, including the old Mail Rd, which passes by Fasta Åland's main attractions.

Trip plan: If you stay in Mariehamn, it's possible to explore much of Fasta Åland by bus or bike, but travelling by car is much more convenient. Book in advance to bring a car on the ferry.

Need to know: Fasta Åland is the main attraction, but the outer islands – accessible by commuter ferries – are intriguing, offbeat destinations for a day trip or a bike ride.

Other months: Oct-Apr – low season, some tourist businesses close; May & Sep – shoulder season; Jun-Aug – peak season, long days, sunny.

THE BERKSHIRES
USA

5-16 Why now? Summer music and dance in a mountain idyll.

From late June to late August, the Berkshires' quiet mountain villages come alive with summer festivals featuring world-class music and dance to delight all ages. Many performances take place outdoors, taking full advantage of the scenic mountain environs. The most famous summer festival is at Tanglewood, in Lenox, summer home of the Boston Symphony Orchestra. The BSO is the main attraction, but Tanglewood also hosts their contemporary counterpart, the Boston Pops, as well as chamber music, choral ensembles, jazz groups and the occasional pop act. Most performances take place in the Koussivitzky Music Shed, an outdoor stage with covered seating and a vast lawn – perfect for families with kids who can listen, picnic and dance (or fall asleep). Nearby Lee stages Jacob's Pillow, a terrific festival of dance and movement, from classical ballet and Indigenous ceremonial dance to hip-hop and acrobatics. Besides the incredibly varied performances (indoor and outdoor), there are free events, including family-oriented music and dance classes.

Trip plan: Berkshires lodgings are expensive in summer, but there are some good campgrounds at local state parks. You'll need a car to get around.

Need to know: Lawn tickets at Tanglewood are generally free for kids. There's also special family programming, usually on Sunday mornings.

Other months: Nov-Apr – cold, attractions close; May-Aug – peak season, summer festivals; Sep-Oct – cool, crisp, fall foliage.

SANTIAGO DE CUBA
CUBA

5-16 Why now? Costumes, conga drums and elaborate parades.

Cuba's rich traditions of music and culture are on full display throughout the month of July, especially in Santiago de Cuba. It starts with the Fiesta del Fuego, a formal presentation of world music and dance, and culminates in the more raucous Carnival festivities. Unlike many pre-Lenten festivals, Cuban Carnival celebrates the Mamarrachos, or saints' days, which coincided with the end of the sugar-cane harvest. The streets come alive with conga rhythms and spontaneous dancing, as well as spectacular costumes and choreography at Céspedes Plaza. Hot days and late nights can be overwhelming for kids, who might prefer the smaller-scale Children's Carnival that takes place the weekend before the main event. During this time, towns along the Santiago coast also host water carnivals, where festive boat parades and beach parties offer relief from the heat.

Trip plan: To watch the processions in comfort, reserve seats in the stands or book a room or a table at the rooftop bar of Hotel Cubanacan Casa Granda, overlooking the plaza.

Need to know: Before travelling to Cuba, do your research and get your documents in order (insurance, travel card, Cuba D'Viajeros registration form). Note that the currency of choice is euros. Credit cards are not widely accepted and US dollars are not recommended.

Other months: Nov-Apr – dry season, sunny skies, crowded beaches; May-Jun – shoulder season, rain possible; Aug – summer vacation, scorching hot; Sep-Oct – stormy weather, potential hurricanes.

(A) Summer in
the Great Lakes at
Mackinac Island;
(L) Pembrokeshire
coasteering, Wales;
(R) Swinging down
from the slopes in
Bariloche, Argentina

138

MACKINAC ISLAND
USA

0–16 Why now? Summertime bliss on a historic, car-free island in the Great Lakes.

In the northern waters of Lake Huron, floating between Michigan's Upper and Lower Peninsulas, Mackinac Island is a delightful destination for old-fashioned summer fun. Measuring only 10 sq km (4 sq miles) and covered in parkland, the island is perfectly suited for walking or biking – which is a good thing, because cars are prohibited from these historic streets. If you want to catch a lift, it will be in a horse-drawn carriage, just as it has been since 1869. A weekend on Mackinac Island involves riding bikes (or horses), exploring historic Fort Mackinac, frolicking in the fresh waters of Lake Huron and eating plenty of fudge. Hiking trails lead to unusual geological formations with intriguing names like Arch Rock and Crack in the Island. Best of all, the incredible Great Lakes are all around, inviting exploration by canoe, kayak or charter boat.

Trip plan: Ferries depart from Mackinaw City (at the northernmost tip of the Lower Peninsula) and St Ignace (in the Upper Peninsula) for the 20min ride to Mackinac Island. You'll pay a fee to bring bikes on the ferry, or you can rent them on the island.

Need to know: Book ferry tickets in advance. Consider combination tickets that include additional attractions such as carriage rides or fort admission.

Other months: Jun-Aug – peak season, long sunny days, many special events; May & Sep-Oct – shoulder season, lower prices; Nov-Apr – low season, limited ferry service.

BARILOCHE
ARGENTINA

5–16 Why now? Sweet snow sports in Argentina's adventure (and chocolate) capital.

Nestled among Andean peaks, beside lovely Lago Nahuel Huapi and deep in the picturesque Patagonian Lake District, Bariloche is outrageously beautiful year-round, but in winter it tempts with tasty and exciting experiences for families to enjoy. From July to October, this is arguably Argentina's best winter sports destination, with sensational skiing and snowboarding conditions on- and off-piste. There are super-challenging, long and exciting runs for experts, but also plenty of gentle slopes for younger kids and beginners. Cross-country enthusiasts can explore a wealth of incredible backcountry routes, threading through alpine woodlands and exposed mountainsides with stunning views. Bariloche is also famous for gorgeous chocolate – there's even a museum dedicated to the stuff (Havanna Museo del Chocolate, offering tours and tastings). For après-ski activities, wander around the pretty Centro Cívico, where kids can enjoy taking selfies with a barrel-carrying St Bernard dogs; or explore the many delights of Parque Nacional Nahuel Huapi.

Trip plan: Bariloche is 1680km (1044 miles) from Buenos Aires; an 18hr drive (with lots to see), a long bus trip or short flight. There's also a once-weekly train service between coastal Viedma and Bariloche.

Need to know: Argentinians are speedy speakers; you'll struggle to keep up with just school/Duolingo Spanish.

Other months: Dec-Feb – sunny, ideal for outdoors weather; Mar-May – autumn colour, National Chocolate Festival (Easter); Jun-Aug – snow; Sep-Nov – wildflowers.

PEMBROKESHIRE
WALES

12–16 Why now? Clamber across cliffs under the Celtic sun.

A super-exciting way of exploring the dynamic intertidal zone, coasteering involves scrambling and clambering along rocky shorelines, climbing across cliffs, jumping into plunge pools and swimming across coves and through sea caves, tunnels and arches. Now internationally popular, the sport was born (as a guided activity) on the craggy coast of Wales in the 1980s, when pursuit-pioneer Andy Middleton began leading groups around the cliffs of Pembrokeshire. Britain's only coastal national park, Pembrokeshire is still the perfect place to experience coasteering, especially in midsummer, when temperatures are ideal and the sun glints off translucent water, projecting spellbinding reflections onto cave walls; seals, dolphins and other wildlife can often be spotted in the warm months, too. It's a family-friendly escapade, suitable for children aged eight upwards; jumps are always optional, giving teenagers ample opportunity to test their mettle and show off (or not).

Trip plan: Several guiding companies (including the original operators, TYF) are based in St Davids, at the tip of the Pembrokeshire peninsula. From Cardiff or Swansea, drive west along the M4 or explore the coastline on small roads.

Need to know: Go with a guide; the depth of the sea changes by the hour and local knowledge is crucial. Wear a wetsuit, flotation device and helmet (supplied), and footwear with grip and protection.

Other months: Dec-Feb – freezing; Mar-May & Sep-Nov – unpredictable sea conditions, but quieter; Jun-Aug – summer, busy, optimal coasteering conditions.

PERUVIAN AMAZON

12-16 | Why now? Explore real jungle during the dry season.

It's hard to imagine a more exciting place to visit than the Amazon jungle. Some families might be put off by the rainforest's intimidating immensity, remoteness and wild reputation, but if you take sensible precautions and travel with a guide in the dry season (May to October), it's a fantastic, life-changing place to visit with kids. Children are treasured in local Indigenous culture, and there's plenty here to enthuse young explorers, not least the chance to see the extraordinary boto – the playful pink dolphins of the Amazon, which often approach small boats. Boat cruises and eco-tours often incorporate small-boat trips, when youngsters can paddle along small tributary rivers and among semi-submerged forests in vast wetlands. Such trips can be arranged in areas like Peru's Reserva Nacional Pacaya-Samiria, known as the 'jungle of the mirrors' for the endless reflections in its still waters. Besides botos, you might see (and/or hear) macaws, caymans, sloths and howler, squirrel and tamarin monkeys, and encounter multiple frogs, insects, lizards, snakes and the occasional tarantula (it isn't a destination for the faint-hearted).

Trip plan: Take a guided trip. Most start from the jungle city of Iquitos, gateway to the Peruvian Amazon (served by frequent flights from Peru's capital, Lima).

Need to know: Mosquitoes and bugs are brutal – take strong Deet-based repellent (spray clothes, not skin), lightweight long sleeves/trousers and protective nets.

Other months: Nov-Apr – rainy, humid, relentless bugs; May-Oct – dry season.

LOCH NESS
SCOTLAND

5-16 | Why now? Long, sunny days make for marvellous monster-spotting conditions.

It's one of the world's most famous legends, but do the dark depths of Scotland's Loch Ness really harbour an enormous monster? At 37km (23 miles) in length, and up to 230m (755ft) deep, the immense loch is Britain's biggest body of fresh water, and there have been thousands of sightings of an enormous beast here, dating back centuries. Cynics put these down to overactive imaginations, tricks of the light, waves and floating logs, but still the stories come. Could it be a species of dinosaur that somehow survived the extinction event 65 million years ago? Or maybe the monster is just a yet-to-be-identified aquatic animal? To examine the facts, visit the excellent Loch Ness Centre, where you can learn all about the legend and the loch, and even help search for the monster by taking a cruise on the sonar-equipped *Deepscan* boat. Bigger (braver) kids will enjoy swimming and canoeing on the loch, too.

Trip plan: Buses run along the loch, through the Great Glen, between Inverness and Fort William. Explore Urquhart Castle while you're here, and learn the gory story behind the Well of the Seven Heads, found on nearby Loch Oich.

Need to know: The Loch Ness Centre is open year-round. Cruises run April to October (subject to conditions).

Other months: Oct-Mar – cold, no cruises; Apr-Jun – quieter, cooler, less midges; Aug-Sep – sunny, more midges, perfect for paddle sports and swimming (if you dare).

QUEENSTOWN
NEW ZEALAND/ AOTEAROA

0-16 | Why now? Prime snow time in this top alpine resort.

Queenstown wears its crown as the 'Adventure Capital of the World' with class – there's no better place to keep the family entertained. Hit the slopes during the day (either on skis or snowboards) at nearby Coronet Peak or the Remarkables, or head further afield to Cardrona or Treble Cone. If you've a passion for cross-country skiing, head up to the Snow Farm, high above the Cardrona Valley. There's seldom snow on the ground in the Wakatipu Basin, so on fine days in winter, you can rent bikes in town and hit the 130km (81 miles) of off-road tracks that make up the Queenstown Trails. The Skyline Queenstown gondola runs year-round, presenting unbelievable views, while the luge tracks (part go-kart, part toboggan) at the top will keep kids excited for hours. Don't forget, bungy-jumping was invented in Queenstown, and it takes kids a while to get tired of watching people diving off Kawarua Bridge with a rubber band tied to their ankles. Jetboats, another Kiwi invention, virtually fly across Lake Wakatipu and on the Shotover and Kawarau Rivers. Warm up with a soak in Onsen Hot Pools to finish your day.

Trip plan: Queenstown has one of the country's busiest international airports. Stay at least a week.

Need to know: Queenstown is an extremely popular resort; book accommodation and a rental car well ahead of your arrival dates.

Other months: Nov-Mar – summer with great hiking & biking; Apr – autumn colours; Jun-Sep – ski season; Oct – spring.

WARRNAMBOOL
AUSTRALIA

5-16 Why now? Watch whale mums nurse newborn calves from the beach.

Each Australian winter, female southern right whales return to the relatively calm waters of Logan's Beach near Warrnambool, in Victoria, to give birth and nurse calves through their early months. Observing massive 18m-long (60ft) mothers teaching their behemoth babies (which weigh a ton, literally) to surface and take a breath – often within 100m (330ft) of the shore – is a goose-pimple-producing sight, especially in the company of your own children. 'Right' whales are so-called because they were considered the correct animals to harpoon (due to the high oil content of their bodies), and these magnificent beasts were hunted almost to extinction in the 19th century. Thankfully, populations have bounced back since whaling ceased, and the animals seem to know they're safe here. This eco-friendly, utterly unobtrusive whale-watching experience can be enjoyed for free from the beach, where there are viewing platforms. Clued-up locals and regulars often recognise returning right whale mums by marks on their tail flukes.

Trip plan: Warrnambool is a 260km (160-mile) direct drive from Melbourne, but take the scenic route along the gorgeous Great Ocean Road, pausing to see iconic surfing spots (including Bells Beach), vibrant coastal towns like Lorne, Apollo Bay and Port Fairy, and wonderful wildlife-rich woodland areas such as Great Otway National Park.

Need to know: Bring a coat (it gets chilly) and good binoculars.

Other months: Dec-Feb – beach weather; Mar-May & Sep-Nov – comfortable temperatures, ideal for hiking.

RĪGA
LATVIA

0-16 Why now? See Latvia's countryside under dry skies.

Discount airlines put Latvia's art nouveau capital on the tourism map, but architecture is just the start of the Rīga experience. On a family break to Latvia, you can kick off in the capital, exploring elegant churches, eclectic museums and busy markets, then set off into the green, serene countryside. The warm, dry days of July were made for getting outdoors: connect through the central town of Dobele to reach Tērvete Nature Park, with carved wooden gnomes, animal pens, log-built playgrounds and villages of miniature houses that kids can clamber around and explore, dotted between the pines in its Fairy Tale Forest. East of Rīga, Sigulda has plenty to keep kids entertained – twin castles, a cable car, ziplines and bobsled runs, mountain-biking trails, kayak and boat trips on the Gauja River. Stay in rural hotels, village guesthouses and campgrounds to fully immerse yourselves in Latvia's green spaces.

Trip plan: AirBaltic, Ryanair and other European airlines fly to Rīga, or you can get here by ferry, train or bus from Stockholm, Tallinn or Vilnius. A rental car is handy for exploring the countryside; trains run to Sigulda and buses to Dobele and Tērvete Nature Park.

Need to know: The *pirts* (sauna) is a Latvian institution; the riverside campground at Jaunzāģeri near Sigulda has a traditional wet bathhouse and kayaks, canoes and rafts for hire.

Other months: Dec-Feb – cold, snowy; Mar-Apr & Oct-Nov – damper, cooler temperatures; Jun-Sep – dry, warm.

INNSBRUCK
AUSTRIA

5-12 Why now? They love bees in Innsbruck – especially at the end of July.

In and around the Tyrolean capital, bees are the in thing – department stores host hives on their roofs, locals have set up bee colonies in the surrounding countryside, and at Patscherkofel, around 45 minutes' drive from Innsbruck, young children can play at being beekeepers for the day while walking the Kofele's Bee Trail. Along the way, they'll get to observe the bee colonies here, which produce unique Alpine-rose honey, and discover interesting facts about nature's little helpers. If you time your visit for the end of July, kids can join the annual 'Kofele becomes a beekeeper' event, where a local apiarist will teach them all about beekeeping and let them taste local honey. With its distinctive rounded peak, Patscherkofel is a ski resort in winter, and a popular hiking spot in summer; the trails here are especially suitable for families thanks to the easy gradient. There's more apiarian interest back in Innsbruck, where the Alpenzoo's interactive Sumsi World exhibit celebrates the sensory abilities of bees.

Trip plan: Visit one of the mountain-hut restaurants dotted around Patscherkofel to fuel up on tasty Tyrolean dumplings, strudel and Käsespätzle, a cross between macaroni cheese and gnocchi.

Need to know: There's another 2km (1.2-mile) bee nature trail at Sistrans Mühlteich pond, a 20min drive from Innsbruck.

Other months: Dec-May – cold, snow; Jun – summer weather; Aug-Sep – still warm; Oct-Nov – getting colder.

141

Scan the shoreline
for fossils along the
Jurassic Coast

JURASSIC COAST
ENGLAND

0-16 Why now? For Dorset days
spent playing on the sand or
searching for fossils.

If there was a capital of the Jurassic Coast,
it would be Lyme Regis. It was here, in
the 19th century, that Mary Anning's
discovery of a near-complete ichthyosaur
first captivated the world, turning the town
into a renowned fossil-hunting spot. If you
walk along the beach towards Charmouth
with your eyes trained firmly on the shingle,
you'll likely find a souvenir, even if it's not
as impressive as an ichthyosaur. Look out
for the coiled whirl of ammonites, squid-
like creatures that lived between 240
and 65 million years ago – their fossils
are common in this area. Stretching from
Exmouth in Devon to Studland Bay in
Dorset, the Jurassic Coast has museums,
guest centres and fossil-hunting spots
that will keep young dinosaur enthusiasts
happy. But the wide, coppery-sand
beaches are as big a draw, and fill with
families on sunny weekends.

Trip plan: Bridport is a lovely base from
which to make day trips. A two-day stay
allows you to focus on fossils, while up to
a week gives you relaxing beach time. The
Jurassic Coaster bus service operates from
Poole to Axminster, and from Lyme Regis to
Seaton, stopping along the coast.

Need to know: Lyme Regis beach can
be cut off at high tide, and the cliffs are
dangerous in places, especially after rain.
Summer should bring warmer days and
fewer downpours.

Other months: Nov-Feb – cold, dark;
Mar-May – spring, pleasant, fairly quiet;
Jun-Aug – summer, coast busy; Sep-Oct –
getting cooler.

© Cavan Images / Getty Images

California dreaming: (R) Santa Cruz; (B) Monterey Bay Aquarium

© David A Litman / Shutterstock

CALIFORNIA USA

5-16 **Why now?** Tailor a road trip around summer sunshine in the Golden State.

After exploring Los Angeles, hire a car and set the GPS for the Pacific Coast Hwy (Hwy 1). Before you arrive in beautiful, bougie Santa Barbara, call in at Malibu for beach vibes and a look at the bizarre natural asphalt lakes at the Carpinteria Tar Pits. Overnight in Santa Barbara, where older kids may relish peering down through the glass rooftop of MOXI (aka the Wolf Museum of Exploration + Innovation); younger kids will not want to leave. Hit the road for Monterey, but first try your luck spotting sea otters at Morro Bay. Teens might appreciate the lavish excesses of Hearst Castle, and some time hiking at Big Sur. Overnight at Monterey, visiting the Monterey Bay Aquarium and, for little ones, El Estero Park's Dennis the Menace Playground, before journeying on

to Santa Cruz, where the Beach Boardwalk Amusement Park beckons. Beyond boho San Francisco, keep the road trip going on an inland detour to incomparable Yosemite National Park. Famed for its granite cliffs and ancient sequoia trees, it does get busy in summer, but if you're prepared to take the family hiking, it's easy to avoid the crowds.

Trip plan: You'll be covering a lot of ground, so hire a car with unlimited mileage (and pack your walking shoes, too).

Need to know: Sea fog can roll in; be prepared for limited visibility.

Other months: Nov-Apr – off-season discounts, rain; May-Jun – overcast mornings, warming up; Aug-Sep – sun, crowds; Oct – mild, still dry.

© photocritical / Shutterstock

VAL D'AZUN FRANCE

12-16 **Why now?** Immerse in nature on a child-pleasing donkey-hike adventure.

In high summer, ditch the beach and head up into the French Pyrenees, where the temperatures are far more pleasant, to enjoy some tranquil family time on the trails without seeing a soul for hours. But what if the kids won't walk for hours? In the Val d'Azun, they have a powerful secret weapon in the form of pure-bred local donkeys, which accompany hiking groups to provide the ultimate distraction. While your kids

will be busy leading, feeding, brushing and constantly fussing over your new four-legged friend (who will also helpfully know the route and the best rest spots), adults can drink in the bright and bucolic mid-mountain landscapes. You'll navigate beautiful green forest, bubbling streams, farming villages and remote lakes, while surrounded by incredible mountain panoramas including the Pic du Midi d'Arrens, Col de Bazès and Col de Couraduque. Accommodation is a mix of local hotels and tents under the stars, while your donkey grazes nearby. The only

downside will come when your children have to say their (often tearful) donkey goodbyes.

Trip plan: This five-day loop begins in Arras-en-Lavedan and ends in None.

Need to know: Book donkey hikes through La Balaguère (minimum age is seven). Expect average daily walks of 3hr to 4hr. The donkeys are there as companions, not to transport your luggage, though they can carry some things for the day.

Other months: Dec-May – wintry, snowy; Jun-Sep – warm (donkey hikes Jul to Aug); Oct-Nov – cool to cold.

SERENGETI NATIONAL PARK
TANZANIA

5-16 | **Why now?** Catch the Great Migration across the Serengeti in full swing.

Seeing Tanzania's wonderful wildlife in the flesh will blow the mind of any child who grew up on books like Roald Dahl's *The Enormous Crocodile* and Eileen Brown's *Handa's Surprise*. From June to August, vast herds of wildebeest undertake the epic migration from Tanzania's Serengeti National Park to Kenya, accompanied by hordes of zebras and gazelles (and the hungry predators that prey on them). To see ginormous crocs in real life, head to the Grumeti River in the west of the Serengeti, or the Mara River in the north, where migrating herbivores run the gauntlet of ravenous reptiles. With kids on safari, stay in safari lodges or semi-permanent tented camps; there's often a pool to splash in, and an on-site waterhole for easy wildlife sightings. Don't overlook smaller wildlife –

kids can enjoy encounters with half-tame rock hyraxes, as well as looking out for bobbing hoopoes or the dangling nests of weaver birds.

Trip plan: Arusha is the main hub for safaris; flights arrive from Dar es Salaam, other African capitals, and a few cities in Europe. Numerous agencies can arrange safaris – budget packages focus on the east of the reserve and the Ngorongoro Crater; allow more days to visit the west and north of the Serengeti.

Need to know: Wildlife is most active mornings and evenings, so prime the kids for early starts and bring drinks and snacks in case of delayed dinners.

Other months: Nov-Apr – warm, wet; May-Aug – cooler, dry, lots of wildebeest; Sep-Oct – warm, dry.

Wildebeest congregate
en masse on Tanzania's
Serengeti savannah

CENTRAL NETHERLANDS

0–16 **Why now? Dreamy summer weather on the waterways.**

A quarter of the Netherlands lies below sea level, so it's only fitting to explore by boat, an idyllic family adventure in the warm, sunny month of July. Rivers and canals connect Amsterdam with Friesland to the north and Utrecht and the province of South Holland to the south, opening up days of gentle cruising by canal boat, dropping in on interesting towns such as canal-crossed Leeuwarden and Gouda (of cheese fame). En route, you'll pass sprawling flower gardens, grassy meadows dotted with windmills, and landscapes that inspired Rembrandt, Van Gogh and Vermeer. Kids will likely love taking a hand at the wheel or tiller, and acting as honorary captain while you navigate locks and bridges. Most boaters start in Amsterdam, exploring the city on foot or by bike before picking up a canal boat or motorised barge from boatyards outside the capital, but there are plenty of downtown moorings, so it's possible to cruise right up to some of Amsterdam's top sights.

Trip plan: Most people arrange a rental boat before travelling to Amsterdam by train, plane or ferry (via IJmuiden). Le Boat and Locaboat are the biggest operators; smaller Dutch companies also rent out boats with bedrooms, bathrooms and kitchens on board.

Need to know: No licence is required for boats of less than 15m (49ft) in length, with a max speed of less than 20km/h (12.4mph), which covers most rental boats here.

Other months: Dec-Feb – cold, foggy, poor for boating; Mar-Apr & Oct-Nov – damper, cooler; May-Sep – dry, sunny, busy.

Puttering along Amsterdam's tree-lined canals

July

REYKJAVÍK
ICELAND

5-12 Why now? Scan the lava flows for elves as Iceland warms up for summer.

There's more to Iceland than whales and volcanoes; this Nordic island is also reputed to be the home of the Huldufólk – a race of 'hidden people' who have been part of Icelandic folklore since Viking times. Superstitious islanders still adorn their homes and gardens with tiny doors to earn the favour of these tutelary spirits, and certain locations are strongly associated with the Huldufólk. On a summertime break to Reykjavík with younger kids, set aside a day to visit Hafnarfjörður, an outer suburb that is said to be a favourite elf haunt; the tourist office here has a map of top elf locations, including Hellisgerði Park and the rocky cliff known as Hamarinn. Continue your Icelandic adventure in the city's magma-heated thermal pools (including Laugardalslaug, with its waterslides and botanical gardens; and the beachside pool at Nauthólsvík); go whale-watching; and discover Viking history at the Saga Museum, Maritime Museum and the National Museum.

Trip plan: Reykjavík is a short flight from mainland Europe; many travellers visit on a stopover en route to New York or Boston with Icelandair. There's no need to hire a car – sunshine-yellow Straeto buses trundle around downtown Reykjavík, and Bus 1 runs regularly to Hafnarfjörður.

Need to know: Alfar (alfar.is) runs guided elf walks around Hafnarfjörður on Tuesdays and Fridays (Fridays and Saturdays in winter), exploring this hidden world and its folklore.

Other months: Dec-Mar – icy and dark; Apr-Jun & Oct-Nov – warmer, brighter.

© trabantos / Shutterstock

Eisbachwelle surfers and spectators

MUNICH GERMANY

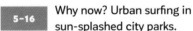

5-16 Why now? Urban surfing in sun-splashed city parks.

The Eisbachwelle in the middle of Munich was recently voted one of the world's top 100 most-beautiful beaches – pretty impressive, considering it's not a beach and the nearest seaside is in Venice, over 300km (190 miles) away. There is, however, a strong surf culture here. The Eisbachwelle (Eisbach wave) is an aquatic roller near the entrance to the Englischer Garten (English Garden), where the artificial Eisbach River emerges from beneath the Haus der Kunst art gallery and breaks over a stone step, creating a standing wave that's been attracting urban surfers for 40 years. It was once illegal to ride the wave, but now boarders come year-round, testing their skills on the Eisbachwelle night and day. A tricky wave with a powerful fast flow and hazards, it's for advanced surfers only, but during summer it draws crowds of spectators (and is especially popular with kids). Beginner surfers can take to the water themselves at another (wider) standing wave further upstream, close to the Zum Flaucher beer garden, and a third, smaller wave at Flosslände in Thalkirchen.

Trip plan: The Englischer Garten is a 30min stroll from München Hauptbahnhof Station. Besides surfing spots, the park has 65km (40 miles) of trails to explore. (And four big beer gardens...)

Need to know: Munich is famous for books, beer and BMW; car-crazy kids love the BMW Welt and the BMW Museum.

Other months: Apr-May – Springfest; Sep-Oct – Oktoberfest (crowds, rivers of beer); Nov-Dec – Christmas markets.

August

WHERE TO GO WHEN WITH KIDS

We want to...

HAVE AN ADVENTURE

TAKE US OUT FOR...

MEMORABLE FEASTS ———— • FAROE ISLANDS P167

SPECIAL SNACKS, TREATS AND SWEETS ———— • BRITTANY, FRANCE P157

Snack on Brittany's baguettes, stinky cheese and sweet and savoury crêpes and galettes

Join puffin patrols on Heimaey Island, home to the world's largest puffin colony

TAKE US...

OUTDOORS

FOR SOME KID-FRIENDLY FUN
- • WYOMING, USA P160
- • GDAŃSK & HEL PENINSULA, POLAND P157
- • SAAS FEE, SWITZERLAND P154

FOR A WET AND WILD TIME
- • BEIJING WATER CUBE, CHINA P156
- • GOTHENBURG, SWEDEN P163

TO A FESTIVAL
- • ALICE SPRINGS, AUSTRALIA P161
- • JAPAN P167

CHILL OUT/ HEAD OUT

Swim, surf and chill on the beach in laid-back and lovely Carrapateira

Wander through Wyoming for Wild West shootouts and gorgeous geysers

Snaffle lobster rolls and ice-creams as you soak up the summer scene in Cape Cod

TAKE US TO THE BEACH

TO BUILD SANDCASTLES AND SWIM
- • CAPE COD, USA P164
- • CORAL COAST, FIJI P161

TO SNORKEL OR SURF ———— • CARRAPATEIRA, PORTUGAL P156

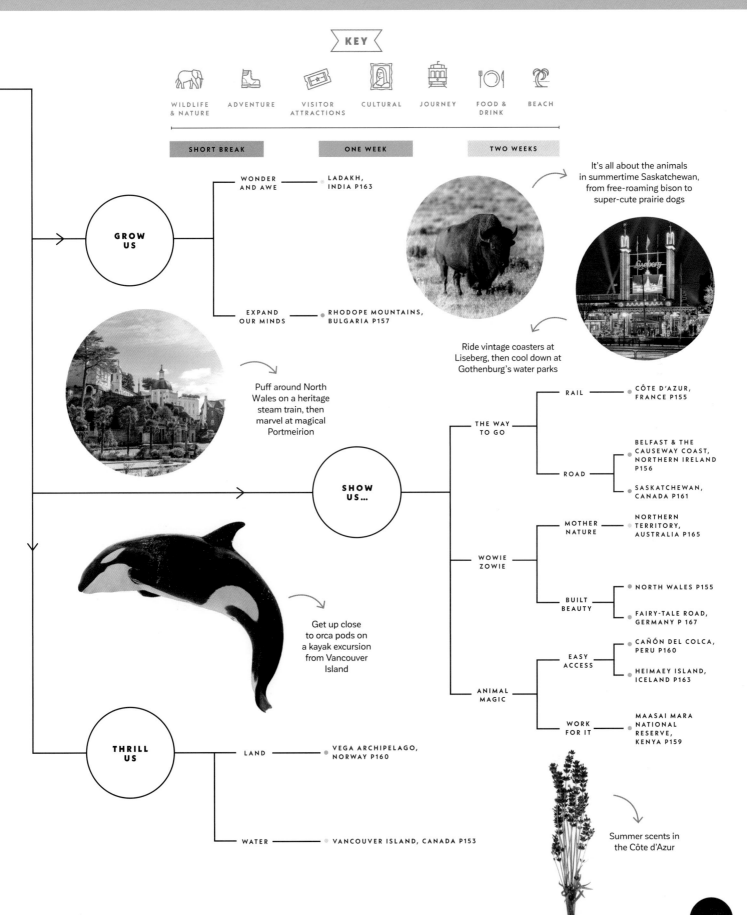

KEY

WILDLIFE & NATURE   ADVENTURE   VISITOR ATTRACTIONS   CULTURAL   JOURNEY   FOOD & DRINK   BEACH

SHORT BREAK   ONE WEEK   TWO WEEKS

GROW US

WONDER AND AWE — LADAKH, INDIA P163

EXPAND OUR MINDS — RHODOPE MOUNTAINS, BULGARIA P157

It's all about the animals in summertime Saskatchewan, from free-roaming bison to super-cute prairie dogs

Ride vintage coasters at Liseberg, then cool down at Gothenburg's water parks

Puff around North Wales on a heritage steam train, then marvel at magical Portmeirion

SHOW US...

THE WAY TO GO
— RAIL — CÔTE D'AZUR, FRANCE P155
— ROAD — BELFAST & THE CAUSEWAY COAST, NORTHERN IRELAND P156
— SASKATCHEWAN, CANADA P161

WOWIE ZOWIE
— MOTHER NATURE — NORTHERN TERRITORY, AUSTRALIA P165
— BUILT BEAUTY — NORTH WALES P155
— FAIRY-TALE ROAD, GERMANY P 167

ANIMAL MAGIC
— EASY ACCESS — CAÑÓN DEL COLCA, PERU P160
— HEIMAEY ISLAND, ICELAND P163
— WORK FOR IT — MAASAI MARA NATIONAL RESERVE, KENYA P159

Get up close to orca pods on a kayak excursion from Vancouver Island

THRILL US

LAND — VEGA ARCHIPELAGO, NORWAY P160

WATER — VANCOUVER ISLAND, CANADA P153

Summer scents in the Côte d'Azur

Events in August

OBON
Kyoto, Japan
Let kids stay up late to see Kyoto lit up by lanterns, while bonfires shaped into Japanese characters blaze on the mountains around the city.

GANESH CHATURTHI
Mumbai, India
Huge effigies of the elephant-headed god are paraded and immersed in the sea – a spectacle to rival anything made by Marvel or DC.

MT HAGEN CULTURAL SHOW
Mt Hagen, Papua New Guinea
Adventurous kids who love edge-of-the-envelope travel will be gobsmacked by the dances, rituals and costumes of PNG's diverse Indigenous peoples.

LOLLAPALOOZA
Chicago, Illinois, USA
If you're going to do a big US music festival with kids, make it this Chicago spectacular, with a dedicated Kidzapalooza for tiny rockers.

LA TOMATINA
Buñol, Spain
There's a special tomato fight just for kids aged 4 to 14 as Buñol turns to tomate frito during this legendary summer fest.

FESTIVAL OF ST LOUIS
Sète, Languedoc, France
Take jousting re-enactments to the next level at this medieval fair – bargemen battling with lances is guaranteed to grab kids' attention.

FLIGHT OF THE PUFFLINGS
Heimaey, Vestmannaeyjar, Iceland
The annual rescue of lost puffin chicks on this volcanic Icelandic isle gives kids a chance to get close to these charming, clown-like birds.

FERIA DE LAS FLORES
Medellín, Colombia
Bathe children in a sea of colour at this fragrant celebration of Colombia's famous blooms, marked by flower displays, parades and music.

Inner wheel labels:
- August (or September) — $
- Mid-August (or September) — $$
- Last Wed in August (last Sat for kids) — $$
- August to September — $$
- Early August — $
- Mid- to late August — $
- First week of August — $$
- Mid-August — $$$

● BRITTANY, FRANCE

● CORAL COAST, FIJI

● CARRAPATEIRA, PORTUGAL

Race to the
lighthouse in
Cape Cod

● CAPE COD, USA

Kayak along Fiji's
Coral Coast

● GOTHENBURG, SWEDEN

Spot elephants in
the Maasai Mara
National Park

Follow Germany's
Fairy-Tale Road to
Bremen

Learn about Native
American culture
and history in
Wyoming

● NORTH WALES

● BEIJING WATER CUBE,
CHINA

● SAAS FEE,
SWITZERLAND

● BELFAST & THE CAUSEWAY COAST,
NORTHERN IRELAND

● CÔTE D'AZUR, FRANCE

● SASKATCHEWAN, CANADA

Shop for souvenirs
in Belfast, home of
the *Titanic*

● MAASAI MARA NATIONAL
RESERVE, KENYA

● WYOMING, USA

● HEIMAEY ISLAND, ICELAND

● NORTHERN TERRITORY
AUSTRALIA

● FAIRY-TALE ROAD,
GERMANY

● JAPAN

● GDAŃSK & HEL PENINSULA,
POLAND

Wander a traditional
turf-roofed village in the
Faroe Islands

The sandy shores
of Poland's Hel
Peninsula

Eider ducks
flock to Vega in
Norway

● CAÑÓN DEL COLCA, PERU

● RHODOPE MOUNTAINS,
BULGARIA

● ALICE SPRINGS,
AUSTRALIA

● FAROE ISLANDS

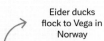

On the road
to Alice for a
boat race in
the desert

● LADAKH, INDIA

Andean condors
soar on thermals
in Peru's Colca
Canyon

● VEGA ARCHIPELAGO,
NORWAY

Mountainside bonfires
are a summer Obon
tradition in Kyoto

● VANCOUVER ISLAND, CANADA

VANCOUVER ISLAND CANADA

12-16 **Why now? For wild encounters, record-breaking totems and mountain biking under the summer sun.** Imagine paddling across silvery-still mountain waters, while ahead of you the sleek black-and-white heads of a pod of orcas (killer whales) loop and bob. The Johnstone Strait, the channel of ocean between Vancouver Island and the mainland, is a feeding ground for some of the world's largest pods of these incredible animals, and kayak excursions get you close to them in their natural habitat. This nature-rich region is the ancestral home of the 'Namgis First Nation, and Alert Bay on Cormorant Island (Yalis) is one of the best places in BC to absorb Indigenous culture; gaze skyward at the world's tallest totem pole, and take in exhibits at the peerless U'mista Cultural Centre. There's no shortage of adventure inland, but fans of mountain biking will love a visit to the central-island village of Cumberland. Recently rejuvenated by a local community group, the extensive and unique trail network here has rides for all abilities.

Trip plan: Allow one to two weeks. Alder Bay is one entry point for kayaking excursions; from Victoria or Nanaimo, follow Hwy 19 North. Alert Bay is a 4hr drive from Nanaimo, then a short ferry ride. Cumberland is a 1hr drive north from Nanaimo up Hwy 1.

Need to know: Dolphins and whales, including baleen and orca, come to feed in the Strait from May to October.

Other months: Nov-Mar – dramatically stormy; Apr-May – mild; Jun-Jul – peak season, busy, warmest; Sep-Oct – quiet.

(L) Orca breaching in the Johnstone Strait;
(R) Paddling Vancouver Island's coastline

Marmot mealtime
in Saas Fee

SAAS FEE
SWITZERLAND

0–16 **Why now?** It's midsummer in the mountains and the marmots are out.

Hemmed in by a magnificent amphitheatre of 13 implacable peaks over 4000m (13,000ft) high, and backed by the threatening tongues of nine glaciers, the village of Saas Fee looks somewhat tiny in the revealing light of summer. This affluent, carefree resort may be teeming with snowsports enthusiasts in winter, but come the summer months it's a haven for families looking to enjoy some Swiss Alpine time. Riding the underground Mittelallalin funicular up through the mountains to stupendous views at 3500m-high (11,482ft) Allalin viewing deck is a must; the kids' bucket-list choice might be a ride on the Spielbodenbahn cable car to Spielboden, at 2448m (8031ft), to see marmots. Known for their shrill whistle, these small Alpine mammals spend 90% of their lives underground (sleeping, hiding from predators and in hibernation), but in the warm days of summer, marmots pop out of their painstakingly dug tunnels and burrows beneath the slopes to stretch their legs – to the delight of kids. These Valaisian marmots show little fear of humans, and will happily eat carrots, peanuts and bread from the hands of whoever turns up to feed them. Purchase marmot food at the Spielboden restaurant.

Trip plan: Saas Fee village has lots of accommodation and eating options; stay for a couple of nights.

Need to know: Unlike neighbouring Zermatt, one valley over, Saas Fee is not accessible by train. You'll have to come by car or bus.

Other months: Dec-Apr – ski season; Jun-Jul – summer visitors .

CÔTE D'AZUR
FRANCE

0-16 Why now? For sun-drenched Nice beaches and a steam train into the hills.

There's a reason the Riviera is so popular in summer. Nice is at its most beautiful when skies and sea are a deep azure, and its honey-hued buildings are lit in high-definition sunlight. Give kids an overview of the city by taking the free lift (or climb the steps) up to the Colline du Château for magnificent vistas across Nice's terracotta rooftops and coastline. This shaded, wooded park used to be the site of a medieval castle and has a lovely garden with play areas and an impressive (artificial) waterfall. For a totally different Côte d'Azur perspective, young transport enthusiasts will love the Train des Pignes, a steam loco which chuffs from the glittery seaside to the medieval village of Annot, providing stunning, ever-changing views along the way. With its shiny black engine and gleaming varnished-wood benches, this line is the only remnant of the metre-gauge Chemins de Fer de Provence that once crisscrossed southern France.

Trip plan: For the Train des Pignes, take a standard train from Chemins de Fer de Provence Station in central Nice to Puget-Théniers, from where the steam train takes 1hr 20min to reach Annot (via Entrevaux).

Need to know: The Train des Pignes (traindespignes.fr) runs every Sunday between May and October; book tickets in advance.

Other months: Feb – Carnaval de Nice; May – Annot's St Fortunat Festival; Jun – Train des Pignes heritage days; Oct – Halloween-themed Train des Pignes rides; Dec – Nice Christmas markets.

© D. Pimborough / Shutterstock

Rafting on the Tryweryn River near Wrexham

NORTH WALES UK

0-16 Why now? Castles, trains, coast and a surrealist nod to Italy.

North Wales is beautiful year-round, but in August you'll (hopefully) enjoy more rain-free days, and can take in special events staged to coincide with the school summer holidays. Wrexham's excellently preserved Chirk Castle has plenty to entertain young children, including a model farm with a play area, and events like a medieval knights' training camp. Lovely Llangollen is close by, from where the heritage steam and diesel trains of the Llangollen Railway follow a 40-minute route to Corwen, through stations restored to their Victorian heyday. Heading west, the Llŷn Peninsula's wild beaches have glorious views and plenty of space to build your own castles in the sand. But for some surreal North Wales magic,

head to Portmeirion. Set on its own tranquil peninsula reaching into the Dwyryd Estuary, the village's colourful Italianate buildings have an otherworldly feel. A forest train tours the peninsula's wooded interior on a 20-minute circuit (April to October only), and in August the village hosts brass bands and other live music. Grab an ice-cream from its gelateria and enjoy the views.

Trip plan: You could easily spend a week exploring North Wales. Book in advance for Portmeirion tickets.

Need to know: Chirk Castle has a packed events calendar; check the National Trust website to see what's on.

Other months: Jan-Mar – windy beach walks; Apr – Easter fun at castles; Jun-Jul – dolphins off the coast; Sep-Oct – less busy, often warm; Nov-Dec – festive decorations.

CARRAPATEIRA
PORTUGAL

 Why now? Find sublime sand and sun on Portugal's best beaches.

The Algarve doesn't need much selling as a family holiday destination. In August, the mercury hovers at around 29°C (84°F), skies are cloudless and the beaches shimmer like powdered bullion. For water babies, Portugal's Atlantic Coast is all about the waves – paddling in them, swimming in them, kayaking over them and surfing the rolling breaks. For the optimum combination of sea and sand, base yourself around the beaches of laid-back Carrapateira. There's soft sand for castle-building, horse-riding tours trotting along the shore, guided kayak trips to visit mysterious sea caves, and local surf schools with bodyboards for little ones and lessons for older kids. Break up beach days with coastal hikes, trips to inland hill villages and lazy mornings at Carrapateira's cafes and the tot-friendly Museu do Mar e da Terra (Land and Sea Museum).

Trip plan: Hotels, villas and holiday lets with pools are easy to find in and around Carrapateira, and the beach (and surf school) at Praia da Borderia is close at hand. Rent a car for easy day trips to more dreamy beaches at Praia do Amado to the south and Praia de Arrifana to the north.

Need to know: The Atlantic Ocean isn't as toasty as the Med; water temperatures can dip below 20°C (68°F), so bring sunsuits or wetsuits to keep the kids in the sea for longer.

Other months: Dec-Mar – cold (not freezing), some rain; Apr-May & Oct-Nov – warmer, drier; Jun-Sep – hot, sunny, busy.

BELFAST & THE CAUSEWAY COAST
NORTHERN IRELAND

 Why now? Enjoy Ireland's green hills in glorious summer.

Northern Ireland's hip and happening capital, Belfast is moving on from the Troubles and throwing everything at the arts, so there's plenty of creative fun for families over the summer. But don't overlook the surrounding countryside – with a rental car, all manner of road trips await. Take a few days to climb up Cave Hill and explore the multimedia Titanic Belfast museum, then plot a route north via beachside Carrickfergus Castle, the vertiginous Gobbins Cliff Path and the Dark Hedges – the eerie tunnel of trees made famous in scenes from *Game of Thrones*. Cap off the trip by parking the car and riding the nostalgic Bushmills Railway to the otherworldly Giant's Causeway. Big kids can have a go at scrambling from rock to rock; keep younger children engaged with tales of the giant Fionn Mac Cumhaill (also known as Finn McCool), who reputedly stacked up these eye-catching basalt columns.

Trip plan: It's just 97km (60 miles) from Belfast to the Giant's Causeway; you can see it on a day trip or fit in overnight stops. Close to the Causeway, the village of Ballycastle has long beaches and reputedly haunted ruins, and you can stroll the coast path to time-toppled Kinbane Castle.

Need to know: The Giant's Causeway is most atmospheric when it's quiet; book tickets online, be there when the site opens at 9am, and ideally avoid weekends.

Other months: Dec-Feb – cold, wet, grey; Mar-May – warmer, spring flowers; Jun-Jul – warm, dry, busy; Sep-Oct – cooler, autumn colour.

BEIJING WATER CUBE
CHINA

 Why now? Stay cool in the pool during the red-hot heat of Beijing's summer.

After the 2008 Summer Olympics in Beijing, the National Aquatics Center built for the Games – where 25 world records were set – was completely reimagined as a watery wonderworld for the public. A state-of-the-art aquatic centre, the Water Cube boasts enough splashing space for 30,000 swimmers, as well as more than 50 slides and 18 rides. Its shape symbolically represents 'Earth' in Chinese philosophy (with the nearby dome of the Bird's Nest Stadium reflecting the 'sky') but it's all about H20 here, with wet and wild features including a wave pool, a lazy river and a spa. Star attractions for thrill-seeking kids include the Tornado (a four-person ride that hurtles down stomach-rearranging drops and rushes around tight bends); the Aqualoop (with a 12m/40ft free-fall); the frighteningly fast Serpentine Speed Slide; and the Bullet Bowl, which whooshes people around a whirlpool before plunging them down a dark, steep drop.

Trip plan: The Water Cube is open daily (10am-9.30pm). To get there, catch Subway Line 10 to Beitucheng, change to Line 8 and travel to Aoti Zhongxin (Olympic Sports Center) Station; take exits B1 or B2.

Need to know: Seemingly made from giant bubbles, the building's brilliant construction helps heat the pools, harness natural light and capture rainfall (which is recycled), making it one of the world's most eco-friendly water parks.

Other months: Dec-Feb – very cold; Mar-May & Sep-Nov – variable weather, fewer crowds; Jun-Jul – Beijing's hot and busy peak season.

BRITTANY
FRANCE

0-16 Why now? For rose-tinted beaches, rockpooling and plenty of crêpes.

Brittany is one of the few regions in France where you can sit on a sandy beach in August, facing a clean, Caribbean-like sea with few other souls in sight. While the rest of the coast heaves with visitors, Brittany's reputation for changeable weather – usually undeserved in August – means there's often space to spare. From the Côtes d'Armor to the shores of Belle-Île-en-Mer through the Pointe du Raz, Crozon and the Quiberon Peninsula, you'll find yourselves marvelling at the quintessentially Breton contrast of inviting beaches suddenly giving way to weathered cliffs. And one of Brittany's natural wonders awaits around Penvern, Trégastel and Ploumanac'h: a delightful coastline of pink- and russet-coloured granite known as the Côte de Granit Rose. The marvellously shaped natural boulders are great for a clamber and the shoreline is ripe for rockpooling (keep an eye on tide times). Brittany without crêpes would be like passing on pizza while visiting Naples; treat the family to an extensive sampling of sweet (crêpe) and savoury (galette) toppings.

Trip plan: Plan to stay for a weekend to a week. St-Malo is the main Breton stop for ferries from southern England. The closest airport is Rennes; you can also come by train from Paris.

Need to know: In August, around 700,000 people visit Lorient on Brittany's south coast for the Festival Interceltique (festival-interceltique.bzh), with parades of traditional costumes and live music.

Other months: Dec-Mar – rainy, dramatic views; Apr-May – spring, tulip fields; Jun-Jul – summer, high prices; Sep-Oct – surfing waves.

RHODOPE MOUNTAINS
BULGARIA

5-16 Why now? Peaceful perfection in the Bulgarian summer.

The bucolic countryside of medieval woodcuts and fairy tales still exists in Europe – if you know where to look. Bulgaria's Rhodope Mountains are crisscrossed by gorges, pockmarked with caverns, carpeted by forests and dotted with farms and villages that feel far removed from mass tourism and the modern age. Bring the kids to a farmstay or to a family-owned guesthouse here and you'll trade the screens and devices for days eating farm-fresh produce, hikes far from traffic noise, and basking in front of soul-restoring mountain views. Older kids with a taste for the spooky might enjoy seeking out landmarks tied to local legends, like the Devil's Throat Cave near Gyovren and the dramatic Devil's Path near Borino. Lucifer's face is said to appear in the reflection of the Devil's Bridge near Ardino, and his footprint can reputedly be spotted on nearby rocks.

Trip plan: The Rhodopes spill along the Greek border in the south of Bulgaria; Plovdiv has the nearest airport (served by low-cost airlines). Accessible by bus from Plovdiv, the spa town of Devin is a good base for hikes; hire a car in Plovdiv to reach rural farmstays and guesthouses.

Need to know: The 3hr circuit around Devin's Struilitsa Ecotrail is a good starter hike, linking the mineral baths to medieval ruins in the hills. For longer walks, take a local guide – there are wolves and bears in the forests.

Other months: Dec-Feb – cool, dry, crowded; Mar-May & Oct-Nov – warmer, quieter; Jun-Sep – scorching.

GDAŃSK & HEL PENINSULA
POLAND

5-16 Why now? Perfect weather for Baltic beaches and city sights.

Facing the Baltic Sea, Gdańsk is a historic shipbuilding and trading city – Poland's most important seaport since the Middle Ages. Reconstructed after WWII, its centre evokes this long history, with ornate and colourful architecture along the Royal Way. Wander the old streets, take a boat tour for a scenic overview, and visit the interactive Hevelianum science centre and the expansive Park Ronalda Reagana for outdoor play. It's also an easy day trip (40 minutes by train) to the well-preserved 13th-century Malbork Castle, a vast historical playground for kids. You can hit the beach in Gdańsk or nearby Sopot (part of the Tri-City set-up, along with Gdańsk and Gdynia), or take a fun ferry across the Bay of Puck to the Hel Peninsula, a 35km (20-mile) spit of sand that's lined with wide and beautiful beaches. The ferry docks at the Baltic resort of Hel at the peninsula's tip, with an aquarium and seal sanctuary, a climbable lighthouse with incredible views from the top, and a picture-perfect, shop-lined main street. To escape Hel's beach crowds, take the train (or walk) to smaller Jastarnia.

Trip plan: Stay in Gdańsk for at least a day or two before heading out to Hel.

Need to know: Inside Gdańsk's Gothic Mariacka Basilica, a 15th-century astronomical clock displays the time, date, phase of the moon, zodiac sign and saint's day. Don't miss the daily 'procession' atop the clock at noon.

Other months: Oct-Apr – off season; May-Jun & Sep – shoulder season; Jul – peak season.

157

MAASAI MARA NATIONAL RESERVE KENYA

🐘 👢

5-16

Why now? Cross the savannah with a Maasai guide during the cool season.

The Great Migration from Serengeti National Park reaches Kenya's Maasai Mara National Reserve by August, and multitudinous wildebeest are just the start of the wildlife bonanza. The acacia-dotted plains can be explored by 4WD, on horseback, by hot-air balloon and – best of all – on foot with guides from the Maasai community, who are incredibly well-informed about the wildlife here. Kids usually love seeing the savannah through the eyes of its Indigenous Maasai residents, spotting edible and medicinal plants and myriad smaller critters – darting birds, dung beetles, mongooses, lizards, leopard tortoises – alongside the headline-catching Big Five (elephants, lions, leopards, rhinos and African buffalo). Stay in a tented camp where you might wake up to find elephants and antelopes strolling between the tents, and you'll have an adventure that your kids will be telling their kids about a few decades down the line.

Trip plan: Arrange a bespoke safari from Nairobi to one of the Maasai-owned wildlife conservancies flanking the Maasai Mara National Reserve – Mara North, Naboisho and Ol Kinyei are good for families. Agencies can put together a package with transfers, game drives, accommodation in semi-permanent tented camps, and walks with Maasai guides.

Need to know: Fees at conservancies are slightly lower than the fees for the National Reserve; kids aged nine to 17 pay half price, and under-eights are free.

Other months: Nov-May – warm and wet; Jun-Jul – drier and cooler; Sep-Oct – warmer, still quite dry.

Lounging lions in Maasai Mara National Reserve

CAÑÓN DEL COLCA
PERU

5-16 | **Why now?** Watch condors soaring over the Colca abyss.

Twice as deep as Arizona's Grand Canyon, Cañón del Colca is an enigmatic mountain valley, rich in culture, history and mystery. A family-friendly highlight is a dawn visit to Cruz del Cóndor viewpoint, opposite Nevado Mismi – an impressive peak towering 5597m (18,358ft) above the canyon – to observe humongous Andean condors emerging from their nearby nesting spot and soaring over the chasm. Kids of all ages can delight in the sight of these gigantic raptors, with a wingspan of around 3m (10ft), as they gracefully glide on thermals rising up the ravine walls; those same walls plunge dramatically to the Río Colca, over 1200m (4000ft) below. Members of the vulture family, Andean condors feature large in Inca culture and the folklore of the Colca's Indigenous people, as you'll learn in the excellent Museo Yanque. For more spectacular canyon views, visit Mirador de San Miguel in Cabanaconde; nearby Chivay romises alpaca encounters and stargazing at a planetarium, and everyone enjoys relaxing in volcano-warmed water in La Calera thermal pools, 4km (2.5 miles) from Chivay.

Trip plan: Chivay, gateway to the Cañón del Colca, is 163km (101 miles) from Arequipa, along roads offering views of volcanoes and vicuñas (a wild alpaca-like animal). The easiest way to visit is on organised trips from Arequipa.

Need to know: Take binoculars and arrive at viewpoints early so that kids can get a good position.

Other months: Dec-Mar – wet season, rain, poor visibility; Apr-Nov – dry season, busy.

VEGA ARCHIPELAGO
NORWAY

12-16 | **Why now?** The home of the duvet is packed with teen-friendly activities.

Teenagers are duvet-loving creatures, so they'll likely feel at home on remote Vega. For centuries, it was home to hardy fishers and their even hardier wives who stayed here, while their husbands went to sea, to farm and tend to the native eider ducks whose discarded down was sold as the world's finest duvet filling. This sustainable practice persists today, but this scenic archipelago of 6500 islands, islets and reefs is also a boon to active families keen to make the most of its hiking, kayaking, cycling and climbing potential, especially on the main island of Vega. And August is a great time to visit, as the summer crowds begin to wane. Highlights include kayaking around the inlets, and hiking the 2000-plus stairs of the Vegatrappa path, which runs from the beach to the top of Mt Ravnfloget and rewards with breathtaking coastline views. To up the adrenaline ante, try the Ravnfloget via ferrata, where you're clipped into iron cables fixed to the mountain; it includes a leg-trembling suspension-bridge section.

Trip plan: From Brønnøysund on the mainland (with daily flights from Oslo), get the ferry to Vega (40min).

Need to know: Hire touring ebikes (at Brønnøysund tourist office) for a fun way to navigate Vega's rolling hills. Stay at Base Camp Vega, at the foot Mt Ravnfloget, in wooden camping pods inspired by the traditional eider house design.

Other months: Jan-Apr – cold, wet; May-Jun & Sep – quieter, cooler; Jul – sunny, peak season; Oct-Dec – dark, cold.

WYOMING
USA

5-16 | **Why now?** Wild West shootouts and Native American dancing amid towering mountains and pristine wilderness.

No place has a more intriguing combination of Wild West scenery and culture than Big Wyoming, where the Great Plains meet the Rocky Mountains. Split your time between Yellowstone and Grand Teton National Parks for abundant wildlife and incredible displays of Mother Nature's grandeur, with a healthy dose of family adventure. Besides the obligatory stop at Old Faithful, there's sleeping under the stars and 'Old West' cookouts in Yellowstone; in Grand Teton, kids can boat and hike around the mountain lakes, with stunning scenery all around. When it's time to return to civilisation, head to Jackson Hole and Cody, with unique, family-friendly attractions that highlight local nature and history, including nightly (staged) gunfights – Western-style drama at its best. For a fascinating window into Native American culture, attend a powwow at Wind River Indian Reservation or catch one of the weekly performances by the Eagle Spirit Dancers, featuring drumming, singing and dance, with performers decked in elaborate ceremonial regalia.

Trip plan: Wyoming is a great place for a road trip. Make a circular loop north from Jackson Hole through the national parks, east to Cody and south to Riverton (via Thermopolis).

Need to know: Book national park lodgings and activities well in advance – preferably six months to a year ahead for stays in the summer months.

Other months: Oct-Apr– off-season, many roads and visitor centres close; May & Sep – shoulder season, lighter crowds, cooler; Jun-Jul – peak season, crowded, events.

CORAL COAST
FIJI

0-16 Why now? Lovely weather and minimal crowds.

'Bula!' ('hello' or 'welcome' in Fijian). August is a great time to hit the resorts of the Coral Coast in the southwest of Viti Levu, Fiji's main island. It's cooler, there's less rain and, as Kiwi and Aussie kids are in school, there are fewer families taking beach-break getaways. Despite the name, the Coral Coast doesn't offer the best snorkelling, but the beaches are decent and there are a host of well-set-up resorts – from full-on luxurious to budget and boutique – to keep everyone happy, most with swimming pools, family-friendly restaurants, kids' clubs and activities to entertain children. From Fiji's gateway airport in Nadi, Queens Rd snakes around the coast, and most resorts are reachable by road within 30 minutes to two hours. The region is peppered with small towns such as riverside Sigatoka (sing-a-to-ka), a commercial hub and a popular off-resort day trip for families, with a bustling produce market, supermarket and souvenir shops. Other day-trip options include taking a jetboat up the Sigatoka River; riding the rails of the defunct coastal railway on a solar-powered electric bike; or visiting the turtles and iguanas at Kula Wild Adventure Park.

Trip plan: Fly into Nadi International Airport and pre-arrange transfers to Coral Coast resorts. For a relaxing break, stay for a week.

Need to know: Local currency is the Fiji dollar; tipping is not expected.

Other months: Nov-Apr – hot and humid summer, southern hemisphere cyclone season; May-Oct – cooler and drier, busy high season.

ALICE SPRINGS
AUSTRALIA

5-16 Why now? Experience a unique dry-river boat race.

Held in mid-August, when Australia's Red Centre is at its bone driest, the Henley on Todd Regatta in Alice Springs (Mparntwe) is a boat race without water. Competing vessels – including bottomless kayaks, Oxford tubs, rowing eights and yachts, some made entirely from beer cans – remain completely dry as red-faced runners carry them Fred Flintstone-style (with frantically scurrying legs coming out the bottom) along the sandy bed of the Todd River, which usually only flows during the Wet season. (In 1993, the regatta was cancelled because surprise rainfall meant the river was running.) A high-spirited shindig with a carnival atmosphere, this idiosyncratic event is fun for all ages, with pirate galleys and other themed larger 'ships' wheeling around while firing water from canons during the Battle of the Gunboats, and all sorts of shenanigans going on during races. There's a BYO boat category and plenty more opportunities to get involved.

Trip plan: Fly to Alice from any large Australian city, drive the epic 2720km (1690-mile) Stuart Hwy, or catch a train from Adelaide or Darwin. While here, explore the Tjoritja/MacDonnell Ranges, learn about Indigenous Arrernte culture and visit the fascinating School of the Air to discover how Outback kids are educated.

Need to know: Bring warm clothes for the chilly evenings.

Other months: Dec-Feb – hot, humid; Mar-May – autumn, pleasant for hiking and biking; Jun-Jul – warm days, cool nights, busy; Sep-Nov – spring, warmer, rain.

SASKATCHEWAN
CANADA

0-16 Why now? The prairie dogs are yapping!

If ever there was a cute little critter to keep kids enthralled, it's the black-tailed prairie dog that inhabits Grasslands National Park in southwest Saskatchewan. These playful, social little animals, a favourite among visitors, spend the first two hours after sunrise foraging and eating, then chill out for the rest of the day dustbathing, grooming, stretching and socialising. Prairie dogs greet each other with a nose-touch 'kiss' and warn of the presence of humans from atop their burrow with a comical yap. You'll see (and hear!) plenty of them in the prairie landscape around the 20km (12-mile) Ecotour Scenic Drive, about 15km (9 miles) east of the national park Visitor Centre at Val Marie. At the other end of the animal-size scale, you may even spot plains bison, symbolic of the prairies, reintroduced after 120 years of absence in 2005. Bison roam free in the park, so keep your eyes open. For a mind-boggler for kids, drive 120km (75 miles) west to Eastend and its T-Rex Discovery Centre, home of Scotty; discovered nearby in 1991, this intact, 65-million-year-old T-Rex skeleton is a whopping 4m (13ft) tall and 12m (40ft) long, and is the largest ever found.

Trip plan: Val Marie is a 3hr 30min drive from Saskatchewan's capital, Regina.

Need to know: Regina's Royal Saskatchewan Museum displays a full-scale replica of T-Rex Scotty.

Other months: Nov-Apr – winter trail and road conditions, no National Park services; May-Oct – Grasslands' Val Marie Visitor Centre and campgrounds are open.

161

(A) Traditional dance in Leh, Ladakh;
(L) Puffins on the Heimaey coast;
(R) Liseburg thrills in Gothenburg

© Lab Photo / Shutterstock

LADAKH
INDIA

12-16 Why now? Hit the high Himalaya when the weather is warm.

It takes weeks of strenuous trekking to reach some corners of the Himalayas, but not lovely Ladakh. Direct flights from Delhi and Mumbai drop into Leh, the mountain-ringed capital of this former Buddhist kingdom, avoiding the bone-shaking two-day trip by road. Using Leh as a base, families can ease straight into the Ladakhi way of life with gentle walks to medieval monasteries, towering stupas and mountain viewpoints, as well as dipping their toes in the diamond-clear waters of the Indus River. Stay in a traditional stone and mud-brick guesthouse with a garden or rooftop terrace – they're colourful, cosy and comfortable, and pizzas, pasta and rice dishes are easy to find for low-stress family meals. Keep teens engaged with longer hikes into the arid mountains around Leh, or rafting trips on the Indus.

Trip plan: Leh gets busy in summer, so book flights and accommodation ahead. Take younger kids on gentle excursions to the Shanti and Gomang Stupas, the hike up to Leh Palace and the glorious monastery at Thiksey, where you can sit in on daily prayer ceremonies and watch monks make sand mandalas and butter sculptures.

Need to know: Leh sits at an altitude of 3520m (11,615ft); to reduce the risk of mountain sickness, keep kids hydrated and avoid being too active for the first few days.

Other months: Nov-Mar – cold and quiet, roads close, flights continue; May-Oct – warmer and busier, road passes open.

GOTHENBURG
SWEDEN

0-16 Why now? Get wet without leaving the city in the balmy Swedish summer.

Stockholm and Lapland draw the summer crowds, but things are a little calmer in Gothenburg (Göteborg), Sweden's affable second city. During the short but sweet Scandinavian summer, this historic port gets plenty of sunshine and everyone heads for the parks and the water. For families, the 100-year-old Liseberg fairground is a great place to start, with an impressive clutch of coasters, flumes and rides, as well as carousels, fairy-tale castles, adventure playgrounds and shows and concerts that should thrill everyone from giddy toddlers to teenage adrenaline junkies. For watery fun in the centre, head to Jubileumsparken, with swimming pools, playgrounds and a sauna spilling into a revamped section of the harbour. Half a dozen museums will fill cooler days, while warmer days invite forays inland to castles and forts, and boat trips around the city's fringing archipelago.

Trip plan: Flights run to Gothenburg from most European hubs, or you can take the train or ferry from Denmark. Stay downtown – plenty of Airbnbs offer more space than hotels – and explore by bus, tram or rented bike, or hire a car for easy day trips.

Need to know: Foraging is a legal right in Sweden, and August is the start of berry season; Vättlefjäll Nature Reserve, about 13km (8 miles) northeast of Gothenburg, is perfect for blueberry-fuelled forest walks.

Other months: Dec-Feb – cold and dark, brightened by twinkling lights; Mar-May & Sep-Nov – cooler, spring growth and autumn colour; Jun-Jul – long warm days and crayfish parties.

HEIMAEY ISLAND
ICELAND

5-16 Why now? See puffins take flight from a volcanic island.

Volcanoes and Vikings, hot springs and hotdogs – Iceland is a blast for kids at any age, but late August is particularly good for younger travellers. Heimaey in the Vestmannaeyjar (Westman Islands) is home to the world's largest puffin colony, and the beginning of autumn is the time for one of Iceland's loveliest traditions. Every year, as the days shorten in August, hundreds of puffin chicks emerge from their burrows in the cliffs, but many are lured towards town by the bright lights, so locals form evening 'puffin patrols' to gather up lost pufflings and release them safely from the sea cliffs near the island's tiny airstrip – and visiting families can pitch in to help. Puffins collected, extend the trip with visits to cute museums, clifftop hikes, boat trips and detours to hidden waterfalls and buildings toppled by lava flows from the Eldfell volcano.

Trip plan: Reach Heimaey on the Herjólfur car ferry; services leave daily from the port of Landeyjahöfn, a 130km (80-mile) drive southeast of Reykjavík. Include a trip to Vestmannaeyjar on a road trip along Iceland's south coast, visiting the cave-backed Seljalandsfoss and Skógafoss waterfalls, the black volcanic sands at Vík and iceberg-filled Jökulsárlón lake.

Need to know: Prime the kids for Heimaey by reading Bruce McMillan's *Nights of the Pufflings*. Bring gloves and seek local advice on the best practice for rescuing pufflings safely.

Other months: Nov-Apr – dark, icy cold; May-Sep – milder, plentiful puffins, bright summer nights.

CAPE COD USA

Sailing past Long
Point Lighthouse,
Cape Cod

0-16 | **Why now?** Classic Cape Cod summer, with beach-hopping, bike riding and drive-in movies.

Long days at the beach, beachcombing and wave-jumping; riding bikes through dunes and marshland; afternoon breaks for ice-cream and lemonade; evenings at the drive-in movie theatre. This may sound like a scene from another century, but that's still how summer goes on Cape Cod – this long, hooked arm of Massachusetts is packed with old-fashioned fun. More than 100 beaches face the calm waters of Cape Cod Bay or the wild Atlantic. This includes the Cape Cod National Seashore, a magnificent 64km (40-mile) stretch of oceanfront land – beach, dunes, marsh and forest – in the outermost section of the Cape. All along this coastline, there are waves to catch, trails to hike (and bike),

lighthouses to climb and seafood to scarf. By night, you can take the family to see a flick at the classic Wellfleet Drive-In, dating from 1957. Top it off with a cone from the dairy bar, and your kids will understand what you mean by the 'good ol' days'.

Trip plan: Summer traffic on the Cape can be a nightmare. Instead of driving to attractions in distant towns, choose your homebase and enjoy the beaches, trails and restaurants nearby.

Need to know: Cape Cod's shark population has exploded in recent years. Watch for warning signs on the beach, and don't swim if you see seals or schools of fish in the water.

Other months: Nov-Mar – winter, many tourist-oriented businesses close; Apr-Jun & Sep-Oct – shoulder season, cooler, lower prices; Jul – peak season, hot, humid.

Sunrise over Uluru
and Kata Tjuṯa

NORTHERN TERRITORY
AUSTRALIA

0–16 Why now? Fine weather and cooler temperatures.

The Northern Territory certainly packs a wallop when it comes to an excitingly wild family adventure. Gateway to the Top End, Darwin is Australia's only tropical capital, and its coolest attraction for kids is its massive waterfront wave lagoon, with 10 different wave patterns perfect for boogie-boarders, and a shallow-water play area for younger children. The city's Crocosaurus Cove is home to the world's largest display of Australian reptiles, including the iconic 'saltie' (saltwater crocodile). Alice Springs won't win any beauty contests, but it's the perfect base for exploring some of central Australia's most stirring landscapes, and the 100-plus species at the Alice Springs Reptile Centre run from thorny devils to bearded dragons. Northern Territory has two UNESCO-listed national parks: Kakadu is Australia's largest national park; Uluṟu-Kata Tjuṯa is home to the world-famous Uluṟu (Ayers Rock) and 36 fascinating weathered rock domes known as Kata Tjuṯa (the Olgas). And the region has more than 50 other national parks and reserves to explore: enjoy a cave tour at Cutta Cutta Caves Nature Park, then a soak in the natural thermal waters of Katherine Hot Springs, on the banks of the Katherine River.

Trip plan: Fly into Darwin International Airport or Alice Springs, and pick up a rental car for a week or more.

Need to know: There are some big distances out here – it's 1500km (932 miles) from Darwin to Alice Springs.

Other months: Dec-Mar – monsoonal rains, fewer visitors; Apr-Sep – dry, milder temperatures; Oct-Nov – humid, heavy rains possible.

© marcobrivio.photography / Shutterstock /

(A) Coastline at Gjógv, Faroe Islands; (L) Marburg's 'Cinderella' castle, Germany; (R) Osaka's Naniwa Yodogawa Fireworks Festival, Japan

FAROE ISLANDS

 0-16 Why now? Fresh air, wildlife and outdoor fun in the best of the weather.

With mythical sea stacks, black-sand beaches and roads jammed with fuzzy sheep, the Faroes – a string of jagged volcanic islands rearing up out of the Atlantic – are the kind of place where it feels like magic can happen. There's space and freedom here for children to roam, with local stories and legends adding fuel to the imaginative fire. Little ones can make black-sand castles at broad Tjørnuvik beach, popular with local families; teens can take to the waves and surf in view of the epic sea stacks known as Risin og Kellingin (the 'Giant and the Witch'). With their seemingly hand-drawn proportions, bright beaks and comical hop, puffins are a major highlight, but they aren't year-round Faroes residents; in August, you'll catch them before tours end for the season. Book a wind-whipped boat trip to Mykines Island and visit their nest sites on white-streaked sea cliffs, also home to raucous colonies of guillemots, gannets, kittiwakes and other seabirds. And get a window into daily life by dining out at a heimabliðni, a relaxed, supper-club-style restaurant in a farm or family home. This is Faroese hospitality at its finest, and offers the opportunity to chat with your local hosts.

Trip plan: Fly to the Faroes' only international airport, Vágar, then hire a car.

Need to know: Weather changes rapidly here, so a flexible schedule is best in case ferry or helicopter departures are delayed.

Other months: Oct-Apr – colder, wetter, many facilities closed; Jun-Jul & Sep – warm, drier, long days.

JAPAN

0-16 Why now? Summer festival and fireworks season.

For a family cultural experience, time a trip to Japan to coincide with Obon, the annual Buddhist festival for commemorating ancestors, whose spirits are believed to temporarily return to this world to visit their relatives in mid-August. While many Japanese travel to their ancestral homes to honour their forebears, it's also a time of street parties. The island of Shikoku comes alive with Kōchi City's exhilarating Yosakoi festival, followed by Japan's largest and most famous bon dance, the Awa-odori, in Tokushima City. At the mountaintop monastery complex of Kōya-san, enjoy the atmospheric Rōsoku Matsuri (Candle Festival), with some 100,000 candles lit on 13 August. Kyoto celebrates the end of Obon with Gozan Okuribi, massive bonfires on five mountains around the city, lit to send ancestors back to the spirit world; floating lanterns are put into rivers, lakes and seas around Japan for the same purpose. While Tokyo's massive Sumida-gawa Fireworks Festival is on the last Saturday in July, Osaka's Naniwa Yodogawa Fireworks Festival is in early August, and there are huge hanabi (fireworks) displays throughout the country this month – families with a passion for pyrotechnics can plot a route based on the best of these booming, whizzing extravaganzas.

Trip plan: Book accommodation well in advance, perhaps in a nearby town or city.

Need to know: August is hot and humid; expect big crowds at festivals and during Obon week.

Other months: Jan-Feb – winter festivals; Apr – cherry-blossom viewing; Oct – harvest festivals.

FAIRY-TALE ROAD
GERMANY

0-16 Why now? Follow the Fairy-Tale Road through Germany's lesser visited interior in the glow of summer.

The kitschly-named Fairy-Tale Road (Märchenstrasse) isn't actually a single road; instead, it's a collection of sites all linked by association (allegedly) with the works of Grimm brothers Jakob (1785–1863) and Wilhelm (1786–1859). Made up of cities, towns and hamlets in four states (Hesse, Lower Saxony, North Rhine-Westphalia and Bremen), the 600km (373-mile) route takes you into Germany's pastoral centre, through old-growth forests and into picture-book villages of half-timbered houses. The original dark, sometimes frightening Grimm fables have since been sprinkled with Disney fairy dust, but the route's forests – the muse to the deep dark woods, home of wolves in grandma's clothing and poisoned apples – make for a beautifully atmospheric wander. While younger family members may miss half the references on display, they'll likely get a kick out of touches like Rapunzel's 'hair' hanging over a balcony in Trendelburg; the 685-year-old 'Sleeping Beauty' castle in Sababurg; 'Cinderella's' castle in Marburg (complete with giant glass slipper); and the weekly rat musical in the town of Hamelin.

Trip plan: The route begins in Hanau, passing through over 50 places celebrating the brothers and their fairy tales all the way to Bremen. Plan on at least four days.

Need to know: The calendar of summer events includes shows, installations and special trails for children; check the website (deutsche-maerchenstrasse.com).

Other months: Jan-Mar – cold, dark; Apr-Jun – warmer, flowers; Jul – peak season starts; Sep-Oct – golden leaves, quieter; Nov-Dec – Christmas markets.

September

WHERE TO GO WHEN WITH KIDS

HAVE AN ADVENTURE

We want to...

TAKE US OUT FOR...

SPECIAL TREATS AND MEMORABLE FEASTS

- DOLE PLANTATION, HAWAI'I P179
- İSTANBUL, TÜRKIYE P186

Stock up on treats like *lokum* (Turkish delight) and nougat at İstanbul's marvellous markets

Take a river cruise under Ljubljana's Dragon Bridge, then hit the city's interactive museums

TAKE US...

OUTDOORS

FOR SOME KID-FRIENDLY FUN
- LJUBLJANA & UPPER CARNIOLA, SLOVENIA P181
- DALMATIAN COAST, CROATIA P175

TO GO HIKING OR BIKING
- TRAIL OF THE EAGLES' NESTS, POLAND P176
- BOHUSLÄN COAST, SWEDEN P179

TO A FESTIVAL
- OSAKA, JAPAN P181
- TUSCANY, ITALY P180

CHILL OUT/ HEAD OUT

Try local snacks like courgette fritters on a ferry-hopping Greek Islands tour

Explore medieval cities and the island-speckled Adriatic along the Dalmatian Coast

Meet wild donkeys and swim at blissful beaches on Aruba, Bonaire and Curaçao

TAKE US TO THE BEACH

TO BUILD SANDCASTLES AND SWIM
- LIDO DI JESOLO, ITALY P176
- GREEK ISLANDS P182

TO SNORKEL OR SURF
- ARUBA, BONAIRE & CURAÇAO P187

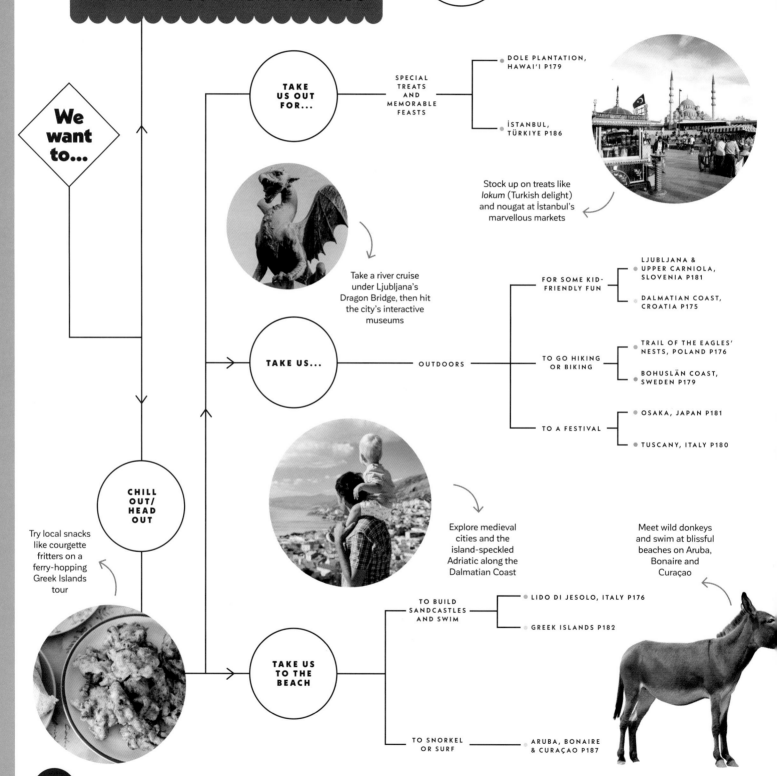

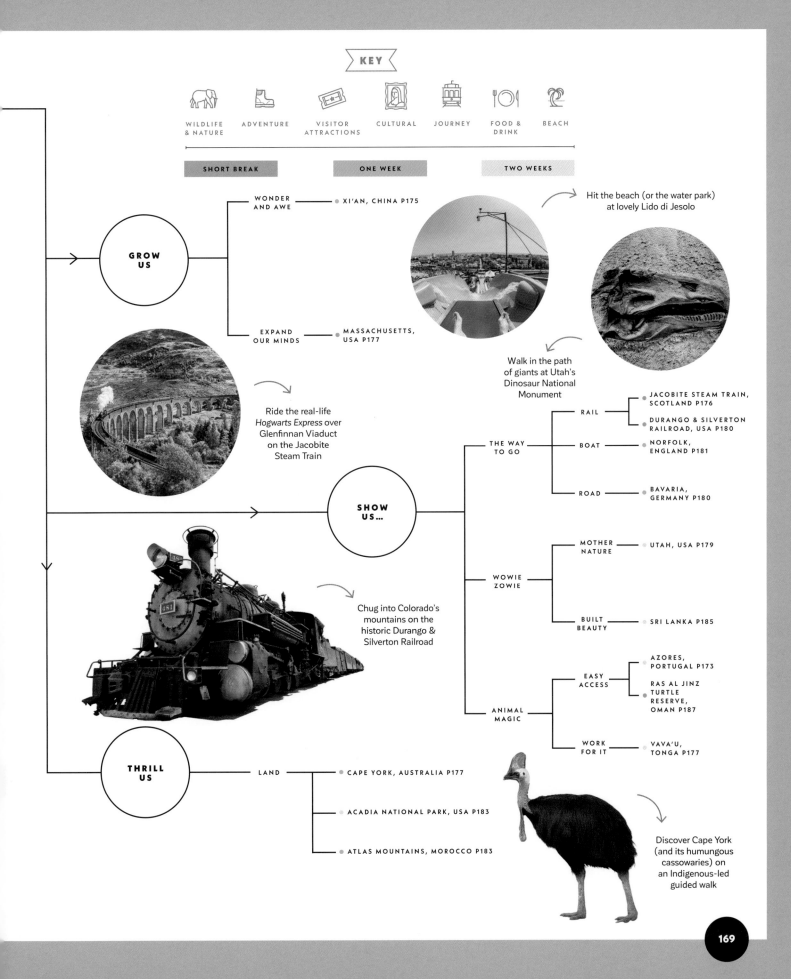

KEY

WILDLIFE & NATURE ADVENTURE VISITOR ATTRACTIONS CULTURAL JOURNEY FOOD & DRINK BEACH

SHORT BREAK ONE WEEK TWO WEEKS

GROW US

WONDER AND AWE —— ● XI'AN, CHINA P175

EXPAND OUR MINDS —— ● MASSACHUSETTS, USA P177

Hit the beach (or the water park) at lovely Lido di Jesolo

Walk in the path of giants at Utah's Dinosaur National Monument

Ride the real-life *Hogwarts Express* over Glenfinnan Viaduct on the Jacobite Steam Train

SHOW US...

THE WAY TO GO

RAIL —— ● JACOBITE STEAM TRAIN, SCOTLAND P176
—— ● DURANGO & SILVERTON RAILROAD, USA P180

BOAT —— ● NORFOLK, ENGLAND P181

ROAD —— ● BAVARIA, GERMANY P180

WOWIE ZOWIE

MOTHER NATURE —— ● UTAH, USA P179

BUILT BEAUTY —— ● SRI LANKA P185

ANIMAL MAGIC

EASY ACCESS —— ● AZORES, PORTUGAL P173
—— ● RAS AL JINZ TURTLE RESERVE, OMAN P187

WORK FOR IT —— ● VAVA'U, TONGA P177

Chug into Colorado's mountains on the historic Durango & Silverton Railroad

THRILL US

LAND —— ● CAPE YORK, AUSTRALIA P177

—— ● ACADIA NATIONAL PARK, USA P183

—— ● ATLAS MOUNTAINS, MOROCCO P183

Discover Cape York (and its humungous cassowaries) on an Indigenous-led guided walk

Events in September

ALOHA FESTIVALS
O'ahu, Hawai'i
Garlands, ukuleles and grass skirts are very much in evidence in this family-focused cultural celebration, culminating with a monster street party.

BRAEMAR GATHERING
Aberdeenshire, Scotland
A historic celebration of all things Caledonian – kids will be awestruck by the caber tossing and tug-of-war bouts between burly Scots.

VENDEMMIA
Tuscany, Italy
Tuscany's grape harvest is always an excuse for a party, and the whole family can kick off shoes and join in the juicing.

CHUSEOK
Seoul, Korea
A focus on treats like tasty rice-based hangwa will keep children sweet at Korea's autumn harvest festival – look out for promotions at Seoul theme parks.

MIDDELEEUWS TER APEL
Ter Apel, Netherlands
The year 1465 comes vividly to life at this celebration of all things medieval, with duelling knights in armour and fairground games.

BURNING MAN
Black Rock City, Nevada, USA
Artistic expression and community spirit are key to this famous countercultural celebration in the Nevada desert, with plenty of kid-focused fun.

REGATA STORICA
Venice, Italy
Families flock to the floating city to watch competitive boatmen in traditional dress racing gondolas along the Grand Canal.

HERMANUS WHALE FESTIVAL
Hermanus, South Africa
Returning southern right whales are welcomed with festive fun: music, kids' events, a parade of vintage cars and lots of whale-watching.

Inner ring labels:
- All month — $$
- First Saturday of September — $$
- All month — $$
- Late September or early October — $$
- 7–8 September — $$
- Late August to early September — $$
- First Sunday in September — $$$
- Late September — $$

● RAS AL JINZ TURTLE
RESERVE, OMAN

Support tiny turtles
as they race to the
sea in Oman

It's harvest time
in Tuscany, Italy

● MASSACHUSETTS, USA

● DOLE PLANTATION,
HAWAI'I

● LIDO DI JESOLO,
ITALY

Relax on the
waterways of the
Norfolk Broads in
England

● NORFOLK, ENGLAND

Start early in the
morning if you wish
to scale Sigiriya in
Sri Lanka

● SRI LANKA

● DURANGO &
SILVERTON
RAILROAD, USA

● DALMATIAN COAST, CROATIA

● AZORES, PORTUGAL

● JACOBITE STEAM TRAIN,
SCOTLAND

Sample different
fillings for your
okonomiyaki
(pancake) in Osaka

● OSAKA, JAPAN

● TUSCANY, ITALY

Pick up a
pineapple at the
Dole Plantation

● XI'AN, CHINA

● ACADIA NATIONAL PARK, USA

● UTAH, USA

● CAPE YORK, AUSTRALIA

Be served traditional
bush tucker in Cape York,
Australia

Go canoeing on the
rivers and lakes of
Bavaria, Germany

● ARUBA, BONAIRE
& CURAÇAO

● BAVARIA, GERMANY

● LJUBLJANA &
UPPER CARNIOLA,
SLOVENIA

● VAVA'U, TONGA

Snorkels are
essential for
Aruba, Bonaire
& Curaçao

● İSTANBUL, TÜRKIYE

Pack hiking boots
for exploring Acadia
National Park

● GREEK ISLANDS

● TRAIL OF THE EAGLES' NESTS,
POLAND

The Terracotta Army was
buried with Emperor Qin
Shi Huang Di in Xi'an

Viewing the
Telouet Kasbah
in Morocco's
High Atlas

● BOHUSLÄN COAST, SWEDEN

● ATLAS MOUNTAINS, MOROCCO

AZORES PORTUGAL

5-16 **Why now?** Time your trip to see dolphins congregating off the Azores' wave-lapped shores.

The islands of the Azores were thrust up from the North Atlantic by submerged volcanoes, and the ocean on all sides provides a deep-water haven for numerous cetaceans, including common, bottlenose, striped and Risso's dolphins. On a late summer break to São Miguel – the largest of the Azores – dolphin-spotting boat tours will take you within splashing distance of megapods comprising hundreds of individuals. Kids will be thrilled at the sight of young calves being tutored by their peers before heading out to deeper waters. On land, there are volcanoes to climb, lighthouses to hike to and historic towns to explore, in between unwinding on clean, quiet beaches and kayaking on volcanic lakes and lagoons. Travellers of all ages will get a buzz from splashing about in the Caldeira Vehla natural hot springs and waterfall; kids 14 or under pay half-price, those under six go free.

Trip plan: Ponta Delgada-João Paulo II Airport on São Miguel island is the gateway to the Azores, with regular flights from mainland Portugal and European, US and Canadian hubs. Ferries and flights connect São Miguel to the rest of the archipelago; top stops for families include history-rich Terceira, volcano-topped Pico and beachy Santa Maria.

Need to know: Dolphins aren't the only cetaceans to visit the Azores – sperm whales can be seen year-round, and blue, fin and sei whales migrate through the archipelago in spring.

Other months: Nov-Feb – cooler, rainy; Mar-May & Jul-Oct – mild, quieter, good for hiking; Jun-Aug – warm, dolphin season.

(L) Striped dolphin pod in the Azores' waters; (R) Sete Cidades scenery, São Miguel

Summer scene in Hvar Harbour, Croatia

DALMATIAN COAST
CROATIA

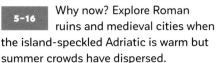

5-16 **Why now?** Explore Roman ruins and medieval cities when the island-speckled Adriatic is warm but summer crowds have dispersed.

The Dalmatian Coast has lots to capture the imaginations of curious kids – and ferry-hopping between the historic cities of Split and Dubrovnik and out to offshore islands delivers a fabulous maritime adventure. Split grew up around the ancient palace of the Roman emperor Diocletian, and its streets and courtyards now bustle with shops and restaurants – get lost among narrow alleyways and explore arcaded basements. Further south, Dubrovnik is the jewel of the coast, its mighty walls and drawbridge entrance straight out of a fairy tale; take a walk along the city walls for views over the terracotta rooftops. Between the two cities, there's a sea of enticing islands to discover. Korčula is a favourite for its eponymous walled city, smaller but no less evocative than Dubrovnik. Hvar and Brač are popular for their inviting Adriatic beaches and easy access. Or, take a longer cruise to the outermost island of Vis, a quieter spot with hidden coves, pebbly beaches and hillside hikes.

Trip plan: Ferries travel between Split and Dubrovnik, stopping at Korčula, Hvar and Brač on the way. Vis is accessible by ferry from Split only.

Need to know: Beware of the summer crush, especially in Dubrovnik. Here and in Split, swerve cruise-ship crowds by exploring in the early morning and late afternoon.

Other months: Oct-Apr – winter, low season, fewer ferries; May – shoulder season, quieter; Jun-Aug – high season, hot, crowded.

Xi'an's iconic
Terracotta Army

XI'AN CHINA

5-16 **Why now?** Late summer means cooler temperatures when visiting the Terracotta Army.

China's terracotta warriors need no introduction, but perhaps they deserve one – each of these 8000-plus pottery soldiers is different, down to their facial features, expressions and hairstyles. The three huge pits containing the clay army are just one part of a vast necropolis spanning 98 sq km (38 sq miles), centred on the unexcavated tomb of Qin Shi Huang, first emperor of China. Introduce kids to this ready-to-go school project in September, as the summer heat fades and tourist numbers start to thin. The terracotta warriors are just an hour by bus from cosmopolitan Xi'an, where kids can haggle for trinkets in colourful Muslim Quarter markets, explore Ming Dynasty watchtowers, climb the evocatively named Big Wild Goose Pagoda and cycle around the medieval city walls (tandem bikes make the trip easy for families).

Trip plan: Flights land in Xi'an from across Asia, with connections to Europe, Australia and America through Beijing, Shanghai, Singapore, Bangkok and other hubs. Three to four days will give you time to explore at an easy pace before you head on by train to other parts of China.

Need to know: If you visit Huashan Mountain near Xi'an with kids, skip the precarious hike and ride the cable-car to the viewpoints atop the west and north peaks.

Other months: Dec-Feb – icy cold, but dry; Mar-May & Oct-Nov – mild, quieter, some rain; Jun-Aug – hot and humid, often uncomfortably so.

LIDO DI JESOLO
ITALY

5-16 **Why now?** Jesolo's summer season goes out on a high.

When Italians think of summer holidays around the Venetian Lagoon, they look north of Venice. With 15km (9.3 miles) of clean, well-looked-after beaches, sparkling Blue Flag waters and a plethora of shops and places to eat, the exemplary resort of Lido di Jesolo has a special place in the country's affections – and a family visit in the quieter tail-end of the summer means you can enjoy the atmosphere before everything shuts up for the season. Jesolo is situated at the north end of the peninsula that separates the lagoon from the sea; on its lagoon-side coast, the cool, green pine forests invite bike rides and shady walks, and the water is perfect for kayaking and sailing. The beach side, with its candy-striped parasols and sunbeds, has everything you need for a relaxed seaside day, with surfing and paddleboarding providing some active pep for older kids. After the sun has set, the *movida* (local 'scene') hots up on Jesolo's main boulevard, Via Bafile, as young Italian holidaymakers congregate in their finery before heading out for the night.

Trip plan: Roads can get busy and parking is limited. Transport options from Venice include buses, trains and ferries.

Need to know: It's wise to book Jesolo accommodation ahead. The beach is divided into *stabilimenti*, each with their own rows of distinctive-coloured parasols, which you'll need to rent.

Other months: Nov-Mar – quiet promenade walks; Apr-May – warming up; Jun-Jul – sandcastle competitions; Aug – busy, fireworks and an airshow; Oct – warm.

© Nahlik / Shutterstock

TRAIL OF THE EAGLES' NESTS
POLAND

5-16 **Why now?** Hike past fairy-tale castles and rural villages in the cool calm of autumn.

Running between Częstochowa and Kraków in southwest Poland, the Trail of the Eagles' Nests (Szlak Orlich Gniazd) is a rambling, rocky 163km (101-mile) hiking – or biking – route connecting about a dozen medieval castles and castle ruins, constructed at the behest of Kazimierz the Great to protect the then-southern border of Poland from the advances of the King of Bohemia. Most are in ruins today, but a few (Będzin, Bobolice, Ogrodzieniec, Ojców) have been restored and are open to explore. Romantic and mysterious, the age-old structures sit atop the limestone cliffs of the Polish Jura highlands, like eagles' nests high up in the trees. Traversing scenic landscapes and picturesque villages, the trail delivers a unique and rewarding multiday hike or bike ride (of course you're not obliged complete it all). Two fortresses anchor either end of the route: the fortified Jasna Góra monastery in Częstochowa, and the majestic Wawel Royal Castle in Kraków.

Trip plan: There are plenty of hotels and guesthouses in towns and villages along the way, in addition to camping. The trail's website (orlegniazda.pl) has route info.

Need to know: Download a route map from Mapa Turystyczna (mapa-turystyczna. pl). The trail is generally well-marked and is mostly easy-going; there's a separate (slightly longer) gravel-bike trail. It's also possible to drive to most of the castles.

Other months: Nov-Apr – winter, muddy trails; May-Jun & Oct – cool, no crowds; Jul-Aug – hot, trail busier.

JACOBITE STEAM TRAIN
SCOTLAND

5-16 **Why now?** Take a magical steam-train journey into the Scottish Highlands.

Generations of children have gawped at cinema screens, spellbound, as the *Hogwarts Express* puffs across the arches of a vast viaduct, transporting Harry, Hermione, Ron and their wand-wielding classmates to the school of witchcraft and wizardry – but did you know that the steam train and bridge featured in the *Harry Potter* films is real? And you can catch it. But don't wait at Platform 9¾ in London's King's Cross Station (where a luggage trolley is embedded in the wall and a shop sells official merch). Catch the Jacobite Steam Train at Fort William (beneath Ben Nevis, Britain's highest mountain) for the 67km (82-mile) journey to Mallaig, passing monstrous lochs, soaring highland peaks, wild stag-stalked moorland and – of course – the photogenic Glenfinnan Viaduct, which hops across the River Finnan via 21 elegant arches, sending the train around a 300m (1000ft) arc, 30m (100ft) high in the sky.

Trip plan: JK Rowling wrote the *Harry Potter* books in Edinburgh, and scenes from the films were shot across Scotland. Explore Glen Coe to find the location of Hagrid's hut, and look for reflections of Hogwarts Lake in deep Loch Morar, near Mallaig.

Need to know: The steam service runs every morning from late March to late October, with an extra afternoon service between May and September. You can travel one-way, but all fares are priced as return trips. Tickets sell out fast; plan ahead and book online.

Other months: Oct-Apr – wild winter weather, diesel trains run on the line.

MASSACHUSETTS
USA

0-12 **Why now?** Mild autumn weather, early-turning leaves and outdoor art.

DeCordova Sculpture Park, around 25km (15 miles) northwest of Boston, is an ideal art venue for little people with busy minds and active bodies – its contemporary, three-dimensional pieces are oversized and extravagant, demanding attention and (often) interaction. Some 60 sculptures are scattered about 12 hectares (60 acres) of fields and forests, with plenty of room to run and skip, hide and seek, wiggle and wander. A scavenger hunt gives kids specific things to look for, and favourite installations include Jim Dine's *Two Big Black Hearts*, which are indeed two big 3.6m-high (12ft) black (bronze) hearts, covered with handprints. Made from mirrored glass, Dan Graham's *Crazy Spheroid* invites kids to play with distorted reflections of themselves and their surroundings. After the art, it's a short drive to Walden Pond for sandcastle-building, minnow-catching and walking the 2.4km (1.5-mile) trail circling the pond. About 11km (7 miles) west in Acton, the smallish Discovery Museum is another terrific destination for curious kids; its indoor and outdoor exhibits offer countless opportunities to play, pretend, experiment, engage and learn. All three venues get packed in summer, but once school is in session, your kids might have the places to themselves.

Trip plan: Concord has a decent selection of lodgings and easy access to Walden Pond and both museums (though you'll need a car).

Need to know: Book in advance for DeCordova and the Discovery Museum.

Other months: Nov-Mar – cold, wet, shorter museum hours; Apr-Jun – showers, spring flowers; Jul-Oct – clear skies, higher prices.

CAPE YORK
AUSTRALIA

5-16 **Why now?** Meet the original rainforest people, try bush tucker and go jungle surfing.

With roots burrowing back 180 million years, the trees and vines of Daintree National Park in Far North Queensland are part of the planet's most ancient rainforest. And September – well into the Dry season – is the best time to meet representatives of the Kuku Yalanji people, who share their culture (one of the world's oldest) with visitors. From magical Mossman Gorge, join an Indigenous guide for a fascinating forest tour, learning how plants have been used for food and medicine for millennia, with life-sustaining knowledge passed down countless generations over 50,000 years. Sample seasonal bush tucker (witchetty grubs will either delight or horrify), hear all about the forest's animals, including cassowaries (ferocious human-sized roosters) and crocodiles, then cool off in croc-free freshwater streams and let the kids try throwing spears and boomerangs. Looking for an extra buzz? Try 'jungle surfing' and go zooming through the tropical canopy on a zipwire, skimming between high treetop platforms.

Trip plan: Fly into Cairns; join a trip there or hire a car and drive 77km (48 miles) along beautiful beach-lined Captain Cook Hwy to Mossman, exploring Palm Cove and Port Douglas en route. With extra time, continue to Cape Tribulation.

Need to know: Look for 100% Aboriginal-owned and operated tours.

Other months: Nov-Apr – the Wet (humid, less visitors, better waterfalls); May-Oct – the Dry (perfect for hiking and beaches).

VAVA'U
TONGA

5-16 **Why now?** Spot (and swim with) humpback whales at the peak of the migration season.

Shaped like a giant jellyfish with tentacles dangling south, Vava'u (va-va-ooh) is picturesque at every turn. Those tentacles are made up of spectacular islands, 61 in all, intertwined with turquoise waterways and encircling reefs that have created one of the planet's most popular sheltered cruising grounds for yachts, and a perfect place to take your family for an unforgettable whale of a time. Vava'u is an important breeding ground for humpback whales, which migrate to its warm waters between June and October. This is the ideal spot to swim with these gentle giants, watching them raise their young in the calm, reef-protected waters, and maybe witness their elaborate mating rituals – male humpbacks sing during courtship routines, their songs carrying up to 100km (62 miles) through the open ocean. Predictable migration habits that once made them easy prey for whalers now make them easy finds for whale-watchers. There are a number of good, licensed whale-watch-and-swim operators on Vava'u, plus decent places to stay and eat in the main town of Neiafu, overlooking the picturesque harbour of Port of Refuge. Small-island adventures, beaches, snorkelling and watersports abound here.

Trip plan: Fly to Vava'u from Tonga's main island and entry point, Tongatapu.

Need to know: There are strict regulations to protect the whales. Don't pressure operators to 'chase' whales to keep customers happy.

Other months: Nov-Mar – hot, humid; Jun-Oct – whale season.

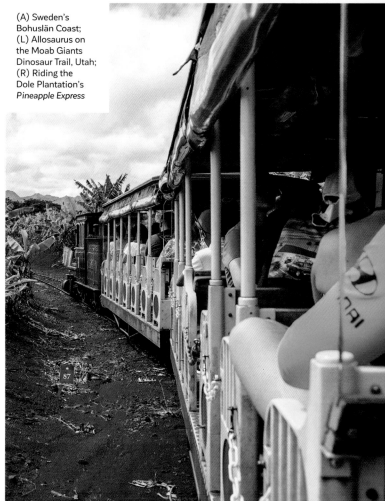

(A) Sweden's Bohuslän Coast;
(L) Allosaurus on the Moab Giants Dinosaur Trail, Utah;
(R) Riding the Dole Plantation's *Pineapple Express*

BOHUSLÄN COAST
SWEDEN

12-16 **Why now?** Hike or run along trails with dramatic, photogenic backdrops.

If you want to entice teens off their screens and out into nature, the smooth, pink-granite rocks and dazzling coastal backdrop at Ramsvik, on western Sweden's magical Bohuslän Coast, is a great place to start. This is partly for its unique geology and ethereal charm, but also because it presents many a photo opportunity, which your kids can then share with their friends when they're next online. Scenic hiking trails (coastal, forest, boulder-strewn) crisscross the 8000 islands of this extensive archipelago – some large enough to house major settlements, others barely big enough for a cormorant to perch on. And September is a lovely time to visit as the Swedish schools will already be back, adding to the tranquillity. Plus, the sea is at its warmest (though still fresh!) for post-walk dips.

Trip plan: Hike from a base at Ramsvik Stugby & Camping or, for more of a challenge, sign up for the early-September Icebug Xperience West Coast Trail event. Participants complete 77km (48 miles) over three days, either hiking, trail-running or a mix of the two, with the emphasis very much on enjoying the scenery and experience as opposed to racing.

Need to know: Children under 15 are allowed to enter the Icebug Xperience if they're accompanied by an adult, and lots of sporty Scandi families take part. There is also a kids' camp for younger children, which includes sailing, crab fishing and mini hikes.

Other months: Nov-Apr – cold; May & Oct – pleasant, quiet; Jun-Aug – sunny, busy.

DOLE PLANTATION
HAWAI'I

0-16 **Why now?** Quieter times as US summer vacations are over.

Your family holiday to Hawai'i may well be built around time on the beach, but a visit to the Dole Plantation in Wahiawā, in central O'ahu, will keep youngsters entertained and focused on something completely different: pineapples. Expect a sweet, sticky overdose of everything *ananas* at Dole, where activities include the Pineapple Garden Maze, declared the world's largest (pineapple) maze in 2008. Among over 4km (2.5 miles) of pathways and 14,000 colourful Hawaiian plants, seek out eight secret stations that lead to the mystery at the heart of the labyrinth. The *Pineapple Express* mini-train takes visitors on a whistle-stop tour through the plantation and Hawai'i's pineapple story, though the highlight for kids may well be picking up pineapple-laced chilli dogs, pineapple soft-serve ice cream or a chocolate-covered pineapple. If you become a tad pineappled out, drop into nearby Green World Coffee Farm, a roadside coffee extravaganza, with free sampling. It's only a 15-minute drive north from Dole to Hale'iwa and on to the legendary North Shore beaches, so it's easy to include a plantation stop as a component of an around-the-island trip.

Trip plan: The Dole Plantation is a 40-minute drive from Waikīkī, also accessible by TheBus.

Need to know: There is no admission to enter the Dole Plantation Visitor Center, but there are charges for the Pineapple Express train and Pineapple Garden Maze.

Other months: Dec-Mar – cooler; Apr-May & Oct-Nov – shoulder season; Jun-Aug – hot and crowded.

UTAH
USA

5-16 **Why now?** Road-trip through Utah to see deserts and dinos without the searing midsummer heat.

Most kids love dinosaurs like Christopher Robin loves Winnie the Pooh, and in the legendary Dinosaur National Monument, Jurassic-era giants lie where they fell millions of years ago, frozen inside cliff walls. The reserve straddles the borders of Utah and Colorado, but Utah's Quarry section has the pick of the skeletons (everything from Stegosaurus and Diplodocus to dagger-toothed Allosaurus). More bones can be spotted on the 4km (2.4-mile) Fossil Discovery Trail – a pleasant, kid-friendly stroll in late summer as temperatures start to cool. Visit on a desert road trip from Salt Lake City, dropping into the town of Dinosaur (where snaps of dino-themed road signs are almost mandatory) and heading on to Moab, where you can hike and bike bankside trails or kayak and raft on one of the most gorgeous sections of the Colorado River.

Trip plan: Salt Lake City is the most convenient international airport, or you can fly into Vernal, which has the closest non-camping accommodation. A Utah–Colorado loop via Rte 40, State Hwy 139 and the I-70 will clock up around 1120km (700 miles) – rent an RV to take advantage of state park and national park campsites along the route.

Need to know: Eight walking trails meander around the Utah section of Dinosaur National Monument – the short Box Canyon Trail is fun for kids of all sizes (bring water and sun protection).

Other months: Dec-Feb – cold can be bitter; Mar-May & Oct-Nov – cooler days and nights; Jun-Aug – peak desert heat.

TUSCANY
ITALY

12-16 Why now? Explore the Tuscan hills during the grape harvest.

In Tuscany, the end of summer is a time to celebrate – September ushers in the *vendemmia* (grape harvest), with festivals to honour wine and viticulture that would make the great Bacchus proud. The *vendemmia* is a family occasion, drawing Tuscans of all ages to the vineyards of Chianti and other wine regions. Book a family stay at an *agriturismo* (farmstay) at harvest time and there's every chance you'll be able to join in the communal harvesting and crushing. Most kids will love squishing grapes under their bare tootsies, and adults will enjoy quaffing the previous year's output. Use wine tourism as the anchor for a week without the summertime crowds, visiting country *castellos* (castles) and dramatic *duomos* (cathedrals) in Florence and Siena (as well as sampling delicious gelato), and taking country walks surrounded by warm, late-summer colours.

Trip plan: Florence is the main air hub in Tuscany; rent a car to roam out to vineyards and *agriturismi* in Chianti and other wine regions. The Movimento Turismo del Vino (movimentoturismovino.it) has listings of member vineyards to approach about opportunities to join in the harvest.

Need to know: Wine festivals abound in September: Greve in Chianti's Expo del Chianti Classico, Panzano's Vino al Vino, Montecarlo's Festa del Vino and the Festa dell'Uva (grape festivals) in Impruneta and Scansano are all worth investigating.

Other months: Dec-Mar – cold, often grey; Apr-May & Oct-Nov – mild, calmer; Jun-Aug – hot, sunny, busy.

DURANGO & SILVERTON RAILROAD USA

0-16 Why now? Ride vintage trains through dramatic mountains and canyons in crisp, colourful autumn.

Since 1882, steam and diesel trains have been running on the narrow-gauge railway between Durango and Silverton in Colorado. The locos originally hauled gold and silver ores, mined in the San Juan Mountains; nowadays, historic trains ply the route, trundling passengers through the spectacular landscape of the Animas River Gorge. In Silverton, visitors can tour the Old Hundred Gold Mine, descending 550m (1640ft) underground; train buffs will also appreciate the Durango & Silverton Railroad Museums in the depots at both ends of the line. The railway is bound to be a highlight for little trainspotters, but Durango is an all-round excellent destination for family travel, with access to hiking on the Colorado Trail, biking along the Animas River and soaking in the Durango Hot Springs.

Trip plan: Stay in a historic hotel in downtown Durango or a lodge or campground out of town. You can get around downtown without a car (free trolley shuttle), but you'll want a vehicle to explore the surrounding countryside.

Need to know: The train takes 3hr 30min to travel from Durango to Silverton, and the same on the way back; opt to return by bus (1hr 30min) if you want to shorten the overall trip. In summer, round-trips on the Cascade Canyon Express take 5hr.

Other months: Nov-May – low season, limited Cascade Canyon Express trains only; Jun-Aug – high season, Silverton line and Cascade Canyon Express running; Sep-Oct – shoulder season, Silverton line only.

BAVARIA
GERMANY

5-16 Why now? Explore a fairy-tale vision of Bavaria in the calm of late summer.

So close to Czechia you can almost smell the beer bubbles and *trdelník* cake, Bavaria's Upper Palatinate district is a gentle sprawl of low mountains, scenic lakes, shady forests, spire-topped castles and historic townships plucked straight from a Brothers Grimm folktale. From the Danube city of Regensburg, you can whisk kids by hire car to fairy-tale settings far from the tourist crowds. Start by exploring the Gothic churches of Regensburg and playing games of Poohsticks on the Steinerne Brücke, the city's 900-year-old stone-built bridge, then meander through the terracotta-tiled medieval centre of Amberg and stroll the shady forest trails of the Naturschutzgebiet Waldnaabtal nature reserve. With older kids, give the fable a Brothers Grimm hue at Waldsassen, where the baroque Stiftsbasilika Waldsassen church enshrines the skeletons of 10 medieval martyrs, transformed into gleaming works of art with lavish layers of gold, silver and jewels.

Trip plan: Fly into Nuremberg and pick up a rental car for the drive southeast to Regensburg to begin this Bavarian adventure. Amberg and Waldsassen are handy bases for exploring this rural idyll, or there are small, family-friendly hotels and Airbnbs at Windischeschenbach, close to Naturschutzgebiet Waldnaabtal.

Need to know: Warm late-summer days are perfect for getting out on the water – kayaks and stand-up paddleboards can be hired at scenic Steinberg am See, north of Regensburg.

Other months: Dec-Mar – cold, ski season in the mountains; Apr-May & Oct-Nov – cooler, cloudier and rainier; Jun-Aug – mild, often warm, but busy.

LJUBLJANA & UPPER CARNIOLA
SLOVENIA

0-16 Why now? Mild days and smaller crowds around Ljubljana and Lake Bled.

Slovenia is often eclipsed by its larger, more famous neighbours, but a calm mood descends over this green haven for families at the end of the summer, and September is still plenty warm enough for forest hikes, mountain biking, canyoning and splashing around in (and on) Lake Bled. Kick off a family break in Ljubljana: hit the museums (the science-focused House of Experiments and the interactive City Museum are especially kid-friendly), take the funicular to Ljubljana Castle and cruise along the Ljubljanica River. To see more of Slovenia, it's a short train and bus ride to Lake Bled, where you can paddle at lakeside beaches and charter a *pletna* (gondola) or rowboat to meander over to the irresistibly photogenic Church of the Assumption on Bled Island. Use Bled as a hub for a restorative week of walking, cycling and soaking up the clean air of the Julian Alps.

Trip plan: Flag carriers and low-cost airlines fly into Ljubljana's Jože Pučnik Airport, but you can also come by train from Austria, Italy, Hungary and Croatia. Trains and buses run north from Ljubljana to Bled; explore the lakeshore by taxi, bicycle or horse-drawn carriage.

Need to know: Bled is great for cycling; the Radovna Cycling Path starts just north of the lake, following the Radovna River for 13km (8 miles) into Triglav National Park.

Other months: Nov-Feb – cold, snowy, good skiing; Mar-May & Oct – mild, quieter; Jun-Sep – warm and bright.

NORFOLK
ENGLAND

5-16 Why now? Quieter days for exploring wonderful waterlands.

Among England's most scenic waterways, the Norfolk Broads were created by accident, when peat-cutters breached the banks of local rivers, creating a watery wonderland spanning 303 sq km (117 sq miles). Navigating the flooded channels is a great family adventure – out of the ordinary, but accessible enough that kids won't mind being dragged away from their screens (especially if they get a go at steering). Rent a day-boat, houseboat or overnight cruiser and you can drift for as long as the fancy takes you – swimming, fishing, birding and dropping in on ancient churches, country pubs and offbeat museums exploring the life of Norfolk's peat-cutters and eel-catchers. Essential family stops include St Helen's Church at Ranworth, the nature trails and mini museum at Toad Hole Cottage and Stalham's nostalgic Museum of the Broads.

Trip plan: Norwich is the Broads' gateway, served by fast trains from London and a handful of European flights. Buses connect to Hoverton and Wroxham, where you can rent boats or take cruises with Broads Tours, Richardson's or Barnes Brinkcraft. Alternatively, head to Simpson's Boatyard in Stalham.

Need to know: If skippering your own boat sounds like too much responsibility, book a family-friendly kayak or stand-up paddleboard tour with the Canoe Man, departing from Wroxham.

Other months: Dec-Feb – cold, misty, poor boating weather; Mar-Apr & Oct-Nov – damper, cooler days; May-Aug – busy, sunny, mostly dry.

OSAKA
JAPAN

0-16 Why now? Experience one of the wildest festivals in Japan.

Often overlooked by travellers, Osaka is an exciting place to take your family. Renowned for its tasty street food, it's a spirited, bold and brash kind of place that has shed the conservatism found elsewhere in Japan – and this exuberance is exemplified by the Kishiwada Danjiri Matsuri. Held over the third weekend in September, it's a kind of running-of-the-bulls, but with massive wooden *danjiri* (festival floats), many weighing over 3000kg (6600lb). The *danjiri* of Kishiwada's 34 neighbourhoods are hauled through the streets on ropes by hundreds of people, at barely believable speeds. Take care, stand back, and don't park your family on the outside of a corner that the *danjiri* take at speed – they've been known to topple! Expect lots of drumming, music, chanting and excitement. There's plenty more interest in Osaka for the kids, too: Universal Studios Japan is here, as well as the vast Osaka Aquarium Kaiyūkan. Shinsaibashi is the city's lively shopping area, while the castle, Osaka-jō, is well worth a visit. And don't miss trying local specialties like *takoyaki* (octopus balls) or *okonomiyaki* (savoury pancakes).

Trip plan: Osaka is the main city of the Kansai region, which also includes Kyoto, Nara and Kōbe; it's easy to base yourselves in one and visit the others.

Need to know: Kishiwada Danjiri Matsuri is held twice a year – first in late September and again in mid-October.

Other months: Nov-Mar – winter; Apr – cherry blossoms; Jun-Aug – hot and humid.

© saryanto yanto / Shutterstock

Start your Greek
Islands odyssey
on Mykonos

GREEK ISLANDS

12-16 **Why now? The hot summer peak has passed and the Med is still warm.**

Greece needs no introduction for teens who've studied history (or discovered its mythology via the *Percy Jackson* novels). Kick off by discovering Athens on a Percy Jackson Scavenger Hunt tour (or create your own), then head out to the islands. Start in Mykonos, with a hiking or e-biking tour along scenic backroads to historic sights and remote beaches. Next head to Paros, for boating across crystal-clear waters to Marcello Beach, navigating the coastline by stand-up paddleboard and exploring the caves and coves of Paros Park. Naxos is one of the most family-friendly islands, with calm shores and relatively quiet streets; take a horseback tour and walk to the unfinished ruins of Portara (the Temple of Apollo), overlooking the sea. The ancient sites continue on Santorini, where the Minoan city of Akrotiri lies preserved by volcanic ash; sporty teens can tackle a hike on the offshore island of Nea Kameni (good fitness and quality shoes required). Finally, head to Milos, where you can marvel at views from the hilltop village of Plaka and the old Venetian fortress beyond it. Other islands to consider for your Greece family stay include Crete, Rhodes and Corfu.

Trip plan: Get around by boat, and use local tours to see the island highlights.

Need to know: The sun can be blazing, with little shade. Expect steep walks and a lot of stairs.

Other months: Oct-Apr – quiet, cool, low season; May-Jun – shoulder season; Jul-Aug – hot, peak tourist season.

ACADIA NATIONAL PARK USA

5-16 Why now? Rugged hiking and biking, chilly swimming and spellbinding scenery, without the summer crowds.

On the scenic rocky coast of Maine, Acadia National Park a prime destination for adventurous fun. You can pack it into a weekend, but it's easy to fill a week (or more) at this outdoor playground. There are hiking trails for all skill levels, from the stroller-friendly Cadillac Summit Loop to the strenuous ascent of Acadia Mountain. For an added challenge, sure-footed kids can tackle the rung-and-ladder trails over granite cliffs, like the Beehive Loop. Acadia is also home to around 70km (45 miles) of carriage roads that are off-limits to motorised vehicles. Crisscrossing the forests and skirting the lakes, this trail network is an unbeatable place for a family bicycle outing. Cool off at Sand Beach, an unexpectedly long and luscious shore tucked in between coastal mountains – and with the water at around 13°C (55°F), you *will* cool off! From the beach you can also hike out to Great Head, with craggy coast and crashing surf all around.

Trip plan: For your base of explorations, pitch a tent in an Acadia campground or book a room at a Bar Harbor seaside inn. You'll need a car and/or bicycles to get around.

Need to know: In addition to the park visitor's pass, vehicles need a reservation to drive the Cadillac Mountain Summit Rd; buy via the National Park Service website.

Other months: Nov-May – low season, some roads and tourist facilities close; Jun & Oct – shoulder season, pleasant weather, lighter crowds; Jul-Aug – high season, big crowds.

Ancient mudbrick kasbah in the Atlas Mountains

© Roberto Moiola / Sysaworld/ Getty Images

ATLAS MOUNTAINS MOROCCO

12-16 Why now? The midday sun is less fierce and skies are clear for stargazing by night.

After a few days acclimatising to the sights and smells of Morocco in Marrakesh (and pointing out dramatic Atlas Mountains peaks from a riad rooftop), head for the hills. Book a tour ahead if time is limited, but for more freedom and autonomy get to Imlil and arrange a series of day treks, or a multiday adventure, directly. Many travellers are here to climb Mt Toubkal, and older teens with previous mountain-hiking experience might be tempted by the four-day trek, via traditional Berber villages and stunning high-altitude passes. With younger children, seek out a reputable guide and organise a mule trek in the Aït Bougmez Valley, past mudbrick villages, burbling streams and smallholdings tended by Berber families. Before heading out atop your mules, ensure you have plenty of snacks, water and hand sanitiser accessible. On a private tour, you can ask to stop when you need to, but bear in mind that your guide will have an agenda, including meal stops, booked ahead (a collective afternoon nap may also be on the schedule).

Trip plan: Book a private car or take a *grand-taxi* from Marrakesh to Imlil, from where you can head out on hikes or mule treks.

Need to know: Mules are sure-footed coming down mountains, but if any family members suffer from vertigo, this might not be the right adventure.

Other months: Oct-Apr – snowy peaks, roads can close; May-Jun – warming but not too hot; Jul-Aug – baking sunshine.

SRI LANKA

5-16 **Why now? See Sri Lanka's ancient cities before the crowds (and rains) arrive.**

Sri Lanka's beaches are everything you've imagined – golden, palm-shaded and lapped by bathtub-warm waters – but it would be remiss to come all this way without introducing the family to the island's rich history. At Anuradhapura, an easy detour inland from the coast, towering *dagobas* (stupas) that have survived two millennia of monsoon rains spill from bird-thronged tracts of forest, perfect for firing up young imaginations. Charter a tuk-tuk for the day and you can drift back through the centuries at toppled temples and vast ceremonial domes, some crumbling and silent, others thronged with Buddhist pilgrims. Continue the trip through time at the hilltop shrine of Mihintale (climb up via the long ceremonial staircase, or drive part-way to save little legs). Teens will be wowed by dizzying views from the rock-balanced palace of Sigiriya, but the near-vertical steps can be a challenge – with smaller kids, try Dambulla, with its vividly painted, statue-filled caverns.

Trip plan: Anuradhapura is an easy add-on to a trip to Sri Lanka's west-coast beaches – laid-back Negombo is a 3hr bus ride away. Connect back to the coast via Mihintale, Sigiriya and Dambulla by local bus, or charter a car and driver.

Need to know: Try to visit Anuradhapura on a *poya* (full moon) day, when white-robed pilgrims wrap the stupas in rolls of fabric. Bring socks – shoes must be removed, and the stones underfoot can be scorching!

Other months: Jan-May – heating up, more rain Apr to May; Jun-Aug – warm, dry; Oct-Dec – cooler, northeast monsoon.

Reclining Buddha at Isurumuniya Vihara, Anuradhapura

Preparing traditional
maraş ice-cream
in İstanbul

İSTANBUL
TÜRKIYE

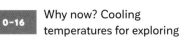

0-16 **Why now? Cooling temperatures for exploring İstanbul's bazaars and backstreets.**

The sun beams down on İstanbul in September, but crowds shrink and temperatures dip as the month wears on, and you won't face such a long wait to view the lavish interiors of Topkapı Palace or the Hagia Sophia Grand Mosque. With kids along for the ride, mix up sightseeing with micro-adventures – boat rides on the Bosphorus, climbing the Galata Tower, shopping for *nazar boncuğu* (eye amulets) in the Grand Bazaar, or spotting medieval birdhouses built onto the walls of Ottoman-era buildings, still in use by the city's avian population today. Line up little treats – *lokum* (Turkish delight), baklava, nougat rolls and theatrically prepared Turkish ice cream – as rewards for good behaviour. Most children can only handle so many historical sights, so build in some 100% kid-focused fun at the rollercoasters, flumes and old-school swings of Vialand theme park; at Miniatürk, explore landmarks from all over Türkiye, re-created at a kiddie scale.

Trip plan: Flights buzz into İstanbul Airport (with easy bus transfers to Sultanahmet) and Sabiha Gökçen International Airport, but you can also come by train via Bulgaria or Romania. For a week or long weekend of exploring, get around using the Metro, ferries and İstanbul's nostalgic trams.

Need to know: İstanbul is home to 200,000 cats – well-fed moggies loitering at shops and cafes in tourist areas are usually friendly, but discourage kids from petting strays in the street.

Other months: Nov-Feb – cool, sometimes rainy, quiet; Mar-May & Oct – warm, quieter; Jun-Aug – hot, sunny, busy.

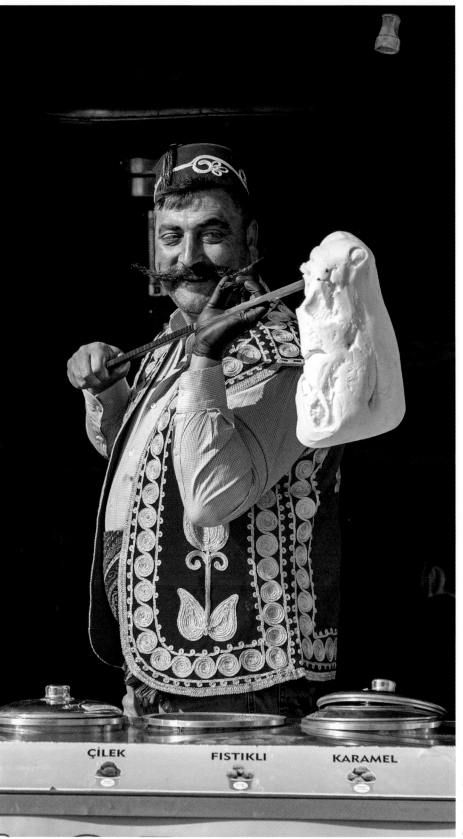

ÇİLEK　　FISTIKLI　　KARAMEL

© grandbrothers / Shutterstock

(R) Trest Trapi Bay, Aruba;
(B) Green turtle offshore of Bonaire

© fokke baarssen / Shutterstock

ARUBA, BONAIRE & CURAÇAO

5-16 Why now? Snorkelling with sea turtles, snuggling with donkeys and exploring desert-island landscapes.

Hurricane season scares travellers away from the Caribbean between August and October, but the 'ABC Islands' of Aruba, Bonaire and Curaçao are generally safe from the seasonal storms, as they lie south of the normal hurricane zone. While Aruba is well developed as a resort destination, Bonaire and Curaçao retain an appealing unsullied vibe. Both are popular scuba destinations, with dozens of dive (and snorkel) sites that are accessible from the shore – a real money saver for families who like to hang out with the fish. Bonus: snorkelling with sea turtles! And if your kiddos (age 10 and up) want to go deeper, this is a great place to get certified for scuba diving. Out of the water, the ABC Islands are arid and starkly beautiful, studded with cacti and populated by flamingos and

wild donkeys. Meet the braying beasts at donkey sanctuaries on Aruba and Bonaire.

Trip plan: Bonaire is small, quiet and quaint, attracting divers to boutique resorts. Larger Curaçao has more restaurants, culture and local life, bigger resorts and more amenities for kids (beaches, water parks etc). All three islands enjoy fine weather year-round.

Need to know: These three islands were formerly known as the Dutch Antilles. Aruba and Curaçao are both autonomous countries within the Kingdom of the Netherlands; Bonaire remains a 'special municipality' of the Netherlands.

Other months: Dec-Apr – high season, higher prices; May-Oct – low season, lower prices.

© Gilmanshin / Shutterstock

RAS AL JINZ TURTLE RESERVE OMAN

5-16 Why now? Hatchling turtles, stunning beaches.

An ancient sultanate on the southeast of the Arabian Peninsula, Oman is dripping with fascinating history and culture and blessed with wonderful wildlife, including loggerhead, olive ridley, green and hawksbill turtles. From June to August, amid Oman's searing summer heat, female turtles come ashore to flipper out holes in the sand and lay eggs; two months later (mainly in September), the tiny hatchlings emerge and tumble chaotically down the beach to reach

the relative safety of the sea. There are strict rules in place to protect the vulnerable turtles during this time. Different species habitually lay in various places (many off-bounds to visitors), but the best – and the only legal – place to watch hatchling greens is Ras Al Jinz Turtle Reserve on the peninsula's easternmost point. It was created by the Omani government to shield and study these endangered animals, and guides are present to stop people disturbing them. Viewing times are 9pm and 6am; dawn sessions tend to be quieter and better for

seeing emerging babies. The reserve also has a family-friendly interactive museum, plus research laboratories and visitor amenities.

Trip plan: There's no public transport to Ras Al Jinz – hire a car and drive the 250km (155 miles) south along the stunning coast road from Muscat. The resort offers accommodation (turtle-viewing included).

Need to know: When viewing turtles, don't use flash photography, stay minimum 10m (33ft) away and use red-beam torches only.

Other months: Apr-May – blooming roses; Oct-Mar – high season, cooler, festivals.

October

WHERE TO GO WHEN WITH KIDS

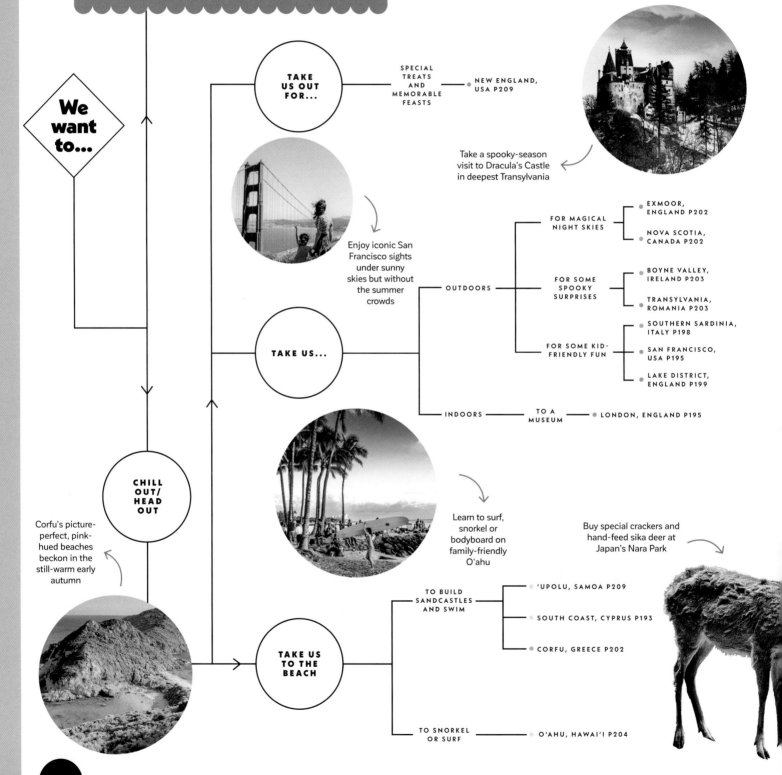

HAVE AN ADVENTURE

We want to...

TAKE US OUT FOR... — SPECIAL TREATS AND MEMORABLE FEASTS — • NEW ENGLAND, USA P209

Take a spooky-season visit to Dracula's Castle in deepest Transylvania

Enjoy iconic San Francisco sights under sunny skies but without the summer crowds

TAKE US...

OUTDOORS
- FOR MAGICAL NIGHT SKIES
  - • EXMOOR, ENGLAND P202
  - • NOVA SCOTIA, CANADA P202
- FOR SOME SPOOKY SURPRISES
  - • BOYNE VALLEY, IRELAND P203
  - • TRANSYLVANIA, ROMANIA P203
- FOR SOME KID-FRIENDLY FUN
  - • SOUTHERN SARDINIA, ITALY P198
  - • SAN FRANCISCO, USA P195
  - • LAKE DISTRICT, ENGLAND P199

INDOORS — TO A MUSEUM — • LONDON, ENGLAND P195

CHILL OUT/ HEAD OUT

Corfu's picture-perfect, pink-hued beaches beckon in the still-warm early autumn

Learn to surf, snorkel or bodyboard on family-friendly O'ahu

Buy special crackers and hand-feed sika deer at Japan's Nara Park

TAKE US TO THE BEACH

- TO BUILD SANDCASTLES AND SWIM
  - • 'UPOLU, SAMOA P209
  - • SOUTH COAST, CYPRUS P193
  - • CORFU, GREECE P202
- TO SNORKEL OR SURF
  - • O'AHU, HAWAI'I P204

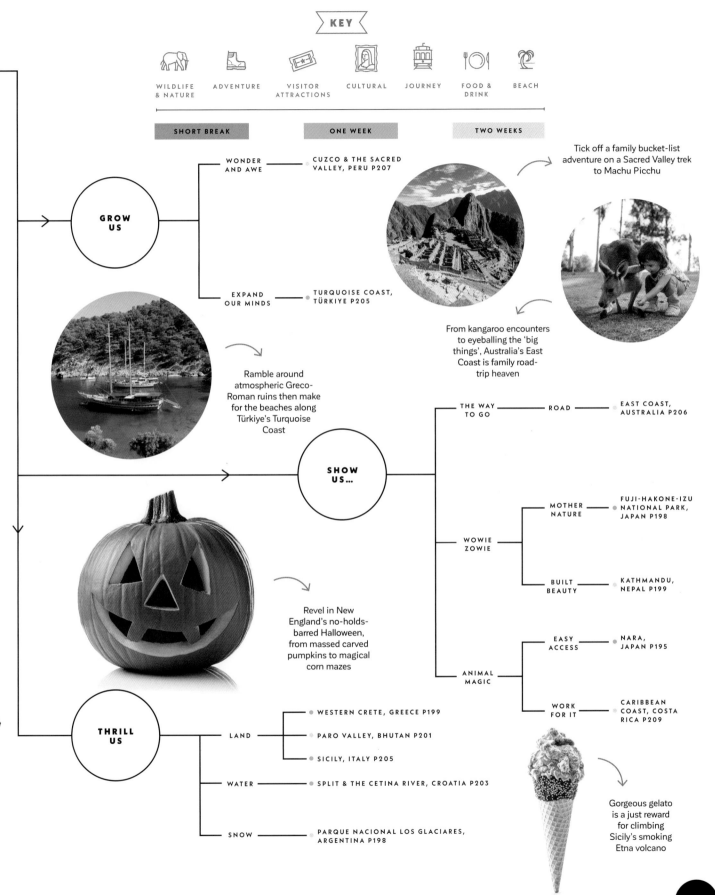

KEY

WILDLIFE & NATURE | ADVENTURE | VISITOR ATTRACTIONS | CULTURAL | JOURNEY | FOOD & DRINK | BEACH

SHORT BREAK | ONE WEEK | TWO WEEKS

GROW US

WONDER AND AWE — CUZCO & THE SACRED VALLEY, PERU P207

Tick off a family bucket-list adventure on a Sacred Valley trek to Machu Picchu

EXPAND OUR MINDS — TURQUOISE COAST, TÜRKIYE P205

From kangaroo encounters to eyeballing the 'big things', Australia's East Coast is family road-trip heaven

Ramble around atmospheric Greco-Roman ruins then make for the beaches along Türkiye's Turquoise Coast

SHOW US...

THE WAY TO GO — ROAD — EAST COAST, AUSTRALIA P206

WOWIE ZOWIE — MOTHER NATURE — FUJI-HAKONE-IZU NATIONAL PARK, JAPAN P198

— BUILT BEAUTY — KATHMANDU, NEPAL P199

ANIMAL MAGIC — EASY ACCESS — NARA, JAPAN P195

— WORK FOR IT — CARIBBEAN COAST, COSTA RICA P209

Revel in New England's no-holds-barred Halloween, from massed carved pumpkins to magical corn mazes

THRILL US

LAND — WESTERN CRETE, GREECE P199
— PARO VALLEY, BHUTAN P201
— SICILY, ITALY P205

WATER — SPLIT & THE CETINA RIVER, CROATIA P203

SNOW — PARQUE NACIONAL LOS GLACIARES, ARGENTINA P198

Gorgeous gelato is a just reward for climbing Sicily's smoking Etna volcano

Events in October

ALBUQUERQUE BALLOON FIESTA

Albuquerque, New Mexico, USA
Jaws will drop at the sight of 500 hot-air balloons filling the sky over Albuquerque; family balloon rides are de rigueur (bravery and budget allowing).

EXMOOR DARK SKIES FESTIVAL

Exmoor National Park, England
Drag the kids away from their screens to discover the delights of the night sky on the Devon and Somerset moors.

HALLOWEEN

Anoka, Minnesota, USA
Americans love to do things bigger and better, and Anoka goes into overdrive at Halloween, with scary costumes, candy and spooky decorations.

NEW HAMPSHIRE PUMPKIN FESTIVAL

Laconia, New Hampshire, USA
Tens of thousands of jack-o'-lanterns adorn the town as residents try to try to beat the most-in-one-place record.

CÍRIO DE NAZARÉ

Belém, Brazil
There's a fairy-tale magic to this vast procession, centred on a flower-decked palanquin bearing Our Lady of Nazareth; look out for stalls selling wooden toys.

KANELBULLENS DAG

Sweden
Swedes celebrate Cinnamon Bun Day with gusto: head to any café and you'll find piles of these sweet treats waiting for keen kiddies.

OKTOBERFEST

Munich, Germany
The beer drinking continues late into the night, but families can enjoy rides, pretzels and shows until 8pm (there's even a dedicated Family Day).

MASSKARA FESTIVAL

Bacolod, Negros, Philippines
Young and old come together for music, dancing, parades, concerts, extravagant masks and costumes – and lots of grilled chicken.

Early October — $$$
Mid-October to early November — $$
31 October — $$
Late October — $$
Second Sunday in October — $$
4 October — $$
Late September to early October — $$
Fourth Sunday in October — $

● NARA, JAPAN

Autumn colours at
Lake Kawaguchi and
Fuji-Hakone-Izu
National Park, Japan

Take a boat trip
across England's Lake
Windermere

● LAKE DISTRICT, ENGLAND

● SOUTH COAST, CYPRUS

Mask dances are a
part of Bhutanese
culture

● SAN FRANCISCO,
USA

Bring back a toy
memento of San
Francisco's cable cars

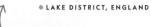

Leaf peep fall foliage in
New England, USA

● LONDON, ENGLAND

● PARO VALLEY,
BHUTAN

● CORFU, GREECE

● NEW ENGLAND, USA

● SOUTHERN SARDINIA,
ITALY

The Library of
Celsus on Türkiye's
Turquoise Coast

● FUJI-HAKONE-IZU
NATIONAL PARK, JAPAN

● EAST COAST, AUSTRALIA

● TURQUOISE COAST, TÜRKIYE

● O'AHU, HAWAI'I

● SICILY, ITALY

● KATHMANDU VALLEY, NEPAL

● EXMOOR, ENGLAND

Curious alpacas roam
Peru's Sacred Valley

Red deer rut in
Exmoor National
Park in October

● NOVA SCOTIA, CANADA

The scent of the
state flower, a
hibiscus, fills the
air of Hawai'i

● SPLIT & THE
CETINA RIVER,
CROATIA

● CARIBBEAN COAST, COSTA RICA

There's more
to Transylvania
than Dracula

● 'UPOLU, SAMOA

● WESTERN CRETE, GREECE

Canoe in Costa Rica's
Tortuguero National Park
on the east coast

● CUZCO & THE SACRED
VALLEY, PERU

Dive into the
To Sua Ocean
Trench, a Samoan
swimming hole

● PARQUE NACIONAL LOS
GLACIARES, ARGENTINA

● BOYNE VALLEY, IRELAND

● TRANSYLVANIA,
ROMANIA

SOUTH COAST
CYPRUS

0–16 **Why now?** Cyprus sun and sea, without the summer crush.

Summer sees Cyprus in full swing, with fierce competition for sun loungers and beach-towel space, and noisy nightlife that isn't always conducive to early bedtimes. But the balmy temperatures outlast the summer holidays, and the sea stays warm enough for swimming into October, with plenty of bright sunshine for sandcastle-building and relaxing on the beach. Prices also come down in family-oriented resorts such as Pafos, Polis and Lemesos, where you can divide your time between kid-friendly beaches, medieval castles, Greco-Roman ruins and walks through thyme-scented dunes and peaceful pine forests in the hills. Rent a car for family picnics in the Troödos Mountains (home to Mt Olympus, the island's highest peak) and day trips to centuries-old villages and the empty, secret beaches of the unspoiled Akamas Peninsula.

Trip plan: Cyprus is split in two by the UN-controlled Green Line between the Greek-Cypriot Republic of Cyprus to the south and the Turkish Republic of Northern Cyprus, but it's easy to hop between both sides. The best beaches are on the south coast of the Greek republic, close to the airports at Larnaka and Pafos. Cars can be hired inexpensively and distances are small, so pick a hub and explore the coast and mountains on day trips.

Need to know: The long warm summer brings lots of seasonal fruit to shops and markets in the autumn – look out for tasty pomegranates, oranges and grapefruits.

Other months: Nov-Feb – cool, quiet, many resorts close; Mar-May & Sep – warm, dry, fairly quiet; Jun-Sep – busy, scorching sunshine.

(L) Greco-Roman ruins at Nea Pafos; (R) Quiet coastline on the Akamas Peninsula

(A) Sika deer in Nara Park, Japan;
(L) London's Science Museum Space gallery;
(R) Sea lions sunbathe on Pier 39, San Francisco

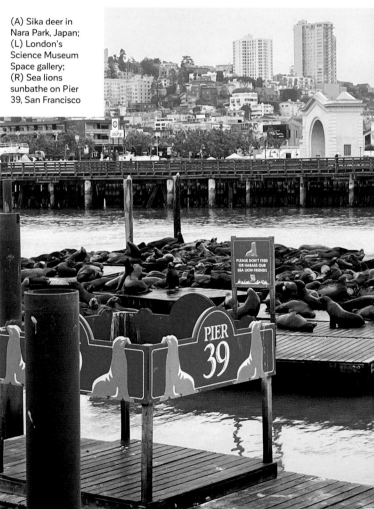

NARA
JAPAN

0-16 Why now? Autumn colours and roving deer.

The country's first permanent capital (before Kyoto), Nara is a must-see on your family's Japan visit – and Nara-kōen (Nara Park) is likely to be one of your children's highlights. More than 1000 sika deer roam freely here; designated as a 'National Treasure', they have become a symbol of the city. Deer crackers are for sale around the park, and some of the surprisingly tame deer have even learned to bow to visitors to ask to be fed. Turn up in October and Japan's famous autumn colours, along with the friendly deer, make Nara-kōen an absolute delight. Also in the park is the Tōdai-ji, one of Japan's best-known temples, home to the awe-inspiring, 15m-high (49ft) Daibutsu (Great Buddha), one of the largest bronze Buddha images in the world. Behind the Daibutsu is a 50cm (20in) hole through the base of a wooden pillar, the same size as one of the Buddha's nostrils – (small) kids crawl through here to be assured of attaining enlightenment. A short stroll away in the eastern part of the park, the vermilion buildings of Kasuga Taisha, Nara's main shrine, make a bold contrast to the surrounding greenery.

Trip plan: Nara is part of the great Kansai metropolis, which also includes Osaka, Kyoto and Kōbe; it's easy to base yourselves in one and visit the others.

Need to know: Of Nara's two main stations – JR Nara and Kintetsu-Nara – the latter is much closer to Nara-kōen.

Other months: Nov-Mar – winter months, cold; Apr – cherry blossom; Jul-Aug – hot and humid.

SAN FRANCISCO
USA

0-16 Why now? Marine life, massive redwoods and San Fran icons.

San Francisco is a treat for families at any time of year, but October is something special – a sweet spot when weather is still nearly perfect, but summer crowds have dispersed. Best of all, the city's famous resident sea lions have returned from their breeding grounds in the Channel Islands, so there are often hundreds of them lounging around at Pier 39, waiting for someone to snap a photo. Other fun San Fran family favourites: riding the cable cars, indulging in the Ghirardelli Chocolate Experience, cycling around Golden Gate Park and touring the creepy island-prison at Alcatraz (book in advance). When your kids need a break from the city, head out of town to Muir Woods or Purisima Creek Preserve, where the massive redwood trees never fail to impress.

Trip plan: It's easy to get around San Francisco without a vehicle; in fact, driving is not recommended. Rent a car for your trip out of town, or catch a ride on the Muir Woods Shuttle (weekends and holidays only). If you do drive, be sure to reserve a parking space at Muir Woods in advance.

Need to know: San Francisco is a big city, with big-city problems, including homelessness, drug use, petty crime and other social ills. Be aware of the sketchy neighbourhoods and stay alert, even around Union Sq and downtown tourist attractions.

Other months: Nov-Mar – chillier, more rainfall, low-season prices; May-Sep – peak season, pleasant weather, dry; Apr-May & Sep – fine weather, lighter crowds.

LONDON
ENGLAND

0-16 Why now? Browse the UK's top museums without crazy crowds.

From June to September, London's famous museums are mobbed. In autumn, when kids across Europe have gone back to school, a sense of calm descends over the capital, and you won't have to squeeze through quite so many bodies to get close to the Science Museum's space rockets or the dinosaur bones at the Natural History Museum. Best of all, the three Kensington museums – the Science (for budding engineers), the Natural History (for would-be naturalists) and the Victoria and Albert (for future fashion designers) – are all free to visit, though donations are welcomed. To avoid culture overload, limit yourself to a museum a day and spend the rest of your time chilling in the green expanse of Hyde Park (where the Diana Memorial Playground has a full-on pirate ship), window-shopping in Kensington and Knightsbridge, or wandering along the banks of the Thames near the Houses of Parliament.

Trip plan: The efficient London Underground makes exploring a breeze, so there's no need to stay in pricey west London. Consider cheaper, roomier digs out east in Islington and Shoreditch or in Camden, then zip down to South Kensington by tube to take in the museums. For more free culture, don't overlook the British Museum, National Gallery and Tate Modern.

Need to know: All three museums offer kids' activities and time-saving highlights tours – call ahead to check start times and prices.

Other months: Dec-Feb – cold, quieter (except over Christmas); Mar-May & Sep-Nov – cooler, calmer; Jun-Sep – warm, madly busy.

Sardinia's Spiaggia di
Cala Domestica, Italy

PARQUE NACIONAL LOS GLACIARES
ARGENTINA

12-16 | **Why now?** Cool glacier views, minus infuriating queues.

In southern Patagonia, tucked up against the ankles of the Andes and close to Argentina's long border with Chile, lies the fantastic frozen landscape of Parque Nacional Los Glaciares, where dozens of glaciers slowly flow into two deep-chilled lakes, Argentino and Viedma. Kids will likely revel in the sense of adventure you instantly feel after arriving in this remote area, where icefields are framed by emerald beech forest and the terrain is constantly reshaped and sculpted by the elements. Much of the park is inaccessible, but it's possible to visit three glaciers – Perito Moreno, Upsala and Onelli – and October is a more chilled time to do it. Families travelling with older children can do guided hikes on Perito Moreno and treks through Magellanic forests. You can also take boat trips across Lago Argentino, sailing past the great wall of frozen water that fronts the glacier, which constantly creaks and cracks like an enormous ice-cube just dropped into a fizzy drink (occasionally, pieces calve off and crash spectacularly into the water).

Trip plan: The gorgeous gateway town of El Calafate is a 3hr 30min flight from Buenos Aires, or a 5hr to 6hr drive through the mountains from Puerto Natales in Chile.

Need to know: Glacier hiking trips are not suitable for younger children (or unfit adults).

Other months: Dec-Feb – peak season, warm, very busy; Mar-May – autumn, mild, fewer crowds; Jun-Aug – winter, snowfall; Sep-Nov – spring, quieter.

FUJI-HAKONE-IZU NATIONAL PARK
JAPAN

5-12 | **Why now?** Milder temperatures and autumn colours around marvellous Mt Fuji.

Autumn in Japan brings a flurry of colour to rival the cherry blossoms of spring, as locals enthusiastically pursue the tradition of *momiji-gari* – literally, 'seeking red leaves'. With temperatures falling from summer highs, this is also a great time to enjoy the lush forest scenery in Fuji-Hakone-Izu National Park, to the west of Tokyo. Trails to the summit of Mt Fuji close in September, but nearby Hakone has Fuji views and hot springs that frame the changing foliage in billowing steam. Add fun to a family trip with a warm soak in an *onsen* (thermal baths) in Hakone, a trip on the 'pirate ship' on the cobalt-blue crater lake of Ashi-no-ko, and a hike around the pungent sulphur vents at Ōwakudani; you can also ride over Ōwakudani on the Hakone Ropeway gondola, connecting Tōgendai and Sōun-zan. More walking trails weave around the forests and rocky headlands of the nearby Izu Peninsula.

Trip plan: Tokyo is Japan's biggest air hub; Shinkansen bullet trains connect Tokyo and Hakone in just 30min. The slower Odakyu Railway offers a special Hakone Freepass, with discounts at the sights and free travel on local buses and trains. The similar Dream Free Pass covers the Izu Peninsula.

Need to know: Many *onsen* are nude and gender-segregated – the easiest option for families is a hotel with in-room baths or a *ryokan* (inn) with a private guest bathhouse.

Other months: Nov-Mar – cool, uncrowded, resorts close; Apr-May – dry, warm, quiet; Jun-Sep – hot, crowded.

SOUTHERN SARDINIA
ITALY

0-16 | **Why now?** For beautiful beaches and a taste of Sardinia in miniature.

Silky beaches, prehistoric treasures, urban bustle and mountains – southern Sardinia's many highlights are even better without the high-season crowds and when bathed in October's gentler heat. The main drawcard is the island's thrilling coastline: east of the historic capital, Cagliari, Villasimius is one of southern Sardinia's most popular resorts and a great base, offering both playgrounds and shallow waters. Alternatively, to the west is the equally alluring resort of Chia, surrounded by rusty-red hills tufted with tough *macchia*. Its pretty pair of beaches – Sa Colonia to the west and horseshoe-shaped Su Portu to the east – have pale sands and gently shelving waters. Located near Barumini, an hour's drive north from Cagliari, the Parco Sardegna in Miniatura presents many of Sardinia's most famous monuments in miniature size. This ambitious attraction also has an archaeological park, a planetarium, a botanic garden and themed zones inhabited by full-size animatronic dinosaurs, designed in collaboration with paleontologists (although they seem to have missed the memo about feathers).

Trip plan: Cagliari Airport is the main entry point; ferries also run from Italy to Sardinia's east coast. The island has a decent rail and bus network, but a car allows you to reach more remote areas.

Need to know: Fancy a road trip? Hit the panoramic SP71, which dips and rises for 25km (15.5 miles) along the beautiful Costa del Sud between Chia and Porto di Teulada.

Other months: Nov-Dec – some rain, resorts closed; Jan-Apr – festivals; Apr-Jun & Sep – mild heat, less crowds; Jul-Aug – peak season, hot.

KATHMANDU VALLEY NEPAL

5-16 Why now? Explore Nepal's ancient cities amid warm weather and dry skies.

There's more to Nepal than mountains. The basin-shaped Kathmandu Valley overflows with magnificent temples and palaces, constructed by rival dynasties locked in an epic battle to see who could create the most extravagant royal capital. Use the dry days following the monsoon for a family journey deep into Hindu and Buddhist mythology in the former city-states of Kathmandu, Patan and Bhaktapur. Meet a living child-goddess in Kathmandu's Durbar Square; leave offerings at pagoda-roofed Hindu temples; light butter lamps at pilgrim-thronged Buddhist stupas; join school-age novice monks in mural-adorned monasteries; and run a gauntlet of cheeky macaques at the hilltop temple of Swayambhunath. Close out the trip with a bonus adventure: a bolt-on safari to Chitwan National Park in search of crocodiles, rhinos and elephants; if you're lucky, you'll encounter one of the park's elusive royal Bengal tigers – a true once-in-a-lifetime experience.

Trip plan: Connect to Kathmandu by air via India or the Middle East, or travel overland from India, passing Chitwan en route. Reach the towns and temples of the Kathmandu Valley by local bus or chartered taxi; three- to four-day Chitwan safaris leave daily from Kathmandu.

Need to know: Keep kids sweet while exploring with treats like hog-plum candy, wild honey, Bhaktapur's creamy 'king curd' and the legendary *lassi* (drinking yoghurt) served at Kathmandu's Asan Tole market.

Other months: Dec-Feb – cold, quiet; Mar-May & Nov – warm, dry, good for trekking and safaris; Jun-Sep – monsoon rains.

WESTERN CRETE GREECE

12-16 Why now? Thinner crowds at the end of the season.

Western Crete offers a host of possibilities for adventurous and outdoorsy families. Hania (Chania), on the northern coast, is Crete's most evocative city, with a magnificent harbour, pretty Venetian quarter and a fascinating covered *agora* (market); it's also the gateway to one of Europe's longest canyons, the Samaria Gorge. While you can hike the gorge in a busy day trip from Hania that includes a bus, 16km (10-mile) hike, ferry and bus back to Hania, it's better to take a few days to enjoy the journey. The hike starts high in the mountains at Xyloskalo at 1200m (3937ft), dropping through the spectacular twisting gorge right down to sea level at the black-sand beach of Agia Roumeli (only accessible by foot or ferry) on Crete's southern shore, where the Mediterranean beckons for a celebratory post-hike swim. Stay in a small hotel here, then ferry east along the coast the next day to the quiet seaside village of Hora Sfakion – or even better, stay a few nights in spectacular Loutro, a pint-sized fishing settlement with no road access. When you're ready, take a bus back over the mountains to Hania and the northern coast.

Trip plan: Allow plenty of time to explore Crete; Hania Airport has direct flights from Athens and seasonally from around Europe.

Need to know: Book Loutro ferry tickets and accommodation in advance.

Other months: Nov-Apr – cold, off-season; May-Sep – Samaria Gorge hiking; Jul-Aug – hot, crowded.

LAKE DISTRICT ENGLAND

5-12 Why now? Explore Beatrix Potter's Hill Top when the farm-framed fells are colourful and uncrowded.

Nestled betwixt Lake Windermere and the much smaller and less-visited Esthwaite Water, Hill Top is a farmhouse that provided a creative retreat and a treasured home for the author Beatrix Potter, who bought the property in 1905 with proceeds made from her self-illustrated books, of which the first published was the children-enchanting *Tale of Peter Rabbit*. This stunningly successful story spawned a further 22 tales starring animals she encountered around Hill Top, from Jeremy Fisher the frog to Jemima Puddle-Duck; they proved phenomenally and perennially popular with consecutive generations, selling in the hundreds of millions. On a visit, kids can seek out familiar scenes from Potter's pages in the house and vegetable garden, explore the bookshop, meet Herdwick sheep (a Cumbrian species the author herself bred), and then wander Windermere's ever-popular shores.

Trip plan: Reach Hill Top by road (B5285) via Ambleside, 10km (6 miles) away, or Coniston, 11.5km (7 miles) away. Trains run to Windermere Station, from where you can catch a ferry across the lake and then take the Mountain Goat 525 bus to Hill Top (mid-March to October).

Need to know: Now owned by the National Trust, Hill Top opens from mid-February to the end of October, but it's closed on Fridays (except in August). No need to book.

Other months: Nov-Feb – cold, Hill Top closed; Mar-May – daffodils and wildflowers, unpredictable weather, quieter; Jun-Sep – warmer, lovely walking conditions, busy.

© pxl.store / Shutterstock

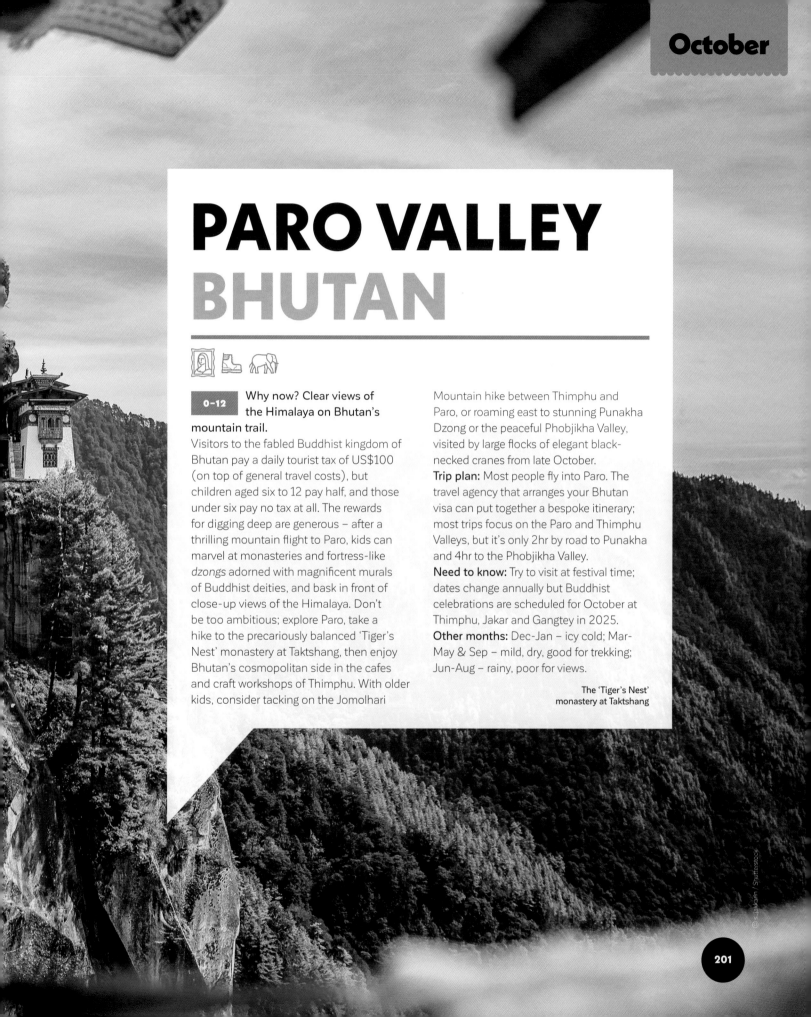

PARO VALLEY
BHUTAN

0–12 Why now? Clear views of the Himalaya on Bhutan's mountain trail.

Visitors to the fabled Buddhist kingdom of Bhutan pay a daily tourist tax of US$100 (on top of general travel costs), but children aged six to 12 pay half, and those under six pay no tax at all. The rewards for digging deep are generous – after a thrilling mountain flight to Paro, kids can marvel at monasteries and fortress-like *dzongs* adorned with magnificent murals of Buddhist deities, and bask in front of close-up views of the Himalaya. Don't be too ambitious; explore Paro, take a hike to the precariously balanced 'Tiger's Nest' monastery at Taktshang, then enjoy Bhutan's cosmopolitan side in the cafes and craft workshops of Thimphu. With older kids, consider tacking on the Jomolhari

Mountain hike between Thimphu and Paro, or roaming east to stunning Punakha Dzong or the peaceful Phobjikha Valley, visited by large flocks of elegant black-necked cranes from late October.

Trip plan: Most people fly into Paro. The travel agency that arranges your Bhutan visa can put together a bespoke itinerary; most trips focus on the Paro and Thimphu Valleys, but it's only 2hr by road to Punakha and 4hr to the Phobjikha Valley.

Need to know: Try to visit at festival time; dates change annually but Buddhist celebrations are scheduled for October at Thimphu, Jakar and Gangtey in 2025.

Other months: Dec-Jan – icy cold; Mar-May & Sep – mild, dry, good for trekking; Jun-Aug – rainy, poor for views.

The 'Tiger's Nest' monastery at Taktshang

EXMOOR
ENGLAND

`5-16` **Why now?** Explore star-studded skies on an autumn campout.

Spanning Somerset and Devon, on England's southwest peninsula, Exmoor is an extraordinary place with a huge variety of landscapes to explore – from craggy shores overlooked by soaring sea cliffs to high moors and deep valleys carved by wild rivers and cloaked in time-forgotten forests. Here, in one day, you might spot a bellowing stag, pass a herd of wild horses and spot dolphins cavorting in secret coves. And in October, when the weather remains reasonable but nights are longer than days, it becomes a passport-free gateway to the galaxy. Europe's original Dark Sky Reserve, Exmoor has low light pollution and on cloudfree moonless nights, visitors who linger after sunset are treated to a mind-blowing display of stars and planets. This month also sees the Exmoor Dark Skies Festival, offering loads of fun and educational events for amateur astronomers and aspirant space travellers of all ages. With trees spectacularly changing colour and the red-deer rut happening, this is an exciting time for family camping trips to one of Exmoor's many scenic sites.

Trip plan: Dulverton, 60km (37 miles) north of Exeter, is a gateway town for Exmoor; alternatively explore the coastal route and come in via Minehead.

Need to know: The National Trust manages sites across Exmoor, with family-friendly activities in autumn (and year-round).

Other months: Dec-Feb – windy coastal walks, snug pubs; Mar-May – wildflowers; Jun-Aug – sun-splashed beaches and riverbanks.

NOVA SCOTIA
CANADA

`5-16` **Why now?** Crisp autumn air, vibrant autumn foliage and black skies full of stars.

With temperatures dropping and the trees turning a thousand shades, from gold glow to scarlet red, shoulder-season October is your last chance to hike through foliage-filled forests and sleep under starlit skies before the winter weather sets in. When the skies are bright, Kejimkujik National Park in Port Joli, southwest Nova Scotia, is decked out in jewel-toned finery, glinting in the sunlight. Your best vantage point to admire the colourscape is from a canoe or kayak on Kijimkujik Lake, or from a bike or hike on Peter Point or Rogers Brook Trail. Designated as a Dark Sky Preserve by the Royal Astronomical Society of Canada, Kejimkujik is even more magical after the sun sets. Rent a 'dark-sky kit' from visitor centres for self-guided stargazing, or enjoy a more curated experience at Deep Sky Eye Observatory, where an expert astronomer will guide you around the vast night sky.

Trip plan: Kejimkujik has two campgrounds and a range of rustic lodgings. Camping equipment, canoes, kayaks and bicycles are all available to rent from in-park Whynot Adventure at Jakes Landing.

Need to know: Kejimkujik is the homeland of the Mi'kmaw people; discover more about their culture on park-run programmes, from touring ancient petroglyph sites at Lake Kejimkujik to watching a Mi'kmaw canoe craftsman at work.

Other months: Nov-Mar – winter, campsites close; May-Sep – peak season, warm, festivals; Apr – shoulder season, cooler, some tourist services close.

CORFU
GREECE

`0-16` **Why now?** Play on pine-fringed beaches and avoid the extreme heat of high summer.

October is made for playing on Corfu's pretty pink-hued beaches, splashing in its still-warm seas, and for long taverna lunches of child-friendly mezze over the gentle course of a week. On the rocky, wind-whipped west coast, roads weave past richly scented pine forests into new-build resorts, up and over into empty tree-lined bays, all with soft, fine sand and clear waters. The photogenic curve of Pelekas Beach is a good family base now that the crowds have gone, while beautiful olive-backed Paleokastritsa's hugely popular azure cove will be all yours in October. Elegant Corfu Town (also known as Kerkyra) stands halfway down the island's east coast and makes a great day trip. Its Old Town is a tight-packed warren of winding lanes, some lined with restaurants and intriguing shops, others timeless back alleys where washing lines stretch from balcony to balcony. Break up the stroll with an ice cream – perhaps with a drizzle of local honey.

Trip plan: Fly into Corfu Town's busy international airport; there are also ferry connections from mainland Greece, Italy and Albania. Hire a car, or stick to the excellent Green Bus route, which covers the island.

Need to know: Average day temperatures are 24°C (75°F) in October; evenings will be cooler, and rain is not uncommon, so pack some sleeves.

Other months: Nov-Apr – very quiet, weather changeable; May – quieter, less expensive, green; Jun – getting busy, heating up; Jul-Aug – peak season, high prices, high heat; Sep – still hot, beaches quieter.

SPLIT & THE CETINA RIVER
CROATIA

5-16 Why now? For end-of-season whitewater rafting and canyoning on roaring river rapids.

In October, Croatia's summer season has ended, the light is softer and the hard heat has given way to gentler days and cooler evenings. But your family is here for the thrilling watersports on the Cetina River, so wetsuits (usually provided) will add a welcome layer of warmth. Omiš, where the Cetina drains into the sea, has multiple operators offering cliff-jumping, rafting, canyoning and swimming, or combinations of each (some activities have a minimum age of eight). From Omiš, the turquoise river carves a channel through karst limestone valleys, with the mountains of the Dinara range providing a scenic backdrop to your joyous leaps and splashes. Along the route of the river there are pools and waterfalls to explore – the 38m-high (98ft) Gubavica Waterfall makes a great spot for a family photo. After your adventure, you're well placed to explore the vibrant Dalmatian Coast city of Split, which is wonderfully uncrowded at this time of year. St Domnius Cathedral's bell tower has fabulous views (although little legs may not be up for climbing all the stairs after all that sport!).

Trip plan: Omiš, your gateway for the Cetina River, is a 40min drive east of Split via the coastal highway. City bus 60 heads here every half hour from central Split.

Need to know: A waterproof camera is a must-have, as there's so much to photograph out on the water.

Other months: Nov-Mar – cool, off-season; Apr – warm; Jun-Aug – hottest, busiest; Sep – quieter, warm seas.

TRANSYLVANIA
ROMANIA

12-16 Why now? Visit 'Dracula's castle' as autumn turns leaves blood-red and bats abound around dusk.

Few characters have sunk their fangs as deep into kids' collective consciousness as Dracula. Treatment of the villainous vampire has varied from horror to humour since Bram Stoker's *Dracula* was published in 1897, with the sharp-toothed titular figure appearing in family-friendly forms such as Drac in *Hotel Transylvania*. Authored by an Irishman who never visited Romania, it's nevertheless known that Stoker's story was inspired by Transylvanian folklore and a real-life Wallachian prince, Vlad Țepeș (aka Vlad the Impaler; Vlad Dracula to his friends). Vlad's Poenari Citadel is ruined, but nearby(ish) Bran Castle – a spectacular hilltop fortress in the Carpathian foothills – looks the part and has links to the backstory. Commonly called 'Dracula's Castle' these days, it holds horror-themed features to chill and thrill kids (and parents) aplenty, including a torture chamber, a time tunnel transporting visitors to Vlad's vicious medieval world, and a 'history of dreads' exhibition that delves into local myths about *strigoi* (vampires), *iele* (nocturnal female spirits), *sântoaderi* (hoofed men) and *solomonari* (wizards).

Trip plan: Bran is 160km (100 miles) from Bucharest; it's a 2hr 30min drive, or get a train to Brașov, from where buses run to Bran.

Need to know: Bran Castle opens afternoons only on Mondays, and shuts at 4pm from October. Look out for events around Halloween.

Other months: Nov-Mar – cold, snowy, quieter; Apr-Sep – warmer, busy.

BOYNE VALLEY
IRELAND

12-16 Why now? Celebrate Halloween on its home turf.

Say 'Halloween' and most imagine costumed kids roaming American streets, clutching jack-o'-lanterns and trick-or-treating themselves towards the scary dentist's chair. But that's a long way from where this ancient autumn festival began. Halloween's roots reach back thousands of years to the pagan harvest festival of Samhain, celebrated across Ireland and the pre-Christian Celtic world as the year darkened. Ireland is rich in prehistoric remains and liberally covered with layers of legend – as epitomised in County Meath's Boyne Valley, home to the Hill of Tlachtga near Athboy (where a fire festival was traditionally held to honour a sun goddess during Samhain), and a passage tomb on the Hill of Tara, built so the main chamber is illuminated by the rising sun around Samhain (which originally spilled into November). Samhain customs have recently been revived in the Boyne, and the all-October Spirits of Meath Halloween Festival is a fun way to celebrate, mixing modern and traditional activities. It features events for younger children (pumpkin carving etc) and for older (13+) kids (Clown Town, Zombie Morgue, Purge Night).

Trip plan: The Boyne Valley is a 20min drive from Dublin Airport.

Need to know: Trim and Athboy's four-day Púca Festival is a music and cultural event from 31 October; it's named after a mischievous folkloric character who wreaks havoc around Samhain

Other months: Nov-Apr – wet and wild; Mar-Sep – best for outdoor adventures.

Calm seas at
Waikīkī Beach

O'AHU HAWAI'I

0-16 Why now? Quiet season for visitors in Hawai'i.

October is the perfect time to holiday in Hawai'i with your family – the weather is ideal, you'll find cheaper flights and more affordable accommodation, and the relative lack of visitors means smaller crowds at beaches and attractions. The island of O'ahu is one of the most family-friendly destinations on the planet, and with so much surf and sand, its coastline could be likened to a giant free waterpark. Most of the accommodation is in Waikīkī, with prices varying according to whether you want to stay right on or further away from the sand, or want a beach or mountain view. There are lots of eating options here, too, plus the opportunity to learn to surf, bodyboard or snorkel. Waikīkī Aquarium teems with Pacific reef marine life, there are tropical species from around the globe at Honolulu Zoo and, of course, plenty of beach options. Don't-miss family-friendly expeditions include climbing Diamond Head; snorkelling at the incomparable Hanauma Bay; and hiking into the island's lush interior on the Mānoa Falls Trail. A trip around O'ahu by rental car is easily done in a day, with lots of fun places to stop along the way.

Trip plan: Fly into Honolulu's Daniel K Inouye International Airport, and stay at least a week.

Need to know: There's no swimming around eight to 10 days after each month's full moon, when box jellyfish are in the waters – follow beach signage and talk to lifeguards.

Other months: Jan-Apr – winter high season, busy; Jul-Aug – summer high season; Sep-Dec – low season.

SICILY ITALY

 5-16 Why now? Cooler, quieter scenes on and around Sicily's famous volcano.

By October, the holiday crowds on Sicily have dissipated, but it's still warm enough for exploring, with daytime highs reaching 24°C (75°F). While the beaches are as lovely as ever (and the water is still warm), autumn is the time to head inland and enjoy Sicily's ancient sites and natural wonders without the queues. Fly into Catania and start the kids off with a geology fieldtrip to puffing Mt Etna – the volcano is active, so join a guided tour, taking the Funivia dell'Etna cable car to Rifugio Sapienza and then a 4WD bus to Torre Del Filosofo before hiking to the craters. Continue with a history lesson at the Greco-Roman ruins of Syracuse and the baroque villages of Noto and Modica, then turn inland at temple-crowned Agrigento for a taste of the interior, finishing up with gelato on Via Etnea in Catania.

Trip plan: Budget airlines fly direct to Catania; a rental car will give you more freedom to explore, and it's also the easiest way to reach the Etna cable car. Spread the circuit over a week, pausing for a few days in Catania, Noto and Agrigento; break the journey back to Catania at Caltanissetta for a gentle hike in the hills.

Need to know: When hiking on Mt Etna, heed local advice about safe areas to visit – there were several small eruptions in 2023.

Other months: Nov-Mar – cool, few crowds, some hotels close; Apr-May – dry, mild and quiet; Jun-Sep – hot, sunny and busy.

© Pic Media Aus / Shutterstock

Ephesus' Library of Celsus, on the Turquoise Coast

TURQUOISE COAST TÜRKIYE

0-16 Why now? Soak up the Türkiye's Turquoise Coast in peaceful calm under sunny skies.

The dizzy days of summer on the Turkish coast can make your head spin; come in October after the sun-and-sand set have departed and you'll see a calmer side to the Med. With lunchtime temperatures reaching 25°C (77°F), it's still warm enough for beach days, but cool enough for exploring ancient sites. Fly into İzmir and kick off with a trip to magnificent Ephesus, one of the best-preserved Greco-Roman ruins in the world and the ideal place to give kids a real sense of what life was like in ancient times. Pack fancy dress clothes for the kids to act out gladiator fantasies on the steps to the Library of Celsus or the stage of the 2000-year-old Great Theatre. Continue the crash course in Mediterranean history at the castle, tombs and legendary Mausoleum of Halicarnassus in Bodrum, then enjoy a few days of sun, sand and boat trips just south at Marmaris.

Trip plan: Seasonal charter flights to İzmir wind down in September, but it's still easy to get here cheaply using budget carriers such as Pegasus Airlines and SunExpress. A rental car will open up rewarding road trips along the Aegean coast – there's plenty in İzmir, Bodrum and Marmaris to fill a week.

Need to know: When the kids need a beach fix, Bitez Beach near Bodrum and İçmeler Beach near Marmaris are worthy detours.

Other months: Nov-Mar – cool, uncrowded, resorts close; Apr-May – dry and warm, quiet; Jun-Sep – hot and crowded.

Kangaroos in Murramarang National Park, NSW

Artisans at work in Chinchero

© Beata Urmos / Shutterstock

EAST COAST AUSTRALIA

5-16

Why now? Balmy days and smaller crowds on Australia's legendary East Coast.

Visiting Australia in summer is the dream, but the reality is high prices and huge crowds. Savvy families drop by in the spring, following the temperature gradient from Melbourne – with daytime highs of 20°C (68°F) – to Queensland, where the mercury can hit 29°C (84°F). This is prime weather for roadtripping, so rent a campervan and track the coast north, stopping in at kangaroo-thronged national parks, sandy surf beaches, scuba-diving hubs, whale-watching townships, hip cities and coaster-filled theme parks along the ritzy Gold Coast. To help the miles pass, plot a route via Australia's famous 'big things' – outsized roadside landmarks that have captured the popular imagination, from the Big Banana

at Coffs Harbour and Woombye's Big Pineapple to the supersized prawn at Ballina.

Trip plan: For the full East Coast experience, fly into Melbourne and out of Cairns, and arrange a one-way campervan hire package – it costs more, but you won't have to repeat the journey. The classic route links Melbourne, Sydney, Byron Bay, Brisbane, K'gari (Fraser Island), Hervey Bay, Townsville and Cairns.

Need to know: Australia's marine wildlife includes sharks, stingrays, poisonous seashells and stinging box jellyfish (the latter migrate past northern Queensland from late October); read up on the dangers and seek out netted beaches.

Other months: Dec-Feb – hot, pricey, crowded, rainy in Queensland; Mar-May & Sep-Nov – mild weather, quieter; Jul-Aug – cool, less busy.

CUZCO & THE SACRED VALLEY
PERU

5–16

Why now? Beat the crowds and the rain on a fantastic family journey through the land of the Inca.

With its stunning Andean scenery and intriguing remains of an ancient civilisation, Cuzco and the Sacred Valley will delight the whole family. (Also, alpacas!) You'll fly into Cuzco, but it's best to head straight to the so-called Sacred Valley to acclimatise to the altitude and bask in the mountain scenery. This fertile Urubamba River valley is dotted with Indigenous villages and Inca sites, including fantastic mountaintop ruins at Pisac, an artisanal textile market at Chinchero and an impressive archaeological site at Ollantaytambo. Your ultimate destination is Machu Picchu, the spectacular 15th-century citadel nestled between two mountain peaks. Adventurous families might get there via a four-day trek on the Inca Trail; alternatively, ride the train alongside the roaring Urubamba River. Either way, Machu Picchu is an astounding display of ancient engineering and awesome beauty that will wow kids and parents alike. Afterwards, circle back to Cuzco for at least a couple of days, allowing time to visit the city's interesting kid-friendly museums (especially the ChocoMuseo!).

Trip plan: It's a short flight from Lima to Cuzco. From there, it's easy to travel around the Sacred Valley by taxi, train and bus.

Need to know: Be careful of altitude sickness, especially in Cuzco, at 3400m (11,152ft). Spend several days at lower altitudes in the Sacred Valley before visiting Machu Picchu and Cuzco.

Other months: Nov-Mar – rainy season, quieter; Apr-May & Sep – shoulder season, dry, lighter crowds; Jun-Aug – dry, maximum crowds.

(A) Paddling at 'Upolu's Togitogiga Waterfalls, Samoa; (L) New Hampshire Halloween bounty; (R) Hang out with the sloths in Costa Rica's forest reserves

© Mira / Alamy Stock Photo

208

'UPOLU
SAMOA

0–16 Why now? The end of the cooler winter season is nigh.

Samoa is one of the most authentic and traditional of all Pacific destinations, a place where the locals cling to *Fa'a Samoa* (the Samoan Way). You won't find mega-resorts or flashy attractions here, but your family is likely to revel in Samoan culture and the intense natural beauty of the place. Most visitors park up for a week or so on the main island of 'Upolu. Apia, the capital, is a bustling place, but you won't have come to this Pacific paradise to hang around in a small city. 'Upolu's southern shoreline presents a dazzling strip of beaches and is dotted with secluded, surf-lapped coves; if you ever wanted to play castaway, this is the place to do it as a family. It's a delight to drive through the villages, where brightly painted houses echo the vibrant colours of the island's native flora. There are also plenty of not-to-be-missed natural spots: To Sua Ocean Trench is like a giant sinkhole with an almost hallucinatory-blue natural pool for swimming; Papase'ea Sliding Rocks is a brilliant spot for skimming down natural slides (actually small waterfalls); and Togitogiga Waterfalls has mesmerising swimming holes.

Trip plan: Fly into Faleolo Airport, on 'Upolu's northwest coast; stay for at least a week on the island.

Need to know: *Fale* is the Samoan word for house; thatch-roofed *fale*-style accommodation is common at budget-style places by the beach.

Other months: Nov-Apr – hot, higher humidity and rainfall; Apr-Sep – cooler, lower humidity.

CARIBBEAN COAST
COSTA RICA

0–16 Why now? Swimming, surfing and wildlife hikes in the coastal rainforest (without the rain).

While the rest of Costa Rica is getting drenched by the heaviest rainfalls of the year, the southern Caribbean coast enjoys a break from wet weather in low-season October, making this a great time to make a beeline for the region's family-friendly resorts. Puerto Viejo de Talamanca promises pristine beaches and reef snorkelling, and is home to a famously challenging surf break, but there are also gentler waves that are ideal for beginners. Nearby reserves offer easy rainforest hikes, with opportunities to spot howler monkeys and sloths in the wild. Meanwhile, it's turtle-nesting season in Parque Nacional Tortuguero, where hawksbill, loggerhead and green sea turtles return to the beaches on which they were born to lay eggs in the sand. In October you're less likely to see mothers nesting, but more likely to see new hatchlings scurrying to the sea – a wondrous witnessing of new life.

Trip plan: Renting a car gives the greatest flexibility and accessibility, but it's feasible to get around using tourist shuttles, and you can't drive all the way to Tortuguero in any case (catch a water shuttle at Moín's boat dock for the 3hr journey through wildlife-rich waterways).

Need to know: Low-season pricing offers substantial discounts on lodging.

Other months: Dec-Apr – peak tourist season, very little rain in most of the country from Jan to Mar; May-Nov – rainy season, slight let-up in rain and uptick in visitors from Jul to Aug; Sep – low season, less rain on the Caribbean coast.

NEW ENGLAND
USA

0–16 Why now? Apple picking, pumpkin festivals, mazes and fiery fall foliage.

New England is magic in October, when the hills – blanketed with maples and oaks – reach peak colour, blazing in vibrant shades of gold and crimson. Families flock to apple orchards where, as well as filling bags with tart, crispy fruits, kiddos can climb trees and enjoy hayrides, petting zoos and apple-cider doughnuts. Pumpkin-picking is also an option, and festivals abound throughout the region, from Pumpkintown in Connecticut's East Hampton (a super-cute village of 'pumpkinhead' people and pets) to the Pumpkin Chuckin' Festival in Stowe, Vermont (a catapult-building competition). Some New England farms construct mazes in their fields for kids to get lost in, one of the largest being the Big Vermont Corn Maze in Danville, where it takes two hours or more to find the way in and out. For good old-fashioned family fun, Massachusetts' Topsfield Fair is a long-standing favourite, with carnival rides, oxen-pulling contests, sheepdog trials and the famous Giant Pumpkin Weigh-In, where competing gourds routinely exceed 454kg (1000lb).

Trip plan: You'll need a vehicle to explore rural New England. That said, there's no need to drive all over the region: build your trip around one or two highlight events or destinations, then take advantage of other attractions in the vicinity.

Need to know: *Yankee Magazine* (newengland.com) is a great source of info on events and attractions around the region.

Other months: Nov-Mar – cold, short days; Apr-May – mild, spring blooms, rain possible; Jun-Aug – hot, humid, berry-picking season; Sep – blue skies, crisp air.

November

WHERE TO GO WHEN WITH KIDS

HAVE AN ADVENTURE

We want to...

TAKE US OUT FOR... — **MEMORABLE FEASTS**
- BANGKOK, THAILAND P217
- PLYMOUTH, USA P225

Snack on sensational street food at Bangkok's legendary night markets

Seek out Schloss Neuschwanstein, the inspiration for Disney's Sleeping Beauty Castle

TAKE US... — **OUTDOORS**

FOR FIREWORKS AND ILLUMINATING CELEBRATIONS
- CHIANG MAI, THAILAND P226
- EAST SUSSEX, ENGLAND P216
- UTTAR PRADESH, INDIA P222

TO A THEME PARK
- DUBAI, UNITED ARAB EMIRATES P229
- TOKYO, JAPAN P223

TO A FESTIVAL
- CENTRAL HIGHLANDS, GUATEMALA P229
- CAYMAN ISLANDS P228

Clamber aboard a tundra-buggy safari in Churchill, the 'Polar Bear Capital of the World'

CHILL OUT/ HEAD OUT

Take in temples, swimming holes and Hanal Pixán, the Yucatán's Day of the Dead

Find theme-park heaven and respite from the heat in Dubai's waterparks

TAKE US TO THE BEACH — **TO BUILD SANDCASTLES AND SWIM** — YUCATÁN, MEXICO P218

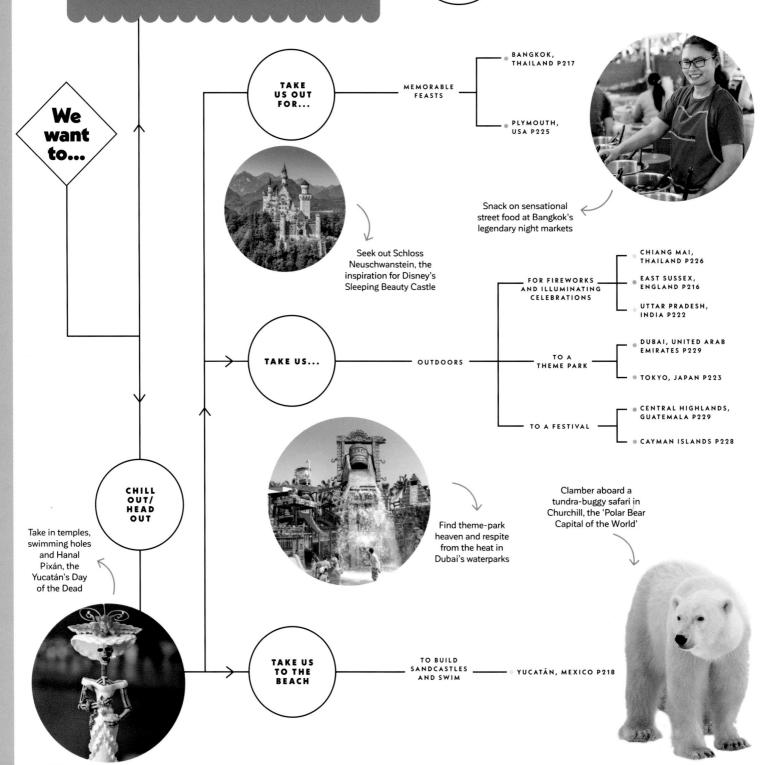

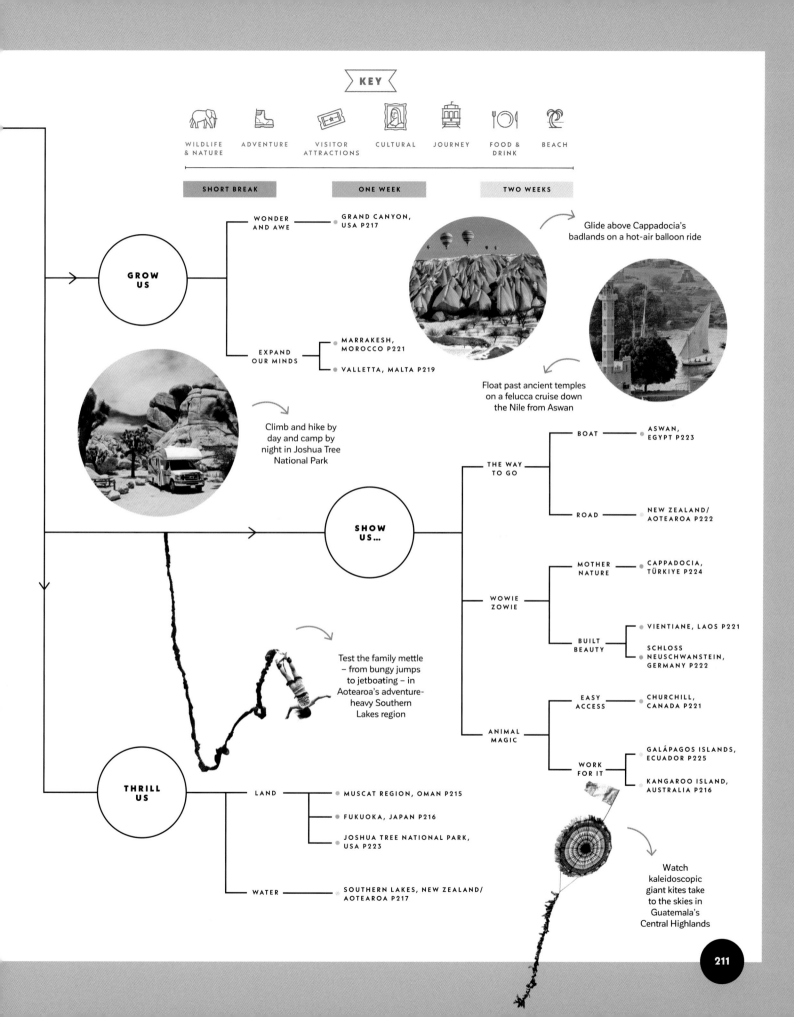

KEY

WILDLIFE & NATURE | ADVENTURE | VISITOR ATTRACTIONS | CULTURAL | JOURNEY | FOOD & DRINK | BEACH

SHORT BREAK | ONE WEEK | TWO WEEKS

GROW US

WONDER AND AWE — GRAND CANYON, USA P217

EXPAND OUR MINDS — MARRAKESH, MOROCCO P221
VALLETTA, MALTA P219

Glide above Cappadocia's badlands on a hot-air balloon ride

Float past ancient temples on a felucca cruise down the Nile from Aswan

Climb and hike by day and camp by night in Joshua Tree National Park

SHOW US...

THE WAY TO GO
BOAT — ASWAN, EGYPT P223
ROAD — NEW ZEALAND/ AOTEAROA P222

WOWIE ZOWIE
MOTHER NATURE — CAPPADOCIA, TÜRKIYE P224
BUILT BEAUTY — VIENTIANE, LAOS P221
SCHLOSS NEUSCHWANSTEIN, GERMANY P222

ANIMAL MAGIC
EASY ACCESS — CHURCHILL, CANADA P221
WORK FOR IT — GALÁPAGOS ISLANDS, ECUADOR P225
KANGAROO ISLAND, AUSTRALIA P216

Test the family mettle – from bungy jumps to jetboating – in Aotearoa's adventure-heavy Southern Lakes region

THRILL US

LAND — MUSCAT REGION, OMAN P215
FUKUOKA, JAPAN P216
JOSHUA TREE NATIONAL PARK, USA P223

WATER — SOUTHERN LAKES, NEW ZEALAND/ AOTEAROA P217

Watch kaleidoscopic giant kites take to the skies in Guatemala's Central Highlands

Events in November

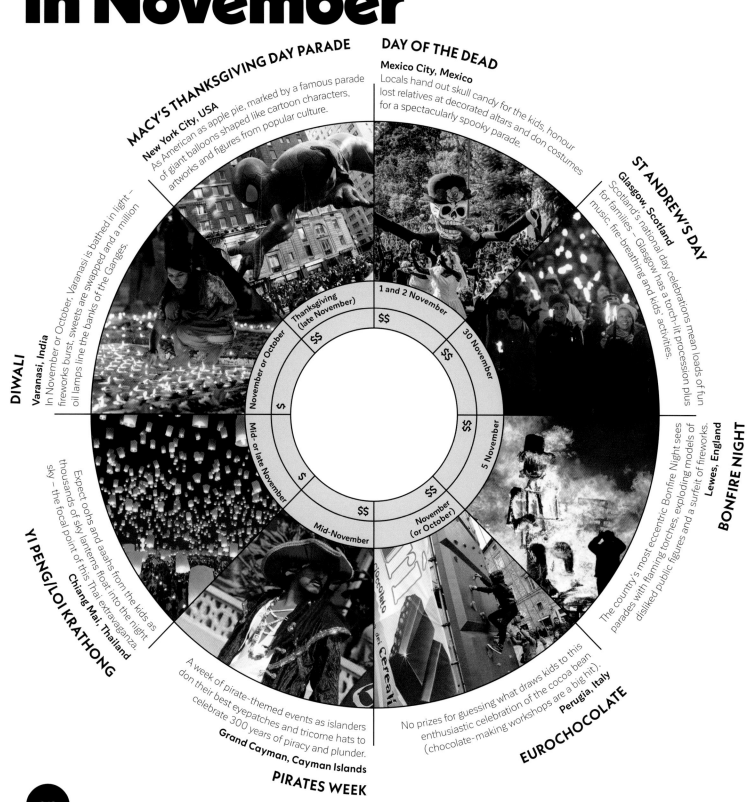

MACY'S THANKSGIVING DAY PARADE
New York City, USA
As American as apple pie, marked by a famous parade of giant balloons shaped like cartoon characters, artworks and figures from popular culture.

DAY OF THE DEAD
Mexico City, Mexico
Locals hand out skull candy for the kids, honour lost relatives at decorated altars and don costumes for a spectacularly spooky parade.

ST ANDREW'S DAY
Glasgow, Scotland
Scotland's national day celebrations mean loads of fun for families – Glasgow has a torch-lit procession plus music, fire-breathing and kids' activities.

DIWALI
Varanasi, India
In November or October, Varanasi is bathed in light – fireworks burst, sweets are swapped and a million oil lamps line the banks of the Ganges.

BONFIRE NIGHT
Lewes, England
The country's most eccentric Bonfire Night sees parades with flaming torches, exploding models of disliked public figures and a surfeit of fireworks.

YI PENG/LOI KRATHONG
Chiang Mai, Thailand
Expect oohs and aaahs from the kids as thousands of sky lanterns float into the night sky – the focal point of this Thai extravaganza.

PIRATES WEEK
Grand Cayman, Cayman Islands
A week of pirate-themed events as islanders don their best eyepatches and tricorne hats to celebrate 300 years of piracy and plunder.

EUROCHOCOLATE
Perugia, Italy
No prizes for guessing what draws kids to this enthusiastic celebration of the cocoa bean (chocolate-making workshops are a big hit).

Inner wheel

- Thanksgiving (late November) — $$
- 1 and 2 November — $$
- 30 November — $$
- 5 November — $$
- November (or October) — $$
- Mid-November — $$
- Mid- or late November — $
- November or October — $

TOTS TO PRE-TWEENS

● CAYMAN ISLANDS

November and December are ideal months to visit Dubai

● DUBAI, UNITED ARAB EMIRATES

America's Grand Canyon inspires awe in all ages

Be mesmerised by hot-air balloons rising over Cappadocia

● CHURCHILL, CANADA

● GRAND CANYON, USA

● CAPPADOCIA, TÜRKIYE

● CENTRAL HIGHLANDS, GUATEMALA

Browse the bazaars of Marrakesh

● SCHLOSS NEUSCHWANSTEIN, GERMANY

● MARRAKESH, MOROCCO

Enjoy quiet beaches, vivid reefs and mellow nightlife in Southern Thailand

● VALLETTA, MALTA

The highlands of Guatemala are rich in beautiful butterflies

EXPENSIVE BUT WORTH IT

GOOD VALUE

● MUSCAT REGION, OMAN

● SOUTHERN LAKES, NEW ZEALAND/AOTEAROA

● KANGAROO ISLAND, AUSTRALIA

Explore the enthralling Muscat region of Oman

Meet Queen Hapshepsut in Luxor, Egypt

● NEW ZEALAND/AOTEAROA

Darwin's finches evolved independently on the Galápagos Islands

● ASWAN, EGYPT

● TOKYO, JAPAN

● GALÁPAGOS ISLANDS, ECUADOR

● FUKUOKA, JAPAN

● BANGKOK, THAILAND

● YUCATÁN, MEXICO

Step back in time at the Plimoth Patuxet Museums in Massachusetts

● VIENTIANE, LAOS

● UTTAR PRADESH, INDIA

● PLYMOUTH, USA

Find golden Buddhas galore in Laos

● CHIANG MAI, THAILAND

● JOSHUA TREE NATIONAL PARK, USA

Bonfire Night in Lewes, East Sussex is unforgettable

● EAST SUSSEX, ENGLAND

OLDER KIDS AND TEENS

MUSCAT REGION OMAN

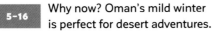

5-16 **Why now? Oman's mild winter is perfect for desert adventures.**
The Arabian Desert sizzles like a hotplate in summer, but temperatures drop to manageable levels – 25°C to 30°C by day (77°F to 86°F) – from November. This is the season for off-road adventures, and desert tours are easy to arrange if you don't feel up to tackling the dunes independently. Kids will get a giddy grin from dune-bashing – thundering across the dunes in a high-powered 4WD – on the Wahiba Sands south of Muscat. Park up and enjoy a different buzz scuttling up the dunes and then sliding or sandboarding down. The heat can build in the middle of the day, so schedule in some time splashing in Oman's emerald *wadis* (seasonal streams). Wadi Shab is an easy drive from Muscat; swimming in the lower pools is forbidden (they're a source of drinking water), but a 2.5km (1.5-mile) hike leads to limpid,

emerald pools where you can take a dip and duck into a hidden waterfall inside a rocky cavern.

Trip plan: Muscat is the main port of arrival for visitors to Oman, and an easy place to arrange 4WD hire and dune-bashing tours. Mix up the desert safaris with time on the coast – try Tiwi Beach near Wadi Shab or gently shelving Bandar Jissah Beach close to Muscat.

Need to know: For a taste of Oman's highlands, drive inland from Muscat to Wakan, where orchards and meadows nestle between ancient stone houses, irrigated by *falaj* water channels.

Other months: Dec-Mar – cool, busier, occasional rain; Apr-May & Oct – warmer, dry; Jun-Sep – baking.

(L) A water-cooled wonderland at Wadi Shab; (R) Walking the dunes at Wahiba Sands

FUKUOKA
JAPAN

12-16 Why now? It's sumō Grand Tournament time in Fukuoka.

Not many images scream 'Japan!' more than two mammoth sumō wrestlers battling it out on a *dōhyō* (packed-earth ring), in front of throngs of screaming fans – and if you visit Kyūshū island in November, when the last tournament of the year takes place in the city of Fukuoka, the whole family can see sumō for themselves. It's a thrilling experience, full of unique Japanese traditions, and it's guaranteed to enthral. This ancient sport dates back some 1500 years and is still very ritualistic, tied to the Shintō faith. Tournaments last 15 days, with Japanese news focused on daily bouts and results. Bouts between lower-ranked wrestlers take place earlier in the day. The real big boys come out after 3pm, with *yokozuna* (the highest ranks) fighting in the last bouts, from around 5.30pm. If you just want to experience sumō, go for a day or two, midweek, early in the tournament. But just as in all sports, excitement peaks as the finals approach. The champion is the wrestler with the best win-loss record. If the result comes down to the last day and it's *yokozuna* vs *yokozuna* to decide the title, everyone in Japan will be feverishly tuned in.

Trip plan: There are six Grand Tournaments every year, each lasting 15 days – three in Tokyo, plus one each in Osaka, Nagoya and Fukuoka.

Need to know: Check schedules and purchase tickets online (sumo.or.jp).

Other months: Jan, May & Sep – Tokyo sumo; Mar – Osaka sumo; Jul – Nagoya sumo.

KANGAROO ISLAND
AUSTRALIA

0-16 Why now? Visit KI before the heat and crowds of summer.

As its name suggests, Kangaroo Island, 13km (8 miles) off the South Australian mainland, is all about animals. A veritable zoo of seals, birds, dolphins, echidnas and – of course – kangaroos, it makes a perfect getaway for budding wilderness and wildlife fans, with plenty of active pursuits, too. There's lots to see under your own steam, including bushwalking trails ranging from short strolls right up to the epic 66km (41-mile), five-day Kangaroo Island Wilderness Trail. The safest swimming is along KI's north coast, where the water is warmer and there are fewer rips than down south; try Emu Bay, Stokes Bay, Snelling Beach or Western River Cove. For surfing, hit the uncrowded swells along the south coast. Pennington Bay has strong, reliable breaks; Vivonne Bay and Hanson Bay in the southwest also serve up some tasty waves. Cycling is a great way to see KI, although road distances can be surprisingly, well...distant.

Trip plan: Day trips are possible from Adelaide, but it'll be hectic; stay a few nights on KI if you can. To make the most of the island, you'll want your own wheels; Sealink runs a car ferry, so you can take a vehicle with you.

Need to know: Ferries between Cape Jervis (mainland) and Penneshaw (KI) take 45min. There are daily flights between Adelaide and KI's Kingscote Airport.

Other months: Dec-Feb – hottest, animals retreat into the bush; Mar-May – warm, calm; Jun-Aug – cheaper, cooler, whales; Oct – start of spring, blooming flowers.

EAST SUSSEX
ENGLAND

12-16 Why now? Bonfire Night in Lewes goes off with a bang.

Celebrating the day Guy Fawkes failed to blow up King James I, Bonfire Night is an English institution, and a great excuse for a family break in the green hills of East Sussex. An easy train ride from London or Brighton, Lewes is the setting for one of the country's most spectacular firework displays. Locals parade through the streets with flaming torches, and satirical effigies of public figures are set ablaze to commemorate the 17 Protestants martyred here in the 1550s. It's a blast for older children, but a bit much for youngsters; bring gloves and ear defenders and give the kids a firework safety briefing before the show. Stay for a few days either side of the celebrations to visit Lewes Castle (for panoramic views and a clamber over the ruins), and to take a stroll on the rolling coastal hills of the South Downs and drop into Brighton for fish and chips and off-season seaside vibes.

Trip plan: Trains run regularly from London Victoria and Brighton to Lewes, but book accommodation well in advance around Bonfire Night. There's limited parking during the festivities; it may be easier to stay in Brighton and travel to the firework display by train.

Need to know: Be wary of flying sparks during the celebrations: arrive early and find a vantage point set back from the action.

Other months: Dec-Feb – cold and windy; Mar-May & Oct – cooler weather; Jun-Sep – warm and dry, good for walking.

SOUTHERN LAKES
NEW ZEALAND/ AOTEAROA

0-16 Why now? Rev up for summer activities in the alpine resorts.

The Southern Lakes resorts of Queenstown and Wānaka have a vibe that reverberates around the globe when it comes to world-class family escapes – no tedium here! Famously the home of bungy jumping, stupendously scenic Queenstown – with the rugged Remarkables mountains towering above Lake Wakatipu – is a vibrant, pulsating place offering oh, so much to do. With younger children, hire bikes and hit easy paths around Queenstown Gardens and along Frankton Track; experienced teen riders will drool over gravity-fed downhill mountain biking from the top of the Skyline Gondola. Another way down is by tandem paragliding (no age restrictions; minimum weight 20kg/44lb). From Skyline's top station, ride the Skyline Luge or hike up Ben Lomond, the peak that rises high above town. Other Queenstown options include skydiving, jetboating, rafting, fishing and lake cruises – it's all here for the active family. Only an hour away by car, Wānaka is quieter, but the gorgeous scenery and activities are no less enthralling. There's top hiking and biking, and for indoor fun, Puzzling World and the Transport & Toy Museum will keep kids entertained for hours – as will simply hanging out at the town beach.

Trip plan: Fly into Queenstown Airport, pick up a rental car and cruise for a week or more; there are lots of accommodation and kid-friendly eating options in both resorts.

Need to know: Partially fed by glacial meltwater, Wakatipu and Wānaka Lakes are 'cool' for swimming.

Other months: Dec-Mar – warmer months; Apr – autumn colour; Jun-Oct – ski season.

BANGKOK
THAILAND

12-16 Why now? Soak up Bangkok's frenetic night markets in the cooler post-monsoon season.

Bangkok's night markets will beguile every teen who loves to shop, with factory-produced bargains spilling out of every other stall at Chatuchak Market on a Friday night. For a more upmarket experience – plus incredible food options – take them to Asiatique, with clothing, handicrafts and an unmissable Ferris wheel on the banks of the Chao Phraya. And for fans of everything retro, there's Talat Rot Fai Srinakharin (Train Night Market), with its nostalgia-inducing memorabilia (regale your kids with all your own childhood memories), including antique toys, quirky signs, vintage cars and other collectibles. Night markets can feel like a sensory overload, with the sizzle of street food, occasional blasts of Thai pop and kids' gadgets that light up as you approach – but cooler temperatures in November at least make it a less sweaty experience. Time your Bangkok trip well and you may catch the water-lantern festival of Loi Krathong, one of Thailand's most photogenic celebrations. (The paper lanterns are sold at night markets and make lightweight souvenirs to take home.)

Trip plan: To reach the markets, take public transport as far as you can, then walk or hail a cab for the final leg.

Need to know: As well as having a plan for reuniting should anyone get lost in the markets, it's wise to set a limit on how long you'll stay, and how much you'll spend (that's you too, parents).

Other months: Dec-Feb – driest; Mar-May – hot; Jul-Oct – rainy.

GRAND CANYON
USA

5-16 Why now? It's a cool, dry and crowd-free time to marvel at the Grand Canyon's beauty and size.

In November, visitor numbers in Grand Canyon National Park are hundreds of thousands fewer than in the summer months – meaning your family will have more space to spread out, hang out and thoroughly absorb the incredible landscape in all its glory. Head to the South Rim, which offers more expansive views and more extensive services than the other access points. A great way to see a lot of the sights and viewpoints is to rent bikes (and trailers, if necessary) from Bright Angel Bicycles and cycle the South Rim Trail, where the Trail of Time delivers a mini geology lesson. Ultimately, a hike into the canyon is one of the best ways to truly appreciate the scale of this most grandiose natural wonder. Follow the Bright Angel Trail, which descends 12.6km (7.8 miles) and 1360m (4460ft) to the fabulous Plateau Point lookout; hiking the whole thing is too much in a day, so choose an appropriate turnaround point based on your family's ability.

Trip plan: In November, it's much easier to get reservations at South Rim lodges, such as the historic El Tovar Hotel or Yavapai Lodge.

Need to know: The North Rim is open for day-use only (the lodge, campground and restaurants are closed) from mid-October to the end of the November, and closes completely December to May.

Other months: Dec-Feb – cold, low prices; Mar-May– cool, light crowds; Jun-Aug – hot, crowded; Sep – cooler, fewer crowds.

217

YUCATÁN MEXICO

Hanal Pixán
in the Yucatán
capital, Mérida

5-16 **Why now? Balmy beaches and brilliant ruins.**

The Yucatán Peninsula probably has a place in your family's collective daydreams. The beaches here – Caribbean-lapped lovelies, all white sand and palm trees – are idyllic; and the hinterland is straight out of a picture book: an adventure playground of thick jungle and azure cenotes (sinkholes) that are perfect for swimming. And it's historically fascinating, too. The Maya civilisation, which flourished from 2000 BCE until the 17th century, built some of their most impressive temples here, from mighty Chichén Itzá to lesser-known Uxmal, from the well-preserved pyramids of Ek' Balam to clifftop Tulum, right by the sea. Clamber to the top of these incredible structures and watch imaginations run riot. Warm, dry November offers perfect beach weather and warm,

calm seas – great for watersports and super for snorkelling – and you can roam the ancient sites among smaller crowds.

Trip plan: Avoid the all-inclusives in places such as Cancún (though the resort's airport is a useful gateway). Instead, seek out community-based tour operators and small Yucatán guesthouses, where you can try traditional food and visit off-the-beaten-track cenotes with expert resident guides.

Need to know: In the Yucatán, Día de Muertos (Day of the Dead) is celebrated as Hanal Pixán, which translates as 'food for the souls' in Maya and is celebrated across three days: 31 October, 1 November and 2 November. You'll see decorated altars at family homes, and lavish offerings of food and drink made to the dead.

Other months: Dec-Apr – warm, dry; May-Jun – hot, wetter; Jul-Oct – hurricane season.

© Loes Kieboom / Shutterstock

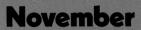

Head from Birgu's colourful harbour to the Malta Maritime Museum

VALLETTA
MALTA

5-16 Why now? Soak up Maltese culture during the mild winter.

Malta is a hedonistic sunshine hub in summer, but there are good reasons to visit this small, history-soaked island in winter. Mild November days are warm enough for building sandcastles, and perfect for clifftop walks and dipping into 8000 years of Maltese culture. Springboard from a cheap, off-season flight into days filled with history (start in Valletta's storied cathedral, palace and fort) and drop in on Popeye Village – a leftover set from the 1980 Robin Williams movie, with added low-key attractions (from playgrounds and inflatables to an assault course and mini golf). Smaller travellers will enjoy Malta's buccaneering history; prime them with stories of rampaging corsairs at Birgu's Malta Maritime Museum, then head out to empty bays such as Imġiebaħ to play pirates. The island's coastal cliffs are riddled with fossils, including the teeth of gigantic prehistoric sharks; the rules say these cannot be taken out of the country, but kids can admire them in situ, and there's a massive reconstructed Megalodon in Mdina's National Museum of Natural History.

Trip plan: Low-cost airlines fly to Malta from all over Europe; try easyJet or Ryanair for discount deals. The capital, Valletta, is the best base for a short winter break; distances are small, but rent a car to reach less-explored corners of the island.

Need to know: Maltese winters can feel warm in the sun, but cool in the shade; bring long-sleeved layers.

Other months: Dec-Feb – cool, quiet (except over Christmas); Mar-May & Oct – mild, dry; Jun-Sep – hot, busy.

© In Green / Shutterstock

219

(A)Vientiane's
Xieng Khuan, Laos;
(L) Polar bear in
Churchill, Canada;
(R) Marrakesh's
Djemaa El Fna in
full swing, Morocco

220

© AndreAnita / Shutterstock

VIENTIANE
LAOS

5-16 | **Why now?** Dry season brings out the colours in laid-back Vientiane.

Laos is the gentle choice in Southeast Asia, and its chilled-out capital, Vientiane, is a great stop for families, particularly in cooler, drier November. Pick accommodation with a garden and a pool and dive into a world of colour – temples decked out with radiant flower offerings; gleaming golden Buddhas; the gleaming spires of Pha That Luang. Blend days in the city with detours to sacred caves, and head over to Patuxai Park to watch fountains dance in front of the city's iconic victory arch, before hitting the night markets for fruit smoothies and chicken with sticky rice. Schedule in a day trip to Xieng Khuan, a riverside garden of fantastic Buddhist sculptures spawned from the imagination of an eccentric monk, then head north to Vang Vieng for a few days of tubing, kayaking, balloon rides and rock climbing by the Nam Song (Song River).

Trip plan: Flights connect Vientiane to key Asian hubs; explore the city by rented bicycle, chartered tuk-tuk or *songthaew* (pick-up taxi). Bus 14 trundles out to Xieng Khuan (1hr) from Talat Sao Bus Station; reach Vang Vieng by VIP bus or minibus.

Need to know: Younger kids may be spooked by the pumpkin-like structure depicting heaven, Earth and hell at Xieng Khuan, but the open-air Buddhas are cheerfully serene.

Other months: Dec-Mar – drier, cooler; Apr-May – hot, increasingly wet; Sep-Oct – hot and drenched by the monsoon.

MARRAKESH
MOROCCO

5-16 | **Why now?** For the imagination-firing sights and sounds of the Medina in the winter sun.

Marrakesh hits the senses in ways few other destinations do, being both a city geared to tourists and a thriving, working hub, full of people going about their day. A walk through the leather- and spice-scented souk alleyways will intrigue and delight. The Medina (Old Town) and Djemaa El Fna are where your kids' natural curiosity can run wild, the latter's sizzling grills giving an introduction to a multitude of novel eating experiences. Both are busiest around sunset; you could avoid this by visiting in the morning, but you will miss out on the atmosphere of the city's pulsing heart. As for where to stay: some Medina riads – traditional courtyard homes turned B&Bs – offer tranquillity and aesthetic charm; hotels in the Hivernage and Palmeraie neighbourhoods and suburbs are ideal for escaping the overstimulation of the city, with spacious gardens and large swimming pools.

Trip plan: Five to seven days gives you exploration and relaxation time. The city centre is easily explored on foot. Babies are best in a carrier or sling; take a lightweight pushchair for toddlers. Children are welcome in most places, and there are many public gardens and play spaces where you can meet and mingle with local families.

Need to know: Few restaurants offer separate kids' menus, but most will include a child-friendly option.

Other months: Jan – off-peak, cheaper prices; Mar-May – blossom, heat rising; Jun-Aug – very hot; Sep-Oct – perfect weather; Dec – busy around Christmas and New Year.

CHURCHILL
CANADA

5-16 | **Why now?** Peak polar bear season in Churchill, Manitoba.

This small, remote town on Hudson Bay is at the end of the line – literally, as it's the last stop on the 1700km-long (1100-mile) train line from Winnipeg. Churchill is also known as the 'Polar Bear Capital of the World', and each October and November, bears that have been forced off their seal-hunting grounds by the melting of ice in Hudson Bay arrive here to await the winter freeze. As soon as the ice is strong enough to carry them, they vanish out onto the bay. But during those weeks while the ice is forming, up to 900 bears are at large in the area around town, making Churchill the most accessible polar bear viewing destination on Earth. The town has a well-established industry, with most tours conducted in custom-made tundra buggies; with indoor/outdoor viewing areas, they can get close to the bears without jeopardising human or bear safety. With a bit of luck, you'll also see Arctic fox, caribou and snowy owls in their natural habitat.

Trip plan: Bear-watching tours range from half-day trips to multiday adventures staying in tundra lodges.

Need to know: Getting to Churchill on the Via Rail Canada network is an experience in itself; it's a two-day, two-night journey, and you may well prefer to fly in. There are no roads from Churchill that connect to the Canadian highway network.

Other months: Oct-May – long, frigid winter; Jun-Sep – short, cool summer, beluga whale-watching Jul to Aug.

UTTAR PRADESH
INDIA

5-16 Why now? Diwali brings fireworks and twinkling lights.

Celebrating the victory of light over darkness – and the return of the Hindu god Rama from exile after defeating the demon Ravana – Diwali is the ideal hook for a family trip to India. During the celebrations in November (or October), homes and gardens are illuminated by *diyas* (oil lamps), sweet treats are doled out (most kids love the milk-based fudge known as *barfi*), and fireworks fill the night with colour. In the sacred city of Varanasi, the Diwali celebrations are followed 15 days later by Dev Deepavali; take a family stroll along the riverside *ghats* (steps) at dusk to see the banks of the Ganges lit up by more than a million oil lamps. Use the time in between to explore the Indian plains – trains and buses provide easy access to Mughal-inspired Agra, British-tinged Lucknow, the holy Hindu city of Ayodhya and the Buddhist pilgrimage centres at Bodhgaya and Kushinagar.

Trip plan: Flying to Varanasi from overseas involves a change of planes in Delhi, Mumbai, Bengaluru or Kolkata; it's more fun to fly into Delhi and take the train. Comfortable, high-speed Vande Bharat trains connect the two cities in 8hr, or you can break the journey in Agra, Lucknow or Prayagraj (Allahabad).

Need to know: Diwali fireworks can be deafeningly loud – bring earplugs or ear defenders for everyone. Check online for upcoming festival dates (utsav.gov.in).

Other months: Dec-Feb – clear skies, cool nights; Mar-May – sunny, but hot; Jun-Sep – cooled by the monsoon rains; Oct – dry and warm.

NEW ZEALAND/ AOTEAROA

0-16 Why now? Road-trip Aotearoa in warm late-spring weather, before summer crowds arrive.

New Zealand's friendly feel and pristine landscapes make it the ideal country for a once-in-a-lifetime family adventure. Land in Auckland to pick up a vehicle, then head north to paddle, surf or sail aquamarine seas at the Bay of Islands. Take a history lesson at the Waitangi Treaty Grounds before venturing to remote Cape Reinga, a spiritually significant spot in Māori culture. Twisting roads back down the west coast can be a challenge with kids, but you'll see ancient kauri forests and black-sand beaches. Next it's Rotorua (via Hobbiton for the Tolkien fans) for everything from mountain biking to luging and dips in thermal springs. In the capital, Wellington, the Te Papa National Museum is an educational must-visit. Then take the Interislander ferry to the South Island. From a base in Nelson, hike and canoe in Abel Tasman National Park, and visit the former gold- and *pounamu*-mining town of Hokitika. Marvel at the (retreating) Franz Josef Glacier, followed by a long, mountainous drive to 'adventure capital' Queenstown – the perfect place for teens keen to (safely) push your anxiety limits.

Trip plan: Most rental outfits don't allow cars and campervans across the Cook Strait; expect to have to change vehicles.

Need to know: Each of these stops could keep you for days – take a whole month if you can.

Other months: Dec-Feb – summer; Apr-Sep – wintry, mild in the north; Oct – spring rains.

SCHLOSS NEUSCHWANSTEIN
GERMANY

5-16 Why now? Fairy-tale Bavaria views without wicked queues.

If your youngster is yearning to see a fantasy castle, you could go to Disney World – but why not visit the real thing? Commissioned by whimsical King Ludwig II of Bavaria in 1869, mountain-framed, multi-turreted Neuschwanstein inspired the Sleeping Beauty Castle that reigns over Walt's Orlando resort. Unlike most 19th-century European royals, the 'Swan King' preferred making music (he bankrolled Wagner) and ornate retreats than war, and was mocked as being mad. Perched upon a rocky rise above his childhood home in the foothills of the Bavarian Alps, where the River Lech flows into the Forggensee, Neuschwanstein was Ludwig's long-held dream project, but he occupied the partially finished palace for just 172 days before being deposed and dying (in suspiciously non-fairy-tale circumstances) aged 40 in 1886, and never got to see its trademark towers. Designed solely for the use of Ludwig and his retinue, Neuschwanstein now greets over a million visitors per year – 6000 each summer's day. It's much quieter and more enchanting in November, surrounded by snow-topped peaks cloaked in colourful autumn foliage – a true fairy-tale vision (you can have a snowball fight in the gardens, too).

Trip plan: Visit via Hohenschwangau, a 2hr-drive from Munich, home to the Museum der Bayerischen Könige (Museum of the Bavarian Kings). Also explore nearby Schloss Linderhof, where the incredible cave-like Venus Grotto includes an underground lake and waterfall.

Need to know: The best Neuschwanstein views are from Füssen's Marienbrücke (Mary's Bridge).

Other months: Dec-Feb – snow; Mar-May – idyllic; Jun-Jul – mad busy.

ASWAN
EGYPT

5-16 **Why now?** Enjoy the Nile in quiet calm, before the crowds descend.

In November in southern Egypt, days are warm and nights are cool – optimum conditions for watching the banks of the River Nile slip by from a traditional felucca sailboat. The classic Nile cruise starts from Aswan, following the river to Luxor over two or three days, with nights spent on cushions and blankets on deck. It's an adventure that will conjure up *Arabian Nights* fantasies for explorers of all ages, and you can choose the level of comfort – the best felucca cruises have support boats with toilets and showers. This is the quiet season, so bookend the river journey with calmer-than-average visits to the Philae Temple complex (particularly the Temple of Isis) and the Nubia Museum in Aswan; the hieroglyph-covered Karnak and Luxor temples; and the Valley of the Kings – last resting place of King Tut and Rameses III – at Thebes, where cute *tuf-tuf* (electric trains) ferry visitors between the Visitor Centre and the tombs.

Trip plan: Domestic flights zip to Aswan from Cairo, but it's more atmospheric to take the overnight train (13hr). Abela sleeper trains run daily; families can book adjoining two-berth compartments for extra space. Felucca cruises to Luxor are easy to arrange through tour operators, or on arrival in Aswan.

Need to know: Don't let Nile mosquitoes distract you from the scenery – cover up with light-coloured long sleeves and trousers, and use bug repellent.

Other months: Dec-Feb – cooler days and nights, big crowds; Mar-May & Sep-Oct – warm, quieter; Jun-Aug – scorching, few visitors.

TOKYO
JAPAN

0-16 **Why now?** For quieter times in this busy city.

Famously crowded, colourful and charismatic, Japan's capital is a parents' dream when it comes to the logistics of travel: it's clean, safe and comes with every modern convenience; and Tokyo is a huge attraction in itself – the uniqueness of Japan is all around you and kids will find a wealth of weird little things to intrigue, from discovering unusual foods in a supermarket to playing with a plethora of buttons that operate functions on a toilet. Of the main kid-centred attractions, high-tech Odaiba district, on reclaimed land in Tokyo Bay, is home to the Legoland Discovery Center and Joypolis, a kid-captivating SEGA-themed indoor amusement park. Japan has a childlike fascination with theme parks, and Tokyo Disneyland and Tokyo DisneySea in neighbouring Chiba Prefecture are its most popular. Back in the city, the 634m (2080ft) Tokyo Skytree is the planet's second-tallest freestanding tower; expect stupendous views, and don't miss the 4th-floor Pokémon Center. Find anime heaven at the Ghibli Museum in Mitaka; the pop-culture-obsessed district of Akihabara is crammed with video game iconography; Harajuku's Takeshita-dōri is a popular haunt for boho youth.

Trip plan: Tokyo has two international airports: Haneda, 15km (9 miles) south; and Narita, 60km (37 miles) east.

Need to know: Avoid riding trains and subways until after 9.30am during the week.

Other months: Dec-Mar – winter, turning to spring; Apr – cherry blossoms; Jun-Sep – hot, humid; Oct – autumn colour.

JOSHUA TREE NATIONAL PARK
USA

5-16 **Why now?** Cool weather for rock-climbing and desert hikes on untrodden trails.

Replete with intriguing rock formations and the twisted contours of its namesake tree, California's Joshua Tree National Park is a place to fire up kids' imaginations amid fantastic, otherworldly landscapes. Miles of hiking trails reward with unusual plant life, old mines to explore, awe-inspiring views and so many rocks to scramble around on. (Don't miss the iconic and creepy Skull Rock.) It's also a climbing and bouldering playground and a great place to take rock-climbing to the next level, with routes for all skill levels – hire a local climbing guide to show you the ropes. Don't want to spend your entire vacation hiking and climbing? Take a break in the town of Twentynine Palms. Dig in to local history at the Old Schoolhouse Museum or paint pottery at the Creative Center; at the Sky's The Limit Observatory, you can walk the Orrery (a solar-system model) or attend a Saturday-night star party (book ahead; they only take place once a month).

Trip plan: The park is a feasible day trip from Palm Springs, but the towns of Twentynine Palms and Joshua Tree are convenient bases for longer stays. You can camp in the park, but be aware that temperatures drop drastically at night.

Need to know: There is no food service and limited water stops in the national park; bring more than you think you'll need!

Other months: Dec-Feb – cooler, possible snow, lighter crowds, lower prices; Mar-Apr – mild, peak season; May-Sep – sweltering; Oct – pleasant weather, lighter crowds.

Hot-air balloons over Cappadocia's fairy chimneys

CAPPADOCIA
TÜRKIYE

5-16 Why now? Balloon rides beckon on crisp, clear mornings.

With its cave homes and fairy chimneys, Cappadocia could have been plucked from a swords-and-sorcery fantasy. Subterranean cities such as Özkonak, Kaymaklı and Derinkuyu are portals to another world, where young imaginations can run wild in maze-like tunnels and hidden rock-cut chapels. Ramp up the adventure by staying in a cave hotel; there are great choices for families in the Göreme. Surrounded by epic sweeps of golden, moonscape valley, this honey-coloured, hollowed-out-of-the-hills village is the main base for hot-air balloon rides over Cappadocia's erosion-sculpted badlands. Get the kids to bed early – most balloon rides take flight at dawn, when winds are steady and the air is crisp and clear. Set aside some time for ground-based activities such as horse and ATV rides, hikes around the fairy chimneys (try the needle spires of the Görkündere Valley), and wandering the fresco-filled chambers of rock-cut churches, chapels and monasteries in Göreme Open-Air Museum.

Trip plan: Nevşehir is the closest airport to Göreme, with daily flights from İstanbul, or you can travel overland by bus. Block out at least three days to explore Cappadocia's badlands, roaming from village to village by dolmuş minibus; services fan out from the Nevşehir's Otogar bus stand.

Need to know: The minimum age for ballooning in Göreme is six years. Wrap everyone up warmly for dawn flights – winter mornings are cool and it's several degrees colder at altitude.

Other months: Dec-Feb – chilly, occasional snow; Mar-May & Sep – cooler, quieter, clearer skies; Jun-Aug – hot and busy.

Galápagos wildlife:
(R) Capturing a marine iguana;
(B) Green turtle

GALÁPAGOS ISLANDS ECUADOR

 Why now? Warm weather, calm seas – and fewer visitors.

Known for their role in Darwin's theory of evolution, the Galápagos Islands may just inspire your kids to think differently about the world. Some of the creatures here – including marine iguanas, the world's only ocean-going lizards – are found nowhere else on Earth, while sea lions, fur seals and beauties such as rainbow-hued Sally Lightfoot crabs abound. The Galápagos is a bucket-list destination, but while many believe that the only way to visit is on a liveaboard all-inclusive cruise, there is a cheaper way to see these unique islands. If you're into independent travel, using inter-island boats and basing yourself at onshore hotels and guesthouses on the islands of Santa Cruz, San Cristóbal or Isabela is the way to go. Staying on land and island-hopping offers a family-friendly experience

and allows for flexibility. Explore beaches, eat where the locals do and take day trips. But note that 95% of the Galápagos' land area is protected by the Galápagos National Park Directorate (GNPD); tourists can visit specific sites only, with park-certified naturalist guides.

Trip plan: Give yourselves as long as you can on your Galápagos adventure.

Need to know: The Galápagos lie around 1000km (600 miles) off the coast of Ecuador. The only way to get here is by air from the mainland, flying into airports on Baltra Island or San Cristóbal.

Other months: Mid-Dec to mid-Jan & mid-Jun to early Sep – peak season; Jun-Oct– cooler, quieter.

PLYMOUTH USA

 Why now? Celebrate the Thanksgiving holiday with food, fun and a history lesson.

Though popular notions of the 'first Thanksgiving' are filled with inaccuracies, they still embrace this day with gusto in Plymouth, Massachusetts, site of the original harvest feast. On the weekend before, Plymouth comes to life as pilgrims, pioneers and patriots parade the streets of 'America's Hometown'. There's also a food festival, concerts, a Wampanoag pavilion and a historic village – all fun for kids. On

Thanksgiving Day, many Indigenous people recognise a National Day of Mourning with a ceremony on Coles Hill, remembering the ancestors who were killed by European settlers. Throughout the week, the Plimoth Patuxet Museums offer special meals and programming that strive to honour the essence of the holiday – gratitude – while also correcting the myths that surround it. Participants learn about the harvest celebration that the Pilgrims and Pokanoket peoples shared, as well as the first official Thanksgiving holiday, some 200 years later.

Trip plan: Lodgings in Plymouth are limited; book ahead if you want to stay in town. Alternatively, take advantage of low-season rates in Boston or Cape Cod.

Need to know: Entertaining and educational for all ages, the three Plimoth Patuxet sites comprise the replica of the *Mayflower*, a 1627 Pilgrim settlement, and a Patuxet homesite. Combo tickets are available.

Other months: Dec-Mar – low season, Plimoth Patuxet Museums closed; Apr-Jun – shoulder season, cooler, some rain; Jul-Oct – peak season, crowded attractions.

CHIANG MAI
THAILAND

5-16 **Why now? Participate in Yi Peng and Loi Krathong,** Thailand's most illuminating spectacles. November ushers in the cool season in northern Thailand, which translates to dry skies and daytime temperatures on the right side of 30°C (86°F). Tourist season is well underway, but you won't mind the company if you arrive during Yi Peng, the Lanna festival of light. Every November, throngs descend on Chiang Mai, releasing untold thousands of paper hot-air balloons, which swarm across the night sky like shoals of illuminated jellyfish. The festival coincides with Loi Krathong, when floating, candlelit offerings are set adrift on rivers, lakes and ponds, and fireworks fill the sky, adding an extra layer of magic. Either side of the celebrations, take some downtime clambering around ancient Buddhist *chedis* (stupas), haggling for trinkets in street markets, swimming in jungle waterholes and eating some of Thailand's best street food.

Trip plan: International flights serve Chiang Mai from across Asia, but things get busy during Yi Peng, so book rooms and transport well ahead. The festival is well organised, and tickets are sold online in advance, granting access to the main lantern-release site, though you can observe the lanterns for free from hotel and bar rooftops.

Need to know: Street vendors sell Yi Peng fire lanterns and Loi Krathong offerings, and visitors are welcome to release their own – but check approved release locations as these move regularly.

Other months: Dec-Feb – cool, dry, busy; Mar-May – hot but quiet, except during Songkran in Apr; Jun-Oct – warm and rain-drenched.

(L) Yi Peng lanterns;
(R) Loi Krathong at Chiang Mai's Wat Phan Tao

Pirates take
to the seas off
Grand Cayman

CAYMAN ISLANDS

5-16 Why now? Live the pirate's life in an island paradise.

Kids of all ages summon their inner Jack Sparrow during the Caymans' unique Pirate Week festival, which celebrates the role of pirates in the island's history. In Grand Cayman, the week-long event kicks off with a theatrical landing ceremony, when 'Captain Morgan' leads a flotilla of decorated pirate ships into George Town Harbour; festivities continue with thematic floats and marching bands parading through the city streets. There follows a week of swashbuckling fun, including a pirate pooch parade, a cardboard boat race and an after-dark illuminated parade, plus live music, street food and fireworks. It's enough to make you want to give up the life of a lubber and run off to sea – until the end, of course. The festival concludes with a public trial, when the pirates are sentenced to walk the plank. Aaaargh!

Trip plan: Most of Grand Cayman's pirating events take place in George Town, near the cruise ship terminal. Staying at an out-of-town hotel – perhaps at one of the many resorts on gorgeous Seven Mile Beach – will enable an easy retreat if your family needs a break from the festivities.

Need to know: Pirate festivals take place on all three Cayman Islands throughout November – the Grand Cayman Pirate Week is usually mid-month, with smaller weekend events on Cayman Brac and Little Cayman in early and late November respectively. November is the Caymans' quieter shoulder season, but Pirate Week brings big crowds.

Other months: Dec-Apr – dry, hot, peak tourist season; May-Oct – rainy season, hurricanes possible.

DUBAI UNITED ARAB EMIRATES

5-16 **Why now?** Enjoy milder weather before the winter-sun crowds descend in December.

Dubai is perfect for small kids looking for big adventures. First stop is Dubai Mall, where you can bounce between KidZania, the aquarium, an indoor trampoline park, ice-skating, cinemas, shopping and places to eat. As the sun sets, head to Burj Khalifa for views of a changing skyline, then take in the Dubai Fountain show. Bring out your inner child next, at IMG Worlds of Adventure (Marvel fans take note) or Legoland Dubai (best for children up to 12). In the Al Fahidi Historical Neighbourhood, the must-visit Sheikh Mohammed Centre for Cultural Understanding offers a window into UAE traditions and customs (look online for sessions pitched to under-10s). Next, take an *abra* (boat) across Dubai Creek to explore dazzling traditional souqs. For more nature-inspired activities, there's the Dubai Safari Park, with Arabian desert or African savannah safari tours; or you can get up close to a South American sloth at the indoor tropical paradise of Green Planet. On a day trip to the desert, ride a camel or take older kids quad-biking in the dunes (children aged nine to 15 can share with a parent). Round off your trip with shopping at the boutique Souk Madinat Jumeirah, Ibn Battuta Mall, Wafi Mall and Dubai Outlet Mall.

Trip plan: Mix up your public-transport trips with *abras* and ferries.

Need to know: Sun protection and plenty of hydration are a must.

Other months: Dec-Feb – milder days, cool nights; Mar-Jun – humidity starts; Jul-Oct – hot.

Getting ready to fly in Santiago Sacatepéquez

© Lucy Brown - loca4motion / Shutterstock

CENTRAL HIGHLANDS GUATEMALA

5-16 **Why now?** Kites of every colour flutter over the highlands.

Every kid loves a kite, and the people of Guatemala's central highlands have been raising kites as big as houses for centuries on All Saints' Day at the start of November. The Festival de Barriletes Gigantes is celebrated most enthusiastically in the towns of Santiago Sacatepéquez and Sumpango, nestled in the hills to north of the former Guatemalan capital of Antigua. Mayan villagers create gigantic, psychedelic kites from bamboo and paper to guide the souls of their ancestors; the giant kites stay tethered to the ground, while smaller octagonal kites dart daintily overhead – snap up a kite from one of the many vendors in the villages and let your kids join in the flying fun. Make the festival the anchor for a week-long tour of Guatemala's highlands, visiting charming, volcano-ringed Antigua, the mask-filled market at Chichicastenango, and outrageously picturesque Lake Atitlán.

Trip plan: Flying into Guatemala City, it's a short trip (1hr to 2hr) by taxi or 'chicken' bus to Antigua. Village buses run regularly from Antigua to Chichicastenango and Panajachel on Lake Atitlán; arrange taxi transport to Santiago Sacatepéquez or Sumpango through your hotel. Book rooms and transport in advance around All Saints' Day.

Need to know: To keep kids entertained at Lake Atitlán, rent a kayak or stand-up paddleboard, take the local ferry to Mayan villages, or book onto a chocolate-making session or a cocoa plantation tour.

Other months: Dec-Feb – drier, cooler; Mar-Apr – hot, humid; May-Oct – rainy, stormy.

229

December

WHERE TO GO WHEN WITH KIDS

HAVE AN ADVENTURE

We want to...

TAKE US OUT FOR...

MEMORABLE FEASTS — HONG KONG, CHINA P239

Join Hong Kong families for a Sunday dim sum feast

Salzburg in the snow – ideal conditions for a visit from the anti-Santa Krampus!

TAKE US...

OUTDOORS

FOR FESTIVE FUN
- JAMAICA P243
- SALZBURG, AUSTRIA P249
- ST-MARTIN P238

TO A THEME PARK
- SAN ANTONIO, USA P239
- COPENHAGEN, DENMARK P244

FOR SOME KID-FRIENDLY FUN — RIO DE JANEIRO, BRAZIL P237

INDOORS

TO A MUSEUM
- LONDON, ENGLAND P239
- KRAKÓW, POLAND P242

CHILL OUT/ HEAD OUT

Swim from blinding-white beaches and snorkel over sculptures in Cancún

Snorkel reef-rich waters off the coast of Rarotonga, Cook Islands

TAKE US TO THE BEACH

TO BUILD SANDCASTLES AND SWIM
- SOUTH COAST, URUGUAY P242
- RAROTONGA, COOK ISLANDS P235

TO SNORKEL OR SURF
- SOUTH COAST, SRI LANKA P238
- CANCÚN, MEXICO P249

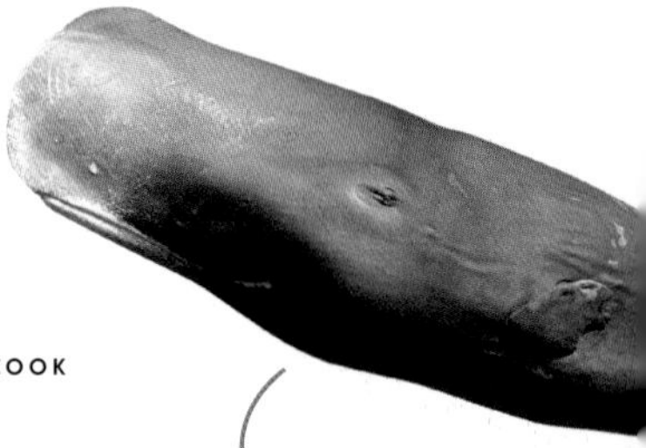

December is the perfect time to see sperm whales off Sri Lanka's south coast

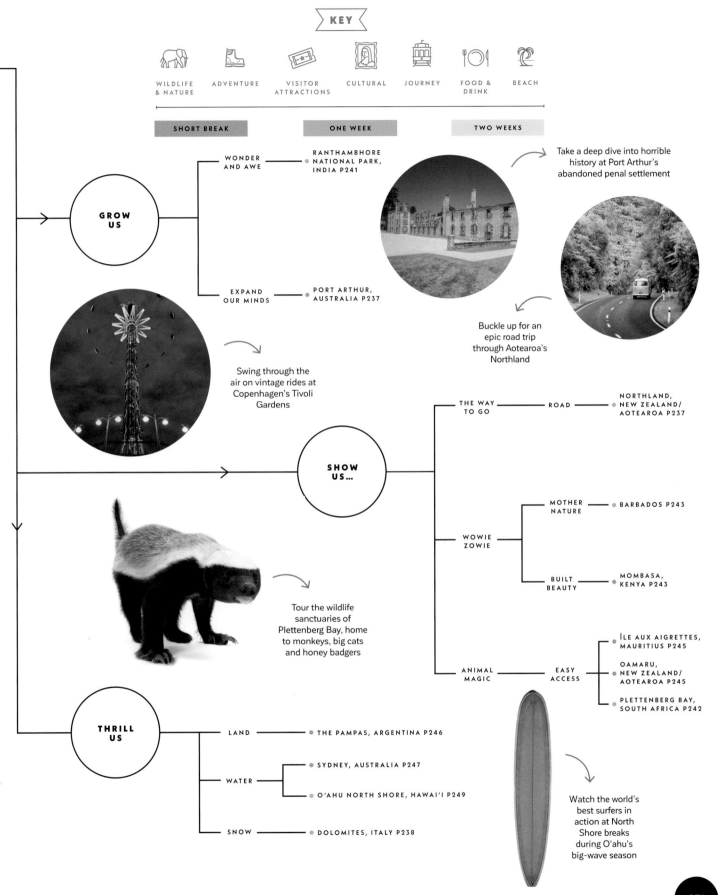

SHORT BREAK   ONE WEEK   TWO WEEKS

GROW US

WONDER AND AWE — RANTHAMBHORE NATIONAL PARK, INDIA P241

EXPAND OUR MINDS — PORT ARTHUR, AUSTRALIA P237

Take a deep dive into horrible history at Port Arthur's abandoned penal settlement

Buckle up for an epic road trip through Aotearoa's Northland

Swing through the air on vintage rides at Copenhagen's Tivoli Gardens

SHOW US…

THE WAY TO GO — ROAD — NORTHLAND, NEW ZEALAND/ AOTEAROA P237

WOWIE ZOWIE — MOTHER NATURE — BARBADOS P243

WOWIE ZOWIE — BUILT BEAUTY — MOMBASA, KENYA P243

Tour the wildlife sanctuaries of Plettenberg Bay, home to monkeys, big cats and honey badgers

ANIMAL MAGIC — EASY ACCESS — ÎLE AUX AIGRETTES, MAURITIUS P245

OAMARU, NEW ZEALAND/ AOTEAROA P245

PLETTENBERG BAY, SOUTH AFRICA P242

THRILL US

LAND — THE PAMPAS, ARGENTINA P246

WATER — SYDNEY, AUSTRALIA P247

O'AHU NORTH SHORE, HAWAI'I P249

SNOW — DOLOMITES, ITALY P238

Watch the world's best surfers in action at North Shore breaks during O'ahu's big-wave season

Events in December

HORNBILL FESTIVAL
Kohima, Nagaland, India
Nagaland's diverse tribal communities come together in Kohima for dances, rituals and trading in this vividly colourful celebration of Indian Adivasi culture.

First week in December — $$

KRAMPUSNACHT & FEAST OF ST NICHOLAS
Innsbruck, Austria
The holidays take a spooky turn in the Tyrol, as demons parade through the streets before St Nick returns to make everything Christmassy again.

5 and 6 December — $$

MONARCH BUTTERFLY MIGRATION
Michoacán, Mexico
Add extra magic to a family trip to Mexico by watching millions of migrating butterflies at the Monarch Butterfly Biosphere Reserve.

October to March — $

TRIPLE CROWN OF SURFING
Oʻahu, Hawaiʻi
Waves can reach 50ft (15m) during this legendary surf comp from November to December, and kids can take on gentler swells in the shallows.

Three events in Nov & Dec — $$

INTERNATIONAL FESTIVAL OF THE SAHARA
Douz, Tunisia
Give children a taste of nomadic desert life at this celebration of Berber and Bedouin culture, complete with camel races, dancing and parades.

Four days in late December — $$

CHICHIBU YOMATSURI
Chichibu, Japan
Kids love the thrill of being out after dark, and this nighttime festival is one of Japan's best, with fireworks, processions and lantern-covered floats.

2 and 3 December — $$$

FIESTA DE SANTO TOMÁS
Chichicastenango, Guatemala
A week of rituals, dancing and festivities, fusing Mayan and Christian traditions – kids will boggle at the elaborate masks and costumes.

21 December — $

GRAND MARKET
Jamaica
See a different side to Christmas markets in towns across Jamaica on Christmas Eve – street stalls are piled high with festive foods, toys and decorations.

Christmas Eve (24 December) — $

● ST-MARTIN

Admire Italy's
Dolomites from the
resort of Cortina
d'Ampezzo

Pay your respects to the
king of the kauri tree
forest in New Zealand

● DOLOMITES, ITALY

The threadfin
butterflyfish is
common in the
Cook Islands

● RAROTONGA,
COOK ISLANDS

● NORTHLAND, NEW
ZEALAND/AOTEAROA

● SAN ANTONIO, USA

● OAMARU NEW ZEALAND/
AOTEAROA

Climb the Gothic
towers of Wawel
Castle in Kraków

● KRAKÓW, POLAND

The Steampunk HQ
at Oamaru in New
Zealand's South Island

● RIO DE JANEIRO, BRAZIL

● SYDNEY, AUSTRALIA

● LONDON, ENGLAND

● SOUTH COAST, URUGUAY

See London from
double-decker bus

● HONG KONG, CHINA

● PLETTENBERG BAY,
SOUTH AFRICA

Ride the Victoria Peak
Tram for views over
Hong Kong

Ring-tailed
lemurs recover
at a sanctuary in
South Africa

● O'AHU NORTH SHORE,
HAWAI'I

● JAMAICA

The festival of
Junkanoo is observed in
December in Jamaica

● BARBADOS

● ÎLE AUX AIGRETTES, MAURITIUS

● THE PAMPAS, ARGENTINA

● SOUTH COAST, SRI LANKA

● RANTHAMBHORE
NATIONAL PARK, INDIA

Beware the scary
figure of Krampus in
Salzburg, Austria

● MOMBASA, KENYA

● CANCÚN, MEXICO

● COPENHAGEN,
DENMARK

● SALZBURG, AUSTRIA

Watch Bengal
tigers from a
distance in
Ranthambhore
National Park

Pause at a wildlife
conservancy
in Port Arthur,
Tasmania

● PORT ARTHUR,
AUSTRALIA

RAROTONGA
COOK ISLANDS

`0-16` **Why now? Summer off-season with fewer visitors.**

It's always a good time to visit this happy, family-friendly isle, the gateway and capital of the Cook Islands. December may be summer – a tad warmer, with occasional tropical showers – but Rarotonga is relatively small and easterly trade winds keep the air moving. It's the perfect playground for kids, and with family values an important part of Cook Islands' culture, you'll be welcomed warmly wherever you go. There's a full range of accommodation – from budget self-catering apartments right up to full-on resorts with all the kid-friendly facilities – and there's lots to do, from swimming and snorkelling to lagoon cruises or cross-island treks; choosing between the clockwise and anti-clockwise public bus for the 40km (25-mile) trip around the island is fun in itself. And with plenty of tropical fruit and seafood on menus, it's also a healthy place to holiday. The not-to-be-missed Saturday morning Punanga Nui Market in Avarua sells delicious cooked food, fresh produce and fish, and features arts, crafts, souvenirs and live entertainment, while Muri's night markets offer up all sorts of delicacies for dinner.

Trip plan: Fly to Rarotonga direct from Auckland, Sydney, Honolulu or Tahiti; stay at least a week, longer if you also plan to stay on the Cook Islands' other top destination, Aitutaki.

Need to know: Lots of Cook Islanders living overseas make the trip home for Christmas and New Year; flights can get booked out later in the month.

Other months: Nov-Apr – summer, warmer, wetter; May-Oct – winter, cooler, drier (whale-watching Jul to Oct).

(L) A crown of leis on Rarotonga
(R) The Cook Islands' underwater wonderland

© Dirk Freder / Getty Images

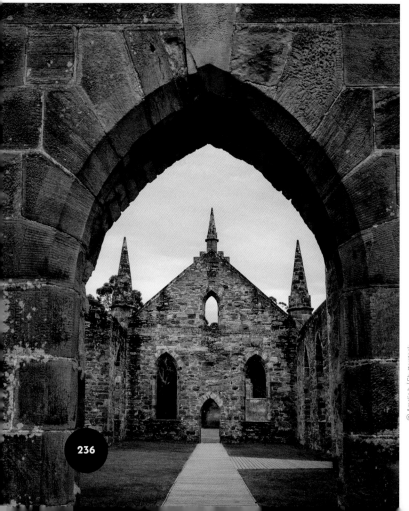

(A) Jumping in at Rio's Ipanema Beach, Brazil;
(L) Explore the ruins of Port Arthur's penal colony;
(R) Sailing the Bay of Islands, Aotearoa

RIO DE JANEIRO
BRAZIL

5–16 **Why now?** See Rio from above and below before the Christmas crowds arrive.

Rio de Janeiro is steamy in December, but the crowds don't gather until Christmas, and evening rain showers take the edge off the heat when it's time to sleep (assuming you don't get carried away by the city's samba beats). Family trips to the Brazilian capital are focused on the beaches – Copacabana has watersports for older kids, while nearby Leblon and Ipanema have dedicated toddler playgrounds – and lush green spaces, particularly the palm-shaded Botanical Gardens (which also has a welcoming play area and cafe). Get a different view of Rio from above by bundling the kids onto the Sugarloaf Mountain cable car or the cog railway to the city-embracing statue of Cristo Redentor (Christ the Redeemer). With older children, tack on a waterfall hike with bonus monkeys – the jungle-fringed Cachoeira dos Primatas and Solar da Imperatriz falls are easily reached from the southern suburb of Horto.

Trip plan: To get the best from Rio after a long flight, stay in Copacabana or Ipanema, and settle in for a week, exploring beaches, gardens, museums and monuments. Get around by metro, taxi or Uber, or the Bike Itaú rideshare scheme.

Need to know: Rio has a reputation for crime but this is a less of a risk in the touristy Copacabana, Ipanema and Leblon districts. At night, be cautious and get around by taxi.

Other months: Jan-Mar – hot, rainy, busy, Carnival; Apr-May & Oct-Nov – warm, drier; Jun-Sep – less rain, cool nights.

NORTHLAND
NEW ZEALAND/
AOTEAROA

0–16 **Why now?** Northland is ripe for a road trip in early December.

North of Auckland lies a land of intriguing NZ history, uncluttered beaches and mammoth kauri trees, perfect for a fun family road trip before Kiwi kids start their summer holidays. Kick off your loop around Northland with a drive up to the Bay of Islands and a cruise on its legendary turquoise waters. Nearby, the Waitangi Treaty Grounds is the birthplace of Aotearoa/New Zealand – a special place in the nation's history and a cultural highlight. Consider spending a night or two in historic Russell, a gorgeous little town that's best reached by ferry from Paihia. Continuing north, fabled Ninety Mile Beach is actually 88km (55 miles) long and an official highway, though not recommended for rental cars; take the sealed inland route instead, but stop off at Ninety Mile's Te Paki Giant Sand Dunes for sandboarding on the massive dunes – likely a big hit with teens. Cape Reinga is as far north as you can go. Heading back to Auckland along the western coast, pay homage to Tāne Mahuta (Lord of the Forest); the grandaddy of all kauri trees, it's reachable via a five-minute walk off SH12, which runs through the Waipoua Forest.

Trip plan: Rent a car in Auckland and drive a loop around Northland; give yourself a week of exploring with the family.

Need to know: If you plan a trip in the busy period from Christmas to New Year, book accommodation well in advance.

Other months: Oct-Apr – warmer, busy; May-Sep – off-season, cooler.

PORT ARTHUR
AUSTRALIA

12–16 **Why now?** Experience the light-and-shade of Tasmania: convicts, ghosts and horrible history, under the Aussie summer sun.

Dangling off the bottom of Australia, the 'Apple Isle' feels idyllic, but Tasmania has such a troubled past that it had to change its name in 1856 – and nowhere is the haunting history of Van Diemen's Land better explained than in Port Arthur's eye-opening penal settlement, where long-dead convicts bring the past to life. It's hard to imagine when you first cross the Eaglehawk Neck isthmus to reach the ocean-stroked Tasman Peninsula east of Hobart, but true horror happened here. While older kids will be fascinated by the prison buildings, ingeniously engaging exhibits and the boat excursion to the Isle of the Dead burial ground, it's during an after-dusk lantern-lit ghost tour that their minds and spines will really start tingling. Regardless of whether you believe in spirits, simply seeing the site at night instead of bathed in the midsummer sun brings home how chilling the events that played out here 200 years ago really were – and if the mortuary doesn't make your hair stand up...

Trip plan: Take the ferry from Port Melbourne to Devonport, then rent a car and spend at least a week touring Tassie: swim in Wineglass Bay on the fantastic Freycinet Peninsula, explore Hobart's historic streets and look for Tasmanian devils around Cradle Mountain.

Need to know: Ghost tours aren't suitable for young children (or anyone susceptible to nightmares).

Other months: Mar-May & Sep-Nov – fewer people, less reliable weather; Jun-Jul – surprisingly cold.

237

WHERE TO GO WHEN WITH KIDS

SOUTH COAST
SRI LANKA

5-16 Why now? Peak whale-watching season on Sri Lanka's sand-sprinkled south coast.

Sri Lanka's dreamy south coast shakes off the rains in December, and the warm days invite long, lazy hours on the sand. Kicking off from the historic, Dutch-flavoured town of Galle, families can drift between palm-fringed surf beaches, taking in easy-going resort towns such as Weligama – one of the best places in the Indian Ocean for newbie surfers, with its shallow bay and small but consistent waves, and surf schools that tutor kids (aged six and up). At Mirissa, the adventure gets even bigger: mighty blue whales frequent these waters at this time of year, accompanied by fin whales, Bryde's whales, sperm whales and megapods of spinner dolphins. Responsible whale-watching operators, such as Raja & the Whales, will get you close (but not too close) to these huge cetaceans, and afterwards you can splash on a sweeping, sugar-sand beach. Other easy-going South Coast stops include Unawatuna (good for diving and yoga) and the surf towns of Ahangama and Midigama, with more gentle breaks for aspiring Kelly Slaters.

Trip plan: Bandaranaike Airport is a 30min drive north of Colombo, from where trains continue to Galle (sit on the right-hand side of the carriage for non-stop coastal views). From Galle, local buses and trains provide easy access to the beach towns.

Need to know: Take a beach break touring cinnamon plantations near Mirissa or Handunugoda Tea Estate near Ahangama.

Other months: Jan-Apr – hot, drier, peak whale season; May-Nov – hot, monsoonal.

ST-MARTIN

0-16 Why now? A French-Caribbean vacation with a festive twist.

The perfect blend of French and Caribbean culture and cuisine, St-Martin is a wonderful family destination, surrounded by windswept beaches and turquoise waters. Whether your family prefers a five-star beach resort or a deserted stretch of sand, you'll find it here; and eco-hikes, snorkel tours and uninhabited outer islands will satisfy young adventurers. In December, residents and shopkeepers compete for the most festive holiday decorations and, until New Year, the streets of Marigot and Grand-Case come alive with street parties, parades and twinkling light displays. On the Sunday before Christmas, residents decorate floats, don elaborate costumes and turn up the music, parading through the streets of Grand Case. Islanders of all ages come out in droves to celebrate and witness the joyful display of creativity and holiday cheer.

Trip plan: You'll have easy access to everything wherever you stay (including on the Dutch side). You'll want a car to get to the beaches and the Grand Case festivities.

Need to know: This tiny island is shared between two countries: St-Martin is an overseas territory of France; Sint Maarten is an autonomous country within the Kingdom of the Netherlands. There's an international border, but no border control. The two sides use different currencies (euros vs US dollars) and speak different languages (French vs Dutch and English).

Other months: Jan-Apr – peak season, perfect weather, festivals; May – shoulder season, discounted lodging; Jun-Nov – low season, more rain, cheaper.

DOLOMITES
ITALY

0-16 Why now? Skiing, sledding and winter fun surrounded by majestic mountains.

With snow blanketing the ground, trees and rugged mountain peaks, all sparkling white against a crisp blue sky, December in the Dolomites is pure magic. Opportunities for winter recreation are endless – skiing and snowboarding, of course, plus toboggan runs on mountain slopes, ice-skating on scenic lakes and horse-drawn sleigh rides through snow-covered fields and forests. Throughout the region, towns and villages host holiday markets and festivals to brighten up the season, with tasty local food, toasty-hot drinks and hand-crafted curios for sale. The largest market – in Bolzano – features a skating rink and other fun activities for kids; smaller events in picturesque mountain villages include the medieval market in Chiusa (Klausen), with fire-eaters and jesters roaming the streets. Lago di Carezza (Karersee) hosts a true festival of lights, with lanterns, bonfires and artistic displays surrounding the lovely moonlit lake.

Trip plan: You can take the train to Bolzano and stay at (or near) a resort like Carezza Ski, with little need to rent a car; you'll need a vehicle to reach the small villages.

Need to know: The northern part of the Dolomites (Alto Adige in Italian, Südtirol in German) was part of the Austro-Hungarian Empire until the early 20th century. It's now part of Italy, but Austrian heritage is prominent and German is widely spoken.

Other months: Jan-Apr – peak ski season; May-Jun – winter snow lingers, muddy/icy trails; Jul-Aug – warm, lush landscapes for hiking; Sep-Oct – cooler, more rain; Nov – cold, dark, wet, many resorts close.

SAN ANTONIO
USA

0-16 Why now? Equal parts education and fun in cool San Antonio.

With thrill rides and water parks alongside historic sites and diverting museums, San Antonio is fabulous family vacation destination. The main attraction is the Alamo, that icon of Texas heritage, where you can learn about the pivotal revolutionary battle in which Texas fought for – and won – its independence from Mexico. Then, walk or cycle through local history along the Mission Trail, linking San Antonio's five Spanish colonial missions (including the Alamo). The unique Witte Museum is another fascinating stop, showcasing dinosaur bones, prehistoric cave drawings, art and textiles, and ecological dioramas. Your kids will thank you if you also include the city's famous theme parks in your itinerary. Six Flags Fiesta Texas now includes a state-of-the-art competitive gaming complex, esix Gaming (you may or may not wish to tell your kids about that!); Aquatica San Antonio is a riot of water slides and wave pools.

Trip plan: Stay downtown to take full advantage of the restaurants and attractions along the Riverwalk; or in the Broadway Corridor, home of the massive Brackenridge Park and the city's best kid museums.

Need to know: San Antonio's signature dish is the puffy taco, featuring a masa (corn-dough) tortilla, deep-fried until it puffs up. Crispy on the outside, soft in the middle, this Tex-Mex favourite was invented in the 1950s by brothers Ray and Henry Lopez, founders of the still-popular Ray's Drive Inn and Henry's Puffy Tacos.

Other months: Nov-Feb – relatively cool; Mar-Apr & Sep-Oct – shoulder season, mild; May-Aug – hot stuff.

HONG KONG
CHINA

5-16 Why now? For Hong Kong lights with added Christmas cheer.

White Christmas? Maybe not. But you're guaranteed a bright Christmas in Hong Kong: dry, mild December brings sunny skies and a truckload of extra sparkle at the city's seasonal Winterfest, when you can take in the Statue Square Christmas tree, fake snow and carol singers from an open-topped antique tram. Hong Kong's most famous tram – the Peak Tram – is actually a remarkably steep funicular railway. It's immensely popular, but the 396m (1299ft) vertical ascent to Victoria Peak is fun and rewards with Hong Kong's best view. Back at ground level, there's no shortage of festive joy at Hong Kong Disneyland, from Christmas shows to decorated trees and the appropriately themed *Frozen* land, World of Frozen. On Sundays, take a break from the holiday-season razzmatazz to join the Hong Kong families who get together for dim sum. Several restaurants run unlimited brunches, so you can try as many glorious steamed and fried dumplings as you can handle. Upmarket Hutong, in Kowloon, has a dim-sum brunch and views across the Victoria Harbour.

Trip plan: Express trains connect Hong Kong Airport to the centre in 25min. Allow two to three days minimum.

Need to know: If you're still here on 31 December, head to Tsim Sha Tsui Promenade, West Kowloon Waterfront or the Central Ferry Pier for the best views of New Year's Eve fireworks.

Other months: Jan-Mar – cool, dry and cloudy; Apr-May – hotter and wetter; Jun-Sep – wettest, typhoons possible; Oct-Nov – warm, dry and sunny.

LONDON
ENGLAND

5-16 Why now? It's elemental: London has a magical, mysterious aura in December.

London's story-soaked streets are lined with houses adorned with blue plaques providing information about famous one-time occupants (from poets and politicians to artists and sporting titans), but the disc on the wall of 221B Baker St is different, as it commemorates an entirely made-up character. This is the imagined address of the world's most famous fictional detective, and the location of the very real Sherlock Holmes Museum, where inquisitive young minds can learn all about Arthur Conan Doyle's eccentric pipe-puffing, deerstalker-hat-wearing super-sleuth, as well as his trusty companion Dr Watson and his evil nemesis, the criminal mastermind Professor Moriarty. Besides browsing books, exploring stories and taking in the Victorian atmosphere, keen-eyed kids can pick up tips, tricks and tools to help them crack cases and solve mysteries of their own from a collection of curiosities and memorabilia.

Trip plan: Baker Street tube station is on the Bakerloo, Circle and Hammersmith & City lines; the museum is just around the corner. The famous Madame Tussauds (home to 250 lifelike renditions of celebs and historical figures) is a 5min walk away, on Marylebone Rd; Oxford Circus (bejewelled with Christmas lights in December) is two stops along the Bakerloo line.

Need to know: The museum opens daily (9.30am-6pm). Children under six are free.

Other months: Oct-Feb – short days, wet and chilly; Mar-Sep – longer days, warmer.

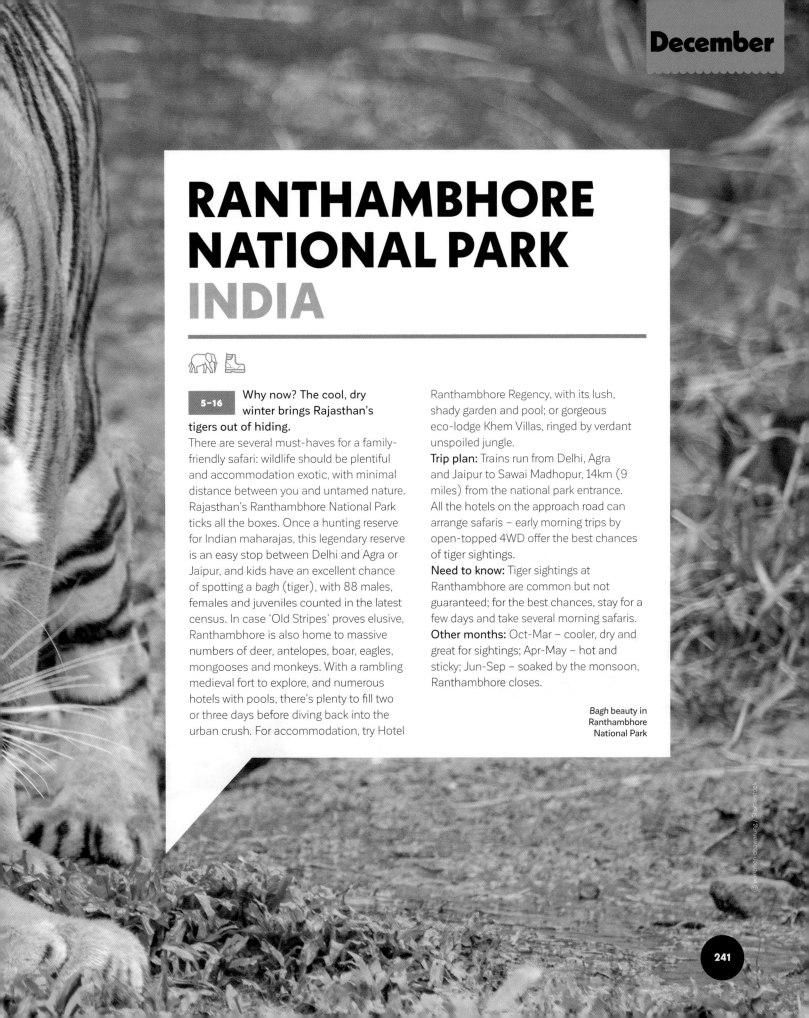

RANTHAMBHORE NATIONAL PARK
INDIA

5–16 Why now? The cool, dry winter brings Rajasthan's tigers out of hiding.

There are several must-haves for a family-friendly safari: wildlife should be plentiful and accommodation exotic, with minimal distance between you and untamed nature. Rajasthan's Ranthambhore National Park ticks all the boxes. Once a hunting reserve for Indian maharajas, this legendary reserve is an easy stop between Delhi and Agra or Jaipur, and kids have an excellent chance of spotting a *bagh* (tiger), with 88 males, females and juveniles counted in the latest census. In case 'Old Stripes' proves elusive, Ranthambhore is also home to massive numbers of deer, antelopes, boar, eagles, mongooses and monkeys. With a rambling medieval fort to explore, and numerous hotels with pools, there's plenty to fill two or three days before diving back into the urban crush. For accommodation, try Hotel Ranthambhore Regency, with its lush, shady garden and pool; or gorgeous eco-lodge Khem Villas, ringed by verdant unspoiled jungle.

Trip plan: Trains run from Delhi, Agra and Jaipur to Sawai Madhopur, 14km (9 miles) from the national park entrance. All the hotels on the approach road can arrange safaris – early morning trips by open-topped 4WD offer the best chances of tiger sightings.

Need to know: Tiger sightings at Ranthambhore are common but not guaranteed; for the best chances, stay for a few days and take several morning safaris.

Other months: Oct-Mar – cooler, dry and great for sightings; Apr-May – hot and sticky; Jun-Sep – soaked by the monsoon, Ranthambhore closes.

Bagh beauty in Ranthambhore National Park

WHERE TO GO WHEN WITH KIDS

SOUTH COAST
URUGUAY

`0-16` **Why now?** Beach-hop Uruguay's coast, from high-rise glitz to dune-backed beauties.

In summer (December to February), holidaymakers hop across borders from Argentina and Brazil to Uruguay on a mission to enjoy its 660km (410 miles) of sandy shoreline. Heading east from Montevideo along the Atlantic coast offers the chance to experience some of Uruguay's best beaches and embrace this corner of South America in vacation mode. Start at the 1930s-vintage resort of Piriápolis for beach-city buzz, before moving on to glitzy Punta del Este for people-watching. Forty minutes further east is boho José Ignacio, known for its sprawling beaches, upscale homes and quaint lighthouse. For a full beach day, keep going to surfer-friendly La Paloma, perfect for building castles on the sand or barefoot walks along the expansive shoreline. Further still, isolated Cabo Polonio is peppered with surf shacks, and is accessible on foot over sand dunes or by 4WD.

Trip plan: Montevideo receives few long-haul flights. For international travellers it can be easier to fly to Buenos Aires and catch the ferry across the Río de la Plata to Colonia del Sacramento (1hr 15min) or Montevideo (2hr 15min). Allow a weekend to a week; a car gives you the freedom to drop into beach towns at your own leisure.

Need to know: December temperatures range from 16°C (61°F) to 27°C (81°F).

Other months: Nov-Feb – warm, dry, busy; Apr-May – autumn, quieter, sea warmest; Jun-Oct – cooler, wetter, southern right whales breed off the coast.

KRAKÓW
POLAND

`0-16` **Why now?** Festive cheer, a fiery dragon and underground worlds.

Every hour, a trumpeter sounds a warning call from the tower of Mariacka Cathedral in Kraków's Old Town. The mournful tune is cut short after only five notes – just as it was 800 years ago, when an arrow from attacking Mongols pierced the bugler's throat. Stories of battles and beasts, kings and castles unfold before your eyes in Kraków. The imposing Wawel Castle is a vast complex of courtyards, cathedrals and royal chambers, with a cave in the hillside below that's said to have been the lair of a dragon; today, to the delight of kids, a bronze statue at the cave-mouth spews fire. Another entrée into Kraków's history lies 4m (13ft) beneath the central market square: Rynek Underground is a high-tech history museum, set among the excavated ruins of the medieval merchant hall. Kids can go even deeper underground southeast of the city at Wieliczka Salt Mine, a vast network of tunnels and chambers carved out of rock salt. Kraków is a delight at any time of year, but all the more so in December, when markets fill the main square and lights twinkle on the snow.

Trip plan: Book a hotel in or near the Old Town for easy access to the main attractions and the Christmas market. Take a bus or a tour to Wieliczka Salt Mine.

Need to know: Both Rynek Underground and Wieliczka Salt Mine require booking in advance.

Other months: Nov-Feb – cold, cheaper; Apr-May & Sep-Oct – mild, lighter crowds; Jun-Aug – warm, long days, busy.

PLETTENBERG BAY
SOUTH AFRICA

`5-16` **Why now?** Enjoy ethical animal encounters during South Africa's sensational summer.

With its glorious white-sand beach, the resort town of Plettenberg Bay makes a stunning stop along the Garden Route's 300km (190-mile) stretch of coastline. As well as revelling in sun and sea, families can head just east to the area around the Crags, where a collection of sanctuaries offers the chance to see and learn about some of Africa's most extraordinary animals. Birds of Eden features the world's largest single-dome free-flight aviary, home to 3500 birds from 220 different African species, rescued from caged environments and being prepared for release into the wild. At nearby Monkeyland Primate Sanctuary, you can seek out 550 free-roaming rescued apes – including capuchin monkeys, ring-tailed lemurs, gibbons and howler monkeys – from a 128m-long (420ft) canopy walk. Jukani Wildlife Sanctuary is home to multiple big cats – lions, tigers, puma, leopards and jaguars – taken in from captive environments where they couldn't be properly cared for, plus raccoons, honey badgers, caracals, zebras, springboks, hyenas and more. Also nearby is an elephant sanctuary and Tenikwa Wildlife Centre, while older kids seeking adventure can join guided kloofing (canyoning) trips at the Crags.

Trip plan: The Crags is a turnoff from the N2 highway near Plettenberg Bay, itself halfway between East London and Cape Town.

Need to know: A combined ticket to Birds of Eden, Monkeyland and Jukani is the cheapest way to visit – experiences can be spread across several days.

Other months: Jan-Feb – summer heat, showers; Mar-May – autumn, cooler, downpours; Jun-Aug – winter chill, dry; Sep-Nov – spring, warm.

JAMAICA

0-16 Why now? Celebrate the season under sunny skies, with traditional parades and pantomime.

The rains are over, the sun is out and the weather in Jamaica is picture-perfect, making December an ideal time to bring your family to this island paradise. The sublime beaches beckon, but there are also waterfalls to climb, caves to spelunk and bioluminescent bays to swim in. Best of all, the calendar is packed with festivities. On Christmas Eve, many towns hold an all-day (and into-the-night) Grand Market, the streets filled with vendors selling food, toys and souvenirs. Boxing Day begins a week of traditional Junkanoo parades, when participants don colourful costumes and creepy masks and dance through streets, acting out ancient stories accompanied by African drums and bamboo fifes.

This is also the season for the National Pantomime, a unique and hilarious form of folk theatre lacing fast-paced musical comedy with plenty of humorous dialogue. The local themes and patois may be difficult for kids to follow, but the costumes and music are always attention-grabbing.

Trip plan: The north coast (between Montego Bay and Ocho Rios) offers fabulous beaches and close proximity to some of the top natural attractions. The capital, Kingston, is the centre for theatre and culture, but there are Grand Markets and Junkanoos in most large towns.

Need to know: In tourist centres, hustlers and touts can be over-aggressive in their sales tactics.

Other months: Jan-Mar – peak season, hot, sunny; Apr – Carnival season; May-Nov – rainy season, discounted prices, light crowds, hurricanes possible Aug to Oct.

MOMBASA
KENYA

5-16 Why now? Explore an ocean-facing fort with holidaying locals, and snorkel with turtles.

Magical, multicultural Mombasa is fronted by the fascinating Fort Jesus, built by the Portuguese in 1593 to protect the port from attackers arriving across the Indian Ocean. During its action-packed history, the fort was besieged for two years (1696–98) before falling to Omani forces, and it changed hands numerous times over the centuries before being commandeered by the British and turned into a prison. Now a UNESCO World Heritage Site, it's an exciting place for kids to explore, with battlements to run around, walls covered in centuries-old graffiti scrawled by Portuguese sailors, the jewel- and weapon-filled Omani House, and a museum displaying finds from Portuguese warships sunk during the siege. Other Mombasa draws for older kids include snorkelling in Mombasa Marine National Park, spotting lionfish and parrotfish among the coral, and looking for leatherback, green, hawksbill, loggerhead and olive ridley turtles. Back on land, colobus monkeys mess around in palm trees above white-sand beaches, and the Old Town's alleyways and Spice Market are full of colour and surprises.

Trip plan: Mombasa is 485km (300 miles) southeast of Nairobi, and is reachable via the Madaraka Express train (4hr).

Need to know: Fort Jesus and the museum are poorly signed; hire an official guide.

Other months: Jan-Feb – hot, dry, Kaskazi winds; Mar-Jun – rainy; Jul-Oct– hot, breezy, good surfing, humpback whale spotting; Nov – humid, wet.

BARBADOS

5-16 Why now? December in Barbados is a time of sun and fun, with festivals and wonderful weather.

Barbados enjoys settled, sunny Caribbean weather during the dry season, but sometimes it's good to beat the midday heat by finding a cooler retreat, and nowhere fulfils this brief better than Harrison's Cave. Kids can delight in exploring this subterranean wonderworld, sculpted by the elements over millennia. On guided trips, part of which take place on a tram (and are suitable for children aged six-plus only), families pass through the mile-long cavern, gawping at gorgeous galleries of stalactites and stalagmites, some of which meet in the middle to form spectacular pillars. At the deepest part of the cave, visitors watch wide-eyed as a cascade of crystal-clear water plunges over a drop into a deep emerald pool. On the Early Explorers tour, kids aged 13-16 can don headlamps and knee guards before creeping and crawling through hidden passages. Back under the blue sky, the adventure continues: at the Harrison's Cave Eco-Adventure Park, kids can take a thrilling zipline ride across the treetops, explore a high-rope obstacle course and nature trail, or take in a bird aviary and wildlife park, home to Barbados' green monkeys.

Trip plan: Harrison's Cave is a 30min drive from Bridgetown. There are buses, but a taxi or hire car is the easiest way to get there.

Need to know: Wear comfy, grippy shoes.

Other months: Jan to mid-Apr – dry season, busy; late Apr to Jun & Nov – shoulder seasons, good deals, quieter; Jul-Oct – quiet low season, showers (hurricanes possible).

Tivoli Gardens
in festive finery

COPENHAGEN
DENMARK

5-16 **Why now?** Copenhagen looks even better adorned with festive lights.

Winter is all about being cosy when it's cold, and nowhere does cosy better than Copenhagen. The tradition of hygge – the pursuit of comfort and contentment – weaves through life in the Danish capital, particularly in the festive season. This might mean browsing jaunty Christmas markets, then retreating for a steaming mug of hot chocolate or *gløgg* (mulled wine for grown-ups) in a snug Nørrebro cafe. It might mean gliding around the Broens Ice Rink or riding nostalgic fairground attractions at the 19th-century Tivoli Gardens amusement park, surrounded by baubles and glittering lights. (Make time for the wooden Rutschebanen rollercoaster, rumbling down the tracks here since 1914.) It's cold out, so plan time around indoor sights such as treasure-filled Rosenborg Castle, the huge Den Blå Planet aquarium and the flagship Lego shop on Vimmelskaftet.

Trip plan: Get to Copenhagen by air or take the train from Stockholm or Hamburg. Renting an Airbnb apartment will give you more warm, indoor space to relax in while you explore. Wrap up well to explore on foot or take the Metro or city buses to hit the sights. Rideshares through the Viggo app are slightly cheaper than taxis.

Need to know: The handy Copenhagen Card covers public transport and gives free or discounted entry to the sights, including Tivoli Gardens (where rides cost extra; the Ride Pass wristband is better value than paying for rides individually).

Other months: Jan-Mar – cold, snowy, windy; Apr-May & Sep-Nov – milder, sometimes overcast; Jun-Aug – warm, dry.

ÎLE AUX AIGRETTES
MAURITIUS

5-16 | **Why now?** Meet a giant tortoise in the land of the dodo, before the humidity hits.

Every giftshop on Mauritius – a tiny teardrop of beach-fringed terra firma in the vast Indian Ocean – sells toy dodos. The island nation's most famous inhabitant was wiped out over 350 years ago, but it lives on as a powerful icon of extinction. And at the Île aux Aigrettes Nature Reserve – a little island dangling off the southeast coast of Mauritius, which has become an ark for endangered species – you'll meet more local animals that have skirted perilously close to oblivion, including the pink pigeon (a direct relative of the dodo) and the flame-headed Mauritius fody. Kids will probably be more excited by an encounter with a giant tortoise like Big Daddy, an alpha male slowly approaching his 100th year, who measures 1.2m (4ft) across the shell and weighs around 300kg (660lb). Sadly, the two tortoise species endemic to Mauritius went the way of the dodo when sailors landed on the island and treated it like a larder, but Big Daddy (an Aldabra giant tortoise, originally from the Seychelles) is part of an attempt to reintroduce these wonderful reptiles.

Trip plan: Reach Île aux Aigrettes via a 10min boat journey from the dock at Pointe Jérome.

Need to know: Île aux Aigrettes is managed by the Mauritian Wildlife Foundation (mauritian-wildlife.org), which conducts excellent eco-tours of the island.

Other months: Jan-Mar – high humidity, heavy rainfall; Apr-Jun – cooler, calmer conditions; Jul-Aug – clear skies, high winds, world-class kitesurfing, amazing stargazing; Sep-Nov – summer heat.

Get up close to little blues at Oamaru Blue Penguin Colony

© Steve Clancy Photography / Getty Images

OAMARU NEW ZEALAND/AOTEAROA

0-16 | **Why now?** Prime penguin-viewing season.

Who wouldn't fall in love with watching cute little blue penguins (korōra) as they make their way home after a day of fishing out at sea? With the Oamaru Blue Penguin Colony almost right in town, at the end of Waterfront Rd, this is family fun easily achieved. In December, rafts (groups) of 30 to 50 birds turn up around dusk each evening – there's safety in numbers – heading for home and announcing their arrival by quacking like ducks. On making alarmingly inelegant landings, they tentatively waddle up the rocky beach, avoiding pesky basking seals, then lean forward and start running for home when they hit flat land. It's all within easy viewing distance of visitor grandstands; a number of penguins take the scenic route by jumping some steps and waddling right past excited families. Before entering their nests, the birds dry off, preen and engage in noisy socialising. It's totally captivating and once one raft has arrived, it might only be a few minutes until the next turns up. Other distractions around town include Elephant Rocks, a filming location for the Narnia movies and a geological wonderland of bizarre rock formations to be clambered over and explored.

Trip plan: Spend at least one night here as the penguins come home at dusk.

Need to know: The little blue is the world's smallest penguin, just 30cm (12in) in height and weighing 1.5kg (3lb).

Other months: Sep-Feb – up to 400 penguins each evening; Apr-Aug – numbers drop drastically.

© Philip Lee Harvey / Lonely Planet

THE PAMPAS ARGENTINA

Horse-drawn
carriage at a
Pampas *estancia*

12-16 **Why now?** Days spent in the saddle as spring eases into summer.

The flat, rolling countryside surrounding Buenos Aires is an area of open grasslands, bird-filled quiet and rich pink sunsets. It is also dotted with *estancias* (ranches) where you can encounter *gaucho* – cowboy – culture, and learn to ride astride an Argentine thoroughbred. Dozens of *estancias* – 19th-century rural estates for raising cattle, or the private getaways of wealthy families – have opened their gates to the public, and many offer a *día de campo* (country day) that's ideal for day-trippers. One of the friendliest and most authentic options within easy reach of Buenos Aires is Estancia Los Dos Hermanos in Zárate. Staying at an *estancia* allows you to really embrace *gaucho* life, with five days giving

you time to learn or brush up on your horse riding on daily excursions into the countryside. Accommodation ranges from grand converted mansions, with pools and polo lessons, to rooms in house-shares. Most feature rides accompanied by *gaucho* guides, but schedules tend to be loose – the most rigorous deadline you'll have is getting back in time for the evening *asado* (barbecue) before the sun sets.

Trip plan: Regular buses operate between Buenos Aires and the Pampas region, around 1hr 30min from the city.

Need to know: Los Dos Hermanos offers riding lessons for all ages and levels, but not all *estancias* do; make sure you check in advance.

Other months: Jan-Feb: peak summer, hot & humid; Mar-Apr: autumn; Sep-Nov: cooler, blossom and wildflowers.

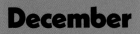

Iconic Icebergs
pool at Bondi Beach

SYDNEY
AUSTRALIA

0-16 **Why now? Beaches and ocean pools beckon.**

There's something special about summer in Sydney – ferries to ride, plenty of sand and surf, plus that classic Australian experience: a swim in a perfectly positioned ocean pool, with the water replenished by ocean waves. Aussies have been doing this for more than 200 years – the first ocean pool was built by convicts in 1819 – and there are over 100 along the coastline of New South Wales. Sydney's most famous ocean pool is Bondi Icebergs, with spectacular views over the golden sands of famous Bondi Beach, a 25-minute drive from the city centre. Bronte Baths, dating back to 1887, is perfect for a paddle, protected from the surf at Bronte Beach in the eastern suburbs. South of Bronte, Coogee Beach offers some excellent options: Wylie's Baths is an ocean pool with views and history, while Giles Baths is a natural rock pool that locals call the 'Bogey Hole'. McIver's Ladies Baths here, open since the 1870s, is particularly popular with women and children. And then there's the seaside suburb of Manly. Take a ferry from the CBD, enjoy the township, the beach, the ocean waves and the Fairy Bower Pool, a top spot for families.

Trip plan: Fly into Sydney Kingsford Smith International Airport. The city has an excellent public transportation network.

Need to know: The easy, 6km (3.7-mile) Bondi to Coogee coastal walk is one of the most scenic ways to see Sydney.

Other months: Nov-Feb – summer; potentially hot and humid; May-Sep – winter, cooler air and sea temperatures.

© Siripong Kaewla-iad / Getty Images

247

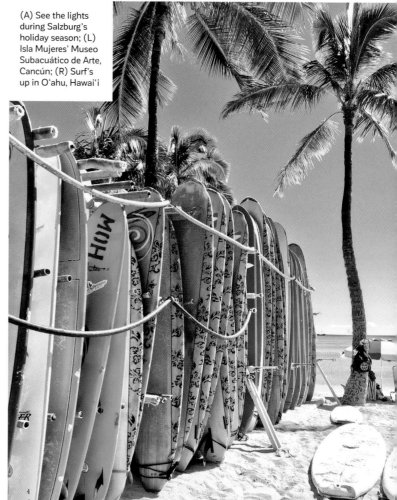

(A) See the lights during Salzburg's holiday season; (L) Isla Mujeres' Museo Subacuático de Arte, Cancún; (R) Surf's up in O'ahu, Hawai'i

SALZBURG
AUSTRIA

12-16 Why now? Meet the anti-Santa during Krampusnacht (naughty kids only).

Part goat, part human, all scary, Krampus is the nasty to St Nicholas's nice. According to folkloric tradition in Alpine Austria (and Bavaria in Germany), the two Christmas characters would travel together on 6 December, visiting children and warning them to behave; those who did got gifts from St Nick, those who didn't suffered a walloping from Krampus – it's the naughty-list origin story. During the 20th century St Nicholas morphed into merry modern Santa Claus, while his snarling sidekick was retired by a conflict-bruised continent. But Krampus never went away, he just hid in the Alpine shadows. Now he's back, and if you have misbehaving kids, consider taking them on a cautionary-tale trip to Salzburg, Austria. Here, in early December, Krampus and Perchten Parades thunder through the Old Town. The Perchten are more frightening folk figures, charged with scaring away winter's dark spirits. There are two types: good ones Schönperchten and evil ones Schiachperchten – the latter look properly scary and, according to legend, in every parade there's one real Perchten.

Trip plan: Salzburg is a 2hr train ride from Vienna. Don't miss the sensational Christkindlmarkt (Christmas market).

Need to know: Some Krampus and Schiachperchten costumes and masks are genuinely terrifying – don't bring little children (unless they're really naughty...).

Other months: Mar-May – spring blooms, climbing the Gaisberg; Jun-Aug – festival season in the city of Mozart and *The Sound of Music*; Sep-Nov – harvest, beer and folk events.

O'AHU NORTH SHORE
HAWAI'I

5-16 Why now? Head to Hawai'i for big-wave season on the North Shore.

Keen to get your kids pumped to learn to surf? There's no better place than O'ahu. In December, the world-renowned big waves are pounding onto the North Shore's legendary surf beaches, home of the planet's top surfing competitions. Take the family to watch the pros in action at Waimea Bay, Sunset Beach and Banzai Pipeline, then give the kids a try, taking lessons on beginner waves at Waikīkī on the protected southeast coast of the island – the waves are slow-rolling here, making it easier for beginners and intermediate surfers to stand up and ride. Waikīkī has good, consistent conditions year-round for lessons and is safe for youngsters. If you're staying in Waikīkī, those surf lessons may only be a few minutes' walk from your hotel. When heading to the North Shore to view those top surfers, ensure you take shade, water, snacks and binoculars. If you really want to keep the family happy, drop into Ted's Bakery at Sunset Beach, home of everybody's favourite local dessert, the chocolate *haupia* (coconut pudding).

Trip plan: Stay in Waikīkī for a week; it's only a 1hr drive to Hale'iwa on the North Shore. The legendary surf beaches stretch east from there.

Need to know: Expect bumper-to-bumper traffic on the North Shore when the waves are pumping and the big competitions are on, between November and February.

Other months: Jan-Mar – winter, cooler; Apr-May – spring, shoulder season; Jun-Aug – hot, crowded; Sep-Nov – autumn, shoulder season.

CANCÚN
MEXICO

5-16 Why now? See Cancún's reefs before they vanish under a sea of snorkellers.

To beat the crowds to Cancún's beaches, it's best to arrive at the start of December. Early birds can enjoy warm days (around 28°C/82°F), cool nights (around 18°C/64°F), balmy waters (around 26°C/78°F) and less company while snorkelling on the coral heads of the Mesoamerican Barrier Reef. Start kids off easy with a snorkelling tour to Isla Mujeres or the Yal-kú Lagoon near Playa del Carmen. Isla Mujeres is also home to the Museo Subacuático de Arte (MUSA), a surreal sprawl of submerged sculptures – coral-encrusted human figures, enormous body parts, a cement Volkswagen Beetle – surrounded by thriving reef systems. Older kids can explore with a mask and snorkel; glass-bottomed boat tours will give younger kids a taste. For time on the sand, skip the busier beaches at the south end of the Zona Hotelera for laid-back Playa Langosta at the north end of Nichupté Lagoon.

Trip plan: Flights drop into Cancún from across the US and Europe. Get around in town by cab (Uber and Cabify rides are cheaper than city cabs) or local bus. Ferries run to Isla Mujeres from Playa Tortugas or Playa Caracol; buses run to Playa del Carmen from Cancún's Terminal Autobuses ADO stand.

Need to know: Cancún's beaches are periodically invaded by sargassum seaweed; snorkelling trips will take you beyond the seaweed zone.

Other months: Jan-Apr – drier, sunny, but busy; May-Jul – rainy and hot; Aug-Nov – stormy, risk of hurricanes.

Index

photo credits

WHERE TO GO WHEN
with **Kids**

Published in May 2025 by
Lonely Planet Global Limited CRN 554153
www.lonelyplanet.com
ISBN 978 18375 8578 6
© Lonely Planet 2024
10 9 8 7 6 5 4 3 2 1
Printed in Malaysia

Written by Joe Bindloss, Joanna Cooke, Sam Haddad, Patrick Kinsella,
Craig McLachlan, Mara Vorhees, Tasmin Waby

Publishing Director Piers Pickard
Publisher, Gift & Illustrated Becca Hunt
Senior Editor Robin Barton
Senior Designer Emily Dubin
Cover Design Lizzie Vaughan
Layout Designer Jo Dovey
Editors Polly Thomas, Nick Mee, Vicky Smith
Image Researcher Heike Bohnstengel
Print Production Nigel Longuet

Lonely Planet Global Limited
IRELAND
Digital Depot, Roe Lane (off Thomas St),
Dublin D08 TCV4

STAY IN TOUCH lonelyplanet.com/contact

Although the authors and Lonely Planet have taken all reasonable care in preparing this book, we make no warranty about the accuracy or completeness of its content and, to the maximum extent permitted, disclaim all liability from its use.

Cover image credits Front: MB Photography/Getty Images; aprott/ Getty Images; ixpert/Shutterstock; George Karbus Photography/ Getty Images; Tetyana Dotsenko/Shutterstock; BlueOrange Studio/ Shutterstock. Spine: evenfh/Getty Images. Back: gracethang2/ Shutterstock; Waj/Shutterstock; Jim Mallouk/ Shutterstock; Kiev. Victor/Shutterstock; Stephen Simpson/Getty Images